HOLLYWOOD IN
THE NEIGHBORHOOD

HOLLYWOOD IN
THE NEIGHBORHOOD

The publisher gratefully acknowledges the generous contribtion to this book provided by the Richard and Meryl Selig Endowment Fund in Film Studies, in Memory of Robert W. Selig, of the University of California Press Foundation.

HOLLYWOOD IN THE NEIGHBORHOOD

Historical Case Studies of Local Moviegoing

Edited by
KATHRYN H. FULLER-SEELEY

UNIVERSITY OF CALIFORNIA PRESS   Berkeley   Los Angeles   London

University of California Press, one of the most distinguished university presses in the United States, enriches lives around the world by advancing scholarship in the humanities, social sciences, and natural sciences. Its activities are supported by the UC Press Foundation and by philanthropic contributions from individuals and institutions. For more information, visit www.ucpress.edu.

University of California Press
Berkeley and Los Angeles, California

University of California Press, Ltd.
London, England

Library of Congress Cataloging-in-Publication Data

Hollywood in the neighborhood : historical case studies of local moviegoing / edited by Kathryn H. Fuller-Seeley.
    p. cm.
Includes bibliographical references and index.
ISBN 978-0-520-23067-5 (cloth : alk. paper)—ISBN 978-0-520-24973-8 (pbk. : alk. paper)
1. Motion pictures—United States—History 2. Motion picture audiences—United States—History. 3. Motion picture theaters—United States—History. I. Fuller-Seeley, Kathryn H., 1960–

PN1993.5.U6H59135   2008
791.430973—dc22   2007016242

17 16 15 14 13 12 11 10 09 08
10 9 8 7 6 5 4 3 2 1

The paper used in this publication meets the minimum requirements of ANSI/NISO Z39.48–1992 (R 1997) (*Permanence of Paper*).

CONTENTS

Part I: Introduction
Setting the Contexts

1. Introduction: Researching and Writing the
History of Local Moviegoing
Kathryn H. Fuller-Seeley and George Potamianos 3

2. Decentering Historical Audience Studies:
A Modest Proposal
Robert C. Allen 20

Part II: Origins
Case Studies

3. The Itinerant Movie Show and the Development
of the Film Industry
Calvin Pryluck 37

4. Early Film Exhibition in Wilmington, North Carolina
Anne Morey 53

5. Building Movie Audiences in Placerville,
California, 1908–1915
George Potamianos 75

6. Cinema Virtue, Cinema Vice: Race, Religion, and Film
Exhibition in Norfolk, Virginia, 1908–1922
Terry Lindvall 91

Part III: Integration and Variations
Case Studies

7. The Movies in a "Not So Visible Place": Des Moines,
   Iowa, 1911–1914
   Richard Abel   107

8. Digging the Finest Potatoes from Their Acre: Government
   Film Exhibition in Rural Ontario, 1917–1934
   Charles Tepperman   130

9. At the Movies in the "Biggest Little City in Wisconsin"
   Leslie Midkiff DeBauche   149

Part IV: Maturity and Crisis in the 1930s
Case Studies

10. Imagining and Promoting the Small-Town Theater
    Gregory A. Waller   169

11. "What the Picture Did for Me": Small-Town Exhibitors'
    Strategies for Surviving the Great Depression
    Kathryn H. Fuller-Seeley   186

12. "Something for Nothing": Bank Night and the Refashioning
    of the American Dream
    Paige Reynolds   208

Part V: Looking Backward, Looking Forward

13. Bad Sound and Sticky Floors: An Ethnographic Look at the
    Symbolic Value of Historic Small-Town Movie Theaters
    Kevin Corbett   233

14. Conclusion: When Theory Hits the Road
    Ronald G. Walters   250

Contributors   263
Selected Bibliography   267
Index   271

Part I

INTRODUCTION

SETTING THE CONTEXTS

1

INTRODUCTION

Researching and Writing
the History of Local Moviegoing

KATHRYN H. FULLER-SEELEY
AND GEORGE POTAMIANOS

Variously termed the new film history, film exhibition history, moviegoing history, local film history, historical reception studies, audience history, or the cultural and social context of moviegoing, innovative approaches to cinema history are some of the most vibrant and exciting aspects of media studies done in the past twenty years. These new research initiatives move outward from a primary focus on films as texts toward considerations of the contexts of their production, distribution, exhibition, and reception by viewers in particular times and spaces and more broadly to analyze the many meanings motion pictures assumed in popular culture and the social practice of moviegoing in everyday life.

Moviegoing history research is characterized by close, detailed studies of specific places, people, and chronologies. It is found at the juncture of several methodological and ideological issues—at intersections of traditional cinema studies with more data-driven research methods such as history, economics, social sciences, and history of readers in literary studies; at intersections of national and international contexts of production with local contexts of consumption; at intersections of modernity and tradition; and at intersections of the culture of the cosmopolitan urban center with the culture experienced by the small-town (and more homogeneous) rural hinterlands. It is also.at the intersections of the persuasive power of movie producers, exhibitors, and film texts with the ability of viewers to make their own sets of meanings from the movies they watched. There should be room in moviegoing history for grand theories as well as specific factual evidence, of psychologically determined viewing positions as well as historically situated, specific audience members, and of examination of reaction to specific films as well as of the practice of moviegoing in which habitual attendance at a theater or exhibition space outweighed the impact of any particular film shown.[1]

Robert C. Allen, Douglas Gomery, Gregory Waller, and Richard Abel have been leading figures in the development of moviegoing history; their influential works have analyzed historical and cultural shifts in film exhibition and reception in localities from rural North Carolina, Kansas, and Lexington, Kentucky, to urban New York City, Chicago, Des Moines, and Cleveland. Growing ranks of media scholars, including Rick Altman, Matthew Bernstein, Jane Gaines, Tom Gunning, Miriam Hanson, Mary Beth Haralovich, Richard Maltby, Charles Musser, Lauren Rabinovich, Jackie Stacey, and Janet Staiger, are researching many aspects of historical reception and moviegoing studies.

At the same time, investigations of moviegoing practices were being undertaken by American historians in the 1980s who studied film audiences in specific communities and the impact of motion pictures on their diverse cultures. Groundbreaking work has been done by Roy Rosenzweig on working-class audiences in the small industrial city of Worcester, Massachusetts; Frank Couvares on social surveys of amusement seekers in Pittsburgh; and Kathy Peiss on gender, ethnicity, and new forms of entertainment among young working-class women in New York City. Their studies have been joined by Lizabeth Cohen's research on immigrants and African Americans using mass culture in their process of adapting to Chicago; Lawrence Levine on the tendency of movie theaters to split American culture into highbrow and lowbrow factions; and Kathryn Fuller-Seeley on the early incorporation of movies into small-town communities. Richard Butsch's research traces similarities and differences among entertainment audiences across 300 years of American history. A steady stream of exciting new work continues to appear that combines historical and cinema studies research to deepen our understanding, and to propose new research questions.

Scholars are at work in the trenches, mining historical details for analysis of moviegoing in scores of communities. We are amassing a cornucopia of moviegoing histories of specific villages, towns, cities, and regions across the nation, uncovering diverse audience groupings, and investigating the impact of a wide variety of film genres and forms (including amateur, art, educational, documentary, and exploitation films) across a range of historical contexts. Moviegoing histories have the potential to turn traditional film histories on their heads, moving outward from the studies of a few key films and great auteurs toward uncovering newly discovered details and new explanations and understandings. Their findings may add fresh nuances to longstanding issues in American film history, such as the longevity of the cinema of attractions; the chaser theory of film's declining popularity on vaudeville theater bills after 1900; the chronology of the nickelodeons' spread and transformation into "vaudefilm" and classical Hollywood–style movie theaters; and patterns of cinema's reception as marked by region, race, ethnicity, gender, class, religion, age, generation, income, or education. The extent to which New York City was a cultural power across a wide, diverse United States may be further uncovered; the mechanisms through which concepts like modernity translated to the hinterlands, and modernity's impact on different types of communities will be explored. The gap between box office favorites and the canons of critically acclaimed films may be wider or narrower in various places across the nation than scholars had previously assumed. Accounting for a significant uniformity of cinema's impact across divergent communities, and/or many fascinating local variations, may be the ultimate outcome of these case studies.

At the Margins of Modernity?
Local Moviegoing and Cinema History

For more than a decade, a number of film historians have explored the many interconnections between cinema and the appearance of "modern life." Emerging at the turn of the twentieth century along with an array of new communication forms and technologically mediated mass experiences (telephone, phonograph, electric light displays, mass-circulation magazines, amusement parks, radio, etc.), early motion pictures seemed to some observers to embody the same "shock of the new" that viewers experienced with the rise of modernity.[2] Modernity was a crisis-like change of Western human experience occurring around 1900, shaped by many facets of the Industrial Revolution, or, as Tom Gunning notes, "a transformation in daily life wrought by the growth of capitalism and advances in technology: the growth of urban traffic, the distribution of mass produced goods and successive new technologies of transportation and communication."[3] Because the sites of early filmmaking were urban, their creation and distribution controlled by corporate capital, and the most visible sites of their consumption metropolitan, some cinema historians have argued that the "modern event" of film production and film's cultural reception was overwhelmingly urban—something that was by, for, and of the big city. Cinema in the "modernity thesis" seems to transform viewers and their culture, the surrounding theaters and streets, into a vast, anonymous, homogeneous mass audience in an equally vast, skyscrapered, fragmented, rapid-paced urban milieu. It is a powerful thesis that goes far to explain the angst and bustle of city life that are well documented in the art, music, film, and literary cultural expressions of the period.

What happened, however, when that same cinematic modernizing force left the big city and ventured into other, less cosmopolitan localities? As Ronald Walters notes in his chapter in this collection, at this point a hitch in the "modernity thesis" seems to occur, for residents of hinterlands locations such as Des Moines, Iowa; Wilmington, North Carolina; Placerville, California; and Lebanon, Kansas, experienced the movies, too. Did early cinema impact them in ways demonstrably similar to or different from what their city cousins experienced? Did change occur as quickly, more slowly, or not at all? Did the towns and their citizens remain as caught between traditional culture and "modern life" as they were before? Robert Allen asks in his chapter on "the 'problem' of the empirical," where and with what theories and methods can we explore these issues?[4]

We have not yet expanded our theorization of the transformative forces of modernity enough to account for variations in audience experience, and we have tended to minimize specific historical moments and contexts of cinema's spread across the United States. The exclusive analytical focus on urban cinema has tended to flatten out the results by leveling all experience into modernity; the narrow focus leads toward broad generalizations that begin to look less solid when we observe cinema's emergence from other angles, those of the local, the peripheral, through specific, empirical case studies. This collection certainly does not wish to criticize the "cinema and modernity" thesis or the excellent work of our fellow scholars, but it does wish to complicate and enrich our understanding of how film and cultural change intersect with and influence each other. These chapters bring magnifying glasses to issues in the early exhibition and reception of motion pictures in local places. We focus on smaller cities, large towns, villages, and rural crossroads. We pay attention to regional variation in customs and racial attitudes—to the complex interplay of social class, gender, and ethnicity.

Modernity: Is It Always a Good Thing?

In *Keywords*, Raymond Williams notes the changing cultural meanings of the term *modern*, which up through the 1800s was used in an unfavorable sense to mean that something historic (such as old buildings, language, clothing styles) was altered in infelicitous ways. At the turn of the twentieth century, the meaning of the term changed dramatically "until modern became virtually equivalent to improved or satisfactory or efficient" and was "normally used to indicate something unquestionably favorable or desirable."[5] The practices of cultural studies urge us to scrutinize the entire range of attitudes and ideas that our culture holds to be natural, inevitable, or "unquestionably favorable or desirable," however. Episodes of resistance to dominant social and ideological norms intrigue us as moments where subordinate groups argue with large institutions about structure and meaning of cultural forms, and historians of early cinema may be lagging behind scholars who have been investigating the struggles that met other media and technological forms when they were first introduced into rural and small-town communities. Enlightening studies include Michael Berger's examination of farmers' ambivalence toward the first automobiles that came tearing down their country roads, and investigations by Claude Fisher, Carolyn Marvin, David Nye, Ronald Kline, and Jane Adams of the diverse reactions of rural people to the introductions of telephones and electricity. Pamela Grundy and Derek Vaillant, writing on early radio audience reception, suggest that rural audiences did not simply accept what was broadcast "for them" over the airwaves but actively shaped the programming through buying sponsors' products, writing letters, and showing their preference for some types of shows (regional sports events) over others (Shakespearean lectures). In American rural history, Hal Barron analyzes the persistence in rural communities of those families and individuals who chose to resist the siren call of urban modernity by remaining on the farm, and Katherine Jellison uses lenses of gender and consumer culture to argue that farm women fought hard to bring the technological advances of domestic modernity within their reach. All these rural and small-town people actively took bits and pieces of "modern life" and melded them with a mixture of traditional community ideologies to invent their own hybrid versions of modernity. Doesn't it stand to reason that small-town movie audiences, at certain times and places, acted similarly?[6]

Let us consider several challenges for investigating early movies, modernity, and nonurban audience contexts. Unlike documented scattered protests against creeping industrialization and commercialization in rural America (resistance to automobiles, electrification, or the telephone), few people outside the big city seem to have rejected the movies outright, at least initially. Histories of moviegoing have not turned up reports of gangs of pitchfork-waving villagers chasing itinerant cinema showmen out of town. No Luddites burned projectors; no frightened rural audiences fled the screened oncoming Black Diamond Express. (Although having not yet located evidence of such occurrences does not mean they never took place, and it would be intriguing to find an instance!) Motion pictures seem to have been well tolerated wherever they were shown in villages and towns across the nation. Many itinerant rural showmen were successful, and nickelodeons cropped up as quickly in smaller towns and cities as they did in Manhattan. Rural individuals may have voted with their feet by not attending movie shows, but this was apparently not done with much organization. Perhaps because cinema was a public entertainment and not a technology meant for the home, workplace, or farm field, rural people were less concerned about the intrusiveness of movie shows into their communities than other technologies. Perhaps because they were outside the large metropolis, the movies appeared only occasionally, brought by itinerant show people to opera houses and church halls, giving communities more of a chance to accept motion pictures as "harmless entertainment" before they became a fixture as regular movie shows in buildings along the small-town Main Streets. Perhaps people outside the major urban centers were more accepting of the movies because there was a dearth of other entertainments that were *not* locally produced. The movies came to rural crossroads that vaudeville, circuses, melodramatic stock companies, and even some medicine shows rarely touched. Perhaps early instances of film censorship instituted by community groups and town governments could be seen as local protests against the encroachment of urban or modern motion pictures into their more traditional cultures.[7]

Without visible early rejection or initial protests against the movies, how can we gauge the extent of audience interest in them (or the lack thereof)? This absence of data creates research challenges for historians of early film reception, questions that Robert Allen raises in his essay: How do we study the people who did *not* go to the picture show? How do we account for competing cultural and social influences on early audiences—a rural population so scattered and poor that gathering even 100 people for a show was too difficult, a local band concert or baseball game drawing more viewers than the one-night-stand movie show? In some communities, conservative religious groups raised objections to movie shows, but, as Terry Lindvall shows us in his chapter, in other localities the church establishment welcomed cinema as an entertainment alternative to the town's saloons and brothels.

Studying Local Audiences:
Bringing Diversity to Cinema and Modernity

If the term *modernity* has generally been met with wide approbation, in contrast, the term *globalization* and far-flung audiences' experience of globalized media have been cause for scholarly concern. For years, academics worried that globalization of media content and control would inevitably lead to a vast homogenization of audience experiences, significant cultural leveling, and reduction of cultural identity and sense of place. A growing number of cultural studies scholars in anthropology and geography investigate the local reception practices of globalized media. They study how the local still operates—products are manufactured centrally for global distribution, but in many important respects have been (and remain) experienced locally; they are made sense of within communities, neighborhoods, and regions.[8] While in other areas of reception studies, scholars utilize the specific case study, ethnographies of fan communities, or studies of Web site communities on the Internet, in cinema studies, scholars have relied for much longer on sweeping generalizations about the mass audience, the urban audience, the urban working-class audience, or the female or male audience.

Michael Curtin demonstrates that in television studies scholarship, the emphasis on globalization of experiences such as the modernity provided by mass media, or "media imperialism," has been tempered by a variety of studies in a variety of approaches that emphasize local context of media consumption, local industrial structures that mediate the centrally produced media product, and "how audiences make unanticipated uses of television programming, often reworking the meanings of transnational texts to accommodate the circumstances of their local social contexts. . . . Rather than simply absorbing U.S. capitalist ideology, 'active audiences' fashion meanings and identities that are hybrid and complex." He concludes that "the play of power in global TV is to be found in the ways that media conglomerates attempt to set structural limits on the production and circulation of meaning and contrarily on the ways in which viewers both comply with and defy these semiotic limits. This play of power requires an understanding of industries and audiences, as well as the diverse social contexts in which the contest over meaning arises."[9]

Here is where moviegoing histories can provide important new insights into the intersections, conflicts, refashionings, and adoption of the mass, the national, the modern, and the urban into the far reaches of the American hinterlands. The chapters in this collection focus on the local, on specific historical developments that both demonstrate the unusual and unique aspects of film consumption in their case study towns and make valuable analytical connections of qualities that those historical experiences have shared with other locations—from big city to small town—across the nation. Contributors to this volume have helped build on this base with research on a variety of local exhibition practices and case studies of reception histories, to make the continual growth of this area of cinema history rich and exciting.

Some Background on Local Places, Towns, and Small Cities in U.S. History

Because this volume's historical and geographic focus is on the first fifty years of moviegoing in small towns and regional centers across the nation, it is useful to provide some background on the place of the "hinterlands" in American history in the first half of the twentieth century. Small-town America was as notable for its economic and cultural distance from New York City in 1900 as for the many ways that distance was closed by the 1960s and 1970s. Changes in mass culture (with the movies at its center) were just as influential as economic and mobility shifts in reshaping the United States across the century. We want to argue that, in the period we find most important for moviegoing, small-town America was a very different place from New York or Chicago.

In the first decades of the twentieth century, there were wide disparities between how everyday life was experienced in the largest cities of the United States and in its small towns and rural areas. In 1910, about 12 percent of Americans resided in the major metropolitan centers of 500,000 or more people, while five times as many people, or 63 percent, lived on farms or in villages with populations smaller than 10,000.[10] New York City, Chicago, Philadelphia, and other great cities had dazzling electric lights, telephones, subways, skyscrapers, and scores of vaudeville theaters. They also had vast differences of social class and ethnicity separating the cities' elites from the immigrant populations that overflowed the working-class districts. The smaller settlements scattered across America's hinterlands, on the other hand, had few urban amenities, and many cultural and economic problems of their own. Nevertheless, they shared at least one thing—an abundance of movie shows.

The vogue for motion pictures spread quickly across the land after their introduction in 1896, appearing everywhere from big-city theaters to small-town opera houses and rural church halls. Of all the new technologies becoming available to American consumers early in the twentieth century (electricity, telephones, automobiles, radio), the movies diffused across the nation the most quickly and thoroughly. Film projectors were portable and relatively easy to operate—without electricity, a projector's light source could come from limelight, or even the headlights of a Model T Ford. The films themselves were mass-produced and could be easily obtained through purchase or rental. Movies found enthusiastic audiences in nearly every corner of every state and territory. A magazine advertisement from 1917 ("And They Both Show the Same Pictures!") emphasized the far reach of the movies across America: "Whether you attend a million-dollar palace of the screen in the big city, or a tiny hall in a backwoods hamlet, you will find that it is always the best and most prosperous theater in the community that is exhibiting Paramount Artcraft Pictures."[11] Although urban places have always been privileged, across the twentieth century, the movies were as much a part of the popular culture landscape of rural and small-town areas as of the nation's largest cities.

However, cinema historians have examined the medium and its audience primarily in a metropolitan context. In a lively debate with Ben Singer in the pages of *Cinema Journal* over the typicality of New York City as a site of early film exhibition, Robert Allen cited population data and concluded, "If we were forced to choose only one locality to represent the way the movies became a part of most communities in America, we would have more reason to choose Anamosa, Iowa than New York, New York."[12] Was the movies' modernizing influence only a phenomenon of the city? The scholars contributing to this anthology argue that it was not. However, then, we must ask, what forms or degrees of impact did the movies have on the less-metropolitan, rural, and small-town Americans, their society and culture? We believe that establishing a nonurban context is crucial to complete our understanding of the birth and growth of the cinema and of American social and cultural history. We find that nonmetropolitan audiences and exhibitors encountered and shaped mass culture in their own ways, in continuing patterns of moviegoing practices that were sometimes similar to and often different from those of their counterparts in large cities. Small-town residents simultaneously engaged mass culture on their own terms and were limited by the contexts established by the business, aesthetic, and institutional practices of mass culture itself.

Although, for decades, scholars have argued for the predominance of urban culture in the United States by quoting the statistic that in 1920 the U.S. census first showed that 50 percent of Americans lived in urban places, they have less often taken into account that the government's definition of *urban* included *all* settlements of 2,500 people or more. For example, the village of Cooperstown, the town of Poughkeepsie, and the borough of Brooklyn were hardly interchangeable places in terms of population and culture, but all were lumped together by the census demographers as equally urban places in New York State. Historical population statistics across the twentieth century tell a more complex story about the size of settlements in which various Americans resided.[13]

The more dramatic story of population change in the twentieth century actually is found in the countryside rather than in the big cities, for residents of the largest regional centers have not represented more than one-third of the nation's total population at any time in the past hundred years. On the other hand, rural and small-town people predominated at the turn of the century—they represented 70 percent of the nation in 1900, but then about half of the population in the 1930s and 1940s, and only about one-third in the latter half of the century. The proportion of Americans who farmed full-time fell from 60 percent in 1900 to 2 percent in 2000. It is easy to oversentimentalize the history of small-town life as a lingering remnant of a mythical past, as a return to some imagined homogeneity, and as representing a conservative sense of community and order. In reality, at the turn of the twentieth century, a great many rural residents were delighted to leave the limited economic horizons and often stultifying social atmosphere of small-town society for the freedom, anonymity, and opportunity of the big city. As cities became larger and more culturally dominant, new urban Americans arrived not only from foreign lands but also from the countryside. After all, Hal Barron has characterized rural residents not as any progressive cultural force but as "those who stayed behind."[14]

Examining only nationwide population averages also obscures significant settlement and cultural variations among geographic regions of the United States, particularly before the 1950s. The Mid-Atlantic States' coastal regions were the most densely populated and were defined by their large cities. Closely spaced small towns, villages, and farms predominated across much of northern New England, upstate New York, and Pennsylvania and outside the industrial centers of the Midwest. Most of the Southeast and Southwest was less densely settled than the North, containing fewer towns and more rural isolation, much more poverty, and sharp racial conflicts that limited everyone's access to the movies. Especially in the years before the Great Depression, midwestern small-town dwellers and farmers tended to be more prosperous than their southern counterparts and had higher rates of automobile ownership (which enabled more of them to attend movie shows on Saturdays). The vast expanses and rugged terrain of the Mountain States and Pacific States affected settlement patterns there; the West contained very large, isolated ranches and small towns spread far apart, but more of its population was concentrated in larger cities than in the Southeast, a situation that created for some residents very limited access to movies, while others had plenty. Hence it was much more likely that farmers in Nebraska and the Dakotas attended the movies than either white or black sharecroppers could in Alabama or Mississippi. Extremely few communities entirely rejected motion pictures, although significant numbers of people in many towns attended only rarely. (As Robert Allen notes in his chapter, this should be an important aspect of our studies of moviegoing, especially in the South, where transportation and expendable income were in short supply, racial conflict created unequal access to theaters, and religious animosity to public amusements was strong.)[15]

Turning to specific local case studies, especially of nonmetropolitan audiences and their moviegoing practices, enables us to address larger debates and issues surrounding the history of cinema and its audiences. As Ronald Walters discusses in his concluding chapter, especially pertinent is the prevailing "modernity thesis," which sees cinema as a product of and agent promoting a perceptual change at the turn of the twentieth century linked to the rapidity, diversity, and anonymity of urban living. Scholars use this thesis to argue that cinema emerged as an amusement especially tailored to the growth of cities. The chapters in this anthology, explicitly and implicitly, question this hypothesis in many ways. For instance, how can we explain cinema's acceptance by rural Americans, situated well outside the allegedly "modern" milieu of the city? Did these Americans undergo the same kinds of perceptual changes that made cinema so attractive to urban audiences, or did rural Americans see something different and put to different uses this mass entertainment than did their urban counterparts? If so, can scholars continue to make such an ironbound connection between cinema and modernity?

Local Moviegoing Case Studies in This Collection

In the opening section of this anthology, Robert Allen establishes a larger context within which the other chapters in the volume fit. Allen makes the case for the importance of giving small towns a prominent place in our understanding of the history of the cinema. He claims that the traditional focus on the largest American cities has resulted in significant misperceptions of cinema history as a whole. Recognition of the importance of rural, small-town, and local moviegoing practices will force scholars to rethink traditional concepts and interpretations common to the standard film histories.

The next four chapters offer an analysis of the itinerant and early phase of cinematic exhibition in rural areas. Diverse geographic locations are represented in this collection, from the South (Gastonia and Wilmington, North Carolina; Norfolk, Virginia) to the Midwest (Des Moines and Anamosa, Iowa; Stevens Point, Wisconsin; the fictional Hilltown, Indiana; Lebanon, Kansas; and rural Ontario, Canada) to the West (Placerville, California; and rural Colorado). Despite geographic and regional differences, however, many of the case studies of early film exhibition follow similar patterns—starting with the historian's search for "the first" local film exhibition or the earliest development of moviegoing practices. These chapters show stages of growth, from a period of itinerant show people to the establishment of nickelodeons whose owners struggled to make connections with their local communities and to work with censors over film and racial issues. The era of traveling amusement shows lasted only a short time in large urban areas, as nickelodeons quickly replaced these exhibitions by 1905. Yet in small towns, itinerants not only brought the first motion pictures to local audiences but also remained an important interface between audiences and moving pictures well into the 1920s (and in some cases, like central Kentucky and the Shenandoah Valley of Virginia, into the 1950s). The late Calvin Pryluck examines the role of rural traveling exhibitors and their audiences before 1910 in a variety of regions of the United States. He calls into question the dominant paradigm of film's origins in an urban, ethnic, working-class milieu.

Three community studies offer a more detailed glimpse at early exhibition. Anne Morey discusses itinerant exhibition and the evolution of stationary theaters in Wilmington, North Carolina, a small regional center in which entertainment stood at the intersection of race and culture. Residents of southern communities mediated mass culture through the lens of analytical dichotomies not prevalent in urban areas at the time. In rural Placerville, California, itinerant exhibition was popular, but the local population would not support a regular diet of motion pictures well into the new century. George Potamianos maintains that for movies to become a dominant amusement in Placerville, an exhibitor had to go to great lengths to shape motion pictures and the theater as an institution worthy of regular local patronage. The exhibitor positioned his theater as a business that would be an important part of Placerville's community identity, not simply a site in which to show films. Rural motion picture theaters differed significantly from urban nickelodeons, in part because local residents expected the theater space to serve a variety of community functions. Finally, Terry Lindvall argues for the importance local religious leaders in actively shaping the acceptability of film exhibition in Norfolk, Virginia, for both white middle-class and black viewers; the context he presents has been largely overlooked in urban analyses or, at best, discussed only in the context of censorship or battles over film content in the second decade of the twentieth century.

Eventually, established motion picture theaters replaced traveling show people. The five contributions to the next part of the book explore the multiplicity of roles these movie theaters played in specific rural communities, with special attention paid to how exhibition in smaller towns fit into state, regional, and national contexts. Richard Abel explores rural movie audiences in Des Moines, Iowa, and the overall discourse surrounding the cinema by scrutinizing the local press, city directories, and magazines. He is interested not only in the types of films exhibited in the community but also in the larger issue of how motion pictures were presented and discussed in the small city. The provincial government of Ontario, Canada, used film as a way to "modernize" rural areas of the province. Charles Tepperman analyzes how rural Ontario residents accepted and occasionally subverted state efforts to shape the countryside through movies. Focusing on the town of Stevens Point, Wisconsin, Leslie Midkiff DeBauche examines three cinematic "moments" in 1916 to explore how the local community interfaced with national discourses: *Birth of a Nation* was exploited locally as part of a national "fashion week" campaign; the new Lyric Theater opened in the context of national "urban beautification" discourses; and national and local advertisements promoted the serial *Gloria's Romance*. Finally, Gregory Waller uses fictional representation of the Llamarada Theater in a series of articles published in the *Saturday Evening Post* and in the film industry trade press to uncover how the national discourse incorporated and regularized the culture of rural theaters and audiences at the edge of late-1920s prosperity as small-town midwesterners entered the 1930s.

Two contributions to the subsequent part explore the impact of the Great Depression on small-town moviegoers and theater managers. Academic examination of film exhibition in the era of "classical Hollywood cinema" (1915–60) has focused for the most part on the largest theaters, the approximately 2,000 lavish urban picture palaces like the Roxy, Strand, and Paramount in New York and the luxurious Balaban and Katz theaters in Chicago, which were owned or controlled by the film studios and which provided the bulk of studio income (as opposed to the more than 12,000 smaller theaters across the nation that were independently owned but nevertheless indirectly controlled by the studios' block booking contracts).[16] Kathy Fuller-Seeley uses letters published in an exhibitors' forum in the industry trade journal *Motion Picture Herald* to argue that the economic collapse imposed greater hardships on rural theater owners who had to employ different strategies than their urban counterparts to retain audiences during a decade of poverty, drought, and pre–Production Code films and block booking. Paige Reynolds details a specific practice common to exhibitors in rural communities in the 1930s, the controversial Bank Night, and positions that practice in the context of changing ideas about the American Dream and ideologies of success.

After a return to prosperity in the World War II era, movie theaters began to close across the nation in the 1950s—both old, worn theaters, in decaying big-city commercial centers, and those that had been at the heart of small-town Main Streets. Everywhere, movie attendance rates dropped by half or more. Big cities reached out into the surrounding countryside through suburbanization. Farmlands turned first into drive-in movie theaters, and then later into subdivisions. Television also spread in the 1950s as a competing form of entertainment, although more isolated farmlands and small towns had to wait years (until the late 1950s) to be within range of TV signals. The new generation of movie theaters built in the 1960s, 1970s, and 1980s were concentrated in suburban shopping malls and commercial centers. Both urban downtowns and a great many rural areas lost all their movie theaters. Typical was Lebanon, Kansas, which in the 1930s was a village of 800 people with a 250-seat theater, the Owl (operated by Gladys McArdle). There were eight to ten other competing movie shows within a forty-mile radius of Lebanon. The Owl closed at the end of World War II. Today the town has only about 300 residents, mostly older people; the younger generations have moved away in search of economic opportunity, and residents have to drive forty to fifty miles to find a movie show.

The last two chapters draw out elements of the bigger picture presented in this volume. Kevin Corbett examines the recent efforts of local exhibitors, preservationists, and community activists to keep the remaining historic small-town theaters viable entities for the present and future. He conducted a series of interviews with small-town central Michigan residents who relayed their experiences at the movie theaters in their communities. Corbett's ethnographic reconstruction argues that there has been a distinctive "rural" practice of moviegoing, a sense of community and shared culture, which preservationists seek to marshal in their efforts to keep old theaters open. In the concluding chapter, Ronald Walters sums up some of the larger themes raised in the volume and offers fruitful directions for future thought and research. He argues that one of the central questions posed by this anthology is the question of what constitutes audiences of popular culture and whether or not the relationship between audiences and cultural texts can be discussed in general terms. Can we ever, in short, make meaningful statements about audiences of popular culture, or is that audience so diverse that nothing systematic and general can be said at all? In particular, he discusses how the contributions to this anthology put the "modernity thesis" to the test. The study of moviegoing practices outside major metropolitan areas paradoxically both clarifies and obfuscates our understanding of the history of the cinema.

Local moviegoing research can be conducted in a variety of ways, with outcomes other than conventional academic articles, and we heartily encourage readers to undertake their own studies into the cinema history of their communities. Our research has developed from interests in the specific and local, in asking questions about how people interacted while attending the cinema, and in uncovering what was unique or unusual in a community's moviegoing practices, and what were parts of larger regional and historical patterns. The range of sources researchers can mine is wide—fire insurance maps, architectural surveys, newspapers, scrapbooks and diaries, county records, newspapers, local histories, and interviews with senior citizens and families of theater workers can all yield information. Library reference and special collections departments may have old theater clippings or photographs. Flea markets, antique dealers, and Internet auctions of old postcards and paper ephemera may offer unusual materials. There is also a growing shelf of scholarly and popular books on local moviegoing history.

Moviegoing history research projects can take a wide variety of forms. Project director Karan Sheldon of the nonprofit moving image preservation organization Northeast Historic Film, in Bucksport, Maine, researched and created an ambitious and multifaceted traveling museum exhibition on the history of moviegoing in northern New England. It was based on extensive archival, oral history, and architectural research, and it received substantial funding from agencies such as the National Endowment for the Humanities. The "Going to the Movies" exhibit has toured several states and is installed in the NHF restored theater/headquarters building (see information on this and other exhibits at http://www.oldfilm.org). David Guss of Tufts University involved graduate and undergraduate students in the research and creation of an exhibit for the Somerville (Mass.) Museum, "The Lost Theaters of Somerville" (http://www.losttheatres.org). Gregory Waller (*At the Picture Show,* 1993) and Kevin Corbett (*Little Palaces: Michigan's Historic Small Town Movie Theaters,* 2000) have created insightful film documentaries on local moviegoing history.

Robert C. Allen of the University of North Carolina, Chapel Hill, has developed a graduate seminar on the history of the social experience of moviegoing, which he has co-taught several times with Kate Bowles of the University of Wollongong, Australia. The course is an experiment to see what challenges and opportunities might arise in trying to use new teaching technologies (especially the "course environment" software packages) to bring together research students around the world with "traditional" on-campus students to study the history of moviegoing. By announcing the course opportunity on film listservs and Web sites, we attracted more than a dozen interested graduate students from around the world: the United States, Great Britain, the Netherlands, and New Zealand. Students were motivated to participate for a number of reasons: some were already doing original research in the field; most were at universities where there were few or no opportunities to take a dedicated course on the history of movie audiences, reception, or moviegoing. One of the course's subsidiary goals was to allow these students to hold a conversation with scholars whose work had shaped the field of the history of movie audiences and reception, and numerous scholars joined them for a week at a time for online discussion of their work. Student research groups in the program have uncovered significant variations in North Carolina film exhibition patterns, who operated theaters and why, how censorship was applied or evaded, and how racial issues shaped moviegoing experiences through segregation. Arthur Knight of the College of William and Mary is working with students to implement the Williamsburg Theater Project (http://www.wm.edu/amst/wtp, designed by Robert K. Nelson), a searchable online database that documents all film programs shown at Williamsburg theaters from the 1920s through the 1960s in the context of local culture.

An international group of cinema scholars has formed the History of Moviegoing, Exhibition, and Reception Project (HOMER). As the group's Web site explains, it "aims to promote understanding of the complex, international phenomena of film going, exhibition, and reception through several means: the collection, scholarly vetting, and sharing, via the world wide web, of new data on film going, exhibition, and reception{ . . . }and dissemination of new models of collaborative research in the humanities that incorporate faculty, graduate students, and undergraduates in long-term projects, and the development of new ways to incorporate such research into cinema studies and cultural history classrooms." The group's Web site (www .homerproject.org) and its links will provide readers with portals through which to explore archival data, case studies, and teaching materials for future potential moviegoing research projects.

Notes

1. Robert Allen, "Relocating American Film History: The 'Problem' of the Empirical," *Cultural Studies* 20 (2006): 44–88.

2. See, for example, Leo Charney and Vanessa R. Schwartz, eds., *Cinema and the Invention of Modern Life* (Berkeley and Los Angeles: University of California Press, 1995).

3. Tom Gunning, "Tracing the Individual Body: Photography, Detectives and Early Cinema," in Charney and Schwartz, *Cinema and the Invention of Modern Life*, 15.

4. Allen, "Relocating American Film History."

5. Raymond Williams, *Keywords: A Vocabulary of Culture and Society*, rev. ed. (New York: Oxford University Press, 1983), 208–9.

6. Claude Fisher, *America Calling: A Social History of the Telephone to 1940* (Berkeley and Los Angeles: University of California Press, 1992); David E. Nye, *Electrifying America: Social Meanings of a New Technology, 1880–1940* (Cambridge, Mass.: MIT Press, 1992); Carolyn Marvin, *When Old Technologies Were New: Thinking about Electric Communication in the Late Nineteenth Century* (New York: Oxford University Press,

American Rural and Urban Population, 1900–1980

Settlement	Percentage of U.S. Population in Each Decade								
Size	1900	1910	1920	1930	1940	1950	1960	1970	1980
Farm and rural	52.1	45.5	40.4	36.4	36.4	29	24.3	21.2	21.4
Small towns 1,000–10,000	16.2	17.5	17.3	16.1	16	16.7	15.5	15.5	15.7
Larger towns 10,000–50,000	9.4	10.4	11.4	12.6	13.2	13.6	18.1	19.3	22.5
Regional city centers 50,000–500,000	11.7	14.1	15.4	18	17.5	17.7	20.2	20.3	21.6
Big cities 500,000+	10.6	12.5	15.5	16.9	16.9	17.6	16	15.6	12.5

1990); Michael Berger, *The Devil Wagon in God's Country: The Automobile and Social Change in Rural America, 1893–1929* (New York: Archon Books, 1979); Ronald R. Kline, *Consumers in the Country: Technology and Social Change in Rural America* (Baltimore: Johns Hopkins University Press, 2000); Kline, "Resisting Development, Reinventing Modernity: Rural Electrification in the United States before World War II," *Environmental Values* 11 (2002): 327–44; Pamela Grundy, "'We Always Tried to Be Good People': Respectability, Crazy Water Crystals and Hillbilly Music on the Air, 1933–1935," *Journal of American History* 81 (1995): 1591–1620; Derek Vaillant, "'Your Voice Came In Last Night but I Thought It Sounded a Little Scared': Rural Radio Listening and 'Talking Back' during the Progressive Era in Wisconsin, 1920–1932," in *Radio Reader*, ed. Michelle Hilmes and Jason Loviglio (New York: Routledge, 2002), 63–86; Hal S. Barron, *Mixed Harvest: The Second Great Transformation in the Rural North, 1870–1930* (Chapel Hill: University of North Carolina Press, 1997); Katherine Jellison, *Entitled to Power: Farm Women and Technology, 1913–1963* (Chapel Hill: University of North Carolina Press, 1993); Jane Adams, *The Transformation of Rural Life: Southern Illinois, 1890–1990* (Chapel Hill: University of North Carolina Press, 1994). For a European context, see Ted W. Margadant, "Tradition and Modernity in Rural France during the Nineteenth Century," *Journal of Modern History* 56 (1984): 667–97.

7. Ted Ownby argues that conservative Christian rejection of motion pictures and other aspects of commercial popular culture only came in the second and third decades of the twentieth century, when the initial period of acceptance in a technological novelty hardened into criticism of the sexual or modern-tinged topics that movies increasingly displayed. Ownby, *Subduing Satan: Religion, Recreation and Manhood in the Rural South 1865–1920* (Chapel Hill: University of North Carolina Press, 1990).

8. Scholars use the term *glocal* to describe a process of the "contested impact of globalization as resulting in combination rather than conquest" for outcome in specific localities "that is both globally connected and locally loyal." Robert Eric Livingston, "Glocal Knowledges: Agency and Place in Literary Studies," *Proceedings of the Modern Language Association* 116 (2001): 145–57; E. V. Swyngedouw and M. V. Kaïka, "The Making of 'Glocal' Urban Modernities," *City* 7, no. 1 (2003): 5–21.

9. Michael Curtin, "Globalisation," in *Television Studies*, ed. Toby Miller (London: British Film Institute, 2002), 43–46.

10. Donald J. Bogue, *The Population of the United States: Historical Trends and Future Projections* (New York: Free Press, 1985), 112–13, table 3.11.

11. "And They Both Show the Same Pictures!" Paramount Artcraft advertisement, *Saturday Evening Post,* September 20, 1919, 9.

12. Robert Allen, "Manhattan Myopia; or, Oh! Iowa!" *Cinema Journal* 35 (1996): 96.

13. Bogue, *The Population of the United States.*

14. Hal Barron, *Those Who Stayed Behind: Rural Society in Nineteenth-Century New England* (New York: Cambridge University Press, 1984).

15. Kathryn H. Fuller, *At the Picture Show: Small-Town Audiences and the Creation of Movie Fan Culture* (Washington, D.C.: Smithsonian Institution Press, 1996), 28–46.

16. See Douglas Gomery, *Shared Pleasures: A History of Movie Presentation in the United States* (Madison: University of Wisconsin Press, 1992); Richard Maltby, *Hollywood Cinema,* 2nd ed. (Malden, Mass.: Blackwell, 2003).

2

DECENTERING HISTORICAL AUDIENCE STUDIES

A Modest Proposal

ROBERT C. ALLEN

In his review of scholarship on the history of American cities, Timothy Gilfoyle notes that American urban historiography remains stubbornly "Gothamcentric." Applied to film history, I would argue, *Gothamcentrism* refers to the related tendencies to place the metropolis at the center of historical narratives of moviegoing and to encourage the assumption that patterns of movie exhibition and moviegoing found there can be mapped to a greater or lesser degree upon smaller cities and towns in all parts of the United States at any given moment in the history of American cinema.[1] The privileging of the metropolitan experience of the movies in American film historiography, as Richard Maltby has pointed out, also mirrors Hollywood's ordering of movie audiences, movie theaters, and theater locations. To use *Variety*'s vernacular from the early 1930s, "metropolites," "deluxers," and "big keys" were at the center of an imagined universe of moviegoing, and "hicks," "dime houses," and the "Silo Belt" were located on the periphery.[2] Supporting this discursive hierarchy was the disproportionate economic importance of big-city movie theaters. As early as 1921, the Federal Trade Commission asserted that 50 percent of studio revenue came from large first-run theaters, and in 1948 the U.S. Justice Department argued in the *Paramount* case that the major studios' control of 70 percent of the first-run theaters in the largest cities in the United States was sufficient to give them oligopoly control over the entire exhibition sector of the film industry.[3] Thomas Cripps has concluded that in the 1920s it was not uncommon for one or two large theaters in New York City to take in more money in a given week than all the theatres in the South put together.[4]

Manhattan has long been at the epicenter of the imagined map of movie audiences and moviegoing—both for the industry and for the field of film history. In the 1920s and 1930s all the major studios operated theaters on

20

Broadway, where they showcased their "superior" films prior to national release, with the assumption that "a success on Broadway would be repeated throughout the United States."[5] In his critique of my own inadvertent contribution to the Gothamcentrism of U.S. film history, Ben Singer argued that the nuances of early exhibition in Manhattan still had a unique claim on the attention of film historians because "Manhattan's nickelodeon boom has played such a prominent role in shaping our conception of early film history, as well as American social history."[6]

The big-city exercises a centripetal evidentiary pull for the film historian as well. With early film production, the national apparatus of show business, and theatrical and motion picture trade papers all located there, Manhattan's moviegoers received more contemporaneous attention than any other audience group in the country—perhaps the world. As I discovered when I first tried to document some of the features of early film exhibition in 1978, if you had the patience to scroll through miles of unindexed microfilmed newspapers and trade papers and the help of a resourceful interlibrary-loan librarian in locating extant city directories and fire insurance maps, it was possible to produce a schematic account of moviegoing in 1907 Manhattan seventy-five years later from hundreds of miles away. Metropolitan movie theaters, moviegoing, and moviegoers also feature in the Progressive Era social reform literature about big-city "problems": white slavery, prostitution, immigration, overcrowding, education and literacy, child labor and child crime, among them. Big cities often (not always) have a sense of their own histories and have large and sophisticated systems for recording and preserving historical data about the physical, economic, social, and political contexts within which movie theaters operated. Judith Thissen's 2001 dissertation on Jewish immigration and popular entertainment in New York City between 1880 and 1914 demonstrates how effectively a wide range of extant material about a city (trade papers, Yiddish newspapers, real estate and architectural records, municipal ordinances, and reform tracts, among others) can be marshaled to support a much more nuanced and complex account of early moviegoing on the Lower East Side than was previously available.[7]

In some ways, then, it makes perfectly good sense to have studied and to keep studying the metropolitan experience of moviegoing in the United States. It is there we would look first if, for example, we were primarily interested in asking, "What were the most economically important sites of moviegoing in the United States between 1921 and 1948?" Or, "From what kinds of theaters in what kinds of localities did the Hollywood film studios derive the largest portion of their box office revenues and profits?" Or, "How did Hollywood imagine the audiences for which its films were being made?"

Problems arise, however, when the historiographical shadow cast by the metropolis obscures other equally important questions and other patterns of moviegoing and social life outside the big city. Assuming the normativity of the metropolitan experience of the movies makes it difficult to see regional or demographic differences as anything other than aberrations or the result of a lag in the pace of modernization. We run the risk of constructing the national audience for the movies as a simple cultural and social hierarchy: *Variety*'s "hicks" and "sophisticates." Or, to use a more contemporary distinction, we risk collapsing a huge and diverse prospective audience for the movies into "the coasts" and "flyover country."

What follows are some reflections on the history of the social experience of moviegoing in the United States made by someone who has spent the past quarter century or so researching and teaching about the movies from a position somewhere between the metropolis and the sticks, and in a region of the country, the South, that provides a very different social, economic, and cultural context for the early history of the movies than is to be found in the urban North or Midwest. I provide examples of the "place" of the movies in the lived experience of people in this part of the country not to suggest that historiographical maps of cinema audience studies should be redrawn with North Carolina at their center but merely to suggest the range of issues that might become more visible when we shift our attention away from the metropolitan.

Removing the metropolis from the center of the study of the social experience of moviegoing makes it easier to ask questions not just about who went to the movies most frequently and where movies and moviegoing were most prominent and best recorded but also about the relationship between the movies as a social phenomenon and what we might call the national social formation as a whole. For example, although the early audience for the movies in the United States was disproportionately centered in large urban areas, most *people* living in the United States in 1910 did not encounter the movies in such metropolitan settings. According to the 1910 census, 63.9 percent of the U.S. population lived in "rural territory," which the Census Bureau defined as unincorporated settlements of *fewer than 2,500 inhabitants*. There were only three cities in the United States in 1910 with populations of greater than 1 million (New York, Philadelphia, and Chicago). The inhabitants of these metropolises represented 9.2 percent of the total U.S. population. An equal number of "urban" dwellers in 1910 lived in the 1,801 towns of at least 2,500 but fewer than 10,000 people.[8]

For example, North Carolina was by no means the most rural area of the country in 1910. It was, in fact, the twentieth most densely populated state, with a mean population density 50 percent greater than for the nation as a whole (45 persons per square mile). However, there were only seven North Carolina cities with more than 10,000 inhabitants (the largest, Charlotte, had fewer than 35,000 people) and a total of only eighteen "cities" of at least 2,500 population in a state that comprised more than 48,000 square miles. Only 14 percent of the state's 2.2 million residents lived in these "urban" centers, and only half of these city dwellers lived in cities with populations of 10,000 or more. Roughly 1.9 million Tar Heels were spread out among nearly a thousand unincorporated settlements of fewer than 2,500 people or lived far enough from population clusters of any size to qualify for my mother's definition of "way out in the country."[9]

Accounts of the metropolitan experience of moviegoing, particularly during the nickelodeon period, place great stress on the "ethnic" character of movie audiences and never fail to mention the prominence of recently arrived European immigrants within those audiences. It is no doubt the case that the newly arrived immigrants who were packed into the most densely populated neighborhoods in the most crowded borough of the largest city in the United States represented a very large part of the audience for the nickelodeons *there*. In 1910 nearly half (47.4 percent) of the *total* population of Manhattan were immigrants, and another third (35.1 percent) were the native-born children of immigrants. Only 17 percent of the people residing in Manhattan (including the 2.6 percent of the population who were African American) were native born residents of native parentage (as the census puts it).[10] In other words, if everyone in Manhattan in 1910 attended the movies at the same rate, we would expect that 83 out of every 100 tickets were sold to immigrants and their children.

In a few other cities in 1910 (most of them in the Northeast), the proportion of foreign-born approached that of Manhattan, but as a part of the country's total population, first-generation immigrants represented less than 15 percent. Furthermore, although the number of immigrants to the United States doubled between 1880 and 1910, the relative proportion of the population they represented over the half century between 1860 and 1910 remained more or less the same.[11] Nor were immigrants evenly distributed throughout the country. More than half of all foreign-born Americans lived in the nine states of the New England and Middle Atlantic regions, and four out of every ten immigrants lived in three states: Pennsylvania, Massachusetts, and New York. Immigrants were most prominent in the largest cities in the United States. They made up nearly a third of the population of cities with more than 500,000 residents, but less than 10 percent in cities and town with fewer than 25,000 residents. Keep in mind that at that time 69 percent of the *total* population of the United States lived in concentrations of fewer than 25,000.[12]

If movie theater entrepreneurs in the sixteen states of the American South had had to rely on recently arrived immigrants—from anywhere—to fill their theaters, there would not have been a single viable movie theater south of Baltimore and east of New Orleans for most of the history of American cinema. In the South, immigrants made up only 2.5 percent of the total population, and in North Carolina only 0.3 percent: 6,092 out of 2,206,287. Of these, nearly half were from the British Isles and Canada. Ninety-five percent of the entire population of North Carolina had been born there, and three out of every four people who moved to North Carolina from someplace else had been born in a contiguous state. In short, in the later decades of the nineteenth century and the early decades of the twentieth, not only was it possible to spend your entire life in North Carolina without ever hearing a foreign language spoken, but it was quite possible, particularly in rural counties, to spend your entire life without cultivating the acquaintance of anyone who had been born outside the state of North Carolina!

Over the past fifteen years or so there has been considerable interest among film historians in drawing connections among cinema, the experience of metropolitan urbanity, and a particular understanding of modernity. Drawing on the work of Georg Simmel, Siegfried Kracauer, and Walter Benjamin, some have argued that modernity involves a historical change in subjective experience as individuals adjust to the new sensory environment of the big city—one characterized by "hyperstimulus." As Ben Singer puts it, "Modernity implied a phenomenal world—a specifically urban one—that was markedly quicker, more chaotic, fragmented and disorienting than in previous phases of human culture. . . . The individual faced a new intensity of sensory stimulation." Singer quotes as a seminal description of what we might call metropolitan phenomenal modernity Simmel's essay "The Metropolis and Mental Life" (1903): "With each crossing of the street, with the tempo and multiplicity of economic, occupational and social life, the city sets up a deep contrast with small town and rural life with reference to the sensory foundations of psychic life."[13]

Immediately after quoting from Simmel's account of the European *metropolitan* experience, Singer moves to equate it with the experience of American urbanity at the turn of the century: "The sudden increase in urban population (which in the U.S. more than quadrupled between 1870 and 1910), the escalation of commercial activity, the proliferation of signs, and the new density and complexity of street traffic . . . made the city a much more crowded, chaotic, and stimulating environment than it had ever been in the past."[14]

To be sure, the decades around the turn of the century saw rapid urbanization in many parts of the country (including my own), but it was not until the 1920 census that, for the first time, a majority of Americans lived in "urban" centers. This hardly means that a majority of Americans lived in metropolises like New York or Chicago: again, the Census Bureau's rather generous definition of *urban* granted that distinction to *all* towns of at least 2,500 residents. Most people's experience of the transition from rural to urban life at the turn of the century was quite different. North Carolina, for example, felt the twin modernizing forces of urbanization and industrialization more sharply than most other American states around the turn of the century. The proportion of the population living in towns of at least 2,500 increased nationwide by 15 percent between 1900 and 1910; in North Carolina the percentage of urban dwellers increased 45 percent over the same period.

Cotton mills, lumber mills, furniture factories, and tobacco factories were built to take advantage of their proximity to raw materials, water power, and cheap labor, and as small farmers, tenant farmers, and sharecroppers were pushed off farms when commodity prices periodically crashed.[15] However, the rapid industrialization and urbanization of North Carolina between 1900 and 1910 did not occur primarily in its "big" cities. More than 90 percent of all factories and mills and 85 percent of all manufacturing workers were located in towns and villages of fewer than 10,000 people.

Even the "big" cities in North Carolina reflected the particularities of southern patterns of industrialization and urbanization. Unlike in northern industrial cities, where worker housing was erected by real estate investors or independent landlords, many southern mill owners built and managed "villages" of rented worker housing around their mills. As a result, the North Carolina cities most greatly affected by rapid industrialization "developed less as real cities than as loose collections of unincorporated mill villages joined by central business districts." Mill villages built on the outskirts of cities "retained a distinctively rural appearance."[16]

Furthermore, just because families undertook what they called "public work" (as distinct from farming) in factories and mills does not mean that they somehow automatically became city folk, leaving behind rural skills, values, ways of understanding, or patterns of social life. Mills recruited entire rural families, not just single men or women, frequently requiring that at least one person per room work in the mill if the family was to obtain mill-owned housing. Men, women, and older children all worked in the same mill. As Jacqueline Dowd Hall and her colleagues note in their landmark study of the southern cotton mill village, "urban" life in the mill village was produced through the dynamic tension between fundamentally rural social structures and values and the demands of first paternal and then corporate industrial capitalism, not by the elimination of the former by the latter. At the same time that metropolitan nickelodeon audiences might have been experiencing the movies as a part of the hyperstimulus of metropolitan modernity, their newly urbanized working-class counterparts in the mill towns of the South still walked to their jobs along unpaved wagon roads; kept chickens, pigs, and cows; tended vegetable gardens; drew water from common wells; and relieved themselves in backyard privies.[17] If there was, as some film historians have suggested, a particular connection between the distinctive experience of metropolitan urbanity and the experience of the movies, then, it seems to me, such theories beg the question of the nature of the relationship among movies, moviegoing, and modernity for the 91.8 percent of the U.S. population who did *not* experience urban life as it tends to be described in these accounts.

Visiting my now eighty-one-year-old mother at Christmas a few years ago, I asked her if she could recall her earliest experiences of moviegoing in the cotton mill town where she and her seven brothers and sisters (and I) grew up. "I didn't go very often," she said, "because the only person who would take me was Faye [her oldest sister, sixteen years older than she], and, of course, we had to keep it a secret from Daddy. He would have had a fit if he knew we went to the pictures." "How many movies do you think your father saw in his lifetime?" I asked. He had been born in 1888 and had died in 1933. He would have been a teenager when the first movie theater opened in Gastonia, North Carolina, in 1907 and had spent most of his entire adult life within a ten-minute walk of its two downtown movie theaters. "None," she immediately and unequivocally replied.

American film historiography in general and studies of movie audiences in particular have assumed that once Progressive Era concerns over insalubrious conditions in working-class metropolitan nickelodeons dissipated with the rise of the picture palace, moviegoing enjoyed early and nearly ubiquitous social acceptance. To be sure, the 1920s and 1930s saw objections raised to particular films and to particular representational practices, but, we have assumed, moviegoing itself became socially unproblematic. How, then, do we explain my maternal grandfather's antipathy toward the movies and, consequently, my mother's own experience of moviegoing as secretive and illicit throughout her childhood? My grandfather's aversion to moviegoing was rooted in the culture and moral theology of the Southern Baptist Church, in which he (along with more than 2 million other white and predominantly working-class people, most of them living in the small towns and rural areas of the South) had been raised and in which he raised his eight children.[18] Whether or not, as my mother believes, he died without ever seeing a motion picture, he had been taught and he taught his children that moviegoing, drinking alcohol, gambling, and dancing were sinful.

Religious attitudes toward moviegoing in the first decades of the twentieth century reflect a larger moral and theological struggle occurring across Christian denominations as believers attempted to reconcile belief and personal behavior, righteousness and secularity within modernity. And religion played an especially significant role in southern culture. The mainstream Protestant denominations most prominent among the working class in the South, the Methodists and Baptists, were also those whose theologies encouraged renunciation of secular values and adherence to codes of social behavior as a sign of conversion.

It is, of course, impossible to know the degree to which organized religious opposition to the movies or personal religious belief and fear of social ostracism by fellow believers impeded the establishment of permanent exhibition venues or inhibited moviegoing in the South or elsewhere. Terry Lindvall's work in Norfolk, Virginia, reveals an accommodationist stance by mainstream Protestant clergy in that naval city, with movies being regarded as less morally objectionable than some other forms of commercial entertainment available to sailors on shore leave. As Greg Waller details in his study of moviegoing in Lexington, Kentucky, in the silent era, religious opposition to the movies in many towns and small cities took the form of Sabbatarianism and attracted support from both fundamentalist and more mainstream Protestant clergy. Attempts by both black and white ministerial associations and the Moral Improvement League to prohibit or restrict the showing of movies on Sundays continued for a decade in Lexington. Waller notes that similar Sabbatarian campaigns in other Kentucky towns produced a variety of outcomes—from outright rejection of such calls to closure of all theaters not only on Sunday evenings but also on Wednesday evenings. In the western Kentucky town of Owensboro, a 1916 municipal ordinance closed white theaters on Sundays but allowed "colored" shows to stay open, on the theory that "negroes would be better off at the picture house than . . . frequenting dives."[19]

But it would be a mistake to regard religious concerns about the movies in general and the propriety of moviegoing among coreligionists as representing the views only of a small fringe element in American Protestantism or as the residue of traditionalist suspicions of the secular world that are swept away as the modernizing influences of the metropolis take hold in the hinterlands. There is reason to believe that religious acceptance of moviegoing was an issue to some degree for all southern exhibitors, and that for many southerners moviegoing fit awkwardly into the fabric of their social and moral lives. In 1966, J. Melville White contributed an essay entitled "The Motion Picture: Friend or Foe" to *Christianity Today,* the magazine founded in 1957 by North Carolina evangelist Billy Graham and circulated to more than 200,000 Protestant ministers and laypersons. In it, he urges evangelicals to engage with the movies and other media forms in order to develop a "discriminating Christian taste" in secular popular entertainment and to explore ways that movies might be used to attract teenagers to evangelicalism. The primary obstacle to the use of movies by evangelicals, he admits, is that "Christians, as a rule, do not attend the movies." In his study of changes in the evangelical stance toward the movies in the 1960s and 1970s, Shanny Luft notes that White's defense of the social and moral potential of the movies proved controversial to *Christianity Today*'s readership. Although a majority of letters to the editor applauded White's "courage" for broaching the subject at all, a significant minority objected to the magazine's implicit endorsement of moviegoing by young people, and one accused it of serving as an "advertising agency for Hollywood's moral vomit."[20]

In situating her pioneering work on movie exhibition in black neighborhoods in Chicago during the Depression, Mary Carbine quite rightly points out that the emphasis on class, ethnicity, and white immigrant audiences in research on early moviegoing has obscured the quite different experience of metropolitan African American audiences. Furthermore, by focusing on the role of moviegoing within white "second-wave" immigrant communities in large cities (Jewish and Italian neighborhoods, especially), she reminds us, film historians have overlooked the fact that the introduction of the movies in America's largest urban centers coincides with the period of the "Great Migration" of southern blacks to those same cities, which saw the number of black residents in Chicago, for example, increase sevenfold between 1890 and 1910.[21]

Carbine argues that in theaters along the black business, shopping, and leisure district of the "Stroll" (South State Street between Twenty-sixth and Thirty-ninth Streets), black audiences were able to incorporate movies and moviegoing into "specifically African-American cultural practices." These movie theaters became important social institutions for building an alternative sense of racial identity and community.

Clearly, more studies of the metropolitan moviegoing experience of African American audiences are needed. However, if we are interested in documenting and understanding the social experience of moviegoing for *most* African Americans living in the first half century of American film history, we need to shift our attention to the parts of the country where most African Americans actually lived: not large cities in the Northeast and Midwest, but the villages, towns, and cities of the Jim Crow South. Although the number of African Americans in New York City increased by 50 percent between 1900 and 1910, they still constituted less than 2 percent of the total city population and only 2.6 percent of Manhattan's during the nickelodeon period. Despite the image we have of the great racial migration of southern African Americans to northern cities in the early twentieth century, in 1910 nine out of ten African Americans still lived in the South, and seven out of ten lived in the rural South—villages and settlements of fewer than 2,500 people.[22]

Race—not ethnicity or social class—was the chasmic demographic, social, economic, political, and cultural divide that ran through every southern state, through every community of whatever size in those states, and through every social and cultural institution in those communities. Race is not just a part of the story of the history of moviegoing in the South; that story cannot be understood except in its relation to race. And once race is placed at the center of that story (where it belongs), it changes from an account of who saw which movies where to an investigation of how the movies functioned as an instrument of social power. Given the fact that during the early decades of the twentieth century, most African Americans lived in the rural South, not the urban North, there is every reason to believe that for at least sixty years—until sometime *after* the civil rights struggles of the 1950s and 1960s, the movies and moviegoing had very different meanings for the majority of African Americans than they had for whites (southern or not) or for the minority of African Americans who lived in big cities outside the South.

Writing the history of the African American social experience of the movies in the South forces us to begin by asking, "Who wasn't a part of the early audience for the movies, why, and for how long?" For example, over the past few years graduate students in my classes on the history of moviegoing have used our library's extensive holdings of local newspapers, city directories, and maps to construct accounts of the first decades of moviegoing in towns of 2,500 to 5,000 inhabitants throughout North Carolina. In almost every case they have found that movie exhibitions were irregular and relatively infrequent (or at least unrecorded by local newspapers) for the first decade of the history of commercial cinema (1896–1906). Towns large enough to have streetcar lines and amusement parks at the end of those lines might feature movies as a summer attraction. Some peripatetic movie showmen set up tents in vacant lots in the early 1900s, but "permanent" movie theaters did not begin appearing on small-town main streets in North Carolina until some time after 1906.

The most important venue for early movie exhibitions in towns in North Carolina and, I think it is safe to assume, throughout the small-town South, was the local opera house. Constructed in almost every town large enough to qualify as such by the Census Bureau by the turn of the century, these grand-sounding structures were often nothing more than the second story of the town hall or courthouse, outfitted with a stage at one end. Always located at the center of the town's business district and frequently the only public secular meeting spaces in town, opera houses were often leased to local managers who brought in traveling theater companies, variety ensembles, minstrel shows, lecturers, *and,* beginning in 1897, motion picture shows.

Newspaper accounts of exhibitions in small-town opera houses typically tell us little if anything about who constituted the audience for these initial encounters with the movies, and, of course, they are silent regarding who was not present. But if we approach the history of moviegoing in the South as a part of history of the institutionalization of Jim Crow racial apartheid, then we can once again make visible that part of the "audience" for the movies who were not allowed to be *in* the audience: by enforced social custom and, in Virginia by state law, blacks were not allowed to sit among whites. The only accommodation made in some public venues was the reservation of a balcony for black patrons or the offering of blacks-only "midnight shows" for some attractions. From municipal records and photographs it appears that some small-town opera houses were large and tall enough to squeeze in a balcony, although the extant historical record is in most cases silent on whether this was to accommodate more white patrons or to provide seating for blacks. Social custom rarely becomes the subject of newspaper articles. Many other opera houses, however, did not have balconies.

So, in addition to suggesting that moviegoing might well have been only a very occasional activity for millions of white southerners for a very long time, this research also suggests that for millions (a majority?) of African Americans living in or near thousands of small towns across the South (and elsewhere?), access to movies was even more limited. It might well have been that many African Americans living in and around towns in which the opera house had no balcony might not have seen a single film until movie theaters were established in some, but by no means all, of these towns more than a decade after they were made daily attractions in big-city vaudeville theaters.

Dedicated movie venues slowly became common features along the main streets of the small towns of the South between 1907 and 1912. Despite the presence of working-class neighborhoods built around mills and factories on the outskirts of these towns, invariably the first and most of the subsequent movie theaters were sited downtown: in the same blocks as the town's stores, restaurants, and courthouse, where the entire white population of the town came to conduct business and where on Saturdays especially many more people from surrounding farms congregated.

Like these other public venues, small-town movie theaters in the South immediately became institutional instruments for asserting and enforcing racial apartheid. Again, it is very difficult to discern from extant sources, but it appears that some theaters in some towns simply refused to admit African Americans at all. Other theaters were built to accommodate a balcony or added one, and blacks were forced to sit there even though they paid the same ticket price as whites. But even this grudging and demeaning accommodation of blacks was not the result of a stunted sense of fair-mindedness on the part of white exhibitors: in many small towns in the South, African Americans made up such a large percentage of the population that exhibitors had to admit them in order to stay in business. Every facet of moviegoing was made a humiliating exercise in racial power: tiny theaters in tiny towns forced blacks to buy their tickets at a separate box office, reach their inferior balcony seats by separate, exterior stairways, and wait for the beginning of the next show not in the theater lobby but on the street—where, ironically, as Chris McKenna has found, they risked being harassed by police *for* congregating outside whites-only lunch counters and hotels. The near ubiquity of "special accommodations" for black audiences throughout the South for half a century or more means that the challenges of conceptualizing and researching the reception of all movies across a huge swath of the American continent are quite literally doubled. I would count among those challenges not only attempting to work through the profound implications of the social experience of moviegoing upon the reception of all movies for millions of African American viewers but also the implications of this racist system for the reception of films by white viewers.

The work showcased in this anthology reflects and contributes to the ongoing reformulation of film history—both as a field of inquiry and as a teaching field—with questions of exhibition, audience, reception, moviegoing, and memory being relocated in the process from the margins of film history to its center. As this occurs, film history finds itself reconfigured in relation to a new set of historiographical challenges and historical literatures. I do not think many film historians, film history textbooks, or film history teachers in 1978 would have regarded oral history, the history of work and leisure, local history, family history, religious history, or the history of everyday life as being directly relevant to the study of film history. In this collection, the relevance of these "other" histories and historiographies does not have to be asserted, much less argued. The immediate and significant contribution these chapters make to our understanding of this phenomenon is both a reflection of the still-fledgling state of this endeavor and a tribute to the resourcefulness and enterprise of a large and growing group of scholars around the world. The work of the scholars gathered here also reflects and contributes to a more general reorientation of the entire project of film history over the past decade or so—both as a field of inquiry and as a taught subject in U.S. universities—around questions of exhibition, audience, moviegoing, and reception. At issue here is not merely whether audiences for the first movie theaters in Anamosa, Iowa, shared a class affiliation with their "fellow" movie fans on Houston Street in 1907. The focus on the metropolitan experience of moviegoing in American film history and the compression of diverse venues of early film exhibition into the catchall term *nickelodeon* have obscured the variety of ways that movies became a part of the social experience of millions of other people living in very different kinds of communities. These chapters remap the social experience of moviegoing and, in doing so, challenge both the film histories and the national social histories of which they are a part.

Notes

Research that formed the basis for this chapter is also drawn upon and discussed in my essay "Relocating American Film History: The 'Problem' of the Empirical," *Cultural Studies* 20 (2006): 48–88.

1. Timothy J. Gilfoyle, "White Cities, Linguistic Turns, and Disneylands: The New Paradigms of Urban History," *Reviews in American History* 26 (1998): 175–204.

2. Richard Maltby, "Sticks, Hicks and Flaps: Classical Hollywood's Generic Conception of Its Audiences," in *Identifying Hollywood's Audiences*, ed. Melvyn Stokes and Richard Maltby (London: British Film Institute, 1999), 23–41.

3. See Ernest Borneman, "United States versus Hollywood: The Case Study of an Antitrust Suit," in *The American Film Industry*, ed. Tino Balio (Madison: University of Wisconsin Press, 1976), 332–45.

4. Thomas Cripps, "The Myth of the Southern Box Office," in *The Black Experience in America*, ed. James C. Curtis and Lewis L. Gould (Austin: University of Texas Press, 1970), 121–23.

5. Maltby, "Sticks, Hicks and Flaps," 28.

6. Ben Singer, "Manhattan Nickelodeons: New Data on Audiences and Exhibitors," *Cinema Journal* 34, no. 3 (1995): 5–35. Singer's point of departure is my 1978 article, "Motion Picture Exhibition in Manhattan: Beyond the Nickelodeon," *Cinema Journal* 18, no. 2 (1979): 2–15. The singular importance of historical interpretations of the Manhattan nickelodeon had also been argued by Robert Sklar in "Oh! Althusser: Historiography and the Rise of Cinema Studies," *Radical History Review* 41 (1988): 10–35.

7. Judith Thissen, "Moyshe Goes to the Movies: Jewish Immigrants, Popular Entertainment, and Ethnic Identity in New York City (1880–1914)" (Ph.D. diss., University of Utrecht, 2001).

8. *Thirteenth Census of the United States (1910), Abstract of the Census—Population* (Washington, D.C.: Government Printing Office, 1913), 59.

9. *Thirteenth Census of the United States (1910), Abstract and Supplement for North Carolina* (Washington, D.C.: Government Printing Office, 1913), 568–69. All the following statistics on North Carolina demography are taken from this source unless otherwise noted.

10. *Thirteenth Census of the United States (1910), Abstract of the Census—Population,* 95.

11. Ibid., 80. Between 1860 and 1910, the proportion of the population made up by immigrants fluctuated between 13.2 and 14.7 percent. Even though the total number of immigrants to the United States increased by more than 1 million between 1890 and 1900, the proportion of the total population they represented actually fell—from 14.7 to 13.6 percent.

12. *Thirteenth Census of the United States (1910), Abstract of the Census—Population,* 91–93.

13. Georg Simmel, "The Metropolis and Mental Life," in *The Sociology of Georg Simmel,* ed. Kurt H. Wolff (New York: Free Press, 1950), 410, quoted in Ben Singer, "Modernity, Hyperstimulus, and the Rise of Popular Sensationalism," in *Cinema and the Invention of Modern Life,* ed. Leo Charney and Vanessa Schwartz (Berkeley and Los Angeles: University of California Press, 1995), 73.

14. Singer, "Modernity, Hyperstimulus, and the Rise of Popular Sensationalism," 73, 95n2.

15. See Jacquelyn Dowd Hall, James Leloudis, Robert Korstad, Mary Murphy, Lu Ann Jones, and Christopher B. Daly, *Like a Family: The Making of a Southern Cotton Mill World* (New York: Norton, 1989), 5–13.

16. Ibid., 116.

17. U.S. Congress, Senate, *Report on the Condition of Woman and Child Wage-Earners in the United States,* vol. 1, *Cotton Textile Industry,* Senate Document No. 645, 61st Cong., 2nd sess. (Washington, D.C.: Government Printing Office, 1910), 531, 534, quoted in Hall et al., *Like a Family,* 119.

18. By 1906 there were 2,009,471 Southern Baptists in the United States, of whom 1,770,303 lived in the South. Baptists were the largest white denomination in the South at the turn of the century. See Rufus B. Spain, *At Ease in Zion: Social History of Southern Baptists, 1865–1900* (Nashville: Vanderbilt University Press, 1961), viii.

19. Gregory A. Waller, *Main Street Amusements: Movies and Commercial Entertainment in a Southern City, 1896–1930* (Washington, D.C.: Smithsonian Institution Press, 1995), 134.

20. J. Melville White, "The Motion Picture: Friend or Foe?" *Christianity Today,* July 22, 1966, 9–11. Changes in the evangelical stance toward the movies in the 1960s and 1970s are discussed by Shanny Luft in his unpublished paper "To Discern between Good and Evil: *Christianity Today* and the Movies" (2004).

21. Mary Carbine, "The Finest Outside the Loop: Motion Picture Exhibition in Chicago's Black Metropolis, 1905–1928," *Camera Obscura* 23 (May 1990): 9–42.

22. *Thirteenth Census of the United States (1910), Abstract of the Census—Population,* 92–95.

Part II

ORIGINS

CASE STUDIES

3

THE ITINERANT MOVIE SHOW
AND THE DEVELOPMENT OF
THE FILM INDUSTRY

CALVIN PRYLUCK

Everyone seems to know of the itinerant movie show, but no one seems to know very much. Yet scattered evidence suggests that a study of the touring movie show may help answer the question implied forty years ago when Mae Huettig asserted: "Without an understanding of the intensity and suddenness of the demand for movies, much of the history of the industry is incomprehensible."[1]

There are reasons why the evidence on touring movie shows has not been assembled previously. In the first place, it is hard to locate; road shows do not leave a dense paper trail. Data have to be collected in scraps, bit by bit. Currently there are full professors who were graduate students when I began this effort.[2]

A more crucial reason has to do with the writing of film history. Film history often falls into the anachronistic fallacy that asserts current importance as the criterion for historical significance. Bernard Berenson could have been speaking for many film historians when he wrote: "Significant events are those events that have contributed to making us what we are today."[3] In such an understanding, the study of the largely rural and now obsolete phenomenon of movie road show men is "an obscure bypath of no importance," as I was told by a scholar whose work I respect. He may be right. I think not.

This attitude is not unique to film history. We know a great deal more about successful revolutions than about aborted efforts, just as we know more about, say, Carl Laemmle than about Ben Huntley, a fellow citizen of Oshkosh, Wisconsin, when both were young men starting their careers in show business. The thrust of my argument is that we will learn much about the dynamics of entertainment industries when we understand the conditions that led one to Universal Studios in Hollywood and the other to the life of a road show man.

We may also learn something about the writing of the history of entertainment. In the process, it may turn out that much of what we think we know about the early days of movies is only slightly true: an elaboration of Huettig's assertion is more complex than commonly thought. Even the revisionist attempts in the past decade may prove to have been too timid. They seem to have accepted the traditional propositions that early development of movies was an urban phenomenon revolving around vaudeville theaters and, somewhat later, immigrant audiences.[4]

The story starts, as we all know, at the end of April 1896 with the first successful commercial showing of projected moving images at Koster and Bial's Music Hall. Many people know that by October 1896, New York audiences could have seen acts featuring at least four, and perhaps six, different projectors: Edison's Vitascope, the Lumiere Cinematographe, A. Curtis Bond's Kineoptikon, the Biograph, and perhaps the Veriscope and Vitagraph.[5]

What we do not know—because we have not looked—is that coincident with these showings, projectors and films became widely available through show business sources and slightly later through nonprofessional rural sources such as the Sears, Roebuck mail-order catalog.

At the opening of the theatrical season in the autumn of 1896, ads started to appear in the show business newspaper the *New York Clipper* offering projectors for sale. Before the first anniversary of the Koster and Bial triumph, ads had appeared for projectors sporting thirteen different names, including Kineoptikon, Vitographe, Gyrographe, Animatographe, Zooscope, Lumiere Cinematographe, "Daisy" Animascopticon, Kineostiscope, Cineograph, Paley's Kalatechnoscope, Magniscope, and Edson's Vietograph.[6]

By the following year, the fall of 1897, many of these names had disappeared from the pages of the *Clipper*. The quality of the projectors is unknown, and some of the ads may have been fraudulent. "Edson's Vietograph" could be easily confused with the product of Thomas Alva Edison, if one reads quickly or poorly. Other ads may have been for inadequately capitalized companies or companies with a defective machine, or both. The data preclude any clear inference beyond the important one that projectors were widely available within six months of the commercial introduction of motion pictures.

The quality of particular projectors is beside the point. A movie projector is a mechanically simple device; once the technological problems of projected moving pictures had been solved, any journeyman machinist could make a usable projection machine. And many did so. The first projector used by Lyman H. Howe, the best-known North American movie road show man, was built by a mechanic in Wilkes-Barre, Pennsylvania.[7]

More to the point is the observation that movies fit into the structure of the entertainment industry as it had developed at the end of the nineteenth century. Entertainment in the nineteenth century was relatively undifferentiated:

dramatic companies included short plays as one of the acts in a bill. Circus is almost defined by acrobats, but acrobatic acts were also part of variety bills. Circuses included minstrel shows as an after-show "concert" for which there was typically an additional charge. Minstrel shows were often variety bills in blackface. Medicine shows included all of the above.

A few examples from the news columns of the *Clipper* may help: "The Clicks, John and Annie, will not take out their farce comedy, 'The Married Man,' this season [1897] but have taken a scene from the second act and will present it as a sketch playing vaudeville houses." The next year, the Marks Bros. Dramatic Co, touring upper Michigan and Canada, reported "We have a strong show with special features between acts making the show continuous and it has caught the public fancy." DeVoe and his movies and Will Malard, a trick bicycle rider, were among the new attractions.[8]

A further characteristic of nineteenth-century show business is that it was an itinerant entrepreneurial occupation in which various troupes and acts were fundamentally independent contractors and subcontractors constantly in competition with each other. There was a premium on novelty; movies gave some of these small-scale entrepreneurs an edge in that competition.

In entertainment as elsewhere, the late nineteenth century was a time of expanding technology. Already by the time of Koster and Bial's historic show there had been other technological entertainments: cyclorama, stereopticon shows, illusions, electricity (itself a circus attraction for several years), phonographs, and shows combining the stereopticon and the phonograph. (One of the sidelights of interest is the number of people who claim to have "invented" talking pictures on the strength of some such combination.)

The moving picture had the attraction of a technological novelty, but it was better than many of the others, since an act performed on a two-dimensional surface is an ideal entr'acte. Up to that point, some performers promoted themselves through the advertising claim "can perform in one" (that is, in front of the curtain while the set was being changed). Now there was an act that could perform not in front of the curtain but better, on the curtain.

Movies also made a good "chaser" (the common description of all closing acts). The headline act or the climax was always next to closing; the closing act was characteristically a dumb act (that is, a silent act, such as a dog act) so that the audience would not be disturbed by those leaving early, yet one whose qualities would leave the audience in a good mood at the end of the show.

Movies were rapidly absorbed into the existing practices of the entertainment industry. In addition to ads offering projectors for sale, the pages of the *Clipper* for the season of 1896–97 included announcements of movies (or animated pictures, as some styled them) as part of the program for various entertainment troupes. Howard and Emerson were illustrating songs with the Phantoscope while the John Stapleton Company featured the Animatoscope showing animated views between acts of a brand-new comedy. W.S. Cleveland's Great Massive Minstrelsy included the "American Biograph, the 'dernier cri' of the art of reproducing light and motion{ . . . }complete corps of operators and electricians{ . . . }films made especially for this organization." Circuses carried movies starting in the season of 1897.[9]

Over the years, the advertising pages of the *Clipper* constituted a busy marketplace for movie-related activities. Dealers offered projectors for sale; there were offers to buy or sell secondhand projectors and films; bookings were solicited for whole programs of movies; several ads solicited bookings while offering machines for sale. There were ads from shows soliciting the service of operators (that is, projectionists) with machines and films; there were ads from operators "At Liberty," including one in 1897 with "nine years experience in electrical show biz. Can do bits."[10]

A single page in the advertising section of the *Clipper* in the fall of 1897 contained two typical ads: "Animated Pictures—Machinist and Electrician who can operate, demonstrate, and improve any machine wants position. Can stop flicker and shake in any machine. H. Thorne care of Clipper." In an adjacent column, P.O. Box 2063 in New York advertised: "Wanted operator for moving picture machine and stereopticon in one night stands. Must understand operating with electricity and gas, attend to baggage, take tickets, and assist generally. Write, stating experience and lowest salary, we paying [*sic*] transportation and hotels."[11] One can wonder whether H. Thorne and P.O. Box 2063 ever got together.

These ads illustrate a central characteristic of show people at that time: they were flexible and versatile. They played in many different kinds of shows and could do several kinds of acts. Many of the ads seeking performers specified that preference would be given to those who could double in more than one act. Motion pictures became just one more act for people already in the business.

David Lano was a sophisticated marionette man whose marionettes performed such plays as *Pygmalion and Galatea*. He was also a knife thrower, a calliope player, an acrobat, a dog and monkey trainer, a ticket seller, and a talker (what civilians called a barker). His wife was only a contortionist and a sharpshooter.

Lano came into possession of a Lubin projector and films of the Jeffries-Fitzsimmons championship fight of 1899 that had previously belonged to a medicine show. At the end of the season the projector went into storage. Lano found himself at liberty in the winter of 1908. He, his wife, and two vaudevillians formed a small four-person show. "I also sent for my motion picture machine, and for the remainder of the winter we did fairly well" until the circus season opened in April.[12]

Projectors and films were also available through nonprofessional—principally rural—sources. Between 1898 and 1907, the Sears, Roebuck mail-order catalogs featured ads for entertainment outfits, including movie equipment and films. These advertisements were printed on the initiative of Alvah Roebuck, who represented the technical side of the partnership with copywriter Richard Sears. The first ads were for a movie projector called the Optigraph, manufactured by a company owned by Roebuck. In 1902, the ads for the Optigraph were joined by ads for the Edison Projecting Kineto-scope.[13]

The films offered for sale in the Sears, Roebuck catalogs include many of those that have come down to us as the classics of the period, such as *The Rice-Irwin Kiss, Black Diamond Express, The Life of a Fireman,* prizefight reproductions, and several that are now less than classic: "'Morning Bath'. This scene represents a dark African mother in the act of giving her struggling pickaninny a bath in a tub of suds. This is a clear and distinct picture in which the contrast of the dark complexion and the white suds is strongly marked." There was also *The Kiss Scene,* described as a "burlesque on the osculatory performance of John Rice and May Irwin. An encounter by two corpulent colored people. One of the funniest views on the market."[14]

The copy made clear the purpose of these outfits. One catalog announced that "$20.00 to $25.00 and more can be made every evening with the Optigraph Moving-Picture Machine"; another offered for sale projectors, films, slides, posters, tickets, and a "rubber stamp printing outfit for filling in dates and places for giving entertainment."[15] Although much of the evidence is thus far circumstantial, I think there are reasons why the importance of sale by Sears, Roebuck should not be underestimated. Direct mail was the only outlet for Sears, Roebuck during this period, and mail-order advertisements are strictly accountable. One knows quickly and continuously how many sales have been generated by a particular ad; a mail-order ad has to pay its way and then some if it is to be continued. And these ads continued for a number of years, suggesting that a profitable amount of entertainment equipment was sold through this source. There is also the claim by Alvah Roebuck in memoirs written thirty years after the event that "the sales of public exhibitor's outfits and supplies{ . . . }continued to be very profitable until after the appearance of the remodeled store motion picture theatres in 1906."[16]

Sears, Roebuck catalogs were distributed widely to the general public in rural areas. My reading of the ads suggests that they were addressed to show business novices; logic suggests that the *Clipper* and *Billboard* would have been better ways to reach an audience of show people. In other words, Sears, Roebuck served as a means for entry into show business for people who had not previously been associated with the entertainment industry. As a consequence, these "Sears, Roebuck" shows opened entertainment venues that had not previously existed.

Unfortunately for our purposes, the relevant records no longer exist. We must draw inferences from the fact that the general catalog ads continued to run for at least six years, to be replaced by a 128-page special catalog of entertainment outfits that also seems to be no longer extant. There is in existence, however, a 534-page mail-order catalog published in 1906 by the Amusement Supply Company, an enterprise formed by Alvah Roebuck after he left Sears.[17]

An impression of the characteristics and magnitude of part of the market may be gained from this catalog. Titled "Amusement for Profit," it includes extensive editorial advice about the operation of an entertainment for profit whether with a gramophone, a stereopticon, a motion picture machine, or a combination of devices. There is an ad for "Motion Picture Exhibition Tents" with seating capacities between 150 and 500. There are more than 40 pages of ads for movie equipment and more than 100 pages of ads for "nearly one thousand" films.

I sense a changing emphasis in this 1906 catalog; the films are priced for sale, but "information regarding rental will be furnished on application." A number of complete outfits are offered: there are five stereopticon outfits and ten combination stereopticon and motion picture outfits "suited to the requirements of the Traveling Exhibitor," while four outfits "are for Nickel Theatres," and six are "adapted to the requirements of those who wish to do Street Advertising."

The movie projector as a mechanical device capable of delivering entertainment, sold in stores or by mail order, opened opportunity for entrance into the entertainment industry to a whole class of entrepreneurs who might otherwise have tried to exploit something like the bicycle craze that was contemporaneous with the introduction of movies. It may have been the glamour that drew these people to "show business," but I suspect that one important factor was the relative ease of entry into the business. Equipment and films could be bought from Sears, Roebuck for substantially less than $200 at a time when a good bike could be bought for $15.75, but a commercial amusement device like a carousel cost thousands of dollars, and a single kinetoscope for an arcade cost $300. The touring movie show was a low unit price, low overhead, cash business with wide popular appeal. Admission was a nickel or dime; other entertainment admission prices were twenty-five or fifty cents; hall rentals were typically a share of the box office gross; a satisfactory show could be put on by one or two people. Living expenses and transportation were the only other overhead costs in addition to the initial investment.

In any case, there were two types of itinerant exhibitors—showmen for whom movies were another kind of act, and men who entered exhibition as a business. It is possible that there were people in the latter group who might have "run away to join the circus" if that were the only choice; at the moment, the evidence is just not there to make this distinction.

The point to the story so far is that the dissemination of movies throughout the entertainment industry was extensive and important. This evidence gives us reason to wonder about film history's cherished folk account about early movies. You know how it goes: Audiences at vaudeville theaters were at first enthralled. They then quickly turned on animated pictures, forcing managers to reduce movies to the ignominious position of chasing audiences out of the theater. Movies then mysteriously lay fallow, only to emerge in 1906 as the shabby yet golden princess of the nickelodeon.

The evidence suggests quite the opposite. Movies easily became part of the entrepreneurial, itinerant, undifferentiated, and flexible structure of the entertainment industry as it existed at the end of the nineteenth century. Wherever there was entertainment, there were movies. There were movies on showboats. There were movies at the height of the gold rush of 1898 in the Klondike near the Alaska-Canada border, thousands of miles from any other settlement.[18]

Weeks short of the third anniversary of the Koster and Bial's showing and a year after the outbreak of the Spanish-American War, the Edison War Projectoscope Company opened the 1899 summer season in Port Washington, Ohio, following a jump of 300 miles. Its plans included a five-week tour of Ohio, a tour through the summer resort areas of northern Michigan and the Northwest, and then on the West Coast.[19]

A five-person company calling itself E. Gorton and Stewart's Cinegraph was also touring Michigan that season; its plans were more localized. Following a three-week tour in April, its plans were to open a store show for five weeks in Kalamazoo, Michigan, a town whose population in 1900 was 24,000. "Then we will go by wagon, making [performing in] small towns."[20]

If it would serve any purpose, recitals of such reports could be repeated to the extent of anyone's patience. One additional piece of evidence may be useful here. Touring troupes were apparently important to the S. Lubin Company, manufacturer of machines and films, that later would be a member of the Motion Picture Patent Company. Portability of equipment was regularly emphasized in its large advertisements; and one ad in the spring of 1899 included a testimonial from the business manager of a show called Sam DeVere's Own Company: "Your films are the greatest moneymaker I ever saw and are wonders of photography."[21]

No evidence supports the commonplace that "audiences got bored" with movies. Box office receipts would be a direct measure of popularity, but we do not have these figures. The large number of shows that included movies offers a better basis for inferences about popularity than does a misinterpretation of the label "chaser."

Given the flexibility of show people, a show or act that failed to please audiences would be abandoned in favor of another potentially more profitable one. There were several live performers who made their careers being good "chasers." The reading of the term given in most interpretations is misleading by being too literal. The term was ironic in the same way as the

North American show business phrase for wishing one good luck, "Break a leg!"

Movies continued to be integrated into the structure of various shows throughout the first decade of their existence. Circuses did not need a "chaser" as this term has been used in film history: the circus band played the audience out of the tent immediately following the spectacular display that was the climax of the performance. The extra admission sideshows served as a coda to the circus experience, in the same way that closing acts did for the vaudeville audience. Sideshow attractions that are not profitable can be changed without diminishing the experience of the midway. Yet the Ringling Brothers Circus had a movie sideshow for at least seven years between 1897 and 1903. In 1900, the John Robinson Circus carried a movie tent, while a small circus, called America's Favorite Pavilion Shows, was adding one.[22]

Even among urban vaudeville houses, there is no reason to believe that movies had lost their popularity. The management of the Masonic Temple Roof Theatre, an important venue in Chicago, preparing to open a summer season of "High Class Vaudeville," advertised in April 1899 for a list of vaudeville acts, adding the comment: "Want to hear from everyone with a good act. Would like to secure a good motion picture or lantern act to close the performance. A season's work for the right act."[23] This does not sound like a man who is looking for an act to chase his audience. Even nineteenth-century showmen were not that foolish.[24]

Itinerant movie shows were principally a rural phenomenon, which raises questions about another truism about the early U.S. film audience as urban, proletarian, and immigrant. There has been some recent discussion about the degree to which the audience was in fact proletarian and immigrant, yet none of these discussions question the characterization of moviegoing as a largely urban experience.

Each of these accounts has added nuance to our understanding of the early development of exhibition; each also shares the urban bias that one of them states explicitly: "In the rural sectors the old prejudice against amusement would continue to hold fast for some time to come."[25]

If nothing else should give pause, population statistics of the United States are worth considering. In the census of 1900 the population was described as 59.8 percent rural; immigrant population represented 13.6 percent of the total population; immigrants accounted for 7.7 percent of the rural population.[26]

With the evidence of touring movie shows and a general understanding of the background, it appears that the only things incontrovertibly urban in early film history are the foundations of subsequent film empires: Fox, Loew, Mayer, Zukor, Cohn, Warner, and Laemmle all started at urban venues. But this part of the story must await another telling.

Any accurate and coherent explanation of the growth of the film industry must take into account the census numbers and the evidence of itinerant movie shows. Such an explanation must also consider regional differences in a country where Portland, Maine, is more than 3,000 miles distant from Portland, Oregon.

It may turn out that the widespread early display of movies was limited to eastern and midwestern locales. There is conflicting evidence about the dissemination of movies in the West. One former traveling exhibitor claimed to have participated as a fourteen-year-old in giving the first movie show in Arizona in 1911–12. However, an animated pictures and illustrated song act was included in at least one show, Hibbard's Trans-Atlantic Star Specialty Company, playing in an adjacent state, Colorado, in 1900.[27]

It may simply be a lapse of memory about events sixty years previous, or that claims like "the biggest, the best, the first," made on the flimsiest grounds, were common among road show people. Nevertheless, the contrast in local distances in various regions is enough reason to suggest that there may have been regional differences in the patterns of development of early motion picture exhibition.[28]

The bulk of the evidence leads to the conclusion that the whole entertainment industry, not just vaudeville, supplied a supporting infrastructure for the infant movie industry. At the same time, itinerant exhibition helped establish the preconditions for the emergence of a separate industry. Itinerant movie exhibition contributed to a separate infrastructure for the film industry by providing a widespread market for equipment and a steady market for a relatively small number of films. The economics of the road show enabled the movie industry to avoid the "chicken-and-egg" difficulty that plagued many other new technologies.

To sell a telephone you have to sell a hundred and build a central exchange. To sell electric lamps you have to supply a power plant and power lines as a source of electricity. To sell automobiles you need paved roads for them to drive on. Movies as an industry did not face this problem, since a touring movie show needed only a machine and a few films over a relatively extended period of time, often as much as six months. As long as there were a few films available, machine manufacturers could sell their machines, and film producers did not have to supply a daily change of attraction, as became the practice in early fixed-location theaters. No participant in the process was required to make a large investment; the total investment was spread over numerous participants.

Although movies in urban vaudeville houses were also touring acts, movie road shows became increasingly a rural phenomenon.[29] The frontier of fixed-location movie theaters constantly displaced the touring movie shows, in cities and in smaller and smaller towns. This development was a manifestation of increasing differentiation between the film industry and the rest of the entertainment industry. Traditional touring shows did not offer regular performances that were central to the rapid growth of the film industry and the moviegoing experience in the period between the introduction of fixed-location movie theaters and the spread of television forty years later.

Only occasionally and certainly not regularly did touring shows return to the same locale during a season. Such occasions were rare enough that a "return date" was a point of comment in the news reports submitted to the *Clipper*. In a transitional stage some touring exhibitors developed a circuit of towns to which they did return on a regular schedule on the same day every week or two weeks.

These developments created a dilemma for movie road show men. Roaming is a central principle in the ethos of the trouper. Terms like *forty-miler* and *coast defender* are sarcastic descriptions of show people who rarely travel far from their homes. The phrase "first of May" used to describe a rookie trouper also implies a desire to wait for the warmth of the late spring instead of enduring hard times on the road, that is, a reluctance to be a real trouper.

These attitudes were dysfunctional in the new world of fixed-location movie theaters. The itinerant movie showman either settled down or remained on the fringes in an increasingly distinct enterprise. By the 1920s the itinerant movie show had indeed become an obscure bypath. One of the oddities of this development is that I have heard stories that I have not been able to verify about movie shows touring into the late 1950s in places like west Texas and eastern Oregon.[30]

The process of differentiation between the film industry and the rest of the entertainment industry evolved into further specialization between the mainstream industry based on fixed-location theaters for majority audiences and the production, distribution, and exhibition of films directed toward marginal audiences, including such specialized forms as rural films, black films, Yiddish films, and pornographic films, Through the 1920s, at a time when the mainstream industry used a rental system for films that was appropriate for fixed-location exhibition, *Billboard* carried advertising offering films for sale to touring movie shows.

One such show was the H. A. Bruce Wild West Moving Picture Show that in 1924 played one-night stands through Ohio and Illinois, showing a single print of a five-reel western and a two-reel comedy. Bruce would arrive two or three days in advance, booking locations and placing advertising posters, always avoiding towns that had a movie theater, while the rest of the company—his wife and teenage son—put on the shows. In 1929, they had four prints, allowing four-night stands. In the intervening years, they toured a literal dog and pony show as the H. A. Bruce Circus.[31]

William F. Dalke can be contrasted with H.A. Bruce. Dalke was an eighteen-year-old-German immigrant who did not like the grocery business but "loved the movies." In 1909 he bought an Edison projector and opened a grind nickelodeon in Washington, D.C. For some reason, he left this location, bought a portable projector, and started touring a movie show in the

Shenandoah Valley, west of the District of Columbia. In the years between 1909 and 1916, he built up a circuit of twelve towns. He would make one-night stands in each location, returning to Washington for a supply of films before going out on the circuit again. In one of these towns, "a little place of about a hundred people," he showed his films in an open field. In other places, he used whatever space was available, often the town's fire hall.

But Dalke "hated to travel." He married a local girl from one of these communities, rented his first theater, and over the years opened other theaters "in the next town and the next town and the next." He eventually had seven theaters in a string along Route 11 in western Virginia. Even today, people in some of these towns remember "old man Dalke" and his theaters. His son and grandson operate the four remaining theaters. Other grandsons are a minister, a lawyer, and an MBA candidate.[32]

In the beginning, Ben Huntley had as much claim as anyone else to a place in what became the mainstream film industry.[33] He was part of the cohort of film pioneers—an early exhibitor who turned to producing. Yet Ben and Myrtle Huntley had reason to share in the ethos of the old troupers. Myrtle was the daughter of Hattie Brandon, eccentric comic, and William Brandon, sometime Dutch comic, sometime Irish comic, and often small-time show business entrepreneur. Around the turn of the century, depending on the circumstances, they were known as the Brandon Duo, Brandon and Fitzgerald, William Brandon's Gilt Edge Show, Brandon Bros. Winter Circus, and the Green Mountain Remedy and Concert Company, among other names. Myrtle was a soubrette with many of these shows. Of the nine people traveling with the Green Mountain medicine show in 1900, five were related to the Brandons: Myrtle and Ben Huntley, her mother and father, and her uncle; three others were also a family. In other seasons, parts of the Brandon family traveled with three different shows.

Ben was eighteen years old when he left his home in Winona, Minnesota, to join the Brandon show as a piano player in 1896; this was the same year that the first Edison performance was given at Koster and Bial's. He acted some, played the piano, did whatever else was needed, and married the boss's daughter.

They retired to Oshkosh, Wisconsin, the Brandon troupe's headquarters town, to start a family; Huntley worked as a cartoonist and advertising salesman at a local newspaper. It was here that he met Carl Laemmle, who was about ten years older. Ben and Myrtle Huntley and two-year-old Howard left Oshkosh in 1903 to go back on the road, playing in theaters in the upper Midwest as the Huntleys and Company Pictorial Monarchs and featuring "an elaborated picture show" with "pictured melodies, special costumes and electrical effects. The most elaborately constructed projection apparatus in the world. None other like it. One big 2-hour performance. Anybody in any seat one dime. 10 c{ . . . }10c." Ben wore a white tie and tails when operating the projector.

The Huntleys toured until it was time for Howard to start formal school-ing at the beginning of World War I. They returned to Huntley's hometown of Winona, where Ben started a business making song and advertising slides for movie theaters. Huntley began to make movies featuring his wife and comedies featuring one of the dozens of Charlie Chaplin imitators then flooding the country. These films were apparently distributed through an in-formal network covering the territory in the Midwest that the Huntleys had toured.

They were back on the road in 1922, playing in tents this time, still using the motion picture projector. The Huntleys toured widely through the Mid-west, putting on a simple vaudeville performance along with the movies. Howard participated as general factotum in business and logistics, such as putting up the tent. "I hated it," Howard said recently. The show went broke and was stranded about 1928 in western Wisconsin near the town of Black River Falls. Ben was fifty years old, Myrtle three years younger. They re-mained in the small resort town, where they lived as people did during the Depression. He opened a picture framing and house painting supply store, and they came to be prominent citizens of the town of 3,200 population. Their grandson is a college dean; their son, Howard, lived out his life in Black River Falls. At seventy-nine, he was still proud of his father's contribution to having the town build a swimming pool after a local boy drowned while swim-ming in a nearby river.

In dealing with a business that numbers its customers in the millions and its assets in the billions, it is a useful corrective to remember a retired road show man and his town's swimming pool. This homespun fact may help re-mind us that the development of the film industry reflected the activities of people like H. A. Bruce, Bill Dalke, and Ben Huntley, as well as people like Carl Laemmle, Marcus Loew, and Adolph Zukor. They were all part of the same cohort of entrepreneurs making decisions about their lives, their work, and what to do about this newfangled device.

We are only beginning to learn about the range of choices, the decisions, and the constraints under which they were made; cumulatively these matters shaped the subsequent course of development of motion picture exhibition history. If we knew more about the opportunities and constraints, perhaps we could better explain, for example, the ten-year gap between the first Koster and Bial showing and the nickelodeon.

We do know that show business was an established and expanding entity during precisely this period. Big-city vaudeville was part of this story. So was legitimate theater, as were minstrel shows, touring dramatic repertory, med-icine shows, and circuses. It seems clear now that early movies fit neatly into the structure of the entertainment industry. Less clear is the pattern of evo-lution between show business and what old-timers came to call the picture business.

It is easy to type out the words *separate infrastructure* to start a theoretical explanation. It is less easy to describe and explain the process. An explanation will include a clearer description than we have of the choices available to road show men and similar entrepreneurs, the people who collected the nickels and dimes that drove the process. As long as touring exhibition was the mode of operation, it continued to be—no matter how obscure—a part of traditional show business. Movies became a distinct industry when a fixed-location movie show became the dominant choice.

If the foregoing is even approximately accurate, research in itinerant movie shows is not merely an eccentric interest. It is concerned with a central question in early film history: What were the conditions that made permanent fixed-location movie shows possible and preferable?[34]

Notes

This chapter originally appeared as Calvin Pryluck, "The Itinerant Movie Show and the Development of the Film Industry," *Journal of the University Film and Video Association* 35, no. 4 (1983): 11–22, and is reprinted by permission from the University Film and Video Association.

1. Mae D. Huettig, *Economic Control of the Motion Picture Industry* (Philadelphia: University of Pennsylvania Press, 1944), 12.

2. The paucity of original sources will account for the heavy dependence in this chapter on circumstantial evidence from the show business newspaper the *New York Clipper*.

3. Bernard Berenson, *Aesthetics and History* (Garden City, N.Y.: Doubleday Anchor Books, 1954), 257–58.

4. See, for instance, Russell Merritt, "Nickelodeon Theatres: 1905–1914: Building an Audience for Movies," in *The American Film Industry*, ed. Tino Balio (Madison: University of Wisconsin Press, 1976), 83–102; Garth Jowett, "The First Motion Picture Audience," *Journal of Popular Film* 3, no. 1 (1974): 39–54, reprinted in *Movies as Artifacts*, ed. Michael T. Marsden, John G. Nachbar, and Sam L. Grogg Jr. (Chicago: Nelson Hall, 1982); Robert C. Allen, *Vaudeville and Film 1895–1915: A Study in Media Interaction* (New York: Arno Press, 1980).

5. First showings with various projectors in New York City were: Vitascope (Koster and Bial's Music Hall), Thursday, April 23, 1896, advertised in the *New York Times*, April 23, 1896, 7; Lumiere's Cinematographe (Keith's New Union Square Theater), Monday, June 29, 1896, advertised in the *New York Times*, June 28, 1896, 11; Curtis Bond's Kineoptikon (Pastor's Music Hall), Monday, August 17, 1896, reported in the *New York Clipper*, August 22, 1896, 392; Biograph (Hammerstein's Olympia Music Hall), October 19, 1896, advertised in the *New York Times*, October 18, 1896, 11. I have been unable to locate independent evidence for first showings of Vitagraph, and Rector's Veriscope mentioned by Terry Ramsaye, *A Million and One Nights* (New York: Simon and Schuster, 1926), 330, 287.

6. See, for instance, the *New York Clipper* for 1896: September 12, 449, 450; September 19, 463, 464; September 26, 480; for 1897: January 16, 738, 739; March 20, 47, 49, 50, 51.

7. Private communication with Carol S. Nelson, Wilkes-Barre, Pennsylvania, producer-director of the film *Lyman H. Howe's High Class Moving Pictures,* Summer 1982.

8. *New York Clipper,* October 9, 1897, 527; October 15, 1898, 556.

9. *New York Clipper,* August 1, 1896, 351; October 31, 1896, 564; January 1, 1897, 739.

10. *New York Clipper,* September 19, 1896, 464.

11. *New York Clipper,* September 25, 1897, 503.

12. David Lano, *A Wandering Showman I* (East Lansing: Michigan State University Press, 1957), 156, 241, passim.

13. Unpublished memoir written by Alvah Roebuck "during the 30s" but otherwise undated and unpaged, Sears, Roebuck Public Relations Department Archives, Sears Tower, Chicago, Illinois 60684. Sears, Roebuck Catalog No. 107 (1898), p. 206; Catalog No, 111 (1902), p. 170. The Sears Archives has a collection of Sears, Roebuck catalogs. Microfilm copies have been distributed to various university libraries, including Duke University, Durham, North Carolina.

14. Catalog No. 107, p. 207; Catalog No. 111, pp. 322–23.

15. Catalog No. 107, p. 206; Catalog No. 111, p. 156.

16. Roebuck memoirs.

17. I have a copy of a 1906 Amusement Supply Company catalog in my personal collection.

18. Philip Graham, *Showboats: The History of an American Institution* (Austin: University of Texas Press, 1951), 99. On the back endpapers there is a reproduction of a poster advertising the Swallow and Markloe Floating Palace featuring "The Greatest Production in Motion Tableaux," *Bold Bank Robber,* copyrighted 1904 by S. Lubin. Mary E. Hitchcock, *Two Women in the Klondike: The Story of a Journey to the Gold Fields* (New York: Putnam's, 1899).

19. *New York Clipper,* April 15, 1899, 129.

20. *New York Clipper,* April 8, 1899, 109.

21. *New York Clipper,* April 1, 1899, 100.

22. Charlotte Herzog, "The Movie Palace and the Theatrical Sources of Its Architectural Style," *Cinema Journal* 20, no. 2 (1981): 24; Lano, *Wandering Showman,* 216; *New York Clipper,* March 10, 1900, 27.

23. *New York Clipper,* April 1, 1899, 100.

24. Robert C. Allen reached a similar but more limited conclusion about the popularity of motion pictures in his *Vaudeville and Film.*

25. Jowett, "The First Motion Picture Audience," 16.

26. Discussion of immigrants and urban audiences for early movies is confounded by the fact that the majority of immigrants settled in urban locales. In 1900, more than 35 percent of the more than 5.5 million total population of New York, Chicago, and Boston were foreign born. Even in smaller cities, those with over 100,000 population, the foreign born and their children represented 65 percent of the total population. In contrast, the same group accounted for 21.3 percent of the total rural population. Since immigrants tended to settle near their countrymen, it is likely that many of the rural foreign born and their children lived in isolated foreign-language communities. I suspect that the pattern of entertainment in these communities was different from the general pattern I have been describing.

27. Daniel A. Spicer, "Memories of a Vaudevillian" (unpublished paper, University of North Carolina at Chapel Hill April 1973); *New York Clipper*, March 7, 1900, 27.

28. In places like New England and parts of the Midwest, towns are three to six miles apart. In the West, including Texas, towns could be ten times as distant. Other transportation conditions such as railroad connections and road conditions also differ between regions and affect the availability of shows.

29. Charles Musser, "American Vitagraph: 1897–1901," *Cinema Journal* 22, no. 3 (1983): 12.

30. I have heard these stories often enough in interviews and conversation to believe them. The lack of reproducible evidence should not be surprising, since these were small companies that likely kept the skimpiest of records. Also, they rarely attracted the attention of newspapers covering the small towns they played. The shows advertised by poster and window cards; their appearance in a town would no longer be news by the time the weekly paper would be published. A brief published mention of itinerant exhibition in the 1950s can be found in Richard Alan Nelson, *Florida and the American Motion Picture Industry* (New York: Garland, 1983), 2:462n143.

31. Interview with Mark Bruce, Evansville, Wisconsin, summer 1981.

32. Interview with William F. Dalke Jr., Woodstock, Virginia, summer 1982.

33. The account of Ben and Myrtle Huntley is based on an interview with their son, Howard Huntley, Black River Falls, Wisconsin, summer 1981; scrapbook and other material made available by Mr. Huntley; and a news report in the *New York Clipper*, March 10, 1900, 27. Kathie Beer of Winona, Minnesota, who has been planning a full-length treatment of the Huntleys, made it possible for me to meet Mr. Huntley.

34. In the years since the late Cal Pryluck published this prescient essay in 1983, other scholars have begun to explore the history of itinerant film exhibition and the impact it had on nonmetropolitan audiences and the shape and meaning of early cinema.

Brief Bibliography on Traveling Exhibition

Fernett, Gene. "Itinerant Roadshowmen and the 'Free Movie' Craze." *Classic Images* 88 (October 1982): 12–13.

Fuller, Kathryn H. "The Cook and Harris High Class Moving Picture Company: Itinerant Exhibitors and the Construction of the Small-Town Movie Audience." In *At the Picture Show: Small-Town Audiences and the Creation of Movie Fan Culture*, 1–27. Washington, D.C.: Smithsonian Institution Press, 1996.

———. "Viewing the Viewers: Representations of the Audience in Early Cinema Advertising." In *American Movie Audiences: From the Turn of the Century to the Early Sound Era*, ed. Melvyn Stokes and Richard Maltby, 112–28. London: British Film Institute, 1999.

Hall, George C. "The First Moving Picture in Arizona—or Was It? The Tragic Tale of C. L. White's Marvelous Projectoscope Show in Arizona and New Mexico Territories, 1897–1898." *Film History* 3:1 (1989), pp. 1–9.

Lowry, Edward. "Edwin J. Hadley, Traveling Film Exhibitor." In *Film before Griffith*, ed. John Fell, 131–43. Berkeley and Los Angeles: University of California Press, 1983.

Musser, Charles, with Carol Nelson. *High-Class Moving Pictures: Lyman H. Howe and the Forgotten Era of Traveling Exhibition, 1880–1920*. Princeton, N.J.: Princeton University Press, 1991.

Stabla, Zdenek. "The First Cinema Shows in the Czech Lands." *Film History* 3 (1989): 203–21.

Toulmin, Vanessa. "'Local Films for Local People': Traveling Showmen and the Commissioning of Local Films in Great Britain, 1900–1902." *Film History* 13 (2001): 118–37.

———. "Women Bioscope Proprietors: Before the First World War." In *Celebrating 1895: The Centenary of Cinema*, ed. John Fullerton, 55–65. Sydney, Australia: John Libbey, 1998.

Véronneau, Pierre. "The Creation of a Film Culture by Traveling Exhibitors in Rural Québec Prior to World War II." *Film History* 6 (1994): 250–61.

Waller, Gregory A. "Robert Southard and the History of Traveling Film Exhibition." *Film Quarterly* 57, no. 2 (2003–4): 2–14.

4

EARLY FILM EXHIBITION IN WILMINGTON, NORTH CAROLINA

ANNE MOREY

The growing literature of film exhibition studies emphasizes the variety of means by which film became established in the United States. Scholars now agree that while New York City, for one, was extremely important to the development of exhibition practices, it does not by itself represent the national picture; New York diverges from provincial patterns both in its continuous exposure to projected film from 1896 onward and in its particular blend of film and vaudeville. Conversely, as Gregory Waller has argued of Lexington, Kentucky, provincial cities might evince a desire to emulate big-city cosmopolitanism while simultaneously viewing some of the attributes of metropolitan entertainment with alarm.[1] And even in communities of similar size, location, and composition, theaters and audiences responded to movies in remarkably individuated ways. Thus, although our understanding of exhibition practices in the South, for example, has been substantially increased by Waller's book-length examination of Lexington, more work designed to sift differences within regions seems warranted. The present chapter focuses on another southern city, Wilmington, North Carolina; as will become apparent, the situation in Wilmington differs in significant ways from that in Lexington, even though the two cities share many geographic and demographic features. While early cinematic reception in Wilmington may not be unique, it nonetheless illustrates a negotiation of a series of oppositions— rural/urban, genteel/working class, black/white, male/female, old/new, and (especially) local/national—not previously categorized.

As a southern, coastal city that was large for its region but small in national terms, Wilmington was unusually industrial by North Carolina standards but undeveloped in comparison to many northern urban areas of similar size. Nevertheless, inasmuch as the city was connected to the rest of the East Coast by six railroads and several shipping lines, it was accustomed to substantial traffic in people and goods, which, coupled with its desire to remain a prominent community in North Carolina, helped forward its project of attracting Northern investment. While Wilmington was for a time the state's industrial center (until 1910 it was North Carolina's largest city), it was never a major metropolis, but it nonetheless saw itself as a regional leader. Moreover, as a consequence of its interconnection with the rest of the East Coast, Wilmington had a long history of theatrical patronage, and its ties to New York and other northern communities were a source of pride. Finally, the city—which in 1900 had nearly 21,000 inhabitants, approximately half black and half white—experienced race relations that were, on the whole, much more uneasy than was the case in Lexington. In short, while in many respects its experience of early film exhibition conforms to national trends, Wilmington serves as an unusual example of a community whose transition to moviegoing took place against a background compounded of southern tradition and northern commercialism, small-town neighborliness and big-city racial hostilities.

Indeed, at the beginning of the twentieth century, racial tensions in Wilmington were such that it is hard to reconstruct film exhibition practices for any but white audiences. The major race riot that the city suffered in 1898 destroyed the black newspaper, the *Record*, effectively silencing African American Wilmington. While Waller notes that in Lexington white-owned newspapers acknowledged the black community through "Colored Notes" columns, the *Wilmington Morning Star* depicted blacks only as criminals, buffoons, or accident victims. One black movie house, the Lyric, which operated circa 1911 through 1915, understandably did not advertise its offerings in the white papers and seems to have left no records; given the *Record*'s violent end, Wilmington blacks may have felt that any high-profile black organization would attract white hostility.

In contrast to its treatment of blacks, Wilmington seems to have been quite hospitable to Jews; it housed the state's oldest synagogue, and Jewish charities and fraternal organizations were well respected. Among the city's Jewish merchants was its preeminent theatrical businessman, S.A. Schloss, owner of what the *Star* termed "the principal theatrical circuit in this part of the South." Schloss's empire extended from Wilmington, where he lived, to Asheville, Charlotte, Concord, Goldsboro, Greensboro, Raleigh, Winston-Salem, and even Virginia and South Carolina; he also maintained contacts in New York City, where he went to book acts.[2] Although his flagship theater, the Opera House (after 1902 known as the Academy of Music), specialized in stock companies and minstrel shows, Schloss also brought traveling motion picture exhibitors to this venue as early as 1897, although he never invested heavily in this new medium. He was otherwise willing to innovate, however, inasmuch as he built Wilmington's first permanent vaudeville theater in 1905, when the Princess Theater Company (run by Schloss and others) opened the Crystal Palace at a reputed cost of $30,000.[3] Film exhibition also attracted other Wilmington Jews, particularly J.M. Solky, who parlayed his success in retailing into theater ownership before eventually retiring to New York. Jewish entrepreneurs appear to have been more likely than many Wilmington businessmen to maintain contacts in the latter city, which may explain their relatively high profile among early theater owners, even though—as we shall see—they were not the most successful group of film exhibitors in Wilmington.

Traveling Exhibitors

While the traveling exhibitor was by definition never part of the community in which he exhibited and thus signals national or regional trends better than local ones, he was always booked through a local opera house lessee or equivalent promoter, who had to gauge community taste so as not to alienate his audience from subsequent attractions. Between 1896 and 1906 most commercial entertainment in communities such as Wilmington—big-city productions and stock companies, minstrel shows and circuses—was itinerant. Moving pictures were similarly peripatetic, but not all traveling film exhibitions addressed the same social class, so it is important to distinguish among the various producers of such programs. While theater managers in any given city would all have drawn upon the same pool, each would book a different combination of attractions, calculated to appeal to a particular local audience representing a particular social mix.

Thus it is important to contemplate not only the content of an entertainment but also the venue in which it appeared. Those whose programs played the opera house, and who exhibited film either as a technological marvel (inevitably, the context for at least the first Wilmington exhibition) or as a bigger and better stereopticon were at the top of the social pecking order; still other traveling exhibitors sought a slightly less refined middle-class or lower-middle-class audience. Films exhibited at carnivals, on the other hand, attracted an audience of all classes, ages, and races.

Nevertheless, the eclecticism of the programs that Schloss booked even into the higher-status Opera House suggests the heterogeneity of Wilmington's early moviegoing audience. The first recorded film exhibitor in North Carolina was the Maryland Projectoscope Company (also referred to as the Edison Projectoscope Company), which, Schloss noted in a communication to the *New York Dramatic Mirror,* drew "fair business; pleased audiences" on 15 through 20 March 1897, presenting a program of broad appeal.[4] Significantly, the entertainment played Wilmington first and for more than one night, suggesting demand for the novelty and possibly repeat visits from some customers. Later exhibitors generally performed on only one date in any city.

The second touring company to pass through the Wilmington Opera House was Brady's Veriscope with an exhibition of the Corbett-Fitzsimmons fight. The fight was filmed in Arizona on 17 March 1897, and the pictures played in Wilmington on 12 and 13 November. Prizefight films, a common early itinerant attraction, might seem a low-status genre; they provoked the ire of the Women's Christian Temperance Union for their effects on the young, exhibited an activity outlawed in most eastern states at the time, and might be thought to exclude women, otherwise the mark of the genteel audience.[5] They nonetheless played opera houses nationwide. North Carolina was no exception, and Schloss continued to book fight films as suitable fare for an opera house audience; for instance, the Gans-Nelson fight pictures played at the Greensboro Opera House (then jointly managed by Schloss and James and Robert Cowan, who doubled as, respectively, the editor of the *Evening Dispatch* and the manager of the Wilmington Wall Paper Company) on 6 December 1906. Likewise, the Cowan brothers scheduled the Britt-Nelson pictures for Wilmington on 6 January 1906, although the exhibition fell through, owing either to problems with the company or to opposition from groups in Wilmington.

Another way in which Wilmington conformed to national exhibition trends is illustrated in Schloss's decision to show a program of films on 30 June 1904 for no admission charge at the Casino, a hotel erected in 1903 at Wrightsville Beach, nine miles via trolley from the city. Schloss was among the hotel's proprietors, and the films were clearly designed to entice the public out to Wrightsville Beach. The beach's commercial potential was later exploited more fully by the Tidewater Power and Electric Company, which built a hotel and dance pavilion known as the Lumina (whose amenities by the summer of 1913 included a large movie screen on the beach with tiered seats for 300 people) and had interests in the trolley line.[6]

As Schloss's example suggests on the local level, even exhibitors who originally aimed at an upscale audience sometimes sought to appeal to the public at large. Nationally, the preeminent traveling exhibitor among those who hoped to lure serious-minded viewers was Lyman Howe. As Charles Musser notes, Howe's success was the result of his astute choice of patronage: he had been among the first "motion picture showmen to cater to a religiously devout clientele. But he was also among the first to see the possibility of creating programs that appealed across rival cultural groupings. . . . He broadened his appeal and wooed those who preferred less righteous and ideologically constrained forms of diversion." The springboard to this new diversity of clients was the Spanish-American War, which caused such an outburst of patriotism (and of interest in actuality footage) that Howe felt free to move his exhibitions from churches and YMCAs to neutral locations such as opera houses, which permitted him to attract a wider audience.[7]

But while Howe spearheaded the penetration of the South by larger itinerant exhibitors and in 1904 created a company expressly for the southern circuit, when films returned to Wilmington, he did not accompany them.

The situation was otherwise with his chief competitor, Archie L. Shepard's "high-class moving pictures." Musser distinguishes Shepard from Howe in several ways: Shepard chose dramatic films over actualities (a harbinger of the preferences of nickelodeon exhibitors); he showed in commercial theaters; he gave Sunday performances (Howe eschewed these to preserve good relations with church sponsors); he used illustrated songs rather than piano overtures during reel changes; his ticket prices were generally lower; and he visited specific towns more frequently than did Howe. In short, Shepard addressed viewers "more likely to be working class and less constrained by religious scruples in their enjoyment of amusement."[8]

Schloss was aware of Howe; he booked him into his Greensboro Grand Opera House on 21 January 1905, describing the event as "very good entertainment, fairly good audience," and into the Goldsboro Messenger Opera House on 7 December 1909, where the show "pleased good business." But for Wilmington, managers evidently preferred the more commercial Shepard, whose pictures played at the Academy under the aegis of the Cowan brothers. Shepard's first appearance in Wilmington was on 5 December 1905; the Cowans reported themselves "pleased." The next, on 16 March 1906, was less successful aesthetically; the report was "fair, to good business."[9] Shepard's last recorded local appearance suggests the difference in tone between the two major exhibition companies in the South. While Howe appealed to the intellect, Shepard pandered to the sensational, a feature played up by the advertisement in the *Wilmington Messenger:* "Among those of more than pleasing interest is 'An Aerial Tragedy,' a dramatic revelation with startling climaxes that are at once powerful and inspiring."[10] But while less cosmopolitan North Carolina communities such as Goldsboro, Greensboro, and Wilson continued to book both Shepard and Howe, neither traveling exhibitor became a significant feature of Wilmington life, a circumstance that may reflect a sense on the part of the city's established theatrical managers that films were not sufficiently "high-class" for a sophisticated audience.

Nickelodeons

Arguably, the exhibitor's personality was at least as important as his wares in shaping the reception of a film during this period. Musser notes that the narrative inadequacies of early films could be corrected via one of two means—either by "the exhibitor introducing live sound through a lecture or behind the screen dialogue . . . [or by] the producer . . . employ[ing] cinematic strategies which made the narrative more accessible without involving the exhibitor."[11] Film's future lay with the second alternative, but this destiny was not determined immediately. In the interim, traveling exhibitors and nickelodeon owners engaged in similar strategies to promote the coherence of their wares, in particular by lecturing and providing missing dialogue. While film itself would become an increasingly standardized and autonomous product, not only in terms of production but also in terms of a number of the conditions of reception, the nickelodeon, like the traveling exhibitor, offered an experience tailored to local conditions. At the same time, the Wilmington record indicates that experience in the entertainment field may have been still more important than long-standing ties to the community where nickelodeon ownership was concerned.

Schloss and the Cowans, to be sure, had both experience and local expertise. But although all these men booked traveling exhibitors, they seem to have preferred legitimate theater to movies. From 1897 to 1907, they vied for the title of preeminent theater manager not only in Wilmington but in all North Carolina, a competition that Schloss eventually won. For all the three men's business acumen, however, none of them recognized that the most promising avenue for theatrical profit would become not the $1.50 seats of the opera houses but the 5- and 10-cent seats of the nickelodeons. The impressive theatrical circuit that Schloss and his rivals dominated among them spanned the state and beyond, but it was James Howard and Percival Wells's movie house circuit within Wilmington that demonstrated that a single community could support a number of one-genre theaters. An advantage of the latter strategy was that it enabled an owner to keep control of his houses himself rather than having to depend on local managers—of whom Schloss, for one, went through five in Asheville alone between October 1906 and February 1908. Indeed, men who managed their own movie houses were the ultimate survivors of the competition of the nickelodeon era here. It was the least pretentious mode of exhibiting moving pictures, the carnival route rather than the opera house route, that became dominant in Wilmington.[12]

Wilmington appears to have been unusual for a community its size in that the original owners of its first nickelodeon maintained control of their property, remained in business through the end of the period of this study and beyond, and were able to expand into the more elaborate structures of the movie palace era (although *palace* is too grand a word for what was on offer in Wilmington after 1911). Accounts from Kentucky and Minnesota suggest that communities of similar size experienced considerable turnover in the ownership and number of theaters, with the beginners long out of the business by the end of the boom times for nickel theaters.[13] Further research is needed to establish whether rapid changes in ownership generally characterize provincial nickelodeons, but in the case of Wilmington a number of factors help to explain the unusual longevity of the Bijou, opened in 1906, which appears to have been North Carolina's first permanent film theater. The theater remained under Howard and Wells's control into the 1920s, by which time their business had absorbed or outlasted all rival establishments.

Howard had begun his career as showman in St. Louis in 1900, exhibiting films as a carnival sideshow with the Gaskell-Mondy Shows, according to a

1922 profile in *Moving Picture World*. Howard coupled these films, typically Pathé and Edison titles, with "either an illusion act or a serpentine dancing act, the films being rather short in those days."[14] He, Wells, and Wells's wife, Alice Fisher, were all experienced performers; Fisher was a singer of musical comedy, while Wells had been a trapeze artist with Barnum and Bailey.[15] None was a Wilmington native, although the wooing of the local market began even before the theater was established. In February 1905, Wells presaged his subsequent career by giving benefit exhibitions for the "Jeff Davis Council No. 63,"[16] which not only advertised him as a potential exhibitor in the not-yet-erected theater but also insinuated permanent film exhibition into the city through the familiar local context of a benefit for a fraternal society. In Wilmington, that could only have been a recommendation; Wilmington's men, in particular, were devoted members of civic groups and were accustomed to mount or commission a wide range of amateur and professional theatricals.

Wells's partnership with Howard brings up another important structural factor, namely, that their theater was a circus tent belonging to Howard and thus permitted low initial overhead, especially since Wells already owned his own projector. That Howard and Wells did not have to rent or buy a building, but instead could merely lease a lot, was clearly an advantage. Indeed, the tent represented not merely an expense avoided but also an element of the Bijou's appeal, inasmuch as this structure—which seated approximately 300 people, in contrast to the average nickelodeon, which usually seated 200 or fewer—was ideally suited to a warm climate. Southern weather, indeed, may well have favored more casual architecture in its initial nickelodeon construction than was the case in the Midwest and the North. In many communities, "airdomes" such as the Bijou were temporary tentlike structures for summer use, set up in vacant lots in the hopes of siphoning patronage away from stuffy converted storefronts; some permanent exhibitors simply closed for the season because attendance was so low during the hot months.[17] For the first six years of its life, the Bijou had only canvas walls and a sawdust floor; a wooden frame was later added to stabilize the structure. Between shows, one memoir relates, the sides of the tent were rolled up to provide "fresh air and light."[18] The contrast between the original Bijou and the elegant theaters managed by Schloss and the Cowan brothers is striking: clearly, permanent film exhibition in Wilmington started at the bottom of the social ladder and slowly made its way up.

The Bijou was located at 205 North Front Street in downtown Wilmington, next door to the Cape Fear Club, a men's club. As of the publication of the Sanborn Fire Atlas of 1904, the area was solidly commercial. The Bijou was just down the street from the Orton Hotel, the post office, and a number of banks, and across from dry goods and furniture stores and the Christian Science reading room. By 1910 its neighbors were a confectionery, the Western

Union telegraph office with an Elks' lodge on the second floor, and an ice cream factory. Perhaps most significantly, a large department store and smaller clothing and shoe stores had moved in across the street, bringing substantial retail trade—and a higher proportion of women—to a block that had formerly been the province of men working at offices, banks, light manufactories, and wholesalers.

The Bijou's address leads to speculation about its first clientele. The only account of regular patrons from this period suggests that children, blacks, and rural families were the most noticeable theatergoers, though not the only ones. The films were old and liable to break, and the patrons were devoted peanut eaters who threw the shells onto the sawdust floor so that the tent was invaded by rodents, in turn controlled by what Robert Fales calls "feline exterminators"; the customers were never sure whether the furry thing brushing against their legs was cat or rat.[19] Presumably this ambience would have discouraged some customers who aspired to elegant living, even while the novelty of attending the city's first permanent site devoted exclusively to film exhibition might simultaneously have attracted viewers across the social spectrum.

The tent was reminiscent of a familiar kind of entertainment, the carnival or midway, which was known to be safe, casual, and, significantly, hospitable to mixed-race gatherings. Contemporary trade papers noted that strict segregation was next to impossible in storefront shows; the original Bijou, in which, in conformity to Jim Crow laws, "the left-hand section of that tent was roped off for negroes who did not like to pass near Caesar [Howard's Great Dane],"[20] at least permitted blacks and whites to sit within sight of each other. Blacks, children, and rural families were united in that all were interested in affordable entertainment in an environment where they would not be made to feel out of place, and none would have been typical patrons of more pretentious and expensive entertainments such as those held at the Academy of Music. It is noteworthy that when the Bijou was rebuilt along more upscale lines in 1912, blacks were relegated to the balcony, the area typically reserved for their use in the South because they were less visible to white patrons there—although the new Bijou maintained contact with its original clientele by continuing to show a downscale (and profitable) program of serials, westerns, and slapstick.[21] But that is not to suggest that the middle class avoided Wilmington's nickelodeons: the children (perhaps mostly boys) who attended from the outset were no street urchins, and it may have been Howard and Wells's circus experience that enabled them to realize that children and blacks had few dependable sources of commercial entertainment. The Bijou thus emphasized the less formal appeal of the sideshow as the ideal packaging for its film programs.

Charlotte Herzog argues provocatively that movie exhibition's first sites affected nickelodeon architecture. The circus motion picture venue was usually a tent—the "black top" that stood among the sideshows on the midway. Herzog notes that "because the circus was a summer entertainment, ticket stands did not have to be connected to and protected by a building. They could be moved out closer to the potential buyer, to persuade him/her to buy a ticket. . . . The nickelodeon box office at the front of the vestibule met its potential customer in the same way and for the same reasons."[22] With their circus experience, Howard and Wells appear to have been the ideal proprietors for their initial audience. At first, the architecture of the Bijou *was* the circus tent. Howard met his customers as aggressively as any showman of the day and indeed was the box office incarnate—McKoy recalls that Howard sat on a stool with a pocket full of nickels, barking his wares: "Never out and never over. Right this way! New picture showing! For five cents, the twentieth part of a dollar!" Similarly, Wells, who exercised the kind of control over his wares typical of this period, both cranked the projector and "told the story that was being portrayed as it went along, using a script that was written out to go with the film."[23] While we can only speculate about the quality of Wells's showmanship, he served as the human relay between a not yet fully autonomous national product and his local audience, which rewarded his theater with remarkable loyalty, considering the competition soon to develop. Howard observed in 1922 that the Bijou, low prices notwithstanding, was always Wilmington's most profitable theater, which warrants an examination of less successful marketing strategies on the part of its rivals.[24]

The Bijou's Rivals

Downtown nickelodeons mushroomed in Wilmington in mid-1907, paralleling the phenomenal growth elsewhere in the country. As Eileen Bowser notes, "In May 1907, the *Moving Picture World* said there were between 2,500 and 3,000 [nickelodeons nationwide] and in November, the figure . . . was 'between four and five thousand.'"[25] Almost as if in response to *Billboard*'s December 1906 identification of North Carolina as one of thirteen states that did not have nickelodeons,[26] *Moving Picture World* announced three nickelodeon openings in the next six months. But only the two neighborhood theaters, the Brooklyn and the Lyric, were to survive for any length of time, and possibly they accomplished their modest success by refraining from competing against the Bijou for the downtown clientele.

The first of the post-Bijou nickelodeons was the Odeon. It opened at 126 Market Street, in a building that in 1904 was divided between a saloon and a shoe repair outfit, suggesting the converted storefronts of the Midwest. The location must have seemed, if anything, better than the Bijou's because it was the former site of another resort of leisure, namely, a saloon, and was opposite the Roundtree and the Bonitz hotels, whose primary clientele, traveling salesmen, would be seeking inexpensive amusement after business hours.

The area was indeed well chosen, since two theaters later opened across the street and did a flourishing business for a time; perhaps the Odeon died because its manager and apparent owner, C. W. Stonebanks, lacked the financial resources to weather the nickelodeon crunch of 1908–9, even though he too could boast of "long experience in the business."[27] Undoubtedly he was at a disadvantage vis-à-vis Howard and Wells, who had lower expenses, a five- or six-month lead, and two families to furnish free labor. In any event, the Odeon was gone by 1910, as was the Theatorium, little more than a block away from the Odeon, which announced its advent in *Moving Picture World* on 1 June 1907.

The last nickelodeon to announce its opening during mid-1907 was the Brooklyn, a storefront operation. Although the 1910 fire atlas lists nothing at the Brooklyn's 1915 location, 810 North Fourth Street, it is probable that this was the theater mentioned in the *Moving Picture World* of 29 June 1907: "It is understood that Messrs. J. J. and W. C. Moore, members of the Police Department, Wilmington, N.C. have decided to open a moving picture theater of the popular type on Fourth Street, between Brunswick and Bladen [the 800 block]. They will not give their time to the operation of the theater, but will have a manager to look after it for them."[28] The Moores present an interesting contrast to Howard and Wells and Stonebanks (who does not appear in city directories until 1908), since they were presumably native Wilmingtonians with no theatrical experience. Significantly, and perhaps because of their inexperience, they chose to operate through a manager rather than controlling their investment directly, which no doubt added to their costs. They chose a modest neighborhood that was largely residential, housing what appears to have been most of Wilmington's small immigrant population.[29] Fourth Street's proximity to the city center (the neighborhood was also on the streetcar line, making it accessible from other parts of town) would have made it an attractive location, especially because the working-class district that housed it and after which the theater was named also "boasted many good retail stores, including the J. H. Rehder Department Store" two blocks to the south, as Fales recalls.[30]

Finally, at 504 Harnett Street—three blocks from the Brooklyn, in a racially mixed neighborhood, and near the epicenter of the 1898 race riot—was the Lyric, then the only black movie house in Wilmington. Apparently opened in 1911 and thus operating concurrently with the Brooklyn, the Lyric disappeared sometime between 1915 and 1917. A contemporary photograph taken in front of the Brooklyn shows an all-white group of two men, four boys, and a girl (posed before advertisements for "High-Class Moving Pictures" and "Illustrated Songs"), suggesting that in addition to its white ownership the theater attracted at least a predominantly white audience. Probably there was little if any overlap between the clienteles of the Brooklyn and the Lyric.[31] Indeed, despite the proximity of the two theaters, the character of the neighborhoods seems different; the Lyric was the only commercial enterprise in its immediate vicinity, and one of only two buildings that served a function other than housing (the other was a white school). As Waller notes, comparatively few of the 112 "colored" theaters estimated to be operating in 1909 were owned by blacks,[32] and in the absence of information about the Lyric's management it is impossible to know to which group it belonged. But Wilmington's general intolerance of African American participation in public life can be gauged from the glee with which a local paper recorded the spread of Jim Crow seating practices to northern locales in 1916 following substantial black migration.[33] It is perhaps hardly surprising that the Lyric disappeared from an area that had just acquired a white school (1914) and may have been undergoing gentrification.

After the Nickelodeon

The next wave of theater building after 1907 began in 1910, when the Grand was erected. The Grand represents an attempt by a wealthy merchant, Jacob Solky, to capitalize on the movie boom by giving customers an elegant environment in which to see films. Solky was the only immigrant among the city's film entrepreneurs, having left Russia in 1880. Sometime before 1898 he came to Wilmington and established a flourishing haberdashery, which he ran concurrently with his elaborate new theater at 25 North Front Street. He hedged his bets similarly when he purchased the site of the Grand and turned the structure into both an office building and a theater, in a location that the *Dispatch* described as "a decidedly central spot."[34] The elegance of the Grand may reflect an awareness that Howard and Wells (still in the circus tent at that point) had cornered the lower end of the nickelodeon business in Wilmington, but it also manifests the beginning of the phase of theater design and film presentation that marks the consolidation of filmgoing as a more upscale entertainment, in accordance with national trends.

The theater opened on Christmas Eve 1910, was closed on Christmas Day, and celebrated what was in effect a second gala opening on 26 December. The Grand seated 500, was carpeted (a contrast to the sawdust, dirt, and peanut-shell floor of the Bijou), had a balcony, and employed both ushers and an orchestra. It continued the tradition of illustrated songs popular at all local theaters; in fact, it had acquired the services of a singer named Horace Baldwin, a former employee of Keith and Proctor in New York.[35] Significantly, the national trade paper noting the emergence of the Grand touted its "modern ventilating plant," although the first genuine air-conditioning did not appear until 1917 in Chicago and then only typically in theaters with 2,000 or more seats, well beyond the scale of anything Wilmington had to offer.[36] Every Wilmington theater that wished to remain in business year-round had to find a solution, however primitive, to the problem of climate control, and even before the advent of reliable air-conditioning local theaters attempted to represent themselves as among the coolest places in town.

Slightly after the founding of the Grand, the Air Dome appeared, opening in 1911 and lasting until about 1914. While it was no doubt designed to attract a clientele similar to the Bijou's, Frank Peiffer, its owner, was handicapped in the contest because national trends were against him. Russell Merritt notes that the movement "toward bigger, more elaborate theaters was unmistakable to anyone reading the frequent theater reports made to the press."[37] While Wilmington movie theaters escaped the threat posed elsewhere by legitimate theaters that began showing movies full-time, by 1910 the middle class had evinced a preference for more elegant theaters that resembled the best legitimate houses, if not outdoing them in uniformed employees and technological marvels such as organs and bigger and better screens and projectors—even the automatic ticket-taking machine advertised by the Royal, a later Howard and Wells theater. The Air Dome could not compete with the Bijou on the one hand and the Grand on the other, especially inasmuch as by late summer of 1915, a national trade paper wrote that new insurance regulations were being applied to the structures, and film exchanges would serve them only on a "cash-in-advance basis."[38] As early as February 1910, moreover, there were articles and a barrage of letters in the *Film Index* about the rivalry between permanent theaters and airdomes, with one article concluding that "as a matter of business fairness an exchange should not supply service to an airdome adjacent to a theatre served by another licensed exchange."[39]

Even the Bijou, as I have already indicated, chose to become a more elaborate exhibition venue when the occasion arose. The tent collapsed in a freak snowstorm on 12 January 1912, and the theater was reborn on 30 May. Three thousand people stopped by to see it on opening night. The revamped theater seated 800: 600 whites in the orchestra and 200 blacks in the balcony, which had a separate entrance.[40] The auditorium was cooled with fans, the screen was thoroughly up-to-date, and two projectors eliminated delay between reels. Howard and Wells had paid $20,000 for the land and $40,000 for the new building and fittings (or, if Fales is to be believed, $75,000 in all).[41] Given the competition from the Grand, if the snowstorm had not intervened, Howard and Wells might well have had to tear down the old Bijou in any case to remain competitive, leaving the airdome niche to the Air Dome until its demise in 1914. After rebuilding, the Bijou did not raise its prices to the dime prevailing at rivals such as the Grand but continued to charge a nickel until the war, in a sign of loyalty to its original clientele.

Waller implies that motion pictures were well on the way to achieving the status of preeminent commercial entertainment in the United States before the nation's entrance into World War I;[42] that Wilmington was no exception to this trend is shown by the pre-1917 openings of the Royal and the Victoria. Opening on 27 September 1915 at 121 North Front Street, Howard and Wells's Royal was less than a block away from the Bijou, right next door to the site of the ill-fated Air Dome. The theater boasted the latest model of projector, and the live orchestra had been replaced by the Seeburg Motion Picture Organ.[43] The features, which changed daily, came from World, Paramount, Metro, and Fox; these brand names were offered as a selling point. Wilmington's theaters now advertised films as national brands, which no doubt had the effect of intensifying competition among them, inasmuch as the same films were on view at theaters that were, by now, similarly appointed (most had been designed by a single architect, B. H. Stephen). The more personal touches, such as Wells's individualized narrations to accompany films, were a thing of the past. In providing and advertising the latest films, the best architecture, or the most recent innovations in efficiency or comfort, Wilmington's theaters were implicitly marking their ability to conform to national standards of good service. Audiences were assured that they were getting the same product that they would get in New York, and at the same time—but for less money.[44]

Small-Time Vaudeville

While competition among local theaters may have promoted standardization as each theater vied to be in the vanguard, it promoted variety in realms beyond mere price and location. Nationwide, the oversupply of theaters and undersupply of films in 1907–8 caused some exhibitors to attempt product differentiation by introducing vaudeville acts, which led by 1909 to the development of a mixed program of film and vaudeville acts known as small-time vaudeville that was enormously successful for big-city entrepreneurs.[45] But small-time vaudeville had its drawbacks. While it had the potential to increase the social cachet of the theater that used it (frequently justifying a rise in the price of admission), it also increased the theater's expenses. A manager might then be forced to select less costly—and consequently less desirable—acts, which in turn fared poorly against all-film programs.[46] Thus, *Moving Picture World* noted in 1909, "The country exhibitors are badly scared at the incursion of the vaudeville acts. . . . If they could show cheap, vulgar vaudeville acts . . . they would not kick so much, but in small towns, where they have to depend entirely on a regular local trade, they cannot show cheap vaudeville acts."[47]

Northern small-time vaudeville was typically the purview of better, more elaborate theaters, which began their appeals to the middle class through their architecture and continued it by providing vaudeville along with film as a certifiably middle-class entertainment. Musser suggests that "vaudeville was a comparative rarity" in the South, and Waller notes that Lexington never had any small-time vaudeville, although such combined bills were common in larger metropolitan centers.[48] Yet there is evidence from trade papers to suggest that small-time vaudeville might have been unexpectedly common even in less populous communities in North Carolina in 1909, and that it operated at the bottom as well as at the top of the theatrical Great Chain of Being. One retrospective account of Wilmington's Air Dome suggests that the theater (about whose programming strategy we otherwise know little) provided small-time vaudeville, and airdomes in Winston-Salem, Raleigh, and Greensboro also offered small-time vaudeville.[49]

When Solky's second theater, the Victoria (briefly managed by Schloss's nephew Marx Nathan), opened on 12 January 1914, it more closely resembled northern models than did the Air Dome. Almost from the beginning, it included B. F. Keith vaudeville and musical comedy in its program. But its owner evidently did not meet with the kind of commercial success in Wilmington that vaudeville often bestowed upon New York managers. An Atlanta businessman, Ralph DeBruler, leased both the Grand and the Victoria from Solky in April 1915, stating his intention to run the Victoria as "a high class feature photoplay theatre, showing only the highest class modern screen productions including the Paramount programme, the productions of the Fox Film Corporation and others, with singers and entertainers of the highest class, but no vaudeville."[50]

The infrequency with which the Victoria advertised in the newspapers before its sale suggests that the theater may have fallen into disfavor; while it may simply have been poorly managed, DeBruler's statement hints that vaudeville may have played a role here. Although the Victoria's exhibition strategy was small-time from the start, it may have chosen this format too late to succeed in a locale in which the competition with similarly appointed theaters showing all-film bills was considerable. DeBruler's comments indicate that in Wilmington at this time, vaudeville may have appeared somewhat unsavory—especially since this city also seems to have catered to audiences of children, for whom mixed vaudeville-movie bills might have been considered unseemly. Children did attend vaudeville at the Crystal Palace, but there was a movement to develop specifically child-oriented programs such as a "children's movie day." In this last regard, Wilmington was responding to national trends visible in other cities; the local paper explicitly cited the example of Atlanta in forwarding the project of children's matinees.[51]

Local and National Advertising Strategies

Clever promotion—the effort to convince audiences, whether children or adults, that shows had been tailored specifically for them—was clearly the best way to get business. In terms of marketing trends, Wilmington illustrates the attempt to reconcile local knowledge of a potential film market with national sales strategies. Gomery contends that film exhibition somewhat tardily "followed the lead of department store and grocery chains, which had precipitated significant changes in mass selling in the United States in the years preceding the First World War."[52] Even before the chain-store approach began to govern local theaters nationwide, Wilmington's theaters reacted to national trends not only involuntarily owing to economic necessity but also deliberately through an emulation of strategies contained in trade papers. After the revamped Bijou opened in 1912, the need to distinguish each theater from its competitors was manifest; Howard and Wells's schemes were marked by their national character, either because they followed lines described in *Moving Picture World* or because they involved a network of theater and studio executives.

One asset of the Howard-Wells partnership was their publicist, D. Montrose Bain, former circulation manager of the *Star*. Bain's connections and savvy were useful in the many contests, promotional articles, and tie-ins related to Howard-Wells projects; for instance, the *Star* printed narrative installments of serials in concert with their Bijou run. But the Bijou's promotions had a national as well as a local dimension. For example, the Brayton baby show, publicized in *Moving Picture World* in May and June 1909, originated in Chicago. Howard and Wells used the idea for their 1912 opening, and, more important, the underlying assumption that it was essential to attract women and children. As the Brayton Slide Manufacturing Company noted, wise managers "know the value of a baby as the advertising medium for the moving picture theater. Women and children make up a large part of the audiences of these places."[53] For the Bijou, this assertion proved true; reported the *Dispatch*, "The ladies and children kept a constant stream to the Bijou and incessant were the ejaculations of admiration and many, many the expressions of gladness at the return of their old favorite."[54] The praise was not merely for the theater's amenities but also for the baby pictures projected onto the curtain, an inducement for the audience both to vote for its favorite infant and to boost the *Dispatch*'s circulation by using ballots cut from the newspaper.

Besides small promotional efforts such as perfume days or souvenir days (every Friday it gave away 2,000 copies of *Photoplay Weekly*, apparently a local fan magazine in this context, although it may have had national affiliations), the Bijou had a fondness for the grandiose. Thus from May through July 1915, the theater cooperated with twenty-one theaters in the Carolinas and Virginia, with several local merchants, and with Universal City in running what it described as a "popularity contest" but what might better be called a ticket-selling contest in which the young woman who sold the most Bijou coupon books would win an assortment of prizes from Wilmington stores and a trip to California with the other twenty-one contest winners. The group of women—chaperoned by the wife of a U.S. senator—not only would visit

community, with the community's interests at stake. At the same time, exhibitors' success in Wilmington also required being au courant with exhibition practices nationwide. Audiences wanted to hear that the films available to them were the same as those playing in New York, or that local personalities and events could be put into newsreels and thus connected with Hollywood products. The success of Howard and Wells, ultimately the preeminent film exhibitors of prewar Wilmington, illustrates that what Wilmington filmdom may have required above all else was a talent for liminality, for positioning oneself as both a resident entrepreneur attuned to the nuances of the city and a businessman capable of understanding and adapting national promotional schemes.

Perhaps a similar point might hold true for scholars engaged in constructing exhibition studies for other local communities.

Notes

I am indebted to Robert Allen for advice and direction, to Shari Novek and Fiona Ragheb for their collaboration on an earlier version of this paper, to Claudia Nelson for editorial comments, and to Beverly Tetterton and Joe Sheppard of the New Hanover County Public Library for help with research questions. Thanks are also due to the *Spectator* for permission to reprint this essay, which appeared in somewhat different form as "Early Film Exhibition in Wilmington, North Carolina, 1897–1915," in *Spectator: The University of Southern California Journal of Film and Television Criticism* 17, no. 1 (1996): 8–27.

1. Gregory Waller, *Main Street Amusements: Movies and Commercial Entertainment in a Southern City, 1896–1930* (Washington, D.C.: Smithsonian Institution Press, 1995), xviii.

2. "S.A. Lynch Purchases the Schloss Circuit," *Star*, 1 May 1915, 5. The *New York Dramatic Mirror (NYDM)* notes that "Manager Schloss has just returned from New York. He reports bright prospects and many bookings of high class attractions for next season"; "Correspondence," 23 April 1898, 6. Schloss's obituary explains that after a false start "in the crockery business," he became an orchestra member for various road shows "and in this manner received his training" ("Mr. S.A. Schloss Is Dead," *Star*, 23 December 1913, 5).

3. Lewis Hall, *Land of the Golden River*, vol. 3 (Wilmington, N.C.: Wilmington Printing, 1980), 326. Wilmington may have been unusual for a community its size in having a regular vaudeville theater by 1905, although Lexington acquired one not long after that time; see Waller, *Main Street Amusements*, 66.

4. "Correspondence," *NYDM*, 27 March 1897, 6. The program included the 1896 Edison films *Watermelon Contest, Lone Fisherman, Tub Race, Feeding the Doves,* and *Black Diamond Express*. Hall's account of the showing lists different titles, but his description suggests that these films were among those shown. He adds that "the pictures were accompanied by selections of vocal and band music played on the new graphophone"; *Land of the Golden River*, 325.

5. In fact, Miriam Hansen reports that in some locales women were a major and eager audience for such displays of the male body. See *Babel and Babylon: Spectatorship in American Silent Film* (Cambridge, Mass.: Harvard University Press, 1991), 1.

6. Waller notes a similar pattern in Lexington, where the local railway company promoted the establishment of a recreation area some distance away from the city center so that residents would make use of the streetcar; *Main Street Amusements,* 53.

7. Charles Musser with Carol Nelson, *High-Class Moving Pictures: Lyman H. Howe and the Forgotten Era of Traveling Exhibition, 1880–1920* (Princeton, N.J.: Princeton University Press, 1991), 93.

8. Ibid., 143; see also 152.

9. "Correspondence," *NYDM,* 4 February 1905, 6; *NYDM,* 18 December 1909, 32; *NYDM,* 16 December 1905, 6; *NYDM,* 31 March 1906, 7.

10. *Wilmington Messenger,* 10 December 1906, 5.

11. Charles Musser, "The Nickelodeon Era Begins: Establishing the Framework for Hollywood's Mode of Representation," *Framework* 22/23 (Autumn 1983): 7.

12. Carnival films reached Wilmington on 14 October 1901, when Edison's Moving Pictures, under the direction of J. T. Potter, gave an exhibition for the Elks grand carnival and street fair.

13. Waller, *Main Street Amusements,* 66–71; David O. Thomas, "From Page to Screen in Small Town America: Early Motion Picture Exhibition in Winona, Minnesota," *Journal of the University Film Association* 33, no. 3 (1981): 3–13.

14. "Howard Left Show to Pitch Movie Tent in Wilmington," *Moving Picture World,* 25 November 1922, 318.

15. Henry Bacon McKoy, *Wilmington, N.C.—Do You Remember When?* (Greenville, S.C.: Keys, 1957), 116. While McKoy holds that Howard and Wells developed the idea of showing moving pictures after both had moved to the city, Robert Martin Fales suggests that they had been traveling exhibitors before settling in Wilmington. See *Wilmington Yesteryear* (Wilmington, N.C.: Lower Cape Fear Historical Society, 1984), 80.

16. "Moving Picture Exhibition," *Wilmington Morning Star,* 10 February 1905, 4.

17. William John Mann writes of Connecticut that nickelodeons lost business during the summers, when they were forced to close owing to the heat and airdomes took their place until September; Mann, "The Movies Come to Middletown: The Cinematic Experience of a Small Town, 1897–1917" (M.A. thesis, Wesleyan University, 1987), 54. In contrast, the Bijou—at the time a canvas tent supplemented with a wooden frame—was able to stay open year-round, reporting "large and well pleased houses" for the week 29 November through 4 December 1909; "Motion Picture Notes," *NYDM,* 11 December 1909, 27.

18. McKoy, *Wilmington, N.C.,* 152.

19. Fales, *Wilmington Yesteryear,* 80–81.

20. "Picture Theatre for Negroes," *NYDM,* 27 March 1909, 13; for the Bijou's segregated seating, see McKoy, *Wilmington, N.C.,* 116. Waller observes a similar arrangement at a Lexington medicine show in 1906; *Main Street Amusements,* 164. Jim Crow restrictions generally became more severe over time, so a racial mixing that was acceptable at the turn of the century might have become impossible fifteen years on.

21. "Howard Left Show," 318.

22. Charlotte Herzog, "The Archaeology of Cinema Architecture: The Origins of the Movie Theater," *Quarterly Review of Film Studies* 6 (1984): 12, 20.

23. McKoy, *Wilmington, N.C.*, 115, 113.

24. "Howard Left Show," 318.

25. Eileen Bowser, *The Transformation of Cinema 1907–1915*, History of the American Cinema 2 (New York: Scribner's, 1990), 4.

26. See Charles Musser, *The Emergence of Cinema: The American Screen to 1907*, History of the American Cinema 1 (New York: Scribner's, 1990), 428.

27. Untitled paragraph, *Moving Picture World* 13 April 1907, 87.

28. Untitled paragraph, *Moving Picture World* 29 June 1907, 266. The 1915 date is problematic; the first edition of the 1915 fire atlas indicates a saloon in this space the second (which is also dated 1915 but may have been emended any time up to 1948) locates a movie theater there.

29. By 1915 the block had become considerably more commercial; only two domiciles remained. A comparison of the 1915 fire atlas plan of the movie theater at 810 North Front with the picture of the Brooklyn suggests that the Brooklyn had been either torn down and replaced or given a substantial facelift.

30. Fales, *Wilmington Yesteryear*, 80.

31. Overlap is unlikely because of the Brooklyn's status as a storefront theater. As the *New York Dramatic Mirror* observed, such facilities had no balconies in which to cordon off their black customers, so that "patronage is generally confined to the whites." The *Mirror* article noted the opening of an all-black theater in Columbia, Missouri; not to be outdone, a correspondent in Vicksburg wrote to report that the latter city "has two of them in full blast and both seem to be doing well." See "Picture Theatre for Negroes," *NYDM*, 27 March 1909, 13; "Theatres for Negroes in Vicksburg," *NYDM*, 15 May 1909, 15. The photograph I refer to is reproduced in Fales, *Wilmington Yesteryear*, 93.

32. Waller, *Main Street Amusements*, 162.

33. "Near 327,000 Blacks Have Left the South," *Star*, 12 November 1916, 10.

34. "Playhouse Beautiful," *Dispatch*, 27 December 1910, 6. Because the trolley ran along Front and Princess streets, passing within a block of every downtown theater, *all* locations were "decidedly central."

35. *Dispatch*, 17 April 1911, 2.

36. *Film Index*, 1 October 1910, 5; Douglas Gomery, *Shared Pleasures: A History of Movie Presentation in the United States* (Madison: University of Wisconsin Press, 1992), 53–54, 75.

37. Russell Merritt, "Nickelodeon Theaters 1905–1914: Building an Audience for the Movies," in *The American Film Industry*, ed. Tino Balio (Madison: University of Wisconsin Press, 1976), 76.

38. *Moving Picture World*, 11 September 1915, 1804.

39. *Film Index*, "A Timely Inquiry," 26 February 1910, 2.

40. Waller observes that in Lexington, balconies for blacks in white theaters were granted and taken away at the whim of the management. Although this capriciousness was not a feature of the Bijou, blacks naturally found separate entrances and seating humiliating and were consequently less likely to attend segregated theaters than were white patrons. See Waller, *Main Street Amusements*, 111, 167; Kathryn H. Fuller, *At the Picture Show: Small-Town Audiences and the Creation of Movie Fan Culture* (Washington, D.C.: Smithsonian Institution Press, 1996), 34.

41. Fales, *Wilmington Yesteryear,* 81.

42. Waller, *Main Street Amusements,* 113–21.

43. "Which," the *Dispatch* promised, "will be operated by an expert musician and music will be rendered in accord with the pictures shown"; "Royal Theatre to Open Today," 27 September 1915, 7.

44. A Victoria advertisement emphasized that patrons could see "the same stars and the same shows that are featured in the leading theaters of New York at $2.00 and $3.00"; *Star* 14 April 1915, 2.

45. Robert Allen, "The Movies in Vaudeville: Historical Context of the Movies as Popular Entertainment," in *The American Film Industry,* ed. Tino Balio, rev. ed. (Madison: University of Wisconsin Press, 1985), 79; Gomery, *Shared Pleasures,* 37.

46. For contemporary commentary on this issue from *Moving Picture World,* see Robert Grau, "Vaudeville in Moving Pictures," 7 May 1910, 726; Thomas Bedding, "Vaudeville Vitiates the Picture," 11 June 1910, 985; "Vaudeville Put in Its Place," 9 July 1910, 93; C. W. Lawford, "Why Vaudeville Was Called Upon," 27 August 1910, 455; J. M. B, "Vaudeville," 15 October 1910, 868; and "Why Vaudeville Is Detrimental," 19 November 1910, 1183. Most of these columns agree that the unsavory in small-time vaudeville arises from revenue too low to recover the cost of good acts; thus adding vaudeville to movies frustrates its original purpose of attracting upscale clients or justifying higher ticket prices. Even so, mixing the two succeeded in Durham, perhaps because of its proportionately larger lower-middle-class and working-class population; Robert C. Allen and Douglas Gomery note in *Film History: Theory and Practice* (New York: McGraw-Hill, 1985), 206, that by 1909 all of Durham's movie theaters had incorporated vaudeville into their programs. For a debate on the classes addressed by metropolitan small-time vaudeville, see Sumiko Higashi, Robert Allen, and Ben Singer, "Dialogue," in *Cinema Journal* 35, no. 3 (1996): 72–128.

47. *Moving Picture World,* 6 February 1909, 142–43.

48. Musser, *Emergence of Cinema,* 428; Waller, *Main Street Amusements,* 66.

49. Hall, *Land of the Golden River,* 328; *Moving Picture World,* 19 June 1909, 5; 25 September 1909, 20; and 9 October 1909, 19. The prevalence and importance of small-time vaudeville in southern airdomes will only emerge with further research.

50. "Atlanta Man Leases the Solky Theatres," *Star,* 10 April 1915, 5.

51. *Star,* 16 July 1915, 15. See Waller for an account of an attempt to upgrade childish tastes; *Main Street Amusements,* 145. According to the *Star,* the sponsors of Children's Movie Day (mostly women) wanted films with "simple plots that are uplifting, entertaining and easily understood by the children. . . . A good plot that contains emotions felt by children portrayed in clean form should be interesting occasionally to grownups and are [*sic*] far better for the children" ("For Children's Movie Day," *Star,* 16 July 1915, 5).

52. Gomery, *Shared Pleasures,* 34.

53. "The Brayton Baby Show Scheme," *Moving Picture World,* 15 May 1909, 632.

54. "Theatre," *Dispatch,* 1 June 1912, 2.

55. Advertisement, *Star,* 25 May 1915, 9. The timing of this contest suggests Carl Laemmle's eagerness to bring the products of the two-month-old Universal City to national attention. Not only was there fierce competition among movie theaters during this period, there was also, as Richard Koszarski observes, equally heated competition among studios to develop facilities of unprecedented size and expense; see Koszarski,

An Evening's Entertainment: The Age of the Silent Feature Picture, History of the American Cinema 3 (New York: Scribner's, 1990), 5–7. Bringing people from the hinterlands to see the studios helped establish the latter as bona fide tourist attractions. Koszarski comments that Universal City was "comparing itself directly to the Panama-Pacific Exposition in San Francisco" during its opening-day ceremony (7).

56. *Star,* 26 May 1915, 3.

57. "Outline Movie Programme," *Star,* 11 August 1915, 5.

58. Although the Bijou did not show films on Sundays, the making of this film awakened the ire of a Sabbatarian who wrote to the *Star* complaining not only because there was an outpouring of people to the beaches on Sundays but also because "we are to have a moving picture exhibition to advertise far and wide how we spend the Sabbath day on the beach! For one, I protest against this." One gathers that the advertising of the Sabbath breaking was a worse infraction than the breakage itself. Letter from Andrew J. Howell, *Star,* 12 August 1915, 4.

59. Elizabeth Ewen, "City Lights: Immigrant Women and the Rise of the Movies," *Signs* 5, no. 3 (1980): S58.

60. Judith Mayne, "Immigrants and Spectators," *Wide Angle* 5, no. 2 (1983): 38.

61. Fuller, *At the Picture Show,* 14.

5

BUILDING MOVIE AUDIENCES IN PLACERVILLE, CALIFORNIA, 1908–1915

GEORGE POTAMIANOS

In 1899, residents of the village of Placerville, California (population 2,600), packed the opera house for a chance to see their first moving picture exhibition. Over the next few years, itinerant film exhibitions drew sizable audiences in the small town. Assuming that the early success of moving picture shows in Placerville meant that the new entertainment had a loyal audience, in 1907 the owner of the local opera house provided a regular program of moving pictures every Tuesday. Less than a month later, a lack of attendance forced the opera house to discontinue its weekly film program. The following year, an entrepreneur established a motion picture theater in Placerville that remained in business for several decades. What drew Placerville audiences to those first exhibitions? Given the successes of itinerant motion picture exhibitions at the turn of the century, why did the opera house face such difficulties drawing a regular Tuesday audience? Why did the opera house's film program fail, but merely one year later a motion picture theater thrive? What did it take for these small-town residents to develop a habit of attending motion pictures? This chapter examines the sources and consequences of the growth of cinematic entertainment between 1899 and 1915, as the movies gradually became the center of Placerville's leisure world.

The story of film exhibition in Placerville is different from both that of the neighboring city of Sacramento and those of larger urban areas. This small town never had a nickelodeon phase, as the village's population could not sustain a theater that exhibited moving pictures to the exclusion of other entertainments. Consequently, when an entrepreneur finally built a movie theater in Placerville in 1908, it resembled the local opera house more than it did an urban nickelodeon. Like the opera house, it offered a combination of live stage performances and moving pictures and adopted additional functions as a dance hall, the high school auditorium, and a forum for local political debates.

In Placerville, movies and other commercial recreations faced tough battles establishing themselves. The people of Placerville were not initially so readily accepting of movies as a regular source of entertainment; therefore, the period of itinerant exhibition lasted much longer than in larger towns. The local opera house, where the first movies were shown, encompassed a vast range of social functions, many of which were local in character.[1] The motion picture theater that finally appeared in Placerville in 1908 opened two years later than the first one in nearby Sacramento.

Demography shaped the reception of mass culture in Placerville and accounts, in part, for the difficulties motion pictures had finding a reliable audience in the small community. Located fifty miles to the east of Sacramento, Placerville, the seat of El Dorado County, witnessed virtually no population growth into the early twentieth century. El Dorado County (population 10,000) was primarily agricultural, with more than 700 farms. Census takers in 1900 identified about fifty nonagricultural firms in the county, with an average of three employees per firm.[2] Most leisure seekers in the county had to drive several miles for their entertainment. The absence of a large permanent population base in the town made it difficult for the owner of a theater to provide amusement on a regular basis. Even more than in larger communities, theater entrepreneurs could not afford to alienate any part of the audience, or they might jeopardize long-term profits.

Late nineteenth-century amusements in Placerville varied greatly, as did attendance. The most popular events were those involving local participants. On September 3, 1898, for example, Placerville held a three-day "Admission Day" to commemorate California statehood. The local band played in the Plaza and the local Native Sons Dramatic Company performed in the opera house. A parade, speeches, athletic contests, a dance, and a baseball game rounded out the activities over the following two days.[3]

Traveling companies generally gained poor attendance in Placerville, especially if their performances conflicted with locally sponsored entertainment. In December 1898, for instance, the Dailey Stock Company performed at the opera house and was "met by a shamefully small audience Monday and Tuesday nights" despite the low ticket prices of 10, 20, and 30 cents. Consequently, the town postponed the regular Saturday night dance "out of courtesy to the Dailey Company"; to reciprocate, the company offered local orchestra members complimentary tickets that night.[4] Conversely, the performance of *Fanchon the Cricket* by local talent for the benefit of the Placerville juvenile band almost a year later, at ticket prices higher than those charged by the Dailey Company, "was played to a full house" and "at the earnest solicitation of many of our citizens the members of the troupe . . . decided to repeat the performance" the following night.[5]

Placerville residents probably encountered moving pictures for the first time outside of their own community, in either Sacramento or San Francisco.

A half-page advertisement in the local press for the Mining Fair in San Francisco between January 29 and March 6, 1898, was the first published introduction of the new medium to the local population.[6] The fair was already a popular attraction because of the importance of the mining industry to the county; railroads offered special rates to and from the fairgrounds, and admission prices were set at 25 and 15 cents. The ad stressed the "free exhibition of Edison's Projectoscope . . . illustrating Pacific Coast scenes, European views, Eastern moving pictures, Klondike scenes, comical views, with lectures," as well as several films of miners and mining.[7] While there is no way to know how many Placerville residents traveled to the Mining Fair, or how many of them actually attended the Edison program, it is clear that prior to the first film exhibition in Placerville in 1899, residents had to travel elsewhere to see the new medium.[8]

The first moving picture exhibitions in Placerville took place in a variety of locales, though the opera house quickly became the most common venue. On February 25, 1899, the opera house exhibited the Corbett-Fitzsimmons fight with the Veriscope at admission prices of 50 cents for adults and 25 cents for children.[9] Moving pictures reappeared in Placerville as a part of the Chautauqua two years later at the local Methodist Episcopal (M.E.) Church. The press hailed the event as a refined version of the stereopticon, which was extremely popular with local ministers who used the projections to illustrate their sermons and give special lectures:

> One very interesting entertainment was a series of moving pictures thrown upon a screen by the stereopticon with accessory appliances for producing the movements. This act has produced really wonderful results, and the motions of a railroad train, of men and animals moving, of gulls flying, and of ships moving are almost as real as if the actual objects were before the audience. One of the most interesting was "The Obstacle Race," representing twenty or more college students running a foot race over rough ground. They could all be seen racing along through mud, jumping into pools of water, and reproducing on the screen every motion of the actual race.[10]

Reviews of these early exhibitions stressed the verisimilitude of the performances and the ability of this new medium to represent real events and places.

Between 1901 and 1903, traveling lecturers brought moving pictures to the Placerville Opera House on an irregular basis. Unlike in larger towns, films did not usually come to Placerville with a vaudeville troupe but were presented with lecturers as a complete evening's entertainment. Moving pictures, therefore, more closely resembled the stereopticon presentations at local churches. Placerville pastors frequently used stereopticon slides to illustrate their sermons or to give special lectures on a variety of topics, most likely to encourage more people to attend church services. In January 1901, the Reverend J. B. Orr conducted morning and evening services at the M.E. Church on the topic "The Final Judgment." The first half hour of the service was dedicated to the display of scriptural scenes by a stereopticon.[11] The local Methodist Church, even more than the M.E. Church, used the stereopticon to present full evenings of amusement, at which the institution charged admission. In March 1904, Reverend King of the Methodist Church presented the chariot race from *Ben Hur,* assisted by local musical talent. The following week, King presented three lectures with the stereopticon on Japan, Ireland, and Scotland.[12] A year later, he projected his own slides of local events and gave a lecture entitled "Placerville, Past, Present, and Future." In one of the first instances of screen advertising in Placerville, King offered to project slides of local businesses for a "small fee," a practice capitalized upon years later by the owner of Placerville's first motion picture theater.[13]

Local audiences thus found in itinerant film exhibitions a familiar format of projected images with a lecturer providing offscreen commentary. In October 1901, the Woodmen of the World brought a multimedia entertainment to the opera house, with moving pictures, a phonograph, and a stereopticon. Many residents attended, probably because the show cost nothing the first night but also because the entertainment was truly novel. As the newspaper review noted, "The house was crowded . . . [and the show] was much better than some of those which charge admission fees." The presentation included films of President McKinley's last speech, with the audio provided by the phonograph.[14] The company changed the program the following week and charged admission fees of 35 cents reserved, 25 cents general, and 15 cents for children. One year later, Captain Ollie Henry and his Boer wife brought 1,600 feet of moving pictures to the opera house to accompany Henry's lecture on the Boer War. Henry, a participant in the war, captivated the audience, one that "taxed the seating capacity of the Opera House," with "thrilling and instructive recitals of the stirring deeds of valor" illustrated with scenes of "all the principal battles and many camp scenes."[15]

Traveling exhibitors continued to present shows in Placerville with increasing frequency through 1907. They began to show more narrative films and fewer travelogues and actualities. Later than in urban areas, Placerville audiences moved away from the notion of film as a representation of reality and accepted moving images as storytelling devices, as amusements that could work without the assistance of a lecturer.[16] In June 1903, Professor Bradshaw brought his moving picture show to Placerville. Bradshaw's program included many story films in addition to the traditional documentary attractions and promised two and one-half hours of continuous film, at prices of 35 cents for adults and 25 cents for children.[17] Two months later, traveling exhibitor Carl Schuman brought moving pictures to the local opera house; for the same prices as Bradshaw's exhibition, audiences saw "an entire series showing the late President McKinley . . . the Dixon and

McGovern fight complete from start to finish . . . a fine series of comics . . . [on Sunday evening] the Passion Play Oberammergau . . . [and on Monday] war and other subjects."[18] The local press labeled the pictures "the best ever shown in this city," and audiences called for a repeat showing of McKinley's funeral and speech on Monday, which Schuman provided.[19]

Later that year, the manager of the opera house experimented with the exhibition of motion pictures on a regular basis. In November, the proprietor contracted with the Laugh Motion Picture Company to furnish motion pictures every Tuesday. For 15 and 25 cents, the opera house promised town residents "illustrated songs, moving pictures . . . [while] the prices have been made very low by the management in order to encourage liberal patronage. It is the intention of the promoters to give the residents of Placerville one evening's entertainment each week at a merely nominal sum, and the entertainment will be clean and enjoyable."[20] The entertainment possessed all the earmarks of success: seats about half the price of typical itinerant exhibitions, a change of program each week, and the promise of morally inoffensive material.

Yet this first attempt to exhibit motion pictures on a regular basis in 1907 failed. By the second exhibition, on December 10, 1907, "the Laugh Motion Picture company did not have a large house, but the exhibition was exceptionally good."[21] By the third week, the management canceled the regular show, though the opera house continued to exhibit films on an irregular basis. Why did movies fail to capture a regular audience in Placerville? Why did commercial recreation take such a long time to penetrate the Placerville market? Though available sources offer no specific evidence, perhaps two factors account for this lag: the nature of the business and the attitudes of residents toward amusement. Traveling exhibitors and other amusement entrepreneurs most likely found the town too small a market to justify putting on a regular show. Perhaps more important were the ways in which residents looked at entertainment. That amusements produced by local residents attracted the largest audiences suggests that Placerville's citizens perceived public amusement as something generated by members inside the community, rather than outside. When the movies first arrived, they had to battle these preexisting attitudes. In counties with low population densities, amusement seekers often had to travel to neighboring towns for entertainment. The manager of the Placerville Opera House was unable to draw a steady audience for moving pictures from the surrounding area. County farmers usually came to Placerville only once each week, on Saturday or for special events.

Moreover, amusements in Placerville tended to occur in short-lived "fads." One commentator, discussing the construction of a roller-skating rink in the town, observed that "as long as people took a fancy to this healthy exercise the hall was crowded every night . . . and for a while all other public places were deserted. [A few years later] [t]his sport gone to rest, the people soon found out that they needed some new attraction, and someone proposed the idea to combine some horse races with the County Fair."[22] Many, perhaps including the owner of the opera house after the failure of the Tuesday movie show, assumed that moving pictures would share this fate. A year later, however, following changes in film production and distribution and numerous marketing gimmicks such as giveaways and free admissions on the part of a new local exhibitor, residents of the small town saw the opening of the first theater dedicated exclusively to motion pictures on a regular basis.

How did Placerville residents become accustomed to the new medium? Given the ubiquitous nature of moving images today, it is easy to assume that this entertainment was innately popular and thus was guaranteed to attract large audiences, yet this was not the case in Placerville. Ultimately, the process of courting an audience was complex, involving changes in the structure of the industry at the national level. Movies, first and foremost, were a business; therefore, a careful understanding of the way the industry changed in 1908 is paramount to an understanding of the overall success of the entertainment. Only when motion picture producers and distributors were able to guarantee a steady supply of products could local exhibitors build a regular audience base for the movies.

Before 1908, there was not a sufficient supply of films to allow for the establishment of a permanent and profitable movie theater in Placerville. Film historian Eileen Bowser explains that "the big problem in 1907 from a business point of view had been the lack of stability, the uncertainty of a source of supply for films, which made it a risk to invest a lot of money in the business."[23] Even contemporary observer George Kleine, the owner of one of the largest film manufacturing and importing companies, understood the problem: "In November last [1906] . . . the average American broker of films could not have supplied one moving picture parlor with three complete changes of film a week throughout the month [without duplication]."[24]

The organization of the Motion Picture Patents Company (MPPC) opened up possibilities for the expansion of movie entertainment in Placerville by creating a stable and predictable system of film distribution, as well as increasing the supply of available films. The changes wrought by the MPPC enabled exhibitors with a small population base to attract enough paying customers by getting them to attend regularly. A theater changing its film program three or more times a week could rely on the repeat patronage of a smaller audience to turn a profit.[25]

In September 1908, an amusement entrepreneur from San Francisco teamed up with a local businessman to establish a movie theater in Placerville. J. B. Travelle leased a former shoe store in the center of the town and remodeled the building into a 200-seat storefront motion picture theater.[26] Local reporters praised his efforts, stating, "Placerville needs a first-class show house where the public can enjoy the best circuit of talent at reasonable prices. . . . they are in a position to put on an attractive entertainment of an hour's duration for ten cents. . . . new life is what we want."[27] In short, Travelle initially had to offer the small community not only moving pictures but a local institution that would provide town residents with a source of local pride. In line with this idea, Travelle called his theater the Elite.

Given the low population density around Placerville, Travelle had to entice people to the theater who lived as far as ten miles away. In neighboring Sacramento and other more urban areas, theaters were accessible to a wide variety of people every day, but in Placerville, audiences had to be cultivated. Travelle first bought advertisements in the local newspaper four times each week. Unlike the theaters in Sacramento and other larger cities, which relied heavily on passersby for clientele and offered the titles of films on signboards outside the entrance to the theater, the Elite presented the titles of every film on the program in its newspaper advertisements.[28] Typically, each program consisted of five or six different films of about one reel each. As in Sacramento, the program emphasized variety with a couple of comedies, a western, a drama, a travelogue or industrial film, and an illustrated song.

Travelle opened the Elite theater at the beginning of October 1908, with a steady supply of Patents Co. films. The Elite offered local residents three reels of film, which changed three times each week, for 10 cents. In the first week of operation, Travelle realized the competitive advantage he held over the local opera house. The first week of October, the Elite offered its standard entertainment, while the opera house booked a traveling theatrical company of fifteen players, "one of the greatest laugh producers of the day," performing *Hooligans of New York,* at prices of 25, 50, and 75 cents. Local residents overwhelmingly chose the Elite's cheaper entertainment. An observer of opening night at the Elite Theater described the scene: "The opening of Placerville's new amusement resort last Saturday night was very largely attended. . . . during the evening four complete shows were given. . . . over five hundred tickets were sold during the evening, and there were many who were deterred from going inside the first night because of the crowd of people who congregated about the entrance all evening. The Elite will hereafter be the most popular resort in the city of evenings."[29] Travelle was not willing to rest on the fantastic success of the opening night. Given the poor long-term track record of moving pictures in Placerville, Travelle realized that he had to discover ways to keep local audiences coming to the theater. He quickly embarked on a business strategy designed to attract and maintain a regular clientele.

Travelle aligned himself with local institutions. This strategy not only promoted attractions at the theater but also positioned the new theater as a legitimate community business worthy of patronage. On October 21, 1908, the local Catholic church sponsored its annual Catholic Fair, a weeklong series of social activities and celebrations. On the twenty-sixth, Travelle presented

The Passion Play, a hand-colored film of the play performed in Oberammergau, Bavaria, in 1904.[30] Travelle thus positioned the Elite as a business enterprise that was a part of the local activities. The following Saturday, the Elite offered a special matinee for children under twelve. At Butts and Quigley's general store, patrons would receive a free ticket to the matinee with a purchase of tea or coffee totaling 25 cents or more.[31] Furthermore, newspaper advertisements presented the Elite as "Placerville's Permanent Home of Entertainment" and emphasized that the Elite "Especially Caters to Women and Children," with "nothing said or done to hurt the feelings of the most fastidious."[32] These gimmicks situated the Elite as a community institution, as worthy of patronage as either the Catholic Fair or the local general store. The creation of a children's matinee and procurement of *The Passion Play* were part of Travelle's overall strategy to convince local residents that, unlike the temporary film exhibitions at the local opera house, the Elite Theater would last and would be an integral part of the town's economic and social environment.

Travelle also voluntarily closed the theater on Sunday evenings. This not only placated local church elites but also mitigated criticism from local religious communities about the morality of motion pictures. The Elite drew large enough audiences from the local population that some citizens even urged churches to express their gratitude to the theater for not monopolizing their congregations: "The churches of Placerville certainly should be grateful to the theater management for ceding to them Sunday night. In other places Sunday is the best patronized night of the week . . . but here the house is dark."[33]

Travelle's strategy, as with his voluntary Sunday closing, was to present the Elite Theater to the local population not as a new business that would run old, established enterprises into bankruptcy but as a business that would support existing community institutions, even competitors. By 1909, the Elite usurped the position formerly occupied by the opera house as the village's central place of amusement. On November 18, 1908, the opera house featured a traveling company performing the play *On Gay Broadway* for the usual 25-, 50-, and 75-cent admission. The show attracted a small audience that, according to one observer, "did not half fill the opera house. It is hard for the best of theatrical talent to play to empty chairs."[34] The performances at the opera house, relatively overpriced and irregular, faced stiff competition for patrons from the Elite theater. Realizing that his competitive advantage would only increase, Travelle bent over backward to give the impression that the Elite supported the community opera house. On November 21, Travelle announced that "hereafter on all show nights at the opera house the doors of this theater will be open at 6:30 instead of 7 p.m. . . . For the benefit of those patrons who desire to witness the performance of the Bostonian Minstrel Maids at the opera house."[35]

The Elite attracted patrons with giveaways during the first few months of its operation. On November 30, it promoted Tuesday and Thursday evenings as "school children's night" and offered a "pretty gift to each child; something that will amuse them" to those who attended the Saturday matinee.[36] However, giveaways were not exclusively the province of children. One week after the children's matinee, the Elite promised a "handsome present" to each woman and child attending the performance.[37] The Elite also emphasized its high standards for the physical environment of the theater, in part as a response to parents' concerns and wider complaints about the safety and morality of moving picture shows. The theater announced that the interior was "well ventilated and fumigated every day to insure our patron's [*sic*] safety from all disease germs" and encouraged "the mothers to send their children, who we promise to treat with all the courtesy due them. Our program is carefully selected."[38]

One noticeable theme in the Elite's strategy to hold a large share of the local market was that the moving pictures themselves were not emphasized in its promotions. It was not the films but the giveaways, the alignments with local businesses, the promises of a clean theater, and the heavy newspaper advertising that attracted the clientele to the theater. This strategy was typical of theaters in other small communities. Charles Huntsberry, an exhibitor in Redwood Falls, Minnesota (county seat of 2,000 people similar to Placerville), explained his battle to establish a theater there: "It takes more than good pictures to keep things moving in these country towns, for expenses are just the same if you have a crowd or not. . . . it keeps me busy thinking of new schemes to keep the people coming."[39]

Within a year, Travelle's business strategies vaulted the Elite to the center of amusement in Placerville. In March 1909, the owner of the opera house pleaded with the city marshal for a reduction in the annual license fee, arguing that business had been "very bad" during the first two months of the year. The city marshal acceded to his request, but this was not enough to save the opera house from bankruptcy.[40]

Building an audience was crucial to the success of the Elite theater. Nothing illustrates this concept better than the efforts of another entrepreneur to establish a competitive venture in Placerville. In 1909, the owner of the opera house leased the building to Fred O'Neil, a local entrepreneur who converted the building into a movie theater. O'Neil promised numerous changes at the new Orpheum Theater: "New improvements will be started at once, including a very attractive front. Good music, illustrated songs, and the best motion pictures will be run with a change of program three times a week [three reels per program]." To differentiate O'Neil's theater from Travelle's, the Orpheum leased its films from independent producers and distributors and argued that these films were "far ahead of anything that the Trust handles on the Pacific Coast."[41] O'Neil's Orpheum opened its doors on

March 29 to a packed house. Ball's Orchestra, Placerville's town band, provided the music to accompany the pictures and illustrated songs.[42]

For two years, the two theaters competed with one another for the town's amusement seekers. They employed strategies beyond the Independent/Trust dichotomy to differentiate themselves. By the beginning of 1910, both the Orpheum and the Elite obtained films from the General Film Company, the distribution arm of the Patents Company. The theaters began to identify one of the films on the program, generally a dramatic picture, as a "feature." Neither theater owner used the term *feature* to refer to multireel films (as it would be defined after 1911), but employed it as a way to highlight the most recently released and most elaborate films on the program. The number of films on each theater's program also became a competitive element between the Elite and O'Neil's. Within two months after O'Neil's opened, the Elite expanded its program from three to six films with an illustrated song, while O'Neil's presented seven films and a song. By May 1909, O'Neil's featured a six-piece orchestra on Saturdays along with a Wednesday matinee. The Elite changed its program four times a week, instead of O'Neil's three, and installed an "electric absorption fan" in the roof over the auditorium, which allegedly "purifie[d] the air every three minutes."[43] In the end, the Elite won the competition for the local audience. On June 11, 1910, O'Neil "retired" from the business and sold his lease on the former opera house to Travelle.[44]

Travelle continued to employ strategies designed to maintain his audience long after O'Neil's closed. His new efforts involved demarcating the Elite as a unique place in the community. At the end of 1911, Travelle completely remodeled the opera house and moved the Elite from its former storefront to the new venue. When the theater reopened in February 1912, the new Elite had a widened front, an inclined main floor, new interior wallpaper and molding, a scenic drop curtain, circular boxes on either side of the stage, three ceiling ventilators, and a front ticket booth.[45] Essentially, Travelle built Placerville's first and only picture palace. Citizens of the town responded with a vaudeville performance featuring local actors, the proceeds of which would go entirely to Travelle to defray some of the expenses involved in remodeling the theater. An organizer of the benefit articulated the purpose of the event as "a way to show Mr. and Mrs. J. B. Travelle, in some substantial manner, [our] appreciation of the public spirit which caused them to provide a comfortable place of amusement here."[46] At the end of 1912, Travelle installed an organ, which provided not only music but also sound effects to accompany the scenes on the screen. One local resident explained that with the new organ, "war pictures will be accompanied by band or martial music, the Indian scenes by tom-tom, kettle drums, etc., and the society plays by the latest orchestral effects."[47]

Travelle used many strategies to build the Elite as a community institution; most involved giving local residents a voice in shaping the theater's space. The

Elite, for example, offered its space for local charity fund-raising. In May 1913, the members of the local St. Agnes Guild negotiated with Travelle to show the four-reel drama *The Prisoner of Zenda* at the Elite. The local group organized the entire evening's entertainment and promised local live talent shows between each reel of the film, as well as a concert by the Placerville Band before the performance. Travelle donated the admission revenues to the St. Agnes Guild to continue with its community church work.[48] Later that year, the Native Sons and Daughters held a moving picture benefit at the Elite, the proceeds of which supported local homeless children.[49] In January 1915, the Elite put on an evening of "juvenile and educational pictures," followed by a performance of the high school glee club.[50] The entertainment was "packed to the doors," and the revenues were used to buy new equipment for the local playground.[51] In 1915, the Elite inaugurated a monthly "child welfare night," essentially a special show for children with films selected by the local PTA.[52]

The theater also provided an important public space for local youth. The Elite acted as an adjunct facility to the local high school. Because the school lacked an auditorium, commencement exercises were held at the Elite theater each year. Moreover, the student drama club used the Elite for all its performances.[53] In January 1911, the theater sponsored a weekly social dance every Saturday and waived the 25-cent admission for women.[54] Placerville youth appropriated the theater, a physical extension of the local school, as *their* space.

In September 1912, Travelle initiated an "amateur night" once each week, thirty minutes before the start of the second program, where local residents competed for prizes on the stage.[55] Two months later, the theater sponsored a drawing for prizes. One week in advance, at each performance, patrons received a coupon for a drawing attached to their tickets. In an effort to encourage and maintain family patronage, at each drawing, prizes were given to a man, a woman, a boy, and a girl.[56]

Travelle also exhibited movies of local events. In 1914, he purchased a moving picture camera and built a developing lab inside the Elite theater.[57] Travelle accumulated footage of the local Memorial Day parade and observances at the cemetery, the congregation leaving the Catholic church, cattle driven through Main Street, and the demolition of one of the oldest local boardinghouses.[58] One spectator of the local films commented, "The pictures are remarkably plain and one has no difficulty of [*sic*] recognizing familiar characters on the streets and at the cemetery."[59]

The case of feature-length films in Placerville best illustrates Travelle's willingness to give the local public a voice in mass entertainment. In 1912, Travelle began to book multireel feature films at the theater. This resulted in doubled ticket prices (which had been such a liability for live entertainments). In the local press, Travelle announced that he had to raise the admission prices for feature films to make up for the increased prices distributors charged for the longer films. Other theaters in the state were also facing problems with admission prices. In June 1912, Travelle attended the San Francisco meeting of the Moving Picture Exhibitors' Association of California, during which he and other exhibitors unanimously supported a resolution objecting to the extra prices charged for the lease of multireel feature films and urging a boycott of all films from distributors until they lowered the price.[60] Despite the protest, Travelle continued to raise his admission prices whenever he exhibited feature films.[61] Travelle, though, refused to raise prices without an appeal to the local public. In 1914, he asked patrons to vote at the theater on whether or not they objected to an increase in admission prices for the longer films. Overwhelmingly, theatergoers supported the admission fee increase.[62] Thus, Travelle's audience legitimized the higher fees.

For Travelle, serials became a primary way in which he ensured regular patronage. In 1914, he booked the serial *Perils of Pauline*. He ran the single-reel episodes one day each week and arranged with the local paper to print the plot of each episode for those who might have missed one. Travelle exhibited new serials after the previous one ran its course.[63] In 1915, he ran two serials during the week. *The Exploits of Elaine* played on Friday evening along with a one-reel comedy and a newsreel, and *The Master Key* played on Saturday with two one-reel dramas. During the week, the theater offered primarily multireel feature films.[64]

In Placerville, audience building was an arduous process. Travelle went to great lengths to present the theater not only as a place to see movies but as an integral part of the social and economic life of the community. The raffles, the giveaways, and the appeals to the public for its approval on raised admission prices were part of a larger strategy to create a business that would remain profitable over the long run in the small town. In the process, audiences in Placerville expected to participate in mass culture and not sit idly by as passive receptors.

This brief case study has demonstrated that examination of the development of film exhibition in one small locality opens to question the standard histories of early film entertainment's reception in large urban areas. Placervillians did not seem innately or automatically attracted to moving pictures when they debuted in the village, several years following their introduction in larger cities like New York. San Francisco, or Sacramento. Film exhibitors did not find easy or substantial profits from early Placerville shows, and they had to be mindful to space their shows out (by traveling a wide circuit of small towns in the itinerant era), by providing significant entertainment value for as low a price as they could bear. They also tried to offer a program that appealed to as broad an audience as possible, attempting to draw the village men, women, and children, farmers and their families, and churchgoers as well as saloon patrons. A local case study can show that even during the spectacular period of growth of nickelodeons, many early attempts at operating stationary opera house movie shows were not successful.

While increased film production by the Patents Company in 1908 enabled exhibitors to construct regular patronage for their theaters, such a process did not occur in small towns like Placerville without challenges, conflicts, and negotiations among producers, exhibitors, and audiences. Small-town film theater owners who were profitable over the long term, like Placerville's J.B. Travelle, endeavored to build a loyal audience base that would patronize his shows multiple times per week, and to create community business and cultural ties to assimilate his new entertainment form into traditional structures of village amusement. By practicing strategies to maintain his audiences once he had established his theater, Travelle, like many rural exhibitors, embellished his show house with amenities, involved local groups in benefit performances, shared his facilities for school functions, showed films of local citizens on his screen, and made patrons feel they had some voice in ticket pricing and film selection. He created not just a movie theater but a community institution, and his promotional tactics focused not on his films so much as on local audiences and village organizations. Examining how even seemingly isolated farming villages like Placerville became enmeshed in motion picture entertainment shows both important anomalies and continuities in the ways in which this process occurred in the nation's largest cities. Further study of the similarities and differences will help us flesh out a much more complete picture of how the movies became a significant part of modern life all across America.

Notes

1. Willis Frederick Dunbar has found this to be true in smaller towns in Michigan as well. "The buildings [opera houses] served a variety of purposes. Lectures, political rallies, high school graduation exercises, and musical concerts, as well as theatrical performances . . . home talent plays, [and] minstrel shows." Willis Frederick Dunbar, "The Opera House as a Social Institution in Michigan," *Michigan History* 27 (October/December 1943): 661–72. Dunbar then asserts that the coming of moving pictures killed the opera house as a social institution. The moving picture theater in Placerville, in fact, usurped the social functions of the opera house. The coming of sound moving pictures, however, does seem to have terminated the theater as a multifunction social site.

2. U.S. Bureau of the Census, "Population by Sex, General Nativity, and Color, by Groups of States and Territories: 1900," Census Bulletin No. 66 (Washington, D.C.: Government Printing Office, 24 June 1901), 5; U.S. Bureau of the Census, "California Manufactures," Census Bulletin No. 136 (Washington, D.C.: Government Printing Office, 11 February 1902), 9. Census takers found in the county 759 farms averaging 276 acres each. U.S. Bureau of the Census, "Agriculture. California," Census Bulletin No. 164 (Washington, D.C.: Government Printing Office, 29 April 1902), 4.

3. "A Memorable Celebration," *Mountain Democrat*, 17 September 1898, 5.

4. "No Saturday Night Dance," *Mountain Democrat*, 3 December 1898, 5.

5. "'Fanchon the Cricket' Played to the Life," *Mountain Democrat,* 21 October 1899, 4. Despite pathetic attendance, the Dailey Company returned in April 1899 and played to "fair houses, although the attendance has not been what the merit of the Company deserve [*sic*]." "Return of the Favorites," *Mountain Democrat,* 15 April 1899, 1.

6. It is impossible to gauge the word-of-mouth publicity moving pictures received in the small community.

7. Advertisement, *Mountain Democrat,* 29 January 1898, 8.

8. Advertisements for theaters in Sacramento did not appear in the Placerville press, though rail fare to the nearby city remained low throughout this period, so it is impossible to ascertain the number of Placerville residents who traveled to the city for amusement and leisure.

9. "Fight To-Night," *Mountain Democrat,* 25 February 1899, 1. I have been unable to find any information regarding the audience for this exhibition, though we can surmise that, at least, the opera house encouraged the attendance of children through reduced admission prices.

10. "The Chautauqua Assembly," *El Dorado Republican,* 18 July 1901, 4.

11. "Church Services: Methodist Church," *Placerville Nugget,* 5 January 1901, 4.

12. "Entertainment Friday Night," *Placerville Nugget,* 1 March 1904, 1; "Stereopticon Lecture," *Placerville Nugget,* 12 March 1904, 1.

13. I was unable to discover exactly what Reverend King charged local businesses for advertising. *Placerville Nugget,* 28 June 1905, 1.

14. *El Dorado Republican,* 7 November 1901, 5; *Placerville Nugget,* 29 October 1901, 1.

15. *El Dorado Republican,* 13 November 1902, 5; "Lecture at the Opera House," *El Dorado Republican,* 20 November 1902, 4.

16. Charles Musser calls these early narratives "story films" and traces the beginnings of their production to about 1899–1900, though they did not become a dominant filmmaking practice until 1903–4. Musser, *The Emergence of Cinema: The American Screen to 1907* (New York: Scribner's, 1990), 267–71, 297, 325–29, 375.

17. "Big Attraction Coming," *Placerville Nugget,* 12 June 1903, 4.

18. "Life Motion Picture Exhibition," *Placerville Nugget,* 12 August 1903, 1; *El Dorado Republican,* 15 August 1903, 4.

19. "Schuman's Pictures Make a Hit," *Placerville Nugget,* 17 August 1903, 1.

20. "Tuesday Night Shows," *Placerville Nugget,* 30 November 1907, 1.

21. *Placerville Nugget,* 11 December 1907, 1.

22. *Historical Souvenir of El Dorado County, California with Illustrations and Biographical Sketches of Its Prominent Men & Pioneers* (Oakland, Calif.: Paolo Sioli, 1883), 215.

23. Eileen Bowser, *The Transformation of Cinema, 1907–1915* (New York: Scribner's, 1990), 36.

24. George Kleine also commented in the same interview that the supply of films between November 1906 and September 1907 increased by 300 percent. "Moving Picture Business Enjoys a Frenzied Boom," *Moving Picture World,* 14 September 1907, 438.

25. A detailed exploration of the changes the Patents Company brought to the film industry is beyond the scope of this chapter. Many excellent secondary sources have traced the history of the MPPC. Among the more comprehensive works are Robert Jack Anderson, "The Motion Picture Patents Company" (Ph.D. diss., Univer-

sity of Wisconsin, 1983); Ralph Cassady Jr., "Monopoly in Motion Picture Production and Distribution: 1908–1915," *Southern California Law Review* 32 (1959): 325–90; David Bordwell, Janet Staiger, and Kristin Thompson, *The Classical Hollywood Cinema: Film Style and Mode of Production to 1960* (New York: Columbia University Press, 1985); Bowser, *Transformation of Cinema;* John Izod, *Hollywood and the Box Office, 1895–1986* (New York: Columbia University Press, 1988); and Robert Anderson, "The Motion Picture Patents Company: A Reevaluation," in *The American Film Industry,* ed. Tino Balio (Madison: University of Wisconsin Press, 1985), 133–52. I have explored the impact of the MPPC's reorganization of the film industry on exhibition in both Placerville and Sacramento in the second chapter of "Hollywood and the Hinterlands: Mass Culture in Two California Communities, 1896–1938" (Ph.D. diss., University of Southern California, 1998).

26. The sources indicate that Travelle had a partner in his theatrical venture, L. J. Werheimer. In all the local advertisements for the theater in the press, however, only Travelle's name is connected with the storefront operation. It is likely that Wertheimer provided most of the capital to start the business, but Travelle, who had experience in the entertainment industry, managed the daily operation of the theater.

27. "Amusement Season," *Placerville Nugget,* 5 September 1908, 3; "Modern Pleasure Resort. Placerville Is Going to Have an Up-to-Date Amusement House," *Placerville Nugget,* 21 September 1908, 1.

28. For details on Sacramento theater advertisements, see my "Hollywood in the Hinterlands."

29. "The New Theater: Opening Night Proved a Gratifying and Unqualified Success," *Placerville Nugget,* 5 October 1908, 1. Using the term *resort* to describe what was, essentially, a storefront nickelodeon indicates an appreciation of the theater as more than simply an outlet for moving pictures.

30. *Placerville Nugget,* 21 October 1908, 4; *Placerville Nugget,* 26 October 1908, 4.

31. "Free Matinee for Children," *Placerville Nugget,* 27 October 1908, 4.

32. The ads appeared weekly in the local press. For one example, see *Placerville Nugget,* 10 October 1908, 4.

33. *El Dorado Republican,* 4 June 1915, 1.

34. " 'On Gay Broadway': A Good Company Received by a Small Audience," *Placerville Nugget,* 19 November 1908, 1, 4.

35. *Placerville Nugget,* 21 November 1908, 4.

36. "Special Notice," *Placerville Nugget,* 30 November 1908, 4.

37. The use of giveaways is important in this instance, because these gimmicks are associated mostly with theaters facing severe financial pressures, as during the Great Depression. The story of the Elite suggests that theaters used giveaways to build an audience and not necessarily to overcome economic downturns.

38. "At the Elite," *Placerville Nugget,* 7 December 1908, 1, 4; "At the Elite," *Placerville Nugget,* 12 December 1908, 1.

39. "Correspondence," *Moving Picture World,* 11 June 1910, 999–1000.

40. "Board of Trustees," *Placerville Nugget,* 5 March 1909, 7. That the town government took responsibility for the financial welfare of the opera house is also indicative of the degree to which places of amusement in smaller towns possessed a civic importance in their communities.

41. "New Theater for Placerville," *Placerville Nugget,* 19 March 1909, 3.

42. *El Dorado Republican,* 25 March 1909, 1, 4; *El Dorado Republican,* 8 April 1909, 1.

43. *El Dorado Republican,* 7 May 1909, 8; *Placerville Nugget,* 21 May 1909, 8; *Mountain Democrat,* 25 December 1909, 1.

44. "Fred O'Neil Sells Out," *Mountain Democrat,* 11 June 1910, 1; *Placerville Nugget,* 17 June 1910, 1; *Placerville Nugget,* 24 June 1910, 6.

45. "The New Elite Theater," *Mountain Democrat,* 17 February 1912, 1.

46. The prominent businesspeople of Placerville called a meeting at the local city hall to organize the benefit. "A Grand Opening Vaudeville," *Mountain Democrat,* 17 February 1912, 1.

47. "More Attractions at the Elite," *Mountain Democrat,* 21 December 1912, 8.

48. "Unusual Attraction Promised," *Mountain Democrat,* 10 May 1913, 1; "Church Benefit a Success," *Mountain Democrat,* 24 May 1913, 4.

49. "Benefit for Homeless Children," *Mountain Democrat,* 15 November 1913, 1; "A Success in a Good Cause," *Mountain Democrat,* 22 November 1913, 8. Every two or three months, the Elite sponsored a charity benefit for some local cause.

50. "Child Welfare Entertainment," *Mountain Democrat,* 23 January 1915, 1.

51. "A Pleasing Entertainment," *Mountain Democrat,* 6 February 1915, 1; "Child Welfare Night at Elite a Pleasing Success," *El Dorado Republican,* 5 February 1915, 2. In May, the theater held another benefit to raise funds to remodel playgrounds and classroom decorations at the local grammar school. *El Dorado Republican,* 7 May 1915, 1.

52. "Child Welfare Night at the Elite," *Mountain Democrat,* 31 July 1915, 8.

53. See, for example, *Mountain Democrat,* 1 June 1912, 8, for an account of the commencement exercises at the Elite.

54. On the origins of the town dance, see *Mountain Democrat,* 18 January 1911, 1.

55. *Mountain Democrat,* 17 September 1910, 1, 8.

56. *Mountain Democrat,* 12 November 1910, 1; "Valuable Presents Given Away," *Mountain Democrat,* 19 November 1910, 3.

57. *El Dorado Republican,* 4 December 1914, 4.

58. *Mountain Democrat,* 26 June 1915, 5; "Movies of Local Scenes to Be Shown Here," *El Dorado Republican,* 2 July 1915, 1.

59. "Movies of Local Scenes to Be Shown Here," 1.

60. "Trying to Head Off a Trust," *Mountain Democrat,* 13 July 1912, 8.

61. On 19 October, for example, the Elite Theater featured both reels of *Ramses, King of Egypt* and a one-reel comedy at a price of 15 cents for adults and 5 cents for children. The following day, for 10 and 5 cents, audiences could see four one-reel films. *Mountain Democrat,* 19 October 1912, 1.

62. *Placerville Nugget,* 8 May 1914, 6.

63. Regarding serials, one newspaper commented, "Travelle knows from the success which has attended the episodes of 'Perils of Pauline,' that the local public is appreciative of a serial service." " 'Zudora,' A New Serial at the Elite Theater," *El Dorado Republican,* 25 December 1914, 1.

64. *Mountain Democrat,* 27 February 1915, 1.

6

CINEMA VIRTUE, CINEMA VICE

Race, Religion, and Film Exhibition
in Norfolk, Virginia, 1908–1922

TERRY LINDVALL

*They will discover that the big cities are not the test of American
opinion. The real acid test of what America thinks—the real gauge
of our prejudice—is in the small towns.*
MACK SENNETT[1]

At the turn of the twentieth century, Norfolk, Virginia, a small but rapidly developing city, received and appropriated the moving picture craze for its own civic purposes. Film exhibition addressed issues of religion and race as relevant constructs in the emergence of alternative community centers. In Norfolk, the realms of race, Protestant religion, and popular culture were continually renegotiating the parameters of film exhibition. In 1900, Norfolk was a growing city of the "New South," busy with its oyster trade, cotton commerce, and railway expansion, erasing its reputation as "that decrepit victim of the slave power, poor old imbecile granny."[2] Norfolk was a small city with urban aspirations. In 1900, it boasted 46,624 citizens.[3] By 1910, the population had grown to 67,400, and by 1920, it was 115,800.[4] This population was diverse, with black constituents making up a significant 38 percent of the census, who lived in segregated wards like Titustown. In 1909, Norfolk still viewed itself as suspended between being a village and a metropolitan center. In 1906, Mayor James G. Riddick was a civic booster who saw the great potential of his city. Although Norfolk boasted a "great white way" and a few taxicabs, its self-conscious manners and cultural style were viewed as comically rustic, with unpaved sidewalks even on the electric-lit Granby Street.

Yet Norfolk in 1900 was also a city of vice, like the much larger metropolises of the North. Surprisingly, however, the emergence of silent moving pictures was counted among the more respectable influences, with its expanding exhibition practices paralleling the growth and reform of the city. In this community, movies arrived with reform movements, often in conjunction with upstanding citizens or as an acceptable alternative to the pervading evils of the saloon or places of prostitution. Known as "the wickedest city in the U.S.," Norfolk had restricted saloons, subsequently spawning more than a hundred "social clubs."[5] Both black and white groups of the Women's Christian Temperance Union castigated a city council that had allowed eighty-one brothels within "the circle of the shadow of one church spire."[6] In this community, movies arrived with reform movements as an acceptable alternative to the prevailing evils of the saloon or places of prostitution.

Motion picture trade journalist Terry Ramsaye identified Norfolk, Virginia, as one of the first localities to experience an exhibition of projected motion pictures, along with Boston and Chicago, in August 1895. LeRoy Latham and his black handyman, Henry Southall, put on a very successful and prosperous show.[7] However propitious its introduction into the Tidewater area, film then slipped quietly into the vaudeville circuit, remaining uncontaminated by association with more visible and notorious amusements.

The arrival of moving pictures may have introduced more respectable amusements for the navy city than many existing illicit entertainments. To view movies as "higher culture" was not a stretch for a city struggling against saloons, taverns, and political corruption and seeking its own reputation as a decent place to live. Whether intentional or not, the local papers connected the burgeoning business of the moving picture houses with community concerns in general and with religion in particular. For two decades, one could not glance at advertisements about local amusements and theater reviews without reading about church activities and specific sermons on the same page. The two were tied together as vital socioreligious elements of both the black and white communities. For a time, the movies functioned as a new mode of representation that altered and destabilized existing cultural forms but was also itself assimilated into the broader cultural landscape of a conservative, southern city.[8]

In an age immersed in an antebellum, Protestant culture, issues regarding religion were paramount. One cannot separate the emergence of film exhibition from the dominant religious culture or the construct of race; they were inextricably intertwined. While various movements around the country aimed at controlling "immoral plays," Norfolk found the high-class vaudeville and moving picture houses as more of an ally than an adversary in the development of a wholesome civic community. As Charles Musser writes, in the 1890s, one "could be a religious person and not only go to a vaudeville house, but one could even find religious inspiration there."[9]

The Wells Brothers

Alongside the economic boom brought by pictures, the primary variable that drew middle- to upper-class audiences into the moving pictures was the sponsorship of respectable Virginia businessmen, such as the Wells brothers. Through a concerted public relations campaign and adept programming, the Wells brothers sold their enterprises as good, clean, wholesome amusement for the city. They were exhibitors, developers, and active community leaders. Otto Wells designed his Chesapeake seaside attraction as the most elegant and best "recognized resort for all Sunday school excursions. . . . a large number of Sunday schools from various points throughout the State are making their annual pilgrimages to this delightful resort where they find every accommodation and amusement clean, refined and dignified."[10]

These two brothers from Memphis cornered the theatrical market of the South, reigning over forty houses from their nexus in Norfolk and becoming "the largest single theatrical business, outside of New York."[11] The run of high-class vaudeville acts, illustrated songs, and motion pictures met with instantaneous success and record business. The Wellses bought both old and new amusement houses for a chain of theaters, including the Colonial, the Strand, the Academy of Music, the Majestic, the Granby, and the Ocean View Resort, the latter of which provided a penny arcade and also exhibited films. On August 26, 1913, they added to their own glory and fame by opening the Wells theater. Local papers punctuated the brothers' prophetic feat: "When President Jake Wells of the Wells Amusement enterprises opened the Wells theatre as a moving picture theatre he did so with the conviction that the screen drama is going to be the foremost entertainment of the future." [12]

The Wells brothers also appealed to the southern prejudice of the community by contracting motion picture views of a large gathering of Confederate veterans for Norfolk.[13] For a patriotic Fourth of July weekend, Otto secured Annette Kellerman's *Neptune's Daughter* for his Ocean View celebrations. Because Kellerman had cured herself of crippling disease through swimming, "the Colonial management issued an invitation to all crippled children in Norfolk to be the guests of the management."[14] The Wells brothers practiced "open doors" for all manner of community activity in their theaters, seemingly recognizing that by inviting church and civic leaders into their houses for various educational, religious, and community events, they would be winning people's hearts and trust.[15]

When controversies regarding theaters did arise, the Wells brothers were astutely aware of where their loyalties lay. They adroitly guided the discussion so that they appeared to be on the side of civic concern and uplift. They were able to divert local censorship by recommending self-regulation.[16] The common knowledge was that "clean, wholesome entertainment has been the watchword of the business. Its success has been founded on that principle."[17]

By March 1912, Otto Wells was able to boast about the "Amusement Enterprises of the Wells' Interests" that "Norfolk leads the South Atlantic seaboard in theatres and its seaside resort."[18] He noted, "From the viewpoint of the theatrical manager, Norfolk is practically ideal. The people are alike liberal and discriminating. They patronize freely the productions which are meritorious; they coldly ignore offerings below their standard of excellence."

No southern cities except New Orleans and Atlanta (with populations of 360,000 and 200,000, respectively) "outrank Norfolk in the novelty of its shows nor in the number or character of its places of amusement." Under the auspices of the Wells brothers, Norfolk had become a hub, regarded by the larger theatrical syndicates as a plum, with their tremendous theatrical organization booking more shows in Norfolk than from "any other spot in the world except the theatrical district of New York."[19]

The Theaters

The *Norfolk and Portsmouth Virginia Directory* of 1909 listed eighteen theaters and places of amusement and seven moving picture supply companies. The Granby and the Majestic held the distinction of being the most popular moving picture theaters. The other high-class vaudeville theaters on Granby Street (the Academy and the Colonial) included motion pictures on their bills equally with stage acts by 1910, while the Majestic and Ocean View used moving pictures more prominently as key attractions. The Star theater, a nickelodeon on the boardwalk of the popular resort, brought the best and latest animated pictures during summer months.[20] The Floating Palace Theatre, anchored at the Ice Pier, offered "Goldie's moving pictures" on the "roof garden" second or theater deck, along with its vaudeville performances. A lower auditorium with private boxes sat 600 people downstairs, and a gallery for colored people accommodated 250.[21]

By this time, theaters in Norfolk were established as significant economic institutions of the city and as centers of community activity. Along with automobiles, appliances, concrete construction, and aerial navigation, moving picture outfits were seen as one of the most promising infant industries in the country's economic growth. A *Virginian-Pilot* article explained that next to the automobile industry, "gauged by the expenditure which it draws from the great American pocket, must be ranged, curiously enough, the moving picture industry. The making and exhibiting of moving pictures is primarily an amusement enterprise, although these views are utilized in industrial lines, in educational work and in a thousand ways that the inventors of the various systems never dreamed of."[22] Individual theaters came and went over the years, but the popularity of movies remained steady. By 1916 the *Tidewater Directory* separately listed fifteen movie theaters for whites and three for colored patrons.[23]

Norfolk's theaters not only adapted to community needs but also ingratiated themselves into the social, educational, and religious functions of the city. Film theaters in Norfolk found themselves being requisitioned for a diverse set of audiences as they reached out to become an integral part of a growing community. As theaters were rented out or donated to various groups, they also won early battles as a site for virtue as opposed to a haunt of vice. For example, the official civic fight against saloons was initiated in the Academy Theatre.[24]

White and black theaters offered their premises for civic events, particularly when connected to public religious ceremonies. More than 1,000 whites and 500 blacks gathered in the Granby to hear Booker T. Washington. While the "galleries were given over to the negroes," the main auditorium was jammed with a standing-room-only audience of progressives who applauded his impressive "preaching."[25] Certain "race events," as they were then known, were even included in the major white theaters after they had "conquered New York City." For example, the Colonial Theatre invited a Negro quartette from Hampton Institute to appear, as their debut in New York City had turned away more than 5,000 people.[26]

As the largest auditoriums in the city, the theaters were generally made available for commencement exercises for the Norfolk High School and for other special assemblies.[27] Films were viewed as proper for all kinds of educational instruction, for social reform, medical and surgical instruction, teaching geography, and in the religious field.[28] Local educators saw tremendous value in this innovation, particularly in the realm of classroom teaching, such as in solving problems of agriculture and public health or in showing geography. They noted wryly that one very peculiar use was the picture of operations intended for display in hospitals and medical colleges.[29]

The *Virginian-Pilot*'s general acknowledgment of positive uses regarding children was a tribute to the moving picture's virtues. Educational films promoted health for local Norfolk physicians[30] warned against rats, hookworms, and mosquitoes;[31] denounced liquor at the Academy'[32] and highlighted a law enforcement address at the Colonial Theater delivered by William Jennings Bryan, under the auspices of the Anti-saloon League.[33] The legal and medical professions both endorsed moving pictures.

Secular theater sites were sanctified by the regular presence of clergy. Annual Lenten noonday services were held by the local Episcopalian churches at the Granby and American theaters.[34] C.E. Heard of New York City intrigued his audience with his timely lecture at the American Theatre on a biblical exposition on "The Fall of Babylon" soon after Griffith's *Intolerance* had played. Seats were free, and he promised to take no collections. Judge Rutherford even took out large ads inviting people to the Colonial Theatre to hear his message: "Millions Now Living Will Never Die." Evangelist Irwin D. Richardson secured the Colonial "because of its large seating capacity" to lecture on the fulfillment of Bible prophecy.[35]

Pastor William Burleigh of the Park View Christ Church gave his sermon "The Sins of Portsmouth, and How to Cure Them" at the Orpheum Theatre, which seemed to suggest that the moving picture theater site was not one of the more nefarious sins.[36] This discourse was a sequel to a sermon delivered by Mr. Burleigh, who allegedly "handled the city's sins, and the sins of many churchmen, with ungloved hands."[37] The Crosman Theatre announced that the Reverend Frank Pratt would speak Sunday nights on such themes as "The Way Our Bible Came to Us." He welcomed strangers to his entertaining Sunday school class, "a school in harmony with the modern spirit."[38] The Arcade promoted Salvation Army evangelists such as Colonel John Dean, who traveled to Norfolk to lecture on crooked women and purity of living.[39] A citywide Baptist revival occurred in the "sacred" halls of the Majestic theater, where the union services "were marked by intense feeling and deep spiritual power."[40]

What is significant about the variety of lectures and sacred concerts at the various theaters was a pervasive sense that theaters enhanced the quality of life and virtue in the community. If one could sing the *Messiah,* hear an evangelistic sermon, or attend charity benefits in a theater, then perhaps other activities in the same place were not too profane.

The Sunday Show Controversy

Norfolk's religious community rarely protested the apparatus or content of moving pictures. What did stir the ire of the faithful, however, was the issue of Sunday moving pictures, a controversy rooted in an objection to Sunday being exploited as anything other than a sacred day of rest. The issue of sabbatical observance would underlie almost all religious objections to the cinema, particularly in Norfolk.

In the year of cinema's invention as a public amusement, the bishops of the Episcopal Church felt compelled to publish a statement declaring that Sunday Sabbath observance "cannot be disturbed without grave evils to the individual and the family, to society and the State."[41] Such sentiments were expressed by Methodist minister John Wesley Hill, who complained that "the red laws of riot, carnival and immorality" had supplanted "the blue laws of Puritanism."[42] Thus, the call, often strident but consistently unyielding, was for a "Blue Sunday."

The prime object of promoting the Christian Sabbath in Norfolk by Methodists was to educate public sentiment in "bringing Sunday work down to the minimum of mercy and necessity, checking the Sunday amusements and securing as great and thoughtful a day as possible."[43] Even as nickelodeons were proliferating in the Norfolk area, judges and politicians were joining clergy in warning against all kinds of Sabbath breaking. Judge Capton minced no words in calling it a crime against God and men. Senator Penrose was joined by Norfolk clergymen to introduce a bill to close down the Jamestown exposition on Sundays but was laughed off the floor of the Senate because his own practice was anything but exemplary.[44] Again at the end of the second decade, Presbyterians and Baptists joined with Methodists to affirm their stance against Sunday film showings. Appropriately, a Presbyterian pastor spoke at the Colonial Theatre, referring to "the movement under way to have the moving picture shows remain open on Sunday" as a digression from his announced topic: "The law of the Sabbath was written in the statute book of Almighty God, Himself, and who shall dare to abrogate it."[45] The same day, Rev. Sparks W. Melton, pastor of the Freemason Street Baptist Church, spoke resolutely against opening picture shows in Norfolk on Sundays, condemning the movement in "most uncompromising" terms. What the newspaper found remarkable was that the "usually liberal" Dr. Melton had established a reputation in Norfolk for never indulging in political controversies or discussion of political questions. His lack of opposition to a prohibition campaign elicited a double surprise for his protest against this movement.[46]

Sunday movie showings were consistently opposed throughout the second decade of the twentieth century in Norfolk, with police willing to arrest any violators. The problem came to the fore with the opening of the Red Circle Theatre on the local military base for the benefit of the servicemen. The naval base theater doubled as a chapel on Sundays. The *Virginia-Pilot* reported, "Twice a week there will be movies and twice a week vaudeville. On Sundays, the theatre will be used both for the Catholic and the Protestant religious services."[47] The Red Circle operated on Sunday with lecturers who gave illustrated talks without charge. Such an educational activity was acceptable, but not Sunday movies. A fierce debate erupted among city council members about whether Sunday amusements could be provided for the servicemen. The Reverend Frank Robertson warned, "The project to throw open the doors of the theatres may possibly conceal an ulterior design. If we let the bars down to provide entertainment for the service men, have we any assurance that things will not gradually widen until the first thing we know we shall have a continental Sunday." The primary fear was that moviegoing was becoming a commercial "wedge" for a variety of antibiblical activities. The real purpose of the movement was not "to provide the service men with entertainment, although that had something to do with it, as it was to provide commercialism with a chance to 'pillage' on the Sabbath. They have six days in which to make money, { . . . } and if they can't make enough on those days they ought to go out of business. Those behind the movement to open the theatres are using the service men as an entering wedge."[48] Charles Musser pointed out that some exhibitors viewed "religious subjects as a crafty device to evade Sunday blue laws," as a wedge to squeeze in all manner of Sunday showings.[49] Major Truxton reminded the council: "But Norfolk, it should be remembered, was a seaport town, and because of that fact was facing certain conditions that few other American cities had to contend with," namely, prostitution. In contrast, moving pictures looked downright pietistic.

Black clergy in Norfolk joined their white counterparts with enthusiasm on the protest and were aligned in common cause; both envisioned the danger of a secular wedge into the Christian community. African American D. F. White, president of the Interdenominational Minister's Meeting of the City of Norfolk, published his views alongside those of the other clergy. Voicing their opposition as a way to protect the colored youth of the city, the ministers gave their "support to those brave and wise white ministers who see an 'entertaining wedge' for the introduction of the 'Continental Sunday.'" They argued that this "wedge" would "curse the negro youth of Norfolk as well as our white youth," because the Sabbath is intended for worship, and if "the church, the Sabbath school, the young people's societies, the Y.M.C.A., the Knights of Columbus, the community Centre, reading rooms, and the Red Circle theatre can not save him from sin, bootleggers and the red light district, neither will the Sunday movie deliver him."[50]

The moral and religious forces of Norfolk supported any city council action "for the eradication of the evils complained of. The armory building must not be used on Sunday for any purpose other than the holding of illustrated talks on travel, health or 'such other educational' lectures as may be given from time to time. [But] Norfolk will not permit the opening of any other place of amusement on Sunday in violation of the laws of the state of Virginia."[51] The issue was well defined in an article that asked: "What is the moral difference between seeing a static or a moving picture?" The editorial suggested that Sunday pictures would not draw people from church. The newspaper writer found it "monstrous to suggest that the churches and the cinematograph are two rival organizations competing as attractions for the masses. Such a view is fundamentally irreligious. A man who wishes to go to church will go there, whatever other ways of spending his time may be open to him. A man who goes to church because he can go nowhere else is not likely to derive any edification from his religious exercises."[52]

Churches as Theaters, Movies as Sermons

By 1912, a survey of ministers of the Methodist Episcopal Church found that two-thirds went to the theaters without regarding it as being sinful. They felt that "John Wesley's injunction leaving the amusement question to the conscience of individuals was the wisest regulation for Americans of the twentieth century."[53] The Reverend H. R. L. Shephard envisioned that the "way in which the cinema might be used for benefiting the lost of the people is perfectly amazing to anyone who has thought at all."[54] Films like *The Wanderer* and George Loane Tucker's *The Miracle Man* took Norfolk by storm in 1919 by bringing "uplift."[55] Such sermonic photodramas were viewed as a way of drawing people to church. Lois Weber's film *The Blot,* which addressed the pitiful wages of teachers and preachers, received high praise when it was shown at the Granby. An invitation to a private showing was sent to all the lawyers, doctors, preachers, schoolteachers, and city officials as an act of community service: "Throughout the story moves the pity-impelling figure of a threadbare young minister of the gospel, hopelessly underpaid and hopelessly in love with America."[56] What poor professional would not find such films an ally?

Not only did Norfolk theaters invite the clergy into their secular space, but Norfolk churches sanctified and blessed the cinematic apparatus by incorporating it into their evangelism, instruction, and worship. An early report by the conservative South Street Baptist Church in February 1906 announced that it was exhibiting Edison Moving Pictures, charging adults 25 cents and children 15 cents.[57] Churches in the Norfolk area followed a tradition of using illustrated sermons with stereopticons usually accompanied by hymn singing. Dr. Adams at the Freemason Church of Christ showed moving pictures portraying in a "vivid manner the customs and habits of the inhabitants of the heathen world, showing how they had been brought under the saving and sanctifying influences of the Gospel of Christ, and the number of preachers, doctors and professors have been sent out by our missionary, who were converts to the Christian faith. Some of these have been converted from cannibalism."[58] Missionary pictures were especially appealing, combining the biblical injunction of the Great Commission with the novelty of the travelogue.[59] Memorial Methodist Church coordinated with social ministries to present films on preventing bubonic plague, fever, and other "dreaded maladies."[60] The Disciples of Christ Church supported the moving picture as a primary factor in enabling the church to understand the "heathen rites" of people it was evangelizing. Moving picture films secured by the Foreign Christian Missionary Society were shown in connection with the lecture "Strange People of Many Lands" at the church.[61]

Headlining the news throughout spring 1914 was an advertising campaign in which readers were admonished to "Go to Church Sunday," all of which culminated in a full-page ad with photos of films announcing: "Man since Creation Seen in Film Pictures." The campaign was designed not for church attendance but as a promotional campaign to prepare the religious community to discover a religious film series. The writers grounded moving picture church evangelism showing how the Sunday school's former use of "many colored lithographs from the Good Book to illustrate a text" led to movies, where "the day of the modern has arrived."[62]

Praised as one of the "most remarkable presentations of the teachings of the Scriptures ever seen in Norfolk," the Wells theater presented an eight-hour spectacle that avoided denominational sectarianism and sought to "harmonize science, history and the Scriptures [in] a very plausible manner."[63] Such optimism was actually grounded more in scientific modernism than in biblical texts, with its sponsors claiming that within a few years high school educators would be using film to bring general knowledge of religious truth to all people with the "greatest efficiency." In fact, they asserted that moving picture exhibitions in the Orient were "the only places where the rich and the poor people of all castes gather at the same time to witness the same performance." However, the organizers saw these pictures as the universal language that would help usher in the millennial era of understanding and peace.

The success of the Creation series at the Wells, as well as the growing interest in the use of films for church purposes, brought opportunities for churches to get into film work itself. The announcement "City Churches to Use Movies" (1914) was a precursor of what churches in Norfolk were to put into practice.[64] While some of the congregation was skeptical, they permitted the pastor of the Calvary Baptist Church to show films in its new $37,000 church edifice. This innovative move to exhibit "Sacred films on Sunday nights" (such as *Queen Esther* or *Joseph of Egypt*) was viewed as a first in the South, "or at least entirely new for church work in the Norfolk area." The church fully approved the film program's use "for evangelism, outreach, and community service."[65]

Rev. Dr. Thompson, pastor of Cumberland Street Methodist Church, called "the mother of Norfolk Methodism," introduced a convenient printed program of Sunday services being adopted by many progressive congregations and announced, "At the Wednesday evening services, which will be held in the auditorium, moving pictures will be used to illustrate religious subjects for some time to come."[66] The pastor then provided brief lectures in connection with the pictures. The same week, the Church of Christ, South Norfolk, announced that on Sunday night, "in connection with the services, feature films will be shown depicting the *Life of Our Savior*."[67]

One of the oldest parishes in the state, established in 1637, built Norfolk's Gothic Christ and St. Luke's Episcopal Church. Designed by the Philadelphia firm of Watson and Huckle, it was erected in 1909–10.[68] Its richly ornamental tower and stained glass windows harkening back to the Middle Ages were inspired by the theme of "How Stones and Glass Speak." Yet, this most traditional of churches also purchased and installed a Moviegraph stand and projector, along with a screening auditorium on its upper floors, to explore how moving pictures might preach messages.

The formal opening of the "handsome" new $80,000 parish house of Christ Episcopal Church in December 1919 was greeted with holiday pomp and ceremony, with an "enjoyable evening" reception and an inspection of the annex. The building of the modern structure of rough granite, supervised by Rev. Francis C. Steinmetz, was celebrated for its innovations: "A large auditorium with a seating capacity of about 500 is on the top floor. A moving picture booth is also equipped, so connected as to be of use in the auditorium."[69] Under the auspices of the Church Federation of Norfolk and Roman Catholic Organizations, churches in Norfolk had undertaken an active moving picture program by 1920.[70]

Conclusion

Norfolk, a naval city of land and sea, saw itself as the gate to the South, yet it aspired to keep the arteries to the big cities vibrantly alive and dynamic. It positioned itself between competing tensions of the autonomous sensibilities and prejudices of a rural community and the tempting glamour and sophisticated images of an urban center. It was a city that, for a season, engaged mass amusements on its own terms: as a conservative religious community, as a stubbornly segregated city, and as a bustling business enterprise.[71] Thus Norfolk found its southern and religious traditions a buttress against too much external propaganda. For a time, Norfolk managed to incorporate the movie culture into the "high-minded" aims of its civic and religious leaders. Thus movies, which in so many other places, urban and rural, were seen as corrupting influences, in Norfolk were used as an acceptable alternative to the usual sin market of a port city.

Notes

1. "Small Town Movie Fan Is Called Real Censor," *Virginian-Pilot* (hereafter *VP*) (December 14, 1924), 14. A large number of articles from Norfolk newspapers were used in this chapter; complete citations will gladly be provided by contacting the author at lindvall4@cox.net.

2. Thomas J. Wertenbaker, *Norfolk: Historic Southern Port* (Durham, N.C.: Duke University Press, 1962), 286–87.

3. Campbell Gibson, "Population of the 100 Largest Cities and Other Urban Places in the United States: 1790–1990," Population Division Working Paper No. 27 (Washington, D.C.: U.S. Bureau of the Census, June 1998), table 13, http://www.census.gov/population/www/documentation/twps0027html (accessed May 17, 2007).

4. "Population of Norfolk Grows 71.6 Per Cent: All Business Has Had Share in Increase," *VP* (May 25, 1920), 1.

5. Thomas C. Parramore, *Norfolk: The First Four Centuries* (Charlottesville: University Press of Virginia, 1999), 256; Carroll Walker, *Norfolk: A Pictorial History* (Virginia Beach: Donning, 1975), 268.

6. Parramore, *Norfolk,* 258.

7. Terry Ramsaye, *A Million and One Nights* (New York: Simon and Schuster, 1926), 185–91.

8. See Charles Musser, "Passions and the Passion Play: Theatre, Film, and Religion in America, 1880–1900," *Film History* 5 (December 1993): 448.

9. Ibid., 447.

10. "Ocean View, Facing Chesapeake Bay, Second to None," *VP* (May 28, 1909), 11. See also Eric J. Dewberry, "Jake Wells, Commercial Entertainment Entrepreneur of the South: A Study of His Career in Richmond, Virginia, 1894–1927" (master's thesis, Virginia Commonwealth University, 2003).

11. "Norfolk: The South's Great Theatrical Center," *VP* (December 24, 1911), 13.

12. "Handsome New Wells Will Open Tonight," *Ledger-Dispatch* (August 26, 1913), 6.

13. "Confederate Reunion Pictures at Wells," *VP* (June 24, 1917), 4.

14. "'Neptune's Daughter Set Town Talking," *VP* (July 2, 1914), 4.

15. "Children at the Colonial Today," *VP* (October 10, 1908), 12; "Salvation Army to Give Annual Outings," *VP* (July 2, 1916), 2; "Kiddies Given Great Outing: For White and Colored Children," *VP* (August 21, 1920), 3; "Ministers Invited to 'After Six Days,'" *VP* (April 11, 1924), 10.

16. "Provides Moving Picture Censors," *VP* (July 12, 1916), 3; "Movie Men Object to Local Censorship," *VP* (July 13, 1916), 5; "Conference on Picture Censorship Ordinance," *VP* (July 29, 1916), 3; "Picture Censorship Meeting on Thursday," *VP* (August 6, 1916), 3.

17. "Otto," *VP* (January 21, 1926), 5; "Movies for Little Folks Saturday, at Wells Theater," *VP* (May 24, 1923), 6.

18. "Norfolk Leads South Atlantic Seaboard in Theatres and Its Seaside Resort," *VP* (March 21, 1912), 12.

19. "First Unit of Chain of Amusement Houses Started 25 Years Ago: Enterprises in Norfolk Now Include Six Theaters and Ocean View Resort; Observe Birthday Week with Special Programs," *VP* (January 24, 1926), 1.

20. "Ocean View to Open Saturday," *VP* (May 19, 1909), 2.

21. "Floating Theatres," *VP* (June 21, 1907), 11; "Floating Theatre Is Vessel, His Opinion," *VP* (March 10, 1908), 3; "Floating Amusement Palace," *VP* (July 19, 1908), 21.

22. "Astounding Growth of Five New Industries," *VP* (June 20, 1909), 13.

23. "Theatres and Places of Amusement," *Norfolk and Portsmouth Directory* (Norfolk, Va.: Hill Directory, 1916), 150: *American, *Arcade, *Bonita, *Columbia, *Crosman, Dixie, Ghent, @Manhattan, *@Palace, Rex, Strand, @Star, Wonderland, Colonial, Granby, Strand, Wells, and Academy hosting both live theater and moving pictures (* denotes moving pictures; @ denotes colored theaters).

24. "To Fire First Gun against Saloons Sunday," *VP* (November 28, 1908), 3; "Temperance Rally at Academy Today," *VP* (November 29, 1908), 9.

25. "Large Crowd Hears Negro Educator at the Granby," *VP* (June 22, 1909), 3.

26. "Negro Quartette Coming Here," *VP* (February 20, 1916), 7.

27. "1908 Senior Class Exercises Held at Granby," *VP* (June 12, 1908), 7.

28. "Uses of Moving Pictures: Films of All Kinds Intended for Class Instruction," *VP* (September 19, 1908), 12.

29. Ibid.

30. "'Boil Your Water' Film at the Bonita Theatre," *VP* (May 15, 1911), 3.

31. "Rat Menace in Movies Will Be Shown in City," *VP* (August 20, 1920), 2.

32. "Liquor Habit Is Worst in World," *VP* (May 25, 1914), 3.

33. "Bryan to Speak Here Tomorrow," *VP* (January 20, 1920), 2.

34. "Holy Week at the American Theatre," *VP* (April 16, 1919), 10.

35. "The Fall of Babylon: How? When? Why?" *VP* (January 12, 1918), 2; "To Lecture on World, War, and Bible," *VP* (January 20, 1918), 4.

36. "Theatre Service Tomorrow Night," *VP* (October 28, 1911), 8.

37. "Curing the City's Sins," *VP* (September 22, 1911), 8.

38. "The Way Our Bible Came to Us," *VP* (October 31, 1915), 2.

39. "Col. Dean to Speak at Arcade Today," *VP* (September 19, 1915), 7; "Baptist Dr. Swope Will Speak at the Majestic Theatre on 'The Way of Transgression Is Hard,'" *VP* (Oct. 9, 1915), 4.

40. "Rain Interferes with Revivals," *VP* (October 8, 1915), 4.

41. "Praise God Every Day: Sunday Protected by Divine Command," *Norfolk Virginian* (October 24, 1895), 1.

42. "Pastors Open War on Sunday Shows," *New York Times* (January 19, 1909), 8; "The Sabbath Was Made for Man," *VP* (May 10, 1903), 4.

43. "Better Observance of Sabbath," *VP* (March 28, 1911), 4.

44. "Sabbath Breaking Crime against God and Men," *VP* (October 31, 1906), 9.

45. "A Man's Sins Will Find Him Out, Says Rev. Dr. Shelton," *VP* (March 24, 1919), 2

46. "Church Opposes Sunday Movies in Resolutions," *VP* (March 24, 1919), 5.

47. "Sailors to Have Own Theatre," *VP* (January 13, 1918), 20.

48. "Nobody Agreed at Meeting on Sunday Movies," *VP* (March 25, 1919), 2

49. Musser, "Passions and the Passion Play," 447.

50. "Nobody Agreed at Meeting on Sunday Movies," *VP* (March 25, 1919), 2; "Colored Ministers Protest," *VP* (March 27, 1919), 6.

51. "No Movies for Enlisted Men on Sundays, Citizens Committee Decides Illustrated Lectures and Travel Talks Sufficient," *VP* (March 28, 1919), 4.

52. Lord Beaverbrook, "Movie Is Poor Man's Book of Travel and Sunday Fun," *VP* (April 17, 1921), 2.

53. "Removal of Ban on Amusements Recommended: Bishops Declare Church Law Prohibiting Dancing, Card Playing Gambling, and Theatre Going Is Obsolete," *VP* (May 4, 1912), 1.

54. "Want Movies Used to Benefit Public," *VP* (December 1, 1918), 8.

55. "'The Miracle Man' Is Unusual Photodrama," *VP* (October 15, 1919), 9.

56. "Lois Weber's Latest, 'The Blot,' Appears at Granby," *VP* (September 11, 1921), 3.

57. "Edison Moving Pictures," *VP* (January 31, 1906), 8.

58. "First Congregational Church," *VP* (January 5, 1908), 21.

59. "China in Moving Pictures," *VP* (May 2, 1908), 8.

60. "Illustrated Lecture on Great White Plague," *VP* (May 15, 1908), 9.

61. "Moving Pictures Show Heathen Religious Rites," *VP* (January 11, 1910), 5.

62. "Go to Church Sunday," *VP* (March 7, 1914), 8.

63. "'Movie' Films to Save Souls," VP (May 15, 1914), 8.

64. "City Churches to Use Movies: Educators and Religious Workers Complete Plans for an Extended Service," *VP* (June 21, 1914), 16.

65. "Moving Pictures to Be Used in Church," *VP* (December 31, 1915), 8.

66. "New Plans of a Venerable Church," *VP* (February 13, 1916), 7.

67. "Feature Films of Life of Christ," *VP* (February 13, 1916), 18.

68. "Norfolk's Christ, St. Luke's Designated Va. Historic Landmark," *Ledger-Star* (April 7, 1979), A4.

69. "Christ Church Parish House Opened," *VP* (December 11, 1919), 3.

70. "Films Show Work of Catholics in War; At Colonial," *VP* (May 2, 1920), 6.

71. As historian Robert Allen has shown, however, provincial communities were empowered to resist and to accommodate the imposing rush of commercial entertainment. See Allen, "Motion Picture Exhibition in Manhattan, 1906–1912: Beyond the Nickelodeon," *Cinema Journal* 18, no. 2 (1979): 2–15.

Part III

INTEGRATION AND VARIATIONS

CASE STUDIES

7

THE MOVIES IN A
"NOT SO VISIBLE PLACE"

Des Moines, Iowa, 1911–1914

RICHARD ABEL

At the turn of the last century, Richard Ohmann writes, the new mass magazines assumed Iowa, like much of America's so-called heartland, was not worth representing, "not a visible place."[1] It was no different in the early trade press devoted to motion pictures. During the height of the nickelodeon period, to be sure, *Moving Picture World* singled out "Des Moines men" for eagerly taking up "the latest hobby": running "moving picture shows."[2] Otherwise, Iowa and its capital city drew little or no attention, and neither would be worth mentioning by July 1916, in the *World*'s special issue on the history of U.S. exhibition.[3] Yet in Des Moines itself, motion pictures enjoyed relatively high visibility. This was certainly the case during the nickelodeon boom of 1907, when at least five new downtown theaters appeared within a matter of months, and Kleine Optical ran a rare ad in the *Register and Leader*, just prior to opening a rental office there.[4]

Beginning in 1911, motion pictures became even more visible, and more consistently, as no less than fifteen new theaters appeared during the next three years. As if to signal the significance of this second, more sustained boom, several companies that rented and/or produced films for the national market—Universal, Mutual, Reliance, Essanay, and Famous Players—placed weekly strip ads in the *Register and Leader* between April and July 1913. Since I have dealt with the earlier years of exhibition in the city, in *The Red Rooster Scare* and in an essay on illustrated songs,[5] I want to focus here on the latter period, using as end points the opening of the first residential theater, in September 1911, and that of the Garden Theater, the first "movie palace," in May 1914. My aim is to recover the discursive record of Des Moines in order to return the city to visibility, to something "worth representing," and thereby reconstruct, in one specific locale, the circulation, exhibition, and reception of motion pictures during what an architectural historian has called "the little noticed . . . period of the early 1910s that bridge[d] the nickelodeon and the palace."[6]

Perhaps not unexpectedly, there are historiographical problems in establishing the basis for such a study in a relatively new, expanding city like Des Moines, an insurance and railway shipping center with many surrounding coal mines, whose population had reached 86,000 by 1910.[7] In their study of New York City, for instance, William Uricchio and Roberta Pearson enumerate a half dozen constituencies competing to shape the discursive terrain within which cinema developed—ranging from Progressive reformers, professionals, and clergy to state or city regulators, the press, and the film industry itself.[8] All these were active in Des Moines, but their presence in surviving records is uneven. Despite the widespread debate about who should exercise control (and how much) over motion picture shows in the interests of public health, for instance, it is difficult to find evidence of the issue, beyond several ordinances between 1907 and 1912 covering the inspection of projection booths, the prohibition of smoking, and the location of theaters on a street corner (or alley).[9] Similarly, although city directories reveal the location of theaters and some sense of their permanence or impermanence, property sales records do not: according to local historian John Zeller, such transactions describe the dimensions of lots but do not often give specific details about the buildings on them.[10] Consequently, the discursive terrain of motion pictures in Des Moines may seem relatively restricted, with its principal constituencies represented in two of the capital city's four major newspapers. Yet however narrowly defined, that terrain, much like the fabled "heartland" Iowa soil, is unusually thick and rich, especially where press and commerce existed in close codependence, in advertising and other forms of publicity.

The only morning paper, the *Register and Leader,* was the oldest and most successful, having built up a large editorial staff and corps of reporters/correspondents after Gardner Cowles gained control in 1903.[11] In an attempt to ensure its dominance, in 1908 Cowles purchased the struggling *Evening Tribune,* originally "an East side journal with a mission to correct the erroneous judgments of the older journals on the West side" or downtown.[12] Together the two papers had a circulation of more than 50,000, and, according to an early history of the city, the *Register and Leader* "ranked seventeenth among journals published west of the Mississippi."[13] A second evening paper was the *News,* an early "penny paper" that had gone through several changes in ownership until it was acquired by the Scripps-McRae League in 1908.[14] Much like the *Register and Leader,* it had grown into "one of the leading State papers," with a circulation of 40,000. The most "sensational" of these—in its choice of stories, headlines, and illustrations—the *News,* like others in the Scripps-McRae chain, had "a very large clientele among the workingmen of Des Moines" (largely on the east side), was "a vigorous supportive of labor interests,"[15] and took a strong position of advocacy for the suffragette movement. E.W. Scripps himself (sounding a bit like Charles Foster Kane) once described his papers as "friends, advisors, and even special pleaders of the ninety-five percent of the population that were not rich and powerful."[16] Interestingly, it was in the *News* that several motion picture theaters began to place advertisements quite regularly from the fall of 1911 on. And it was there, too, that weekly movie listings and reviews as well as frequent stories began to complement those ads in November 1912.[17] Within months, the *Register and Leader* was forced to pay more and more attention to the new amusement, so that, by 1913–14, the two papers were issuing a steady stream of discourse that not only publicized motion pictures but also promoted moviegoing. Given the richness of this material, Des Moines, compared with larger, more researched American cities, arguably offers an exceptional case study of motion picture exhibition early in the second decade of the twentieth century.

The Playhouses and Players of Local Exhibition

As in most other cities, motion picture exhibition in Des Moines developed in close proximity with what newspapers and city directories called "amusements"—that is, legitimate theaters and vaudeville houses. By 1911, motion pictures theaters could be found in two principal areas. The most important was the downtown shopping district (just north of the courthouse and passenger train station), the hub for a network of streetcar lines stretching into all the city's major residential areas.[18] There, the Colonial (opposite Younker Brothers department store) and the Family (within a block of three legitimate theaters) were especially prominent, at least given their ads in both the *News* and the *Register*. A second, smaller shopping district lay down the hill from the state capitol building on the city's east side, where the Elite Theater catered to chiefly white-collar and working-class neighborhood audiences. By late 1911, the new amusement had achieved such a level of profitability that new theaters devoted primarily to motion pictures began to open in residential districts, and all were adjacent to streetcar lines.[19] Charles Namur, owner of the Colonial, initiated this development with a series of theaters—the Idle Hour on University Place, near Drake University on the city's prosperous northwest side; the Highland Park, in a northern middle-class suburb; and a third in the predominantly Italian working-class area on the near south side.[20] Soon small theaters such as the Rex, Crystal, and Cupid were clustered near University Place, and still others such as the Mystic, Isis, Ideal, and Amuz-U could be found in the white-collar/working-class areas ringing the capitol on the east side (where Scandinavian and Jewish immigrants were prominent).[21] At the same time, downtown theaters such as the Unique (700 seats) and the Majestic (1,100 seats) shifted exclusively to motion pictures; the Star and Family (1,000 seats) were renovated extensively;

and still others were newly constructed—the Casino (550 seats), Golden, Royal, Palace (1,100 seats), and Black Cat[22]—confirming a *News* editorial, in August 1912, that asserted "the moving picture show is here to stay."[23] By early 1914, just before the downtown Garden opened, more than twenty motion picture theaters were operating throughout the city.[24]

Most of the men who "boomed the business" in Des Moines had residences on the city's prosperous near west or northwest side and/or came from backgrounds that suited the new amusement. Ben Elbert and John Getchel, who jointly headed one of the city's amusement companies, had opened the Nickeldom (the first motion picture theater in 1906), later renovated it as the Unique, and owned the Majestic. Isaac and Joseph Ruben, who owned the Lyric and Star (and perhaps the Elite for a time), ran a profitable east side clothing store. Namur, who owned a skating rink as well as a circuit of cinemas, also had a prominent downtown drugstore.[25] In parallel with exhibitors in larger cities (but noticeable in a city of chiefly German, Scandinavian, Irish, and English immigrants), many of these men were Jewish.[26] In addition to the Ruben brothers (Isaac would move to Minneapolis after 1910 and, with partner M. L. Finkelstein, operate a large circuit of cinemas),[27] there were J. F. Zimmerman (from Chicago), who had managed the Radium in 1907–8; Jacob Milowslowsky, who turned the Radium into the Family (which went through several renovations) and then opened the Palace; Julius Singer, who first ran the Laemmle Film Service branch office and then headed the Capital City Film Company;[28] and A. H. Blank, who owned a loan office specializing in real estate before acquiring the Star (from Ruben),[29] as well as building the Casino (in partnership with Abe Frankle)[30] and then the luxurious Garden. Blank not only would amass a chain of major cinemas throughout the city and across the state (as would Frankle) but also eventually would become a regional executive for the Publix Theatres controlled by Paramount.[31]

The Circulation of Motion Pictures:
From Variety to Feature Programs

The years immediately after 1910 were marked by several important changes in the American cinema industry, none of which occurred all that evenly or smoothly. The newspaper discourse in Des Moines offers a unique perspective on these changes, beginning with the intense competition between the Motion Picture Patents Company (MPPC) and the Independents, as the latter, loosely organized in the Motion Picture Distributing and Sales Company (or simply Sales), struggled to create a nationwide distribution system matching that of General Film, the MPPC's distribution outlet.

In Des Moines, General Film supplied the Colonial, for years the most consistent advertiser in the *News;* all the residential theaters in Namur's circuit;

two other downtown theaters that advertised infrequently, the Lyric and Star; as well as the Casino, after its construction in late 1912. As testimony to its subordinate position, Sales serviced only the Family, Elite, and Golden, at least of those theaters advertising in the *News* and *Register*. Still, in the fall of 1911, the Elite made a special point of repeatedly promoting the "Famous 'Imp' Pictures [that were] rapidly making friends and steady patrons."[32] Shortly after Sales broke into factions in the spring of 1912, Laemmle's Film Service office in Des Moines became affiliated with Universal, and another rental exchange in the city, H & H Film Service, soon contracted with Mutual.[33] Initially, Universal continued to supply the Family and Elite and added at least one new theater, the Royal, while Mutual heavily promoted its programs at the Unique.[34] The theaters contracted to these two companies fluctuated throughout the summer and fall of 1913, but their total share of the city's market (again, at least according to newspaper ads and movie listings) seems to have reached, by then, a level on par with that of General Film. Film Supply, a third Independent company (which handled Gaumont films, among others), did not have an exchange office in Des Moines—and its film releases never appeared in theater ads. The situation was very different in the smaller city of Cedar Rapids (in northeast Iowa),[35] in which one of two downtown theaters that advertised frequently in the local newspaper (the other got its films from Universal) became an exclusive venue for Gaumont films in the summer and fall of 1912.[36] The contrast is quite suggestive of Film Supply's relative weakness as a distributor, even in a small market like that in Iowa.

A second important change in the industry came with the gradual introduction of multiple-reel films, especially as those reshaped and, in turn, were shaped by rental and exhibition practices. It may seem surprising that, in early 1912, the majority of motion picture theaters that advertised in the *News* offered new programs of films each day, just as they had five years earlier in the first nickelodeons. Yet one has to remember that, by then, both the MPPC and the Independents were releasing more than thirty new film titles per week, with older titles still available through either the distributors themselves or the "secondhand" trade.[37] In other words, Sales and its subsequent factions (Universal, Mutual, and Film Supply) adopted General Film's established practice, as Michael Quinn puts it, of supplying exhibitors with a "complete service"—that is, enough new reels to change their programs daily.[38] Both the Elite and the Unique, for instance, promised "fresh" Independent film titles each day; when the Casino opened in late 1912, it too offered daily changes of new licensed films.[39] Yet ads in the *News* also reveal that nearly as many theaters did not follow this practice. The Family and Golden, both Independent theaters, changed their films three times a week (on Mondays, Wednesdays, and Fridays), as did the Star, a licensed theater.[40] The Colonial alone presented biweekly programs of licensed films (changing Sundays and Thursdays), while all of Namur's other theaters, in residential areas, advertised films changed daily.[41] By the fall of 1913, again according to ads, the downtown theaters with daily changes now included the Majestic and Family, and the Colonial joined the Star, Royal, and Palace in changing programs three times a week. In short, the daily-changed variety package, once a mainstay of the nickelodeon period, still strongly influenced exhibition, supported by the release schedules of the manufacturers and distributors, as well as by the "continuous shows" that many exhibitors continued to champion. The regularity of that variety package also allowed exhibitors to specially promote their more popular films, as the Colonial did in 1912, for instance, with *Pathé Weekly*, often making it the headlined feature of its weekend programs: "Read It in the Papers," one ad proclaimed, and "See It Here."[42]

As two- and three-reel films moved beyond what the *New York Dramatic Mirror* called their "experimental" phase, in late 1911, certain exhibitors were better positioned than others to work them into their highly structured programs.[43] In Des Moines, the Colonial could handle the first licensed special features—from Selig's *Two Orphans* and Kalem's *Colleen Bawn* to Milano's *Dante's Inferno* and Selig's *Cinderella*—with relative ease as the main attraction of the week's opening program (Sunday through Wednesday), confirming its status as the city's "exclusive motion picture house."[44] By the spring of 1912, on Mondays and Tuesdays, the Family also was booking special Independent features from Cines' four-reel *The Crusaders* to 101-Bison two-reel westerns such as *Blazing the Trail* and *The Post Telegrapher*.[45] For at least another year, the Colonial thrived on a relatively steady output of multiple-reel licensed films, from Selig's *Coming of Columbus* in June to Pathé's *Grotto of Torture* in December 1912, while the Family briefly cut back on its promotion (at least) of special Independent features, except for those like *Oliver Twist*, starring the stage actor Nat Goodwin. By early 1913, however, such films had become accepted enough that certain theaters could risk screening them for just a single weekday. The Family now booked Universal two-reelers, such as the Civil War film *Sheridan's Ride*, on Tuesdays, which the Elite then ran for east side audiences a week later.[46] Similarly, when the Unique began advertising a weekly schedule of Mutual films, it booked multiple-reel films even more systematically, with Broncho titles such as *The Burning Brand* playing on Wednesdays, and the "celebrated Kay-Bee westerns" on Fridays.[47] Consistent with Quinn's general argument, then, licensed multiple-reel films led the way in making features a popular attraction in Des Moines, with Universal and Mutual exploiting and extending their popularity by presenting particular genres stamped with brand names on regularly scheduled days of the week. Yet, if General Film "did little to differentiate its features from its [regular] programs," as Quinn claims, the Colonial repeatedly made a point in its ads of marking just such a distinction.[48]

The development of the "state rights" distribution system, whereby an individual or company purchased the licensing right to exhibit one or more special features within a certain territory, seems to have bypassed Des Moines as a profitable market until well into 1913.[49] This is a bit surprising because Famous Players booked its first feature, *Queen Elizabeth* (starring Sarah Bernhardt), for a full week at the Berchel, the city's principal legitimate theater, in mid-September 1912, less than a month after its initial release in New York and Chicago.[50] Yet despite the weeklong engagement of Milano's *Homer's Odyssey* at the Colonial in November and *Queen Elizabeth*'s return for one weekday at University Place in February, no Des Moines theater advertised a "state rights" feature until the spring of 1913.[51] Significantly, the Colonial was in the forefront of booking them regularly (and risked dropping its General Film service in the bargain), most notably with a weeklong run of Ambrosio's *Satan* or *The Dawn of Humanity*, in May.[52] For the next several months, a mix of American and foreign features—from Warner's *Dead Secret* (with Marion Leonard) to Itala's *Tigris* and Éclair's *Zigomar III*—held the screen at the Colonial for three or four days each.[53] That fall, the Colonial booked American features exclusively, from Famous Players' *In the Bishop's Carriage* (with Mary Pickford) and Warner's *Theodora* to Thomas Ince's five-reel *Battle of Gettysburg;* then, in late October, it negotiated an exclusive contract for three to four features a week from Warner's.[54] In some regions of the country, Famous Players may have led the way in establishing the distribution of "regular features," as Quinn argues, but in Des Moines the leader was Warner's.[55] Not until May 1914 would Famous Players' features return on a regular basis to the city, and then at the Star (which also dropped its General Film service), beginning with a much-delayed screening of *Caprice* (again, with Pickford).[56]

Despite the institution of "regular features" from Warner's at the Colonial, the market for features remained relatively open throughout the 1913–14 season. As he had in other cities, for instance, George Kleine contracted with a legitimate theater, the Berchel, in August 1913, for an exclusive weeklong screening of Cines' *Quo Vadis?* Yet, in November, his version of Ambrosio's *Last Days of Pompeii* had to be shown at the Colonial when Pasquali's competing version was booked at the Berchel.[57] The Palace used exclusive screenings of *A Sister to Carmen* (with Helen Gardner) and Famous Players' *His Neighbor's Wife* to promote its opening in late October but then quickly adopted Universal's daily programs.[58] The market also was still uncertain, even "chaotic," as evidenced by the long delays between the release dates of certain features and their exhibition. This was not uncommon, as Quinn notes, for early Famous Players film such as *The Prisoner of Zenda*, which finally played at the Star in July 1913.[59] But it was unusual for others. Pathé's *Les Misérables*, for instance, finally appeared for a weeklong run at the Berchel in April 1914, as did (surprisingly, given its popularity in New York, Boston, Cleveland, and other cities) Universal's controversial *Traffic in Souls* in May.[60] The most egregious delay was for Helen Gardner's *Cleopatra*, which was not booked for more than a year; yet the Star promoted its weeklong run (also in May) with a half-page ad in both the *News* and the *Register*.[61] One can appreciate the risks, then, that the Black Cat took when it opened in late January, determined to offer programs of at least one feature daily.[62] When, by May, the Star and the Garden joined the Colonial in successfully programming "regular features," it was instead for more typical three- or four-day runs (at the Colonial, sometimes a week).[63] Yet the variety format of short films changed daily continued to flourish at the majority of theaters, including the downtown Casino, Unique, Majestic, and Palace—now anchored not only by newsreels but also by biweekly episodes of serials and series, from Selig's *Adventures of Kathlyn* and Pathé's *Perils of Pauline* to Mutual's *Mutual Girl* and Universal's *Lucille Love*.[64]

"Regular features" had a significant yet hardly singular effect on theater ticket prices and newspaper advertising, and hence targeted audiences. Throughout 1911 and 1912, ticket prices at General Film theaters (the Colonial, Lyric, Star, University Place, and Highland Park) consistently were 10 cents, whereas the more successful Independent theaters (the Family and Unique) charged just 5 cents.[65] The Casino, which Blank opened in December 1912, suddenly blurred this distinction with its 5-cent ticket price, and soon other theaters (the Golden and Royal) were forced to follow suit; when the Star came into Blank's possession six months later, its admission price also fell, as did that of the Majestic when it shifted to motion pictures in September 1913. Since nearly all these theaters showed new films daily, the low admission cost now became associated with the constantly changing variety program.[66] By contrast, as the Colonial began successfully exhibiting "state rights" features in the spring of 1913—followed by the Palace, Star, and Garden—the 10-cent admission cost became associated with special features booked for runs of three days to one week. In early 1914, the Black Cat briefly attempted to merge the two, running its daily change of features at a cost of 5 cents, but the experiment quickly failed. The Casino's opening and the Colonial's dedication to "state rights" features also led to changes in advertising, which in turn suggested that audiences for motion pictures were broadening. Throughout 1911 and 1912, theaters had placed ads much more frequently in the *News* than the *Register*. It was noteworthy, then, that Blank advertised the Casino's opening in the *Register* (not the *News*) and that the Colonial also promoted its first features more often there.[67] Blank also chose the *Register* when he began advertising features at the Star and when he announced the Garden's opening in a special four-page spread, in May 1914.[68] This increased advertising in the *Register*, especially that associated with first-run features, has to be read as a deliberate attempt to attract and hold a middle-class audience. Yet, on a daily basis, more ads continued to appear in the *News* (for its predominantly working-class/white-collar readers), and from a wider range of venues, since the *Register*'s came exclusively from downtown theaters.

Newspaper Stories, Columns, and Other Novelties

Reading through the discourse of newspapers such as the *News* and the *Register* gives one a sense of certain patterns in the contours of motion picture distribution and exhibition that not only extend and qualify or modify our thinking about the years immediately after 1910 but also suggest that some of our assumptions and conclusions may need rethinking. If one steps back and looks more closely at the discourse itself, other contours and landmarks become visible, revealing patterns in motion picture promotion and reception. These patterns come into even sharper focus when the Des Moines papers are read in contrast to one another, as well as in relation to papers in other cities, and when the discourse on motion pictures is read in relation to other kinds of newspaper material—all of which made certain assumptions about readers.

In the midst of all the ads and stories that appeared in the *News* throughout 1911 and 1912, easily the most surprising bit of discourse—a truly unexpected landmark—was a front-page story on 11 November 1912. Under a filmstrip banner labeled "The Movies" was a story about the famous wager in Palo Alto, California, in 1872, which led Eadweard Muybridge to "invent" motion pictures. Filling out this story were a variety of "big facts" about the current industry that had grown up from this invention, along with a thumbnail sketch of its "three branches: *manufacturer, renter, and exhibitor.*"[69] The writer was "Gertrude M. Price, the Daily News' Moving Picture Expert," and on the next page was a bold announcement that she would be entertaining readers almost daily with stories about the "MOVING PICTURE FOLKS"—"that Smiley, Golden-Haired Girl [undoubtedly, Pickford] . . . that Beautiful Child . . . that Athletic Young Hero, and that Gun-Toting Cowboy"—because the *News* "recogniz[ed] 'the movies' as the biggest, most popular amusement in the world."[70] The following day, as promised, not only did an illustrated story on Dolores Cassinelli (from Essanay's Chicago studio) appear, but so did another banner story about the movie business in Des Moines, claiming that the city's fourteen motion picture houses had a daily attendance of 10,000—"from the coal miner north of the city who walks a mile or more to attend the picture show in Highland Park to the rich man who stops his automobile in front of the show in University Place"—and that was a "conservative estimate."[71] Throughout the following week, stories sprouted daily and in unexpected places: a "Movies" column claimed that "there were five hundred people in Des Moines who depend for a living on the motion picture industry"; another offered capsule reviews of one or more films being shown at eight different theaters; and other illustrated stories featured Essanay stars Broncho Billy and Alkali Ike, and Selig's "fearless" heroine, Kathlyn Williams.[72]

Because Price was described as the "News' Moving Picture Expert," I first thought that she was a local journalist, perhaps with connections in Chicago.[73]

But as I read through several months of stories, "Movies" columns, and other pieces, that seemed less and less plausible. Whereas the "Movies" columns and some articles clearly had a local angle, many illustrated stories included short sections that read like interviews (obviously not done in Des Moines); moreover, by 1 February 1913, Price was described as writing from the "great California studios where they make your wild west pictures."[74] As this disjunction persisted, it was clear that Price could not be writing all this material; furthermore, it was unlikely that the *News,* alone among the country's newspapers, had sent one of its reporters west to do exclusive stories on the movies. This mystery was solved, at least in part, when I discovered that Price's initial articles also appeared at exactly the same time in several other newspapers, from the *Cleveland Press, Toledo News-Bee,* and *Detroit Times* to the *St. Paul News* and *New Orleans Statesman.*[75] Their placement may have differed—the initial story on page 1 of the *News* appeared on page 2 of the *News-Bee* and page 4 of the *Press*—and several illustrated stories in the *News* did not appear in the *Press* or *News-Bee* (and vice versa), but all were attributed explicitly to Price. That the *News* and several other papers were members of the Scripps-McRae League meant that Price was a writer whose work was syndicated and distributed throughout the chain.[76] Whereas this diminishes any claims about her as a local journalist, it makes her one of the first syndicated writers with motion pictures as her exclusive subject—which also means that she probably was more widely read at the time than anyone in the trade press.[77] That alone would make her writings well worth examining further, but so does the extent of her work in the *News,* together with all the local discourse in the paper, as well as that in the *Register,* because more of her stories appeared there than in any of the other papers.[78]

For at least six months after Price's sudden appearance as a "movie expert" in November 1912, hardly a day went by without a story or column on motion pictures in the *News.* Every Tuesday, beginning on 3 December 1912, an unknown writer filled the "Movies" column with capsule reviews of selected current pictures, as well as tidbits of local information—for instance, interviewing Julius Singer of Capital City Film and noting that "neighbors and others" requested the return engagement of *Queen Elizabeth* at University Place.[79] Whereas Pathé's "sensational" jungle picture, *The Grotto of Torture,* won praise as "a marvelous panorama of stirring events," another "French film at the Golden depicting such things as . . . two suicides, unfaithful women, etc." was condemned as censorable.[80] After a brief absence in late February 1913, the column returned several weeks later, as a permanent feature on Sundays, listing the film titles in weekly programs for a half dozen theaters (which probably paid for its publication).[81] Undoubtedly provoked by all this attention in the *News,* the *Register,* also in February, established a Sunday column devoted to motion pictures (again, the writer is unknown), which seemed to sift the trade press for information considered of interest to Des Moines. The choices are revealing: "keen interest" in producers such as Famous Players and in specific features such as *Cleopatra* and *Les Misérables* (long before they came to the city), and special attention to scientific films, nature films, and travelogues.[82] Not until August 1913 did the *Register* begin printing its own weekly listing of film titles at selected theaters, and Blank's Casino and Star took the lead as sponsors.[83] Unlike the *News,* the *Register* first called its Sunday column "At the Moving Picture Playhouses" and then "News of the Photoplays and Photoplayers." Here, the *Register* was following the trade press, and other papers like the *Cleveland Leader,* in eschewing the slang term *movies,* which the *News* and Price herself preferred, for a more elevated term that cast motion pictures as a legitimate art, with educational effects.[84] But the distinction also clearly revealed the two papers' different readerships, hence the different audiences they imagined as moviegoers.

A Fan Culture of Movie Stars or Personalities

Most of the articles Price signed in the *News,* as well as those she did not, focused on individual screen personalities or movie stars, exploiting a new public interest that the industry (and trade press) was only beginning to use to its advantage.[85] Moreover, all were illustrated with one or more halftone sketches deftly drawn from publicity photos (copyrighted, for the most part, by film companies). It is telling that, although the *Register* never paid as much attention to stars as the *News* did, during the initial weeks of its own Sunday column devoted to motion pictures or photoplays, it too sought to catch readers' eyes by displaying the faces of "famous players" or "celebrities" sketchily depicted in rough line drawings.[86]

The cumulative effect of Price's articles was to suggest how keen an interest Des Moines readers had in movie stars, how the continual circulation of commodified figures as different as King Baggott and John Bunny, or Mary Fuller and Mabel Normand, could produce and sustain their desire to "go to the movies."[87] In short, Price's steady output of articles assumed and fueled an emerging fan culture in which the movie star or personality was the main attraction. One specific sign of that culture was the contest that five theaters sponsored, in February 1913, asking *News*'s readers to name which stars appeared at which houses, using images repeated from Price's articles.[88] Another was the stark difference between one kind of fictional tie-in, promoted long before she appeared in the *News,* and another, shortly after.[89] "Which story in the *Motion Picture Story Magazine* is the best?" a Family Theater ad had asked, in March 1911, announcing a contest with "$250 in cash prizes."[90] The inaugural issue of that magazine, printing the stories of selected MPPC films (illustrated with a few photos), had just been released in February, and moviegoers probably could purchase that or the new March issue at the theater.[91] By the summer of 1913, they could read a very different kind of fictional tie-in. For more than a month, the *News* ran a new short story every Saturday, "with an illustration especially posed for this newspaper" of Vitagraph stars Pauline Frederick and Earle Williams.[92] Sporting captions claiming that famed illustrator Harrison Fisher had called Frederick "the most beautiful woman in America," these images now promoted a cheap version of mass magazine short fiction to *News* readers by exploiting the lure of the movies and, specifically, their stars.

The stars or personalities that Price wrote about at first came from the licensed manufacturers (particularly Essanay, Selig, Vitagraph, and Kalem), but she gradually included those working for the Independents—such as Imp, American or Flying A, Solax, Keystone, Kay-Bee, and 101-Bison (after its acquisition by Universal)—as well as others from Pathé American. Her choice of stars shows several striking patterns. For one thing, at least one out of four or five are described as acting in westerns, and the illustrations support this by having men and women like Jack Richardson and Pauline Garfield Bush (American) decked out in cowboy hats, and others like Mona Darkfeather (Universal) in full Indian costume.[93] Price's texts also underscore that emphasis, as in her description of Kalem's Ruth Roland as "an athletic girl" who "runs, rides, and rows with all the freedom and agility of a boy"—as in one of her "riding pictures," *The Girl Deputy.*[94] Yet Des Moines theaters, unlike those in other cities, did not heavily promote westerns. Essanay's G. M. Anderson, for instance, whether known as Broncho Billy or "Bullets" (as he was called in northeastern Ohio), was rarely a headliner in the city.[95] The multiple-reel westerns of 101-Bison, Broncho, and Kay-Bee occasionally were "celebrated," but not as frequently or intensely as they were in cities such as Cleveland, Toledo, and elsewhere. Price's many stories suggest, then, especially coming after several "Flying A" stories were published in the *News* in early 1912,[96] that she was not alone in her fascination with cowboy, cowboy girl, and Indian figures, and that indeed there was a substantial audience for westerns in the city. In late 1913, she even wrote an exclusive series of nine stories on location about Buffalo Bill Cody's epic reenactment of several battles in the Indian wars of 1876 to 1891, produced by Essanay with U.S. government support.[97] This series is a rare record of what then became *Indian Wars Pictures,* which was shown privately to government officials and clubs, beginning in January 1914, but whose several versions never were widely distributed or exhibited.[98]

Even more striking, however, are the number of stories, at least two-thirds of the total, devoted to women. As might be expected, familiar stars still turn up—from Mary Pickford and Kathlyn Williams to Alice Joyce and Pearl White—but most now are forgotten, and several such as Pauline Bush appear more than once.[99] Among them one can count the "regal-looking Miriam Nesbit," who, supposedly "bored by the world," turned to the movies and "likes rough and ready parts."[100] Or Anna Q. Nilsson, a "movie beauty [who] risks [her] life to put thrill in the pictures" for Kalem—whose story appeared prominently on the newspaper's front page.[101] Or Jessylyn Von Trump, "a capital rider" at American, who "likes herself in a cowgirl costume very much, indeed."[102] Or that "tall woman of the picture players," Anne Scheaefer, who enjoys playing lead roles and character parts for Vitagraph's western unit.[103] Or "dainty, daring" Clara Williams, "who can beat the boys at anything on a horse."[104] Or Leona Hutton, who finds that "being 'almost killed' 365 days in the year is only a hum drum regularity" in her busy life at Kay-Bee.[105] Celebrated as skilled horsewomen and "daredevils," a good number resemble the champion cowgirl riders and sharpshooters, such as Bessie Herberg and Lucile Parr, prominently promoted in performances of the 101 Ranch Wild West that passed through Des Moines at the time.[106] Moreover, complementing them are several successful filmmakers or scenario writers: Alice Guy Blaché at Solax, Lois Weber at Rex, and Nell Shipman.[107]

Certainly Price's stories (with their elaborated, punchy titles) and the accompanying images could have appealed to men reading the *News*. But, overall, they seem targeted primarily at women.[108] After all, most of her favored stars are described as athletic young women, carefree but committed to their work, frank and fearless in the face of physical risk. Strikingly, nearly all are unattached and without children. How desirable they must have seemed to the young unmarried women who formed a core readership of Scripps-McRae newspapers, as well as an emerging fan culture, perhaps especially those in white-collar or even professional jobs in the growing service industries of Des Moines and other cities. For them, the desire "to go to the movies" would have been double: not only did the film roles that women played function as projective sites of fantasy adventure for such spectators—that lashed reading/viewing/consuming into a pleasurable activity—but, as a new kind of active, attractive worker or professional, the stars (and even Price herself) could serve as successful role models to emulate. In short, although never named as such, most arguably could be read as popular figures of a specifically American "New Woman."[109] The political stance of the *News,* as well as that of Price herself, provides a further context for the continual parade of all these women. As a strong advocate of women's suffrage, the *News* had printed stories about special screenings of suffragette films such as *Votes of Women* at the Unique in June 1912.[110] Furthermore, not only did it give front-page coverage to the famous suffragette march on Washington, in early 1913; Price also joined the march to interview one of its leaders.[111] In describing actors such as Pauline Bush, then, the following admiring remark was hardly surprising: that, much like herself, she was "an ardent suffraget."[112] Consequently, in circulating, weekly and even daily for more than a year, a series of influential "New Women" for female fans of the movies, Price's syndicated column takes on special significance for the way it interconnects movies, working women of different classes, and the suffragette movement.

For anyone reading the *News* and, later, the *Register*, the "movie madness" that seized Des Moines between late 1911 and late 1913 must have been difficult to ignore.[113] Much of it was due, of course, to companies such as General Film, Universal, Mutual, and Warner's and to motion picture theater entrepreneurs such as Namur, Elbert and Getchell, Milowslowsky, Frankle, and Blank, and to the way each established and sustained (through extensive advertising) a mix of both variety and exclusive feature programs for an increasingly broad audience. It was due equally to the anonymous writers whose sudden outcropping of reviews, columns, and stories in the *News* and the *Register* were responding, in part, to new marketing strategies promoted by the industry and trade press. Yet none would have succeeded without the emerging fan culture of moviegoers throughout the city, from laborers and white-collar workers to middle-class managers and professionals—particularly young women. Perhaps most crucially, then, the city's "movie madness" was dependent on the previously unheralded writer, Gertrude Price, whose syndicated stories in the *News* played a special role, creating what would become long-lasting bonds of pleasure between female stars and female fans.

Notes

This chapter originated as a paper delivered at the 1995 annual meeting of the Society for Cinema Studies. Based on considerably more research since then, aided by Cowles Library's Interlibrary Loan Services at Drake University, several Drake Faculty Research Grants, and research funds from the University of Michigan, I have written a substantially new essay, small portions of which appeared in another paper delivered at the 2001 SCS conference or were published in "A Marriage of Ephemeral Discourses: Newspapers and Moving Pictures," *Cinéma et Cie* 1 (Fall 2001): 59–83. In order to save space, I have used the following acronyms: *MPW (Moving Picture World)*, *MPN (Moving Picture News)*, *NYDM (New York Dramatic Mirror)*, *NYMT (New York Morning Telegraph)*, *CL (Cleveland Leader)*, *DMN (Des Moines News)*, and *DMRL (Des Moines Register and Leader)*.

1. Richard Ohmann, *Selling Culture: Magazines, Markets, and Class at the Turn of the Century* (London: Verso, 1996), 231.

2. "Trade Notes," *MPW* (25 May 1907), 181.

3. "The Evolution of Exhibiting," *MPW* (15 July 1916), 367–421. The cities nearest Des Moines to receive attention were St. Louis and Kansas City.

4. Kleine Optical ad, *DMRL* (20 October 1907), 3:7.

5. Richard Abel, *The Red Rooster Scare: Making Cinema American, 1900–1910* (Berkeley and Los Angeles: University of California Press, 1999); and Abel, "That Most American of Attractions, the Illustrated Song," in *The Sounds of Early Cinema*, ed. Richard Abel and Rick Altman (Bloomington: Indiana University Press, 2001), 143–55.

6. Maggie Valentine, *The Show Starts on the Sidewalk: An Architectural History of the Movie Theatre* (New Haven, Conn.: Yale University Press, 1994), 31. For a related, yet

broader case study of Lexington, Kentucky (a much smaller city than Des Moines, with a significant black population), see Gregory Waller, *Main Street Amusements: Movies and Commercial Entertainment in a Southern City, 1896–1930* (Washington, D.C.: Smithsonian Institution Press, 1995). Unfortunately, Douglas Gomery skips this period in *Shared Pleasures: A History of Movie Presentation in the United States* (Madison: University of Wisconsin Press, 1992). Although Eileen Bowser focuses on "the newer 'palatial' theaters," she does devote several informative pages to nickelodeons and motion picture theaters after 1910; Bowser, *The Transformation of Cinema, 1907–1915* (New York: Scribner's, 1990), 121–36.

7. The population of Polk County, with Des Moines at its center, was 110,000. The population of Des Moines had increased by nearly 40 percent in the ten years before 1910, and it would increase even more in the following ten years. "Supplement for Iowa," *Thirteenth Census of the United States, with a Supplement for Iowa* (Washington, D.C.: Government Printing Office, 1913), 588, 620, 624. Of the city's 86,000 people, the census listed slightly more than 10,000 as "foreign-born white," with the greatest number coming from Scandinavia, Germany, and Russia (largely Russian Jews). As in many Iowa cities, the majority of the residents of Des Moines were second- or third-generation German immigrants. See also "Des Moines: One of the World's Great Insurance Centers," *DMN* (27 October 1910), 9. Ten percent of the city's population may have been coal miners; *American Newspaper Annual and Directory* (Philadelphia: N. W. Ayers & Son, 1914), 277.

8. William Uricchio and Roberta Pearson, "Constructing the Audience: Competing Discourses of Morality and Rationalizing during the Nickelodeon Period," *Iris* 17 (Autumn 1994): 43–54.

9. Des Moines (Iowa) City Council, "Proceedings of City Council and Ordinances of the City of Des Moines, 1907–1908," Iowa Collection, Des Moines Public Library, Des Moines, Iowa; and "Safe Theaters Provided for New Ordinance," *DMN* (11 June 1912), 2. No fire insurance survey map was done between 1900 and 1920; Fire insurance records, State Historical Society of Iowa. Theaters in Des Moines also were segregated, restricting African Americans to the balcony or back-row seats, but the only mention of this came from a court case in which a "negro justice of the peace of Bussey, Iowa," unsuccessfully sued the manager of the Royal Theater; "Movie Man Freed in Color Case," *DMN* (27 June 1913), 4.

10. Conversations with John Zeller, March 1997. For good models of how directories and property sales records can be used in writing the history of early film exhibition, see Robert Allen, "Motion Picture Exhibition in Manhattan, 1906–1912: Beyond the Nickelodeon," *Cinema Journal* 18, no. 2 (1979): 2–15; Ben Singer, "Manhattan Nickelodeons: New Data on Audiences and Exhibitors," *Cinema Journal* 34, no. 3 (1995): 5–35; and "Dialogue," *Cinema Journal* 35, no. 3 (1996): 72–128.

11. John Brigham, *The History of Des Moines and Polk County*, vol. 1 (Chicago: S. J. Clarke, 1911), 556.

12. Ibid.

13. *American Newspaper Annual and Directory* (1914), 278.

14. Brigham, *History of Des Moines and Polk County*, 557–58; *American Newspaper Annual and Directory* (1914), 277–78. The *News* eluded me while I was writing *The Red Rooster Scare* simply because the only extant microfilm copy is at the Iowa City branch,

rather than the Des Moines branch, of the Iowa Historical Society Library. The fourth newspaper, the evening *Capital,* had a circulation of more than 40,000; like the *Tribune,* it did not issue a Sunday edition and initially gave little attention to motion pictures.

15. Brigham, *History of Des Moines and Polk County,* 558. For more information on Scripps's newspapers, see Gerald Baldasty, *E. W. Scripps and the Business of Newspapers* (Urbana: University of Illinois Press, 1999).

16. Quoted from a 26 February 1906 letter to Robert Paine, the general editor of Scripps's chains, in ibid., 147.

17. Capsule motion picture reviews emerged even earlier, in the fall of 1911, in northeastern Ohio, in such papers as the *Cleveland Leader, Youngstown Vindicator,* and *Canton News-Democrat.*

18. The city's major street car company built a summer amusement park, Ingersoll Park, at one terminus on the western edge of the city; its vaudeville theater showed motion pictures as early as 1902, and one streetcar line allowed east side working-class residents direct access to it, without changing cars downtown. Conversation with John Zeller, March 1997.

19. By contrast, in northeastern textile-dominated cities like Lawrence, Lowell, and Lynn (similar in size to Des Moines), picture theaters tended not to extend beyond the downtown area.

20. Idle Hour University Place Theatre ad, *DMN* (12 September 1911), 8; Namur's (Highland Park) Theatre ad, *DMN* (15 November 1911), 6; "Photo Plays," *DMN* (18 February 1912), 6; Namur's block ad, *DMN* (18 November 1912), 6.

21. The Cupid may have been owned and managed by two women, Mrs. Dodson and Mrs. Baker; "Charter Car to See the Movies," *DMN* (2 April 1913), 5. The immigrant backgrounds of the city's neighborhoods can be gathered from the churches listed in the *Des Moines City Directory.* Theater names and addresses can be found under "Amusements" in the *Des Moines City Directories* of 1910, 1911, 1912, and 1913—each annual volume appeared on December 1 of the designated year. Ten years later, these residential areas would be sites for a rather imprecise survey of Des Moines attitudes toward motion pictures; James L. Arnold, "The Motion Pictures of the Nation and City of Des Moines" (B.D. thesis, Drake University, 1925).

22. "Elbert & Getchel to Make Changes at Unique-Majestic," *DMN* (30 April 1911), 6; "Photo Plays," *DMN* (27 January 1912), 3; the Casino ad, *DMRL* (4 December 1912), 4; the Theatre Royal ad, *DMN* (2 February 1913), 6; the large Casino ad, *DMN* (16 March 1913), 6; "Star Theatre Sold," *DMN* (9 May 1913), 4; "New Movie House," *DMN* (15 June 1913), 13; "Majestic Will Be Turned into Movie Theater," *DMN* (3 September 1913), 5; "New Palace Is Beautiful Theater," *DMN* (26 October 1913), 6; "Black Cat Movie House," *DMN* (2 November 1913), 2. The seating capacities for the Majestic, Unique, Casino, Family, and Palace, respectively, come from "New Vaudeville Theater to Open," *DMN* (20 August 1910), 6; the Unique ad, *DMN* (26 January 1913), 6; the Casino ad, *DMN* (16 March 1913), 6; "New Movie House" (15 June 1913), 13; and the Palace ad, *DMN* (24 October 1913), 10.

23. "Moving Pictures," *DMN* (20 August 1912), 4. For some sense of the prosperity of motion picture theaters in Des Moines, especially those of A. H. Blank, see "Local Men Find Movie Shows Are Paying Ventures," *DMN* (23 October 1913), 2.

24. In December 1913, *Moving Picture World* reported "twenty-seven moving picture houses" in Des Moines, more than are listed in either the 1913 or the 1914 city directory; "Correspondence: Iowa," *MPW* (13 December 1913), 1293.

25. Isaac Ruben's clothing store was located next to the Fair department store. Namur's drugstore was adjacent to his Colonial Theatre. Namur's drugstore was still "the most popular" in the city in 1914; see the large Namur's ad, *DMN* (30 June 1914), 3. Namur himself was included in a series of sixty photographs of "Men Who Are Building a Great City Here," *DMN* (23 June 1907), Illustrated Sunday Magazine, 4.

26. Ranked fifth or sixth among "immigrant" populations in Des Moines, Jews numbered about 5,000 or approximately 5 percent of the city's overall population, with most recent immigrants coming from the Pale region of eastern Europe; *Thirteenth Census*, 624; Robert A. Rockaway, ed., *Words of the Uprooted: Jewish Immigrants in Early 20th Century America* (Ithaca, N.Y.: Cornell University Press, 1998), 168. According to an early study ending in 1895, the majority of Jewish families and businesses were located on the city's east side; Frank Rosenthal, *The Jews of Des Moines: The First Century* (Des Moines: Jewish Welfare Federation, 1957), 38. The prominence of German, Scandinavian, and Irish immigrants in the upper Midwest in the late nineteenth century is detailed in Jon Teaford, *Cities of the Heartland: The Rise and Fall of the Industrial Midwest* (Bloomington: Indiana University Press, 1993), 58–64.

27. "June 2, 1931," *Variety Obituaries II, 1929–1938* (New York: Garland, 1988).

28. "Drama," *Des Moines Mail and Times* (7 June 1907), 26–27; "The Radium," *Midwestern* (July 1907), 59–60; the Family ad, *DMN* (21 April 1912), 6; "The Family Reopens," *DMRL* (24 July 1913), 3; "Brevities of the Business," *Motography* (9 August 1913), 114.

29. "Star Theater Sold," *DMN* (9 May 1913), 4.

30. "March 8, 1944," *Variety Obituaries, III, 1939–1944* (New York: Garland, 1988).

31. *Who's Who in Des Moines* (Des Moines, Iowa: Robert Baldwin, 1929), 31; "August 18, 1971," *Variety Obituaries. VII, 1969–1974* (New York: Garland, 1988).

32. Elite ads, *DMN* (6 August 1911), 6; (3 September 1911), 6; and (10 September 1911), 6.

33. Laemmle Film Service had a branch office in Des Moines by 1911; Sales ad, *MPW* (5 August 1911), 260. Mutual opened its branch office a year later; Mutual ad, *MPW* (17 August 1912), 611.

34. See the large ad for the Unique Theatre and Mutual Films in *DMN* (26 January 1913), 6.

35. Of the more than 30,000 people in Cedar Rapids, the census listed slightly more than 5,000 as "foreign-born white," with the great majority coming from Austria (many of these Czechs); "Supplement for Iowa," 624.

36. See, for instance, the Columbia ads for Gaumont's *The Land of Lions, Cedar Rapids Republican* (31 October 1912), 3, and (3 November 1912), 3; and the Palace ad for Universal's *The Massacre of the Sante Fe Trail, Cedar Rapids Republican* (5 October 1912), 3. A third theater, the Princess, gradually revealed, in generic ads, that its films came from General Film.

37. "'Spectator's' Comments," *NYDM* (31 January 1912), 51. For a thorough overview of the initial production and distribution of American two- and three-reel films, from the standpoint of the trade press, see Bowser, *Transformation of Cinema*, 191–204.

38. Michael Quinn, "Distribution, the Transient Audience, and the Transition to the Feature Film," *Cinema Journal* 40, no. 2 (2001): 40.

39. Unique ad, *DMN* (18 January 1912), 8; Elite ad, *DMN* (28 January 1912), 6; Casino ad, *DMRL* (4 December 1912), 4. In Youngstown, Ohio, the Dome Theater (seating 1,000) also presented daily-changed programs from General Film—according to the full-page ad for the theater's opening in the *Youngstown Vindicator* (22 December 1912), 24.

40. "Photo Plays," *DMN* (31 January 1912), 8; Family ads, *DMN* (19 April 1912), 14, and (21 April 1912), 6; Star ad, *DMRL* (21 April 1912), 5.

41. "Photo Plays," *DMN* (18 February 1912), 6. It was not unusual for most motion picture theaters to offer a daily change of programs and a smaller number to change their programs three or four times a week—as my research on cities such as Toledo, Rochester, and Lynn attests—but the biweekly programs of the Colonial in Des Moines were unusual and most closely resembled those of the Lyric in Minneapolis, managed by S. L. Rothapfel, beginning in September 1911.

42. Colonial ads, *DMN* (30 April 1912), 7, and (14 May 1912), 2.

43. "'Spectator's' Comments," *NYDM* (8 November 1911), 26. The argument that many theaters had only one projector—which mandated a break, an illustrated song, or a vaudeville act between reels, and thus discouraged the screening of multiple-reel films—seems far from tenable in Des Moines, as elsewhere. The Casino used at least two "Powers machines"; Casino ad, *DMRL* (4 December 1912), 4. Although unmentioned, the Colonial probably used two projectors because it consistently stressed its "continuous" programs and, in early 1911, could afford to install the only "Plate Glass Mirror Screen . . . Outside of New York and Chicago"; Colonial ad, *DMN* (17 January 1911), 3. Notably, the Family Theater did not add a second projector until the summer of 1913; "Family Reopens," *DMRL* (24 July 1913), 3.

44. Colonial ads, *DMN* (3 January 1912), 5, and (11 January 1912), 6.

45. Family ads, *DMN* (21 April 1912), 6, and (5 May 1912), 6.

46. Family ad, *DMN* (27 January 1913), 6.

47. Unique ads, *DMN* (21 January 1913), 5, and (26 January 1913), 6.

48. Quinn, "Distribution," 45–46.

49. For a good summary account of the "state rights" distribution system, see ibid., 48–49. Briefly, in "state rights" distribution, a person or firm purchased the right to license a film's exhibition within a particular territory—at legitimate, vaudeville, and/or picture theaters. This differed from "roadshowing," in which a distributor took a film "on the road," renting a legitimate theater on a percentage-of-the-gross basis—a practice made familiar by Monopol's distribution of Milano's *Dante's Inferno* in 1911–12 and by Famous Players' distribution of *Queen Elizabeth* in 1912–13.

50. Berchel ad, *DMN* (14 September 1912), 5. *Queen Elizabeth* first played at Powers Theatre in Chicago, in the middle of August; Famous Players ad, *MPW* (17 August 1912), 679. In much bigger cities such as Cleveland, the film did not open until late October; "Preliminary Peeps at the Peep Shows" and Colonial ad, *CL* (27 October 1912), M3, M4.

51. Colonial ads, *DMN* (2 November 1912), 2, and (8 November 1912), 10; Namur's University Place ad, *DMN* (4 February 1913), 6. To be sure, "state rights" companies struggled throughout 1912 and 1913, and Famous Players even "flirted with bankruptcy in early 1913"; Quinn, "Distribution," 49.

52. Colonial ad, *DMRL* (2 May 1913), 12; "Great Demand to See Satan," *DMN* (8 May 1913), 8.

53. "The Movies," *DMN* (25 May 1913), 6; Colonial ads, *DMN* (1 June 1913), 6, and (29 June 1913), 6. Although the Colonial booked Éclair's *Balaoo* along with *Zigomar III*, French crime thrillers were conspicuous by their absence in Des Moines theater ads. The first of Gaumont's *Fantomas* series was prominently advertised in Cedar Rapids, in early September 1913, but not once was there mention of any of the five titles of the series in the capital city; Crystal ad, *Cedar Rapids Republican* (7 September 1913), 3.

54. "Mary Pickford Is at Colonial," *DMN* (21 September 1913), 6; Colonial ads, *DMN* (25 September 1913), 10, and (9 October 1913), 10.

55. Quinn, "Distribution," 50. First Famous Players and then Warner's began advertising the extent of their arrangements with "state rights" distributors that fall; "Famous Players' Regular Releases," *MPN* (2 August 1913), 31; "P. A. Powers to Provide Exclusive Films," *MPN* (9 August 1913), 15; Famous Players ads, *MPW* (28 August 1913), 854–55, and (4 October 1913), 97; Warner's ad, *MPN* (25 October 1913), 10. Kansas City Feature Film was supposed to supply Famous Players features to Iowa, but contracts with Des Moines theaters seem to have been irregular up to November 1913 and then nonexistent until March 1914. According to my own research, Famous Players did lead the way, closely followed by Warner's, in such cities as Boston, Lynn, and Cleveland; yet Warner's led the way in cities other than Des Moines and as disparate as Lowell, Rochester, and Toledo.

56. Star ad, *DMRL* (19 March 1913), 9.

57. Berchel ad, *DMRL* (27 July 1913), 6; Berchel and Colonial ads, *DMN* (8 November 1913), 2.

58. Palace ads, *DMN* (24 October 1913), 10, and (6 November 1913), 10.

59. Quinn, "Distribution," 50.

60. Berchel ads, *DMRL* (19 April 1914), 6, and (17 May 1914), 6. *Les Misérables* was first advertised by Eclectic Film in *MPW* (5 April 1913) 11; in July, it appeared at the New Grand Central in St. Louis "with great success"; James McQuade, "Chicago Letter," *MPW* (2 August 1913), 520; in September through November, it ran for a record twelve weeks at the Tremont Temple in Boston. Similarly, *Traffic in Souls* opened for multiple-week runs in Cleveland and Boston in December 1913. Several other big French features also appeared that spring: Pathé's *Germinal* at the Star, and Film d'Art's *The Three Musketeers* (eight parts), in an extremely rare sighting, first at the Garden and then at the Berchel; Star ad, *DMRL* (22 March 1914), 6; Garden ad, *DMRL* (17 May 1914), 8; Berchel ad, *DMRL* (24 May 1914), 6.

61. See the Star's half-page ad, *DMN* (24 May 1914), 7. *Cleopatra* ran for two weeks at the Duchess Theatre in Cleveland, beginning on 24 December 1912.

62. "Black Cat Opens Tomorrow," *DMN* (30 January 1914), 8; Black Cat ad (with a weekly list of film programs), *DMN* (7 March 1914), 2.

63. "Book Big Films Solid Week Now," *DMN* (31 December 1913), 5.

64. Another regular weekly feature of the variety format, of course, was the newsreel. For further studies of the first serials, see Shelley Stamp, *Movie-Struck Girls: Women and Motion Picture Culture after the Nickelodeon* (Princeton, N.J.: Princeton University Press, 2000), 102–53; Barbara Wilinsky, "Flirting with Kathlyn: Creating the Mass Audience," in *Hollywood Goes Shopping*, ed. David Desser and Garth S. Jowett (Minneapolis: University of Minnesota Press, 2000), 3–56; and Ben Singer, *Melodrama*

and Modernity: Early Sensational Cinema and Its Contexts (New York: Columbia University Press 2001), 221–87.

65. The residential and east side theaters that often placed ads in the *News* set their ticket prices at 10 cents rather than 5 cents (although Namur's theaters charged 10 cents on weekends), perhaps because their customers saved a nickel by walking rather than having to ride a trolley downtown. Vaudeville houses like the Majestic and Orpheum had admission prices of, respectively, 10 to 25 cents and 10 to 75 cents; legitimate theaters like the Berchel, respectively, 15 to 50 cents and 25 cents to $1.00.

66. In February 1914, there was an unsuccessful attempt to institute a uniform ticket price of 10 cents for all motion picture theaters; "Movie Men Try to Boost Price," *DMN* (23 February 1914), 2. Even as late as 1914, then, relatively poor moviegoers still could attend a half dozen, first-class downtown theaters for the cost of a nickel. Evidence from Denver suggests that working-class families made "the moving picture show allowance" as "much a part of the expense for necessities as . . . the rent and the grocery bill"; see the remarks of the head of the Neighborhood House in "Nickels for the Theatres vs. Nickels for Bread," *NYMT* (12 May 1912), IV.2, 2.

67. The first ad for the Casino did not appear in the *News* until 15 January 1913, more than a month after its opening.

68. "New Garden Theater Will Open This Afternoon," "Builders and Furnishers of the New Garden Theater and Odd Fellows Building. The Finest in Iowa," and Garden Theater ad, *DMRL* (2 May 1914).

69. The quoted phrase is from David Hulfish, "Motography: The Salesman," in *Motion-Picture Work* (1911; New York: Arno Press, 1970), 112.

70. "The Movies," *DMN* (11 November 1912), 2.

71. "The Movies," *DMN* (12 November 1912), 1; "Many 'Dolor's Clubs' Named after This Beauty of the Movies," *DMN* (12 November 1912), 8.

72. "The Movies," *DMN* (13 November 1912), 2; Gertrude Price, "'Alkali Ike' and 'Broncho Bill' Tear Things Up Something Fierce, but 'The Old Sheriff' Jerks 'Em Short with His Six-Shooter," *DMN* (16 November 1912), 3; Gertrude Price, "Nervy as Ever to Act the Most Daring Things Ever Seen on Stage!—Heroine of Movies," *DMN* (17 November 1912), 7; "The Movies," *DMN* (20 November 1912), 7.

73. For a more extensive examination of Gertrude Price's writings, see Richard Abel, "Fan Discourse in the Heartland: Gertrude Price and the *Des Moines News,* 1912–1914," in a forthcoming special issue of *Film History,* edited by Shelley Stamp and Amelie Hastie.

74. "Daily News Reporter Writes from Great California Studios Where They Make Your Wild West Pictures," *DMN* (1 February 1913), 6.

75. "The Movies," *Cleveland Press* (11 November 1912), 1, 4; "The Movies," *Toledo News-Bee* (11 November 1912), 1, 6. In her research on Lois Weber at the Museum of Modern Art, Shelley Stamp recently found a clipping of Price's story on Weber from the *New Orleans Statesman;* the same story appeared almost simultaneously in the *Des Moines News.*

76. Baldasty, *E. W. Scripps and the Business of Newspapers,* 15–20. The Scripps-McRae League was contracted to the United Press Association, which had gathered Scripps's telegraphic services into a single nationwide entity in 1906, so Price's stories would have been available to its more than 200 client papers as well; Baldasty, *E. W. Scripps and the Business of Newspapers,* 21–22.

77. Not until the spring of 1913 was a syndicated service (in New York) suppos-edly supplying "Motion Picture Pages" to subscribing newspapers; Jas. S. McQuade, "Chicago Letter," *MPW* (19 April 1913), 265; Syndicate Publishing Co. ad, *MPN* (8 November 1913), 8.

78. That Price's stories appeared so often in the *Des Moines News* may be due to the presence of Sue McNamera as the paper's "dramatic editor and special feature writer," for McNamera seemed to share Price's interest in travel and interviewing "celebrities"; see A. C. Hasselbearth, "Women Writers of American Press," *Editor and Publisher and Journalist* (6 December 1913), 476.

79. "The Movies," *DMN* (22 November 1912), 4, and (4 February 1913), 5.

80. "The Movies," *DMN* (21 November 1912), 4, and (3 December 1912), 10. The Golden was an independent theater, so probably this "three-reel" French film was an Éclair crime thriller released in 1912, such as *Zigomar II* or *The Mystery of the Bridge of Notre Dame*.

81. Initially, this listing included downtown theaters (the Casino, Family, and Unique), as well as those on the city's northwest and east sides (the University Place, Cupid, and Elite); "The Movies," *DMN* (23 March 1913), 12.

82. "At the Moving Picture Playhouses," *DMRL* (9 February 1913), 7; "Moving Picture News," *DMRL* (23 March 1913), 8; "News of Photoplays and Photoplayers," *DMRL* (1 June 1913), 7.

83. "Movie Programmes," *DMRL* (31 August 1913), 6.

84. Significantly, the Colonial advertised its initial big features in the *Register and Leader* rather than the *News*, suggesting that the targeted audience was more middle class than before. In its Sunday page devoted to motion pictures (perhaps the first in the country), the *Cleveland Leader* several times reported favorably on the continuing protest in the trade press against using *movies* because "it harms the business"; "Photo-Plays and Players," *CL* (10 December 1911), S5; and "Protest against Use of Name, 'Movie,'" *CL* (20 October 1912), S5.

85. The crucial study of the early star system is Richard deCordova's *Picture Personalities: The Emergence of the Star System in America* (Urbana: University of Illinois Press, 1990).

86. "At the Moving Picture Playhouses," *DMRL* (9 February 1913), 7; "Motion Picture Celebrities in the Public Eye," *DMRL* (18 March 1913), 8.

87. Gertrude Price, "King Baggott Detests Sentimental Stuff; Longs to Be Regular Dyed-in-the-Wool Rip Roarin' Jake," *DMN* (7 December 1912), 2; Gertrude Price, "Mary Fuller? Why, of Course, You've Met Mary! And Such a Deep-Dyed Pessimist Is This Slip-of-a-Girl Who Likes Witches, Old People and Poor Folks Most," *DMN* (28 December 1912), 4; Gertrude Price, "Funniest, Fattest Man in the Movies Is John Bunny Who Plays 'Mr. Pickwick,'" *DMN* (29 December 1912), 4; "The Airman's Hoodoo Is What Mabel of the Movies Calls Her Pretty Self," *DMN* (4 March 1913), 7.

88. See the large ad announcing the contest, *DMN* (10 February 1913), 3; and the equally large ad announcing the winners, *DMN* (17 February 1913), 7. Later the *News* also ran a weeklong series of portrait caricatures of several stars, beginning with John Bunny; "Who's Who in the Movies Caricatured by Higgins," *DMN* (12 October 1913), 12.

89. On later fiction tie-ins related to serials, see Singer, *Melodrama and Modernity*, 269–87.

90. Family ad, *DMN* (8 March 1911), 13.

91. For a valuable history of the early development of movie fan magazines, see Kathryn H. Fuller, *At the Picture Show: Small-Town Audiences and the Creation of Movie Fan Culture* (Washington, D.C.: Smithsonian Institution Press, 1996), 136.

92. "Our Saturday Short Story," *DMN* (9 August 1913), 6.

93. "Movie Stars Who Play Leads in Western Dramas at Unique Theater," *DMN* (12 December 1912), 7; "The Great Spirit Took Mona, But in This Girl She Still Lives," *DMN* (6 February 1913), 12.

94. "Runs, Rides, Rows," *DMN* (16 April 1913), 6.

95. In Youngstown, "Bullets" Anderson was so popular that, from fall 1911 through early 1912, one downtown theater could use his name and photo to promote Essanay westerns as headliners on its Sunday programs; "J. Max Anderson," *Youngstown Vindicator* (15 October 1911), 14; Princess ads, *Youngstown Vindicator* (22 October 1911), 17, and (17 December 1911), 24.

96. Early in 1912, American chose the *News* as one of fifty dailies across the country in which to publish "'Flying A' stories" so that people would subsequently "want to see them." Although only three stories ever appeared, they suggest that "Flying A" films circulated and may have been popular in Des Moines, even if no theater advertised them. See the American Film ad, *MPW* (16 March 1912), 980–81; and the first story, "The Grub Stake Mortgage—A Moving Picture Short Story of Western Life," *DMN* (17 January 1912), 10.

97. "Here They Are! Snapshots from 'Wounded Knee,' Where Our 'Movie' Experts Are," *DMN* (23 October 1913), 4; Price, "Indian Braves Adopt Heap Big 'Movie' Man and Call Him 'Wanbli Wiscasa,'" *DMN* (2 November 1913), 4. See also Charles J. Ver Halen, "Bringing the Old West Back," *MPN* (22 November 1913), 19–20.

98. James McQuade, "Chicago Letter," *MPW* (7 February 1914), 660, and (14 March 1914), 1388–1389; "'Buffalo Bill' Picture Shown," *MPW* (March 1913), 1370. For a good discussion of this film's production, distribution, and exhibition, see Joy S. Kasson, *Buffalo Bill's Wild West: Celebrity, Memory, and Popular History* (New York: Hill and Wang, 2000), 257–63.

99. Price, "'Billie Unafraid,'" 7; Gertrude Price, "Stunning Mary Pickford—Only 19 Now!—Quits $10,000 'Movies' Career to Shake Her Golden Locks as a Belasco Star," *DMN* (9 January 1913), 7; "Movie Queen Is Alice Joyce," *DMN* (1 March 1913), 1; "Live with Flowers and Grow Beautiful, Says Girl," *DMN* (29 November 1913), 5.

100. "Bored by the World, Actress Goes to 'Movies' to Get Thrills!" *DMN* (17 March 1913), 8.

101. Gertrude Price, "Movie Beauty Risks Life to Put Thrill in the Pictures," *DMN* (7 February 1913), 6.

102. Gertrude Price, "No One Will Ride Pinto but Dainty, Daring Clara," *DMN* (27 March 1913), 6.

103. "Face Is Fortune of Tallest Picture Player Who Sheds Tears for Sake of Art," *DMN* (26 march 1913), 4.

104. Price, "No One Will Ride Pinto but Dainty, Daring Clara," 6.

105. 'No Thrill to Her to Be 'Killed' 365 Times a Year," *DMN* (24 December 1913), 8.

106. "Daring Girl Rider Coming," *DMN* (27 July 1912), 3; "Summer Amusements," *DMN* (28 July 1912), 12.

107. Gertrude Price, "Charming Little Woman Runs 'Movie' Business by Herself, and Makes Big Success," *DMN* (9 February 1913), 2; "Lucky Thirteen Word Proves to Be a New Money Making Position," *DMN* (15 May 1913), 8; Gertrude Price, "Sad Endings Are All Right, Says This Woman Director," *DMN* (27 September 1913), 5.

108. Like most Scripps papers, the *News* made "a particular effort at providing content of interest to working-class women; Baldasty, *E. W. Scripps and the Business of Newspapers*, 143. See also "Des Moines Women Found in All Fields of Labor," *Des Moines News* (7 July 1907), 9; "Women Are Rapidly Taking the Jobs That Belong to Men," *Des Moines News* (6 October 1907), Sunday Supplement: 3. This sense of a targeted audience is more than speculation, given the many studies of young women at the turn of the last century, sometimes in relation to new amusements; see, for instance, Kathy Peiss, *Cheap Amusements: Working Women and Leisure in Turn-of-the-Century New York* (Philadelphia: Temple University Press, 1986); Elizabeth Wilson, *The Sphinx in the City: Urban Life, the Control of Disorder, and Women* (Berkeley and Los Angeles: University of California Press, 1991); Lauren Rabinovitz, *For the Love of Pleasure: Women, Movies, and Culture in Turn-of-the-Century Chicago* (New Brunswick, N.J.: Rutgers University Press, 1998); Stamp, *Movie-Struck Girls*.

109. In one of her last signed stories, Price explicitly described the "wonderful field which the moving picture has opened" as a "great new field for women folk"—from stars and lesser actors to writers and filmmakers—where a woman's "originality . . . her perseverance and her brains are coming to be recognized on the same plane as [a] man's." Gertrude Price, "Sees the Movies as Great New Field for Women Folk," *Toledo News-Bee* (30 March 1914), 14. That this story was not printed in the *News* demands further investigation. For especially relevant studies of the New Woman, see Lois Rudnick, "The New Woman," in *1915: The Cultural Moment,* ed. Adele Heller and Lois Rudnick (New Brunswick, N.J.: Rutgers University Press, 1991), 69–81; Susan Glenn, "Introduction," in *Female Spectacle: The Theatrical Roots of Modern Feminism* (Cambridge, Mass.: Harvard University Press, 2000), 1–8; and Singer, *Melodrama and Modernity,* 241–53.

110. "Suffragettes See Parade Picture," *DMN* (25 June 1912), 5; "*Votes For Women* in Picture Play," *DMN* (27 June 1912), 5. For more information on *Votes For Women,* see Stamp, *Movie-Struck Girls,* 175–79.

111. Gertrude Price, "A Day with General Jones and Her Army of 'Hikers' on Their Way to the Capitol," *DMN* (23 February 1913), 3.

112. "Western Girl You Love in the 'Movies' Is a Sure Enough Suffrager," *DMN* (11 February 1913), 3. Indeed, Price acknowledged women in the industry as political figures, promoting the early 1914 election of Lois Weber and Laura Oakley as mayor and police chief, respectively, of the newly incorporated Universal City; Gertrude Price, "Only Movie Players Live in This Town," *Toledo News-Bee* (6 January 1914), 13. This story, too, was not printed in the *News.*

113. The secretary of the city's interchurch council had used the phrase in explaining a lack of attendance at Sunday night services; "Des Moines Is Going Movie Mad Says the Rev. J. W. Graves," *DMN* (2 November 1913), 8. Another sign of "movie madness" was the series of "Adolf and Osgar" cartoons that ran for several weeks in the *News,* from "A Movie Actor Must Take All Kinds of Risks to Produce a Thriller," *DMN* (28 April 1913), 6, to "Osgar Pirates the Death Scene in *Queen Elizabeth,*" *DMN* (14 May 1913), 6.

8

DIGGING THE FINEST POTATOES
FROM THEIR ACRE

Government Film Exhibition
in Rural Ontario, 1917–1934

CHARLES TEPPERMAN

We live in the day of the scientist and the expert, and he who closes
his ears to their advice will never dig the finest potatoes from his acre.
HUGO MÜNSTERBERG[1]

When London's branch of the Ontario Vegetable Growers Association met one January evening in 1917, it was treated to a novel feature of the province's information apparatus. "Vegetable Growers See Work in Movies," proclaimed the *London Advertiser,* which went on to describe an audience with both ears *and* eyes wide open: "Grow More Potatoes at Home Is Advice of Expert." The unnamed film showed farmers in Ontario maximizing their yield of onions, tomatoes, celery, and lettuce, as well as the aforementioned potatoes:

> The pictures were taken under the direction of the Ontario Government for educational purposes in order to teach vegetable growers the best methods of production.
>
> S. C. Johnson of the vegetable branch of the Ontario Agricultural Department operated the picture machine and in detail explained the different sections of the film . . .
>
> It is the first time that pictures of this nature have been shown in the city, and the inauguration of the scheme was made the subject of many complimentary remarks by the large number present.[2]

These films were only the beginning of a program that would be carried out on an extensive scale in the future, bringing similar pictures to all corners of the province. Indeed, by the time London's vegetable growers had been treated to these fine films about produce, railway cars fitted with agricultural displays and dubbed "Better Farming Specials" were already crisscrossing the province. The trains carried "everything, even a moving picture machine, which give some very interesting illustrations of advanced methods in various

lines of farming. . . . Evening meetings are held in halls which have been secured, and here the movies entertain as well as instruct."[3]

Entertain and instruct could have been the motto of the Ontario Motion
Picture Bureau (OMPG), the government agency formed to manage the
province's film operations. Between 1917 and 1934, the OMPB organized
film production for a variety of government departments and agencies, and
distributed these films in both urban and rural settings. It was the rural and
nontheatrical distribution of these films, however, that was most actively pur-
sued by the OMPB.[4] Established during a state of heightened wartime activity, the province of Ontario was clearly very interested in "digging the finest
potatoes from its acre." "All eyes turn now to the Canadian Farmer," exhorted
a government press campaign, "for he can render the Empire special service
in this sternest year of the war."[5] Films about vegetable growing, home gar-
dening, and other progressive farming techniques complemented home-
front propaganda of the period.

But the government's interest in film went far beyond potatoes and wartime necessity. The OMPB not only outlived its wartime origins by more than
a decade but also demonstrated, from the beginning, a conviction that motion pictures could act as more than mere disseminators of information. By
adopting motion pictures to entertain and instruct rural audiences, the
province hoped to capitalize on the cinema's perceived powers as a means of
progressive and scientific education; movies were thought to have a particular capacity for getting inside the heads of their spectators. This use of motion
pictures might seem surprising, since the social function of movies in North
American society was still a highly contested subject at this time. For many
governments and social reformers, the explosion in numbers of nickelodeon
theaters and the huge popularity of movies among the urban masses were
cause for some alarm. But there were also progressives who hoped to harness
cinema's powers of "visualization" for more productive and educational ends.[6]

The "visualization" in film of a modern, scientific countryside, I will
argue, was one of the principal and sustaining features of the OMPB's film
operations. In presenting vegetable growers with instructional films, the
government not only was cultivating a more efficient farmer but also was circulating an ideal image of that farmer. From the mind's eye of the government to the mind's eye of the country dweller, and then to his actions: this
concept of "visualization" was one of a variety of scientific and pseudoscientific theories that provided a justification for adopting the new, untested, and
expensive technology of motion pictures in rural Ontario. But since an examination of the OMPB's efforts to *instruct* tells only one side of the story, I
will also discuss how the bureau worked to *entertain* its country dwellers. In
some ways this function was closely linked with the bureau's educational role,
but at other times it could be seen as weakening the propagandistic force of
its films, giving the OMPB something of a split personality. In fact, in addi-

tion to producing instructional films, the OMPB also became a major nontheatrical distributor of commercial films, claiming in 1926 to be the "the largest non-theatrical distributors on this continent and, in fact, in the world."[7] Though it is not possible to discuss the full extent of the OMPB's activities, it is important to consider how the films it distributed were exhibited and received by rural and small-town audiences. Empirical evidence of film spectatorship and reception is always hard to come by, but small-town newspapers can provide us with some information about who saw the bureau's films, and what they thought of them.

Finally, I hope that this investigation will shed some light on the still obscure early history of nontheatrical film exhibition. The Ontario Motion Picture Bureau was not alone in its early foray into instructional and nontheatrical motion picture use. American federal, state, and local agencies were also experimenting with educational and nontheatrical films, and by the early 1920s a movement for "visual education" was in full swing.[8] Visual education inherited the reformer's optimistic vision of films as a force social change, but entertainment and instruction persisted as the unstable dual objectives in many of these agencies. An examination of the OMPB's films and exhibition contexts can suggest some preliminary themes and directions for future inquiry into the motion picture's instrumental use during this period.

Mechanical Brains?

As we have seen, the government of Ontario was commissioning and exhibiting films on a small scale as early as January 1917. The following May, the province's film operations were consolidated under the supervision of the provincial treasurer in the department responsible for film censorship and amusement taxation. Among the new bureau's first acts was the purchase of fifty Pathescope portable film projectors. These hand-cranked projectors did not require electricity and used the 28mm nonflammable safety films that could be legally exhibited without fireproof projection booths. As both of these features attest, one of the bureau's primary goals was to exhibit its films in nontheatrical situations, which included churches, schools, and community halls in rural communities.[9] These projectors were made available to the government's "agricultural representatives," specialists (and usually graduates of an agricultural college) who were responsible for bringing scientific methods and equipment to the farmers in their assigned county. Though records of the agricultural representatives show that their use of motion pictures varied in frequency and technique from county to county, they clearly provided the most regular outlet of bureau-produced films among rural audiences.[10]

Ontario's modern agricultural and industrial technologies went hand in hand with modern bureaucratic and communications strategies. Despite—

or perhaps because of—the chaotic nature of the rural populace and their social, educational and cultural interests, the government's use of film was grounded in a scientific rhetoric of applied psychology and progressive theories of education. Ontario's treasurer, the Honorable T. W. McGarry, called the OMPB's films "educational propaganda" and lauded their success in promoting modern farm practices: "Through the instrumentality of these moving picture shows, which explain to the farmer the manner in which he should proceed with the different operations in connection with farm life, the Department of Agriculture is providing a wonderful object lesson in each particular art of agriculture."[11] While this is not exactly the same concept of propaganda that we are familiar with today, the term *instrumentality* implies that in taking up films as a means of reaching and influencing citizens, the government may have hoped to exploit features of the cinema that were much commented upon by psychologists and progressive reformers of the period: that is, the alleged powers of cinema to influence and persuade certain audiences. Such powers were seen as either detrimental or productive depending on their exploitation. Critics feared the harmful psychological effects of movies that showed violent, lascivious, and criminal themes, leading some to call nickelodeons "schools for crime" and establish review or censorship boards to protect weak minds. The psychologist William Healy voiced a specific concern with the effects of moving pictures in his 1915 study, *The Individual Delinquent,* when he wrote, "The strength of the powers of visualization is to be deeply reckoned with when considering the springs of criminality. . . . It is the mental representation of some sort of pictures of himself or others in the criminal act that leads the delinquent onward in his path."[12]

But some reformers *also* speculated that these "powers of visualization" could be deployed for educational and uplifting purposes. For example, Hugo Münsterberg, one of the founders of applied psychology and an early theorist of film, pointed out that the cinema's technological capabilities rendered it a much more potent medium for conveying stories and information than the traditional theater. Münsterberg found that the key to this power lay in the cinema's capacity for directing viewers' attention and shaping their emotional responses in ways that are much more forceful than dramatic live performances. Echoing Healy, Münsterberg cautions that "it is evident that such a penetrating influence must be fraught with dangers. The more vividly the impressions force themselves on the mind, the more easily must they become the starting points for imitation and other motor responses." But, as Münsterberg also points out:

> While the sources of danger cannot be overlooked, the social reformer ought to focus his interest still more on the tremendous influences for good which may be exerted by the moving pictures. The fact that millions are daily under the spell of the performances on the screen is established. The high degree of their suggestibility during those hours in the dark house may be taken for granted.

> Hence any wholesome influence emanating from the photoplay must have an incomparable power for the remolding and upbuilding of the national soul.[13]

Münsterberg's remarks are representative of many who wished to turn the moving picture's instrumentality toward more uplifting and educational purposes. But they also reflect the variety of elements that were thought to contribute to the cinema's power: for some, it was simply the cinema's ability to *show* things; for others, including Münsterberg, particular elements of film form (for example, the close-up) and narration (drama or comedy) were necessary; finally, many noted the context in which films were shown ("those hours in the dark house") as an important contributing factor.

Despite the lack of a coherent theory or scientifically proven method for using films, by about 1915 many educators were recommending the use of moving pictures in schools. Proponents cited the medium's educational efficiency in support of an "economy of time" doctrine that sought new ways of streamlining an increasingly crowded curriculum and was central to pedagogical debates during this period.[14] It is important to note, however, that like many other reform-minded thinkers of the day, Münsterberg also believed some segments of the population—particularly women, children, immigrants, and country dwellers—to be more susceptible than others to the motion picture's influence.[15] By 1920 a growing number of trade journals about visual education continued to focus on films for children, immigrants, and farmers. A recurring advertisement for the DeVry portable motion picture projector that appeared in *Reel and Slide Magazine* through 1918 gives us a telling indication of the field's conventional wisdom at that time. An illustration shows the portable projector casting a film (*From Grass to Glass*) before a room of captivated schoolchildren; the text beneath the picture explains:

> The first essential in pedagogy, as recognized by the modern educator, is to create in the student a reliable mental visualization of the subject matter of the text. The stimulation of a true mental image at once so vivid as to induce the student to discard any erroneous preconceived ideas he may possess on the subject and so lasting as to insure its retention against possible contradictory influences of later environment has heretofore been dependent on the teacher's ability to draw word pictures. But with the entrance of motion pictures into the educational field the teacher is enabled to give his class a vision of things as they really are.[16]

While this explanation gives a reasonable account of the educational justification for using films, the ad's caption is more blunt. In large letters above the children's heads it asks simply, "Mechanical Brains?" Such an image can give us some idea of what McGarry understood to be the "instrumentality" of the OMPB's "educational propaganda": films could discipline a spectator's mind and rationalize his actions.

Even as the motion picture's powers of visualization were thought to be a potent force for educating farmers about agriculture, a link between the Ontario Motion Picture Bureau's films and their *political* "instrumentality" becomes evident following the provincial elections of October 1919. This election saw the defeat of the province's traditional political parties at the hands of independent candidates united under the banner of the United Farmers of Ontario (UFO). The UFO was, according to its leadership, "an organization whose aim was to provide the farmers of Ontario with means for self-education, not only in matters pertaining to the business of production, as other societies had done, but also along broad lines of citizenship, the study of public questions, and the giving to the rural people a means of making their opinions felt in these matters"[17] The UFO brought with it an even more explicit acknowledgment of the "progressive" potential of moving pictures, as a letter sent to Ontario's new attorney general from a UFO member illustrates: "This wonderful method of visual education and information, if rightly controlled and utilized, possesses potentialities for individualizing and Canadianizing our whole provincial development."[18]

But the relationship between the OMPB's film productions and propaganda is set out most explicitly in a 1921 letter from Filmcraft president Irwin Proctor to then provincial treasurer Peter Smith, under whose supervision the OMPB operated.[19] Proctor bluntly explains the great benefits of using moving pictures for political propaganda, including their ability to reach a larger audience than public speakers alone and, more important, their transmission of undetected messages: "Just imagine the effect of propaganda of this kind being hammered into the entire population week after week. I think that to explain your policy and demonstrate your accomplishments before the people in such a way that they do not know that it is being done, with any purpose in view, is the most effective and surest way in the world to create a favorable impression with the consequent effect at the next election."[20] If this sounds insidious, it seems even more so when Proctor reinforces the secretive nature of producing such films: "The political part of it is something about which there need be no correspondence or discussion but it would be working for you every day of the year, and would be a great help to the progressive movement not only in Ontario, but all over the Dominion."[21] In addition to the visualization of educational messages, the OMPB was also considering the political efficacy of undetected messages; the UFO may have promoted "self-education" and a voice for the province's rural people, but moving pictures could give this government a powerful tool for shaping this education and voice.

Government Films and Lessons

It is tempting to dismiss all this talk of propaganda after looking at the OMPB's film output. By the standards of later and more famous examples of propaganda (like Sergei Eisenstein's *Old and New* [1929] and Leni Riefenstahl's *Triumph of the Will* [1935] or present-day political advertising), the OMPB films appear somewhat clumsy and bland. But there are plenty of reasons to suggest that many OMPB films, both before and after this letter to Smith, were engaged in exactly the kinds of propaganda Proctor sets out. The films produced by the bureau attended to a wide variety of activities in rural life, including practical farming, leisure, and social hygiene.[22] One type of film it distributed was the specialized instructional film, which showed farmers how to make the most productive use of their land and effort. Films like *Celery Culture* (c. 1919), *Successful Farm Methods* (c. 1922), and *Spraying and Dusting Fruit Trees* (c. 1919) offered spectators practical scientific advice, usually originating from the Ontario Agricultural College.[23] Other films suggested how new technologies like tractors or spraying machines could be used to greater advantage on Ontario farms. *Why Not Use a Tractor?* (c. 1919) corresponded to a provincewide initiative encouraging farmers to use tractors to increase labor efficiency during the postwar manpower shortage. To encourage their use, the Department of Agriculture purchased tractors, which could then be rented out to farmers. An intertitle in the film reads: "Have you a tractor? If not, your Agricultural Representative will arrange to do your work at a moderate charge."

Films about the annual Ontario Plowing Match also promoted the use of new farm technologies, but did so in a more festive and public setting. At plowing matches, farmers from Ontario and beyond gathered in very large numbers (20,000 in 1917) to watch or participate in competitions of farming skill. These matches also provided a venue for demonstrations of new tractors and other farm machinery, all set in a community context similar to a county fair.[24] Like an Olympics for agricultural skill, the plowing matches reflected the progressive farmer's interest in refining, testing, and maximizing the productive capacity of agricultural workers. But films about these plowing matches also suggest a Taylorization of agricultural work: *Turning the Furrow* (1920), a one-reel film about the province's eighth annual match, breaks down and demonstrates, through shots of various scales and angles, the different steps involved in plowing a field (making scratch, the first heavy round, and forming the crown), providing an analysis and visualization of the scientific method of plowing. A message about the farmer's duty is expressed in an extremely direct intertitle that reinforces the analogy between agricultural and industrial work:

Good workmanship is as necessary on the farm as in the factory.

To be a good citizen you must learn to improve your own work.

See Government films and—

Apply their lessons.

The equivalence presented here between factory and farm clearly spells out the government's interest in accelerating the technological rationalization of country life; moving pictures stand at the juncture of this meeting between industry and countryside, simultaneously foregrounding economic productivity and modern efficiency as the principal requirements of "good citizenship."

Indeed, films played a significant part in the Ontario government's attempt to harmonize country life with modern technology. Moving pictures were only one of several modernizing technologies that, with government assistance, were radiating outward from cities to the countryside. Aside from the province's train cars—the "Better Farming Specials"—which carried moving pictures and scientific displays as media for disseminating scientific advice, the government was also involved in other aspects of the electrification and industrialization of rural life. To take as a specific example the town of Parkhill, an inspection of the community newspaper in 1917 reveals that modern technology was advancing steadily on rural life: citizens were discussing the cost of bringing electricity to the town (19 April); the agricultural representative was making tractors available for local use (21 June); a drive "over good roads" to the resort town Grand Bend was named a "splendid" summer excursion (12 July); the province established a "Canning Centre" to rationalize the conservation of food (13 September); and before the end of the year the OMPB had made a film of this center's operations and displayed it in Parkhill (8 November, 7 December).[25] Clearly, modern technologies (electricity, paved roads, tractors, moving pictures) were rapidly spreading through the countryside, with the government spurring their progress.

Some of the OMPB's films directly addressed the countryside's integration of modern technology. *The King's Highway* (c. 1922)—which corresponds closely to a subject proposed by Proctor in his memo on propaganda—shows how the rapid adoption of motor vehicles in Ontario necessitated the rationalization of the province's transportation network: one intertitle reads, "Of all the influences for the economic and social advancement of a country there is none more important than the improvement of roads in the rural districts." While one aspect of this project was directed toward lowering the cost of transporting produce from the countryside, "We must also consider the social aspects of country life which react directly on the economic side, making farm life less isolated and more tolerable; a good road stops rural depopulation and increases production." The easy flow of people (and technology) back and forth, between city and country, was seen to benefit attempts at rationalizing country life. The cooperation between these spaces is idealized in the film's final title, which shows an animated drawing of city and country dwellers shaking hands over the caption: "Prosperity." From generating educational propaganda to ordering the movements of Ontario's rural folk, it is clear from OMPB documents and films that its operations were founded on a belief that films could "visualize" and thus help to produce a harmonious and efficient countryside.

But accompanying this faith in the motion picture's instrumentality, there is also a different and perhaps conflicting purpose for the films. "Happiness and recreation are necessary to a contented rural population," one intertitle in *The King's Highway* reads, "which in turn is essential to a prosperous Ontario." Isn't the film's interest in "happiness and recreation" exemplified by the government's relocation of moving pictures—an urban entertainment form—to nonurban locales? The film's intertitles closely mirror the UFO's declared interest in making rural life more urban, through which they hoped to both stave off rural depopulation and reduce the cultural gulf between city and country. Comparing the exhausting monotony of farmwork to the structured divisions of city life—which allowed time for both production *and* leisure—one UFO publication remarks that "the constant mingling of human beings in urban centres, in whatever condition, has the further effect of sharpening their wits and making the individual dexterous in employing what knowledge he has. The farmer's conclusion is that he himself would be well advised to concentrate less on production, and give more hours to the study of how to live well."[26] Government films could provide both education and leisure, but, perhaps more significantly, they could also provide a taste of modern time and urban stimulus to farmers still chained to seasonal time and organic production.

If conveying information about agricultural issues and promoting more efficient techniques were the OMPB's the primary functions, altering the "social aspects of country life" was also a consideration, and for many spectators this may have been the principal appeal of the bureau's activities. A magazine article published in 1919 illuminates the OMPB's plan for film exhibition in Ontario's countryside as follows:

> It is the primary intention of the Bureau to circuit these [films] mainly in those centres not now served by established movie theatres. It is in line with the basic idea that the programs of these rural meetings have been made more attractive by supplementing the regular showing of educational films with comedy and drama reels, featuring Charlie Chaplin, Mary Pickford, Max Linder and other famous people. . . . There is a sound business reason in this move, for beyond the unquestioned benefits the remote rural residents will derive from these comedy films, there is the result of greatly augmented audiences at these educational meetings, and their increased receptivity to educational influences.[27]

With the motion pictures, agricultural representatives improved country dwellers' lives by bringing city amenities and entertainment to them; but they also allowed the state to convey their message, which in turn encouraged the citizens to increase production and improve their lives.

This dual function of OMPB film distribution in rural Ontario is also reflected in the variety of occasions on which films were exhibited, including patriotic pageants, agricultural meetings, and community holidays. The Bolton Victory Loan Concert, for example, placed films within a context of uplifting and rational recreation; songs and recitations were presented alongside " 'The Prince, Britain's Future King,' 'Prosperity,' a Victory Loan booster, and a comic reel," all "designed to boost the sale of Victory Bonds and . . . help along this great national project."[28] At the meeting of the Meadowvale Farmer's Club, movies were shown following a debate about the agricultural merits of "Ontario vs. The West": "Mr. Carrol of the Department of Agriculture was present and gave moving pictures of farm operations, treatment of grain for smut, medical inspections in public schools, also entertaining features."[29] In Elmbank, "several agricultural and educational films, as well as some of comic nature," were shown as part of a Victoria Day celebration that also included singing, dancing, and copious amounts of ice cream. While movies were likely not the only factor in these cases of "reviving community spirit," their role should not be discounted and would certainly be in line with UFO goals. A report in the local newspaper lauded the event for attracting so many young people: "In these days when we hear so much of 'reviving community spirit' and cultivating social relationships in rural districts an evening such as that spent in the hall at Elmbank concluding the holiday is of particular interest. The building was full to overflowing with young people—true there were gray hairs there, but the youthful mirth of girls and boys leavened all."[30]

But the wide variation in exhibition context, film selection, and audience composition must surely have influenced, if not seriously compromised, the supposed instrumentality of films. Though reformers, bureaucrats, and producers could hope for a suggestible audience, primed for "visualization," these groups did not control the selection and presentation of films once they were in the field. Howard Trueman, the agricultural representative for Grenville County, recalls the strange juxtaposition of speeches, songs, and pictures that took place at some meetings featuring films. At the request of a local minister, Trueman exhibited moving pictures to the community club of Eastman's Corners:

> Since it was around Easter, I thought I'd show *From the Manger to the Cross.* I had one of those old machines you had to reverse and rethread. Between the stations of the cross, the member of the club provided the cover up for the work I was doing with the machine. Between the second and third station of the cross, the local elocutionist recited, "When Father Laid the Carpet on the Stairs." And at the next station, the local orchestra played, "There Ain't No

Fleas on Auntie." I thought it was the most incongruous mixture I'd ever witnessed! But they loved it, all of it.[31]

As these examples attest, the exhibition context of films distributed by the OMPB was determined to a large extent by the tone and composition of their audiences. This situation hardly recalls the kind passive and suggestible audience proposed by Münsterberg or Proctor. Though such entertainment may have improved the social quality of country dwellers' lives and encouraged a general feeling of goodwill toward the government, it is not yet clear that entertainment *and* instruction were the natural result of the OMPB's efforts.

The Handicap: A Rube in Ontario

An effort to master the tension between entertainment and instruction can be found in the OMPB's docudramas about health and social hygiene like *The Handicap* (c. 1920). This film offers an example of the government's efforts to pair instruction with entertainment at the level of the film's formal organization, recalling both Münsterberg's theory and Proctor's practical advice. *The Handicap* parallels Münsterberg's observation that while an actuality or educational film has the potential, in certain contexts, to influence an audience, it is really the photoplay (or fiction film) that is most effective in this respect when utilized correctly.[32] To this end, Münsterberg and Proctor suggest that fiction films be structured around illuminating, uplifting, or (in Proctor's case) political themes to achieve the maximum positive effects on audiences.

The Handicap presents a dramatized account (performed by nonactors) of the medical inspection of rural schoolchildren. The main characters of the film are students with undetected health defects that prevent them from behaving as productive young citizens: Joe's blurry eyesight hinders his studies; George "Easy" Irwin has difficulty with any activities requiring energy or thought; and, George's sister Bessie has toothaches that prevent her from eating properly and playing with her friends. Rather than a straightforwardly didactic film that might document the inspection of anonymous children with actual health problems—such as the OMPB's urban health film *Overcoming Life's Handicap* (c. 1922)—*The Handicap* presents characters acting out these roles. As a result, the film combines a didactic direct address that tells the spectator things with an integrative mode of narration that asks the spectator to identify with particular characters or actions. (At times this latter mode even adopts a subjective point of view that approximates Joe's blurry vision with out-of-focus shots.)

Though several episodes show the schoolchildren in narratively motivated scenes, *The Handicap*'s most pronounced effort to entertain comes in the form of its comic relief. The only farmers to appear in this film (which is concerned primarily with students and school officials) are the parents of George and Bessie Irwin, two children who suffer most from medical neglect. While Mrs. Irwin is depicted as a sensible woman who is concerned about her children, her husband is portrayed in a somewhat comical manner. Indeed, Mr. Irwin seems in appearance and action like a caricature of an old farmer, or, in short, a "rube." "You're the best teacher we've ever had," he says when visited by the concerned educator. "But you're not strict enough. You've got to lambaste 'em and make 'em learn—Beat it into 'em—Why when I was a boy—" To which Mrs. Irwin replies: "You've never so much as laid a hand on one of them in all their lives, John. Now do be sensible." This exchange exposes both an outmoded style of education ("lambaste 'em and make 'em learn") and the kind of reaction the bureau expected from some viewers of the film. In a few deft characterizations, however, the film positions those who might object to the government's modern health and educational policies as old-fashioned rubes, if not doddering fools. Indeed, Mr. Irwin reappears near the end of the film to admire the teacher's "new-fangled ideas" and reprise his comic role. Eventually, his recurring use of phrases like "when I was a boy . . . ," which just sort of trail off, signal a gag ("Now do be sensible") that no longer needs to be fully restated.

Aside from the rhetorical (and comic) function of this characterization, it is also important to note that the "country rube" was a stock character of early cinema and other fictional accounts of modernization. The rube is someone unfamiliar with the appropriate behavior around new urban technology; he is depicted as too ignorant to be "sensible." In Edison's film *Uncle Josh at the Moving Picture Show* (1902), a country rube is shown trying to interact with a series of moving pictures, as though not understanding that they are just projected images. When a film showing an approaching train is cast on the screen, Uncle Josh recoils in terror, demonstrating that he is more naive than the film's actual spectator.[33] As we have seen, Münsterberg also understood rural audiences to be more reactive and more receptive to the effects of moving pictures—they seemed to be easily excitable in a way that urban audiences were not. *The Handicap* comically visualizes an excitable farmer's conversion to "new-fangled ideas," in the process both increasing the film's entertainment value and enhancing the audience's already heightened receptivity.

If these entertaining characterizations and episodes provide one pole of *The Handicap*'s style of address, the film's more didactic moments leave little doubt about what message the government hopes to convey to the film's spectators. The middle section of the film shows a doctor and nurse, dispatched by the provincial Department of Education, visiting the school and diagnosing the children's ailments. The film's remarks about George's condition leave us with little uncertainty about its interests:

> If the adenoids are removed George has a chance to pick up. If neglected he will become an inefficient unit and may eventually be a charge on the state. Organized periodic health inspection of school children will safeguard the community and the home against this neglect.

The government's concern with inefficiency is here made very plain—not only does it fear the cost of an unproductive body (or "inefficient unit"!), but it intervenes in an attempt to counteract this "neglect." To drive home this message in visual terms, the children's discolored and decayed teeth are shown in extreme close-up shots, and George is appropriately abject in repeated high-angle close-ups. Certainly, these images are informative, but in filling the screen with an abscess or a decayed tooth, they also recall *curiositas,* or the kind of knowledge Tom Gunning describes as the "lust of the eyes" and a "fascination with seeing." As Gunning reminds us, *curiositas* possesses "the power to lead us astray" or distract, making it an appealing element in the "cinema of attractions" but somewhat less desirable in an instructional film's careful visualization of an action or consequence.[34]

But the diseases and health defects are not the only target of the government inspector's work, as one intertitle attests: "Community health education extends to the parents, who eagerly receive new ideas on personal and community hygiene." If farmers watching the film might initially identify with Mr. Irwin's "rube," the government evidently hoped these rubes would aspire to become a more progressive kind of citizen who recognized their "neglect" of themselves and adopted the film's advice. Such a transformation was even in keeping with the UFO government, which hoped, with the help of progressive and scientific methods, to raise up the "motley crowd" of old-fashioned, tenant, or dirt farmers to more modern standards of production and hygiene.[35]

Beyond the film's use of a fictionalized narrative as a persuasive way of couching its didactic material, *The Handicap* closes on a curious, and slightly clumsy, note. As the now-healthy children cavort in a field, an intertitle interrupts to announce "The hum of an aeroplane." As the children look up, we see two discontinuous shots of an airplane in flight and taking off. The children scramble to pick up flyers, evidently dropped from the sky, and we see a bespectacled Joe reading one (with lips moving) in close-up. The final shot pans across the group of children standing together, each concentrating on a piece of paper dropped from the airplane. This ending is rather abrupt but perhaps anticipates the circulation of a government pamphlet, like the one seen in the film, among the film's audience members.

It is also worth noting how these final moments conflate modern technology, vision, and communication. On one level, an airplane distributing pamphlets is analogous to the government's project of introducing technologies of health and domestic science to rural spaces. In this sense, the fictional success of the medical inspections and the improved health of the children are poetically mirrored in the airplane taking flight. The film also presents symbolic affinities between the airplane and the motion picture itself: both are fascinating modern technologies engaged in the communication of a message to the countryside. Moreover, the communication is specifically mediated by lenses and corrected vision, fictionally represented by Joe's glasses. Indeed, the appearance of the airplane offers a way of understanding how the film viewed its own functioning within a broader context: it shows that modern technologies of communication and vision would improve the lot of country dwellers.

But even if the film offers us a rich way of understanding the government's visualization of modern communication, contemporary spectators may have found it interesting for different reasons. On 4 May 1920, the Brampton Women's Institute had arranged afternoon and evening exhibitions of *The Little Shepherd of Kingdom Come* as a fund-raiser for the School Nurse Fund. But before this U.S. Civil War film was shown, an early version of *The Handicap* was exhibited. The newspaper review noted: "The film showing the medical inspection of some of Peel's schools was run off first. The late J. W. Stark appears leading Dr. McKenzie Smith to the Britannia schoolroom door, where the school teacher, Miss Martin, is ringing the bell. The various steps of the inspection are shown, interspersed with explanatory and suggestive captions."[36] Not only did *The Handicap* show nearby places that were likely well known by the spectators, but the reporter was also able to name some of the key individuals who appeared in it. In contrast to the historical and geographic remoteness of *The Little Shepherd of Kingdom Come, The Handicap* offered these spectators an opportunity to see films that reflected familiar people, spaces, and experiences. The review also refers to the film's poetic value: "This film is full of human notes, which found a responsible chord in the breasts of this audience. The film that shows human nature to itself as in a looking-glass is the successful one. The small boy who got a pair of glasses that made him think the world a very wonderful place, was the happiest touch in the whole admirable picture."

Miniaturization, Motion Pictures, and Rural Ontario

Given the government's efforts to bring new technologies to Ontario's countryside, it is not hard to see how the OMPB's work in film production and distribution belonged to a general project that extended principles of modern scientific management to rural spaces and agricultural production. As James C. Scott points out, this effort to rationalize rural activities was a common goal of modern states. Attempts to make spaces and populations more legible and easily managed went hand in hand with growing bureaucracies, taxation, and progressive reform. In many states, this rationalization was driven by what Scott refers to as a "high-modernist ideology": a faith that borrowed, as it were, the legitimacy of science and technology. It was accordingly, uncritical, unskeptical, and thus unscientifically optimistic about the possibilities for the comprehensive planning of human settlement and production.[37]

In Ontario, modern communication technologies from electricity to paved roads helped governments to extend their project of rationalization outside of urban centers. Moving pictures played a significant role in these projects, as the Ontario government looked to films as a means of informing, educating, and convincing the province's rural public. Beyond subjects that instructed farmers in modern methods, the films also sought to convince rural dwellers to acquire modern implements and even to accept the government's advice on issues of personal and social hygiene, as well as other private matters. That the Ontario Motion Picture Bureau hoped that the modernization of rural Ontario would be most effectively conveyed through motion pictures is hardly surprising, since, as Scott observes, "The carriers of high modernism tended to see rational order in remarkably visual aesthetic terms. For them, an efficient, rationally organized city, village, or farm was a city that looked regimented and orderly in a geometrical sense."[38] Films could provide a visualization—or, in Scott's terms, "miniaturization"—of the modern efficient countryside. More than offering simple "useful tips" or "educational information," these films presented an attempt to modernize rural life, transforming it from an agrarian idyll to a modern scientific ideal.

But clearly this is only a part of how the OMPB understood and justified its activities. In addition to the moving picture's role as instructor, the OMPB also promoted its use as an entertainer and provider of happiness and recreation. In theory this second function could reinforce the film's instructive role by making rural spectators more receptive to "educational influences," but this does not always seem to be the case. It is possible that the tension between entertainment and instruction, work and play, is the result of a flawed strategy on the OMPB's part, perhaps indicating a failure to dictate sufficient control over the films' exhibition and reception. But it more likely results from ambivalence in theories of "educational propaganda" toward the mechanisms of a film's "powers of visualization"; though reformers and psychologists worried about fascinated and suggestible spectators, it was this very fascination with popular films (complete with visual attractions and exciting themes) that progressives hoped to co-opt and redirect as uplifting visualizations. Adapting the purpose of films required a variety of theories and pseudoscientific strategies, but most often it resulted in a concession to playfulness or entertainment, at the level of either the individual film or a program of films. Playfulness or entertainment was thought by some to reinforce instructional themes, but it could also result in distraction, *curiositas,* or fascination that destabilized a film's meaning and undermined its instrumental value. Such playfulness and instability of meaning can even be found in the

"Testing the Mind" films Münsterberg helped produce for Paramount in 1916. These films were designed by Münsterberg as vocational tests and exercises for certain mental activities, such as memory and visual estimates. But as quizzes addressed to a crowd of moviegoers, they probably were, as we can imagine, greeted with loud—perhaps cheerful, perhaps derisive—but hardly scientific "results."[39] At least two of these films were available for rent from the OMPB during the 1920s; one of them, which, according to the catalog, "provides amusement as well as a test of mental power," is appropriately called *Can You Resist Illusions?*[40]

By 1917, modern industrial and communication technologies were steadily transforming everyday life in Ontario's countryside and small towns. As roads and electricity spread outward from urban centers, so too came tractors and moving picture shows. Such modern devices did not always appear in tandem or spread out evenly across the countryside, but it is remarkable how closely their introduction and exploitation paralleled one another. Though modernization may have found its most emphatic and frequently represented manifestation in big cities, rural spaces (at least in Ontario) were not immune to those forces shaping modern experience in the early twentieth century. At once providing ideal visualizations of agricultural efficiency and lively modern entertainment, the Ontario Motion Picture Bureau brought nontheatrical film to the province's countryside. In one sense, the films provided a planned and composed visual counterpoint to the somewhat disorganized and chaotic process of technological and social modernization then taking place in rural Ontario. But entertainment could itself be a disorganized and destabilizing force, as the OMPB films and exhibition contexts demonstrate. In making films appealing to rural spectators, Ontario's government ran the risk of making them objects of distraction or fascination in their own right, detached from any instrumental purpose they might have originally possessed. Finally, the OMPB's films offered Ontario's rural inhabitants a "looking glass" of an unusual kind; by showing familiar people, places, and events, these films may have helped mediate the onslaught of modern technologies in the countryside.

Notes

A version of this chapter was presented at the 2002 Film Studies Association of Canada conference in Toronto. My sincere thanks to all who have supported this work, and especially to Lee Carruthers, Ken Eisenstein, Jim Lastra, Tom Gunning, Michael Geyer and Jan Goldstein, Yuri Tsivian, participants of the Mass Culture Workshop at the University of Chicago, Rosemary Bergeron, Buckey Grimm, helpful staff at the Archives of Ontario and the National Archives of Canada, and the Social Science and Research Council of Canada. Most of all, I would like to thank Bill O'Farrell for introducing me to the OMPB films, and for his unparalleled knowledge and generosity; this chapter is dedicated to him.

1. Quoted in Matthew Hale, *Human Science and Social Order: Hugo Münsterberg and the Origins of Applied Psychology* (Philadelphia: Temple University Press, 1980), 106.

2. "Vegetable Growers See Work in Movies," *London Advertiser*, 25 January 1917, 16.

3. "A Remarkable Train," *Weekly Sun* (Toronto), 24 January 1917, 4.

4. "Financial Statement of Hon. T. W. McGarry, 1919," 35–38, Record Group (hereafter RG) 56-1-1, Archives of Ontario (hereafter AO). For other facets of the Ontario Motion Picture Bureau's activities, see Peter Morris's *Embattled Shadows: A History of Canadian Cinema, 1895–1939* (Montreal: McGill-Queen's University Press, 1979); Shelley Stamp Lindsey, "Toronto 'Girl Workers': The Female Body and Industrial Efficiency in *Her Own Fault*," *Cinémas* 6, no. 1 (1995): 81–99.

5. "Serve, Save, Produce," *Topic* (Petrolia, Ont.), 20 March 1917, 2.

6. Many historians have traced this debate, but for a recent and excellent reassessment, see Lee Grieveson's *Policing Cinema: Movies and Censorship in Early-Twentieth-Century America* (Berkeley and Los Angeles: University of California Press, 2004).

7. George Patton to W. H. Price, 13 January 1926, RG 56-1-1, AO. Commercial films were initially available to nontheatrical exhibitors through the Pathescope Company of Canada (which also produced many of the OMPB films), but in 1925 the OMPB purchased Pathescope's library of films and absorbed it into its own operations.

8. The U.S. Department of Agriculture established its Motion Picture Service in 1912. Public school boards across North America tried out films during the second decade of the twentieth century, as did university extension departments and religious and labor organizations. For more about early nontheatrical film production and distribution in the United States, see Anthony Slide's *Before Video* (New York: Greenwood Press, 1992).

9. For more about 28mm and early nontheatrical film exhibition, see Anke Mebold and Charles Tepperman, "Resurrecting the Lost History of 28mm Film in North America," *Film History* 15 (2003): 137–51.

10. Reports of Agricultural Representatives, RG 16–68-Container 4, OA.

11. "Financial Statement of Hon. T. W. McGarry, 1919," 36–37.

12. Cited in Grieveson, *Policing Cinema*, 64. On reformers and crusades against the Nickelodeon, see Grieveson's section called "Schools for Crime," 58–66.

13. Hugo Münsterberg, *The Photoplay: A Psychological Study*, in *Hugo Münsterberg on Film*, ed. Alan Langdale (1916; reprint, New York: Routledge, 2002), 154–55.

14. Diana Louise Lembo, "A History of the Growth and Development of the Department of Audio-visual Instruction of the National Education Association from 1923 to 1968" (Ph.D. diss., New York University, 1970), 71–72.

15. Roberta Pearson and William Uricchio discuss the perceived susceptibility of certain kinds of spectators in "'The Formative and Impressionable Stage': Discursive Constructions of the Nickelodeon's Child Audience," in *American Movie Audiences*, ed. Melvyn Stokes and Richard Maltby (London: British Film Institute, 1999), 65–66; Münsterberg notes: "The applause into which the audiences, especially of rural communities, break out at a happy turn of the melodramatic pictures is another symptom of the strange fascination" (154).

16. Advertisement, *Reel and Slide Magazine*, July 1918, 13.

17. Melville H. Staples, ed., *The Challenge of Agriculture: The Story of the United Farmers of Ontario* (Toronto: George N. Morang, 1921), 42–43.

18. Richard Rogers to Hon. W. E. Raney, 19 November 1919, RG 56-1-1, AO.

19. Filmcraft produced about half of the films commissioned by OMPB at the time, the other half being produced by Pathescope of Canada. The fierce competition between these two companies provides some important context for Proctor's overture to Smith. See Morris, *Embattled Shadows,* 146–48.

20. Irwin Proctor to Hon. Peter Smith, 15 December 1921, RG 56–1-1-20, AO.

21. This secretive attitude, and a reference to the OMPB director's positive opinion on the matter, suggests that the knowledge of motion picture propaganda, and the "instrumentality" of motion pictures in general, had provided a backdrop to OMPB activities for some time but needed to be spelled out more clearly to Smith.

22. It should be pointed out that the OMPB at first (1917–23) only commissioned and distributed films, but later (1924–34) it established its own production unit. The earlier films were made by, primarily, two companies—Pathescope Co. of Canada and Filmcraft—which produced films based on directions or scenarios provided by the OMPB.

23. This discussion of films produced by the OMPB is based on my own viewing of these films at the National Archives of Canada.

24. Fairs were also the subject of several films: *The Rural School Fair* (c. 1919), *The Fall Fair* (c. 1922), and *Fair Days in Picton* (c. 1922), for example.

25. *Parkhill Gazette.* Unfortunately there are pages missing from the extant issue of 13 December 1917 that would likely have reported on its exhibition, but the film itself, *The Community Canning Centre,* is held by the National Archives of Canada.

26. Staples, *Challenge of Agriculture,* 173.

27. J. Cameron Secord, "Canada Teaches Farmers with Films," *Reel and Slide Magazine,* January 1919, 13.

28. "Localettes," *Bolton Enterprise,* 7 November 1919, 1.

29. "Local Correspondence—Meadowvale," *Conservator* (Brampton), 12 February 1920, 7.

30. "Local Correspondence—Elmbank," *Conservator* (Brampton), 27 May 1920, 3.

31. Howard Trueman, "Reminiscences" (1981), in *Ontario's Ag Reps (1907–1982),* Archives of Ontario, pp. 72–73.

32. Münsterberg, *The Photoplay,* 155.

33. As Miriam Hansen argues, the film "agitates [Uncle Josh] beyond control," and he eventually becomes "altogether infantilized" by what he sees. *Uncle Josh at the Moving Picture Show* quite literally reenacts the supposed effects of cinematic suggestion on the country dweller—he takes the movie to be real and imitates and reacts as though it were. Miriam Hansen, *Babel and Babylon: Spectatorship in American Silent Film* (Cambridge, Mass.: Harvard University Press, 1991), 26.

34. Tom Gunning, "An Aesthetic of Astonishment," *Art and Text* 34 (Spring 1989): 39. Gunning argues that early science films, such as Charles Urban's *Unseen World* series (1903), appealed to people's fascination with disgusting, if thrilling, scenes from the natural world (magnified bugs, for example). Though billed as educational, such films were criticized by reformers for being vulgar. Clearly, the instability of a nonfictional image's meaning (does it appeal to reason or *curiositas*?) was a cause for concern long before the OMPB.

35. Charles M. Johnston, "'A Motley Crowd': Diversity in the Ontario Countryside in the Early Twentieth Century," in *Canadian Papers in Rural History,* vol. 7, ed. Donald

Akeson (Gananoque, Ontario: Langdale Press, 1990), 237. *Motley crowd* was the term used by J. J. Morrison, a founder of the UFO; Johnston describes the great divide in class and education between the progressive, entrepreneurial methods practiced by specialized farmers (livestock breeders, fruit and dairy farmers) and the old-fashioned, unscientific ways of "general" farmers.

36. "Moving Pictures for School Nurse Fund," *Conservator* (Brampton, Ontario), 6 May 1920, 1. Though this review does not refer to *The Handicap* by name, it is clearly referring to some version of this film. The OMPB had produced a film about medical inspections in schools by 1919, but this film was evidently lengthened and reedited (likely to incorporate more fictional material) in 1920 and appeared in the OMPB's 1922 catalog as *Medical Inspection or the Handicap*. The presence of at least two different intertitle styles in the version held at the National Archives of Canada attests to this hybridity. The presence of a card dated June 1920 and some discrepancies in content suggest that the version I have seen is a slightly different (and later) version from that presented in Brampton. It also worth noting that *The Handicap* was produced by the Pathescope Co. of Canada, suggesting that Filmcraft was not alone in its recognition of the cinema's ability to carefully position viewers.

37. James C. Scott, *Seeing Like a State: How Certain Schemes to Improve the Human Condition Have Failed* (New Haven, Conn.: Yale University Press, 1998), 4.

38. Ibid.

39. On Münsterberg's "Testing the Mind" films, see Langdale's essay "S(t)imulation of Mind," 33–34n40, and Münsterberg's "Speech on the Paramount Pictographs," 204–5, in *Hugo Münsterberg on Film*. Scott Curtis also discusses these films in chapter 1 of his dissertation, "'Like a Hailstorm on the Nerves of Modern Man': Cinema, Legibility, and the Body in Germany, 1895–1914" (Ph.D. diss., University of Iowa, 1996); many thanks to Curtis for sending me this material.

40. Province of Ontario Pictures, *Descriptive Catalogue of 28mm Slow Burning Film*, May 1927, Reel No. 3192-b.

9

AT THE MOVIES IN THE
"BIGGEST LITTLE CITY IN WISCONSIN"

LESLIE MIDKIFF DEBAUCHE

In December 1916, an editorial in the *Stevens Point Gazette* challenged the city to take action: "If there is one thing Stevens Point needs more than anything else right now it is a thoroughly organized, aggressive commercial or advancement association." The reason? "It is the modern city's business to advertise itself, to let outside people know what it has, to invite outside capital to come in{ . . . }and it is time that Stevens Point was in a class with other progressive cities in this respect." [1] Stevens Point, located on the Wisconsin River and served by the Soo Line, was a small but growing city of about 11,000 in central Wisconsin. [2] Its economy was both industrial and agricultural. The lumber industry had spawned paper mills, millworks, and furniture makers, and the soil of the area was right for potatoes. The city—with a large Polish and German population—had a brewery and a weekly Polish-language newspaper in addition to the Republican *Stevens Point Journal* and the Democrat *Gazette*. One Catholic church, St. Peter's, provided services in Polish, while St. Joseph's catered to the German residents. Nearer downtown were the city's main Catholic church, Frame Presbyterian Church, the Episcopal Church of the Intercession and a small synagogue. Methodists, Baptists, and Lutherans also had congregations in Stevens Point.

Citizens could shop Main Street and Strongs Avenue for ready-made clothes, jewelry, carpets, musical instruments, and bicycles. There were three banks and as many companies selling all sorts of insurance. Miss C. J. Frost ran a factory making fishing tackle, and, when it was necessary, coffins could also be bought from the Boston Furniture and Undertaking Co. on Main Street. Out-of-state newspapers, including the *Chicago Examiner* and the *Chicago Sunday Tribune,* were available at French, Campbell and

Co., and the public library subscribed to more than forty national magazines.[3]

The city sat at the intersection of highways running north, south, east, and west in the state, and it was also accessible to the long-distance automobile traveler driving the transcontinental Yellowstone Trail. Entertainment came into Stevens Point via the roads and the rails. In their leisure time residents could attend the Chautauqua in July, lectures by visiting experts invited to the state normal school, and political talks held in various venues, including the parish hall at the Episcopal church. Vaudeville and traveling theater companies also passed through town. The Opera House had been built in 1893 and was the first theater to show movies when Lyman Howe arrived in 1904. It closed in 1915, but citizens could see a variety of films every week.

With the opening of the Lyric Theatre on July 1, the number of places where people could watch movies in Stevens Point increased to six. The Ideal, located downtown, was the oldest theater, dating from 1906 or 1907. The Della, on the south side of Stevens Point, and the Gem, located on Strongs Avenue a few blocks south of the downtown area, changed their programs daily. The Empire Amusement Hall, with the largest stage and the greatest seating capacity in the city, was on Union Street at the western edge of the downtown. To the Empire came the special showings, including *Birth of a Nation,* Lyman Howe's Travel Festival, and *Damaged Goods,* a drama about the effects of syphilis, which was denounced from two different local pulpits in March.[4] The parish hall at the Episcopal church, just southeast of downtown, hosted a series of epic films: *The Last Days of Pompeii, Julius Caesar, The Lion of Venice, Antony and Cleopatra, Spartacus, Othello,* and *Cabiria,* programmed by a church member and teacher at the normal school, Professor Frank Hyer.

A close look at moviegoing and the business of film exhibition in Stevens Point, Wisconsin, during 1916 illustrates important facets of the relationship between local and national concerns, indigenous and mass-distributed popular culture. This small city in the middle of the state was shot through with real and metaphoric roads linking it both to other small cities and towns in the region and to the major metropolitan areas of Chicago and New York, as well as to European cities, including Paris, London, and Berlin. Citizens of Stevens Point traveled to visit family in Washington, D.C.; they left to take jobs in New York City and went to Chicago to buy stock for their stores.[5] Those who stayed home received letters and mail-order catalogs, read magazines and newspapers, and also went to movies. At the Gem and the Ideal, the Della and the Lyric, they saw images shot on location in New York and California, among other places. The mise-en-scène of the films they watched revealed contemporary fashion in clothing and room decor, while the themes in the films' narratives expressed the preoccupations of popular fiction. The music played during the screenings incorporated songs whose sheet music could be purchased at French, Campbell and Co. on Main Street.

To show the particular even as I argue for Stevens Point's place on the national map, I will describe three events that took place during 1916. In late March there was a showing, the first in the city, of *The Birth of a Nation* at the Empire Theatre. It was a special screening to complement the other festivities of "Fashion Week," the local emanation of a campaign created and promoted by the retail fashion industry based in New York City. Stevens Point joined other cities and towns around the country in encouraging shoppers to buy new, fashionable clothes so they could "dress up" for spring. Local clothing merchants, city officials, and Russell Gregory, the manager of the Gem Theatre, realized that Fashion Week could promote Stevens Point at the same time it sold suits, dresses, millinery, and men's clothing. Paradoxically, perhaps, a film highlighting the harmful effects of war on the wardrobes of southern women—already the "southern ermine" scene was recognized as brilliant—was a key factor in the success of Fashion Week.[6]

Second, on July 1, the Lyric Theatre opened next to the post office at 454 Main Street. Dr. F. A. Walters, the newly elected mayor, spoke at the opening performance, noting that the Lyric was a grand example of the "City Beautiful" scheme.[7] The work chosen to mark the inaugural and to lead into Fourth of July activities was *The Battle Cry of Peace* (1915), a Vitagraph film advocating military preparedness for war. Here, also, we see the combination of a high-profile film with a civic event. One theme common to both the opening of the new movie house and the Fourth of July festivities was boosterism—the enthusiastic support for the theater, the city, and the nation.

I will conclude this chapter by discussing the promotion and exhibition of *Gloria's Romance* at the Gem Theatre in Stevens Point. This twenty-part serial played nearly every Wednesday from October 18 through December 6. Produced by George Kleine and starring Billie Burke, the series ran while the nation chose between incumbent Woodrow Wilson and Charles Evans Hughes for president; while Mayor Walters warred with Chief of Police John Hofsoos, the local newspapers, and local citizens; and while diphtheria, scarlet fever, and finally smallpox raged throughout the city. Examining *Gloria's Romance* during this time and in this place lets us see how Stevens Point fit into the plans of a national film distribution company. Whereas my first two examples highlight the way that Stevens Point envisioned itself as part of the nation, this third example shows how George Kleine's company needed the Gem Theatre, and theaters in other small cities and towns, in order to make a profit. The promotion of *Gloria's Romance* also demonstrates the extent to which moviegoers in Stevens Point were aware of trends in popular culture.

"Have you heard of a new mode just dawning . . ."[8]

In early spring 1916, *Women's Wear,* an important source of information for the fashion industry, encouraged retailers around the country to join in a national promotional campaign to spark sales. One advertisement featured a young woman looking at her transformed self in a large oval mirror. She was surrounded by seven dwarfs wearing tunics spelling "Dress Up." In answer to her question,

> Magic Mirror hanging there
> What shall I do to be more fair?

the Mirror replied:

> O daughter of a land at peace,
> Whose power and riches e'er increase,
> These words, observed, will beauty bring:
> Cast off your cares—Dress Up for Spring.[9]

This verse was packed with allusions showing how fashion was inextricably connected to cultural, social, economic, and political events. Snow White was the main character, and the fairy tale that had been produced as a play starring Marguerite Clark in 1912 would open as a film, featuring the same actress in the title role, in time for Christmas in 1916. Then, there was war. The European war was of special importance to the clothing trades because Paris was the wellspring of fashion, and Germany was the source of many of the dyes used in the fashion industry. Stories describing battles, heads of state, and struggling populations had filled American newspapers since 1914. The equally persistent—and much closer—civil war in Mexico spilled over the American border in March as Pancho Villa crossed into New Mexico and killed ten American citizens. President Wilson sent troops under the command of General John Pershing on a "punitive expedition" to try to capture Villa.[10] In spite, or perhaps because, of the unsettled state of the nation and the world, American women were urged to take advantage of their good luck to spruce up their spring wardrobes. Nature itself provided the final allusion. "All nature dresses up in the spring. Get in line," ordered an ad in the *Stevens Point Journal.*[11] Easter, a traditional dress-up day, was less than a month away.

C. G. Macnish, the owner of a shoe shop at 417 Main Street, headed up Fashion Week in Stevens Point. By 14 March, the *Stevens Point Journal* reported that thirteen local businesspeople had agreed to participate, and "Mr. Macnish called on several firms this morning and will interview others."[12] Fashion Week began on Monday, 27 March. It featured decorated store windows and shops stocked with the newest modes; a parade of the latest model automobiles was held on Thursday afternoon. Thursday evening, a style show organized by members of the St. Agnes' Guild of the Episcopal

Church, including Mrs. C. G. Macnish, attracted 500 people to the Episcopal parish hall. Local women modeled everything from kimonos through suits to bridal dresses. A three-day screening of *The Birth of a Nation* kicked off the festivities.

Residents of Stevens Point were privy to the advanced planning for this special film showing. Russell Gregory, the manager of the Gem Theatre, booked the film and also arranged for it to be shown in the parish hall of the Episcopal church, which had seating for 800. The film would have fit nicely into this setting. Beginning in January, the Church of the Intercession had hosted a series of epic films in its parish hall. But, while seating capacity was adequate, when T. E. Hughes, assistant manager of the road show company, arrived to inspect the site on 14 March, he found that the stage was too narrow, at twelve feet, to accommodate behind-the-screen noise-making machinery. At this point the film's location changed for the last time, to the Empire Theater.[13] Even though *The Birth of a Nation* had been shown in the neighboring small city of Grand Rapids, Wisconsin, in February, the *Stevens Point Journal* reported that a "good many out of town visitors are expected here for the production." The *Gazette* agreed: "As 'The Birth of a Nation' pictures are to be shown at the Empire theater during 'Fashion Week' prospects for a large outside attendance are excellent."[14]

Promotion for *The Birth of a Nation* covered a forty-mile area around the city, comprising the combined efforts of Russell Gregory of the Gem Theatre, T. E. Hughes, and local merchants.[15] The campaign included large advertisements highlighting the film and linking it with Fashion Week in the local papers, and advertisements placed by local retailers like Mr. Macnish linking the film with his store. In the early planning stages, the *Stevens Point Journal* noted that much good could accrue to local merchants from such "massed advertising." Other selling points for the film—featuring the same advertisements as were used when it played in other parts of the country—included its huge production costs, the large number of people involved in making the film, the excessive yardage needed for costumes, and the historical fidelity of the film's mise-en-scène.[16] Several ads also included the announcement, "Highly Important: 'The Birth of a Nation' will never be presented in any but the highest class theatres and at prices customarily charged in such play houses."[17] Publicity pieces appeared as news stories in the papers and foregrounded the historical value of the film, the genius of its style, the hard work that went into the making of the picture, and the presence in the film of that "favorite among the actors," Mae Marsh.[18]

The Birth of the Nation made front-page news when its company arrived late on Monday, 27 March. The *Stevens Point Journal* also reported that the electrical capabilities of the Empire were tested by the demands of the stage machinery connected with the film, and, as a result, the matinee began forty-five minutes late. Still, the paper gave the film a glowing review. Commending the music for a mixture of the familiar and the evocative, the reporter also praised the film's editing: "The rush of imagination that follows the suggestions of the swiftly flying scenes combine to produce an overpowering effect that is almost paralyzing." At times, the writer noted, the audience seemed stunned to silence, and "handkerchiefs were more in evidence than hand-clapping."[19]

Still, the affinity of a Union audience for protagonists loyal to the Confederacy gave the writer pause:

> It is a peculiar sight to witness a northern audience swept in sympathy with the sufferings of the south during the war and especially during the Reconstruction period and frequently applauding the Ku Klux Klan. . . . Whether justly or not, the effect of the picture tends to prejudice the spectators strongly in favor of the southern whites and to render the negro almost an object of loathing. Almost the best that is given the negro is a laugh at his peculiarities though here and there an instance of that touching devotion for which the colored man was known at times appears.[20]

The equivocal phrase "Whether justly or not" not only manifested a discomfort with the idea of former enemies making such jubilant common cause but also raised the issue of race and cast it as a problem.

According to the 1910 census, no blacks lived in Stevens Point, and there were only five in Portage County. Less than 1 percent of the state's population was black in 1910, and the numbers did not change appreciably in the 1920 census.[21] But news of black people was available in the local newspapers. Throughout 1916, lynchings in the South were reported in Wisconsin. In fact, the week after *The Birth of a Nation* played in Stevens Point, the *Journal* reported, "Negro Lynched by Mob, Seized in Trial Room and Hanged from the Balcony of the Court House." This took place in Idabel, Oklahoma; the victim was accused of attacking a white girl. Because news like this was not the stuff of local editorials, it is difficult to gauge how citizens of Stevens Point reacted to such vigilantism. Another story described an attempt by St. Louis, Missouri, to institute a legal segregation in housing in the city, and a headline in June summarized a sad event: "Gap Too Great to Be Bridged, African Dwarf Disappointed Because He Couldn't Learn Ways of Civilization." In this case Ota Binga committed suicide. This story was accompanied by a drawing showing a very black figure, dressed in a plaid suit and with very white lips.

One further event, whose meaning is not yet clear, at least to this researcher, occurred in Stevens Point during the summer. As planning began for the Fourth of July festivities, it was decided that there would be a parade in the morning, baseball games and horse races in the afternoon, and speeches—including a reading of the Declaration of Independence—and music in the evening. The parade is of interest here. While "patriotism will be the keynote of the day{ . . . }[t]he parade will be made a leading feature, the idea being to make it beautiful and symbolic of deeds and ideals dear to American hearts."[22]

The middle section of the parade was to be a "historical pageant" consisting of those events and individuals that were the foundations for the nation's ideals.[23] Predictably, the Native Americans were followed by Spanish explorers, then British colonists, including John Smith, and even, in 1916, Pocahontas. Next would come Uncle Sam, the Liberty Bell, and Columbia. The Civil War section of this marching time line would include "old soldiers in uniform, representing civil war period, zouaves; sailor boys; group symbolizing the end of the civil war, showing soldier of north and soldier of south clasping hands; Ku Klux Klan on horseback."[24] Stevens Point's history, which began in the late 1850s, would provide personages and floats for the next part of the pageant.

This chronology, whereby the Klan riders stood in for the Reconstruction period, was proposed in a planning meeting and reported in the *Stevens Point Gazette* on 21 June. In the coverage following the parade, the Klan's position, and thus its meaning, had changed. The *Gazette* reported that the parade opened with city officials, clergy from area churches, and, in time-honored tradition, fire trucks. These dignitaries were followed by the historical pageant. The last section in the parade was a mixture of local businesses with floats and delivery cars, the Boy Scouts and Girl Scouts, local members of trade unions, and in between the float for the Women's Christian Temperance Union featuring girls in white representing the cardinal virtues and the prohibition states and Weeks Lumber company entry: a load of logs and workmen holding pike poles and cant hooks, rode the four Ku Klux Klansmen.

The presence of the Klan provoked no special notice by either of the newspapers in Stevens Point. Lon Myers, whose name was connected to it in the articles describing parade planning, was a an auctioneer and a hotel owner in town. He also was a city alderman and a member of the Odd Fellows, in other words, a prominent and well-liked citizen. After forty-eight years of inactivity, the KKK had been revived in Georgia in November 1915, but it did not gain a large following in the Midwest until the early 1920s. Certainly Stevens Point was home to groups that the Klan despised: immigrants, Catholics, and Jews. Still, there is no evidence that the four Klansmen riding in the parade ever acted out the ideology implicit in their regalia. In fact, a joking reference to the Klan was made later in the year when a group of men who were legally banned from saloons attempted to organize to protest their plight. It may be that they were simply another costumed group illustrating a bygone period of American history instead of an active, contemporary fraternal organization. Still, the enthusiastic reception of *The Birth of the Nation* three months earlier may have contributed to a normalizing of the KKK so that its presence in July did not provoke comment.

It was also the case that negative racial stereotypes were familiar, almost a cliché, in the local press. The same day that *The Birth of a Nation* moved its audience to silent awe, Charles Virnowenski was arrested for allegedly stealing twenty-two chickens in Stevens Point. The offense was described as "the familiar old Uncle 'Rastus crime'{ . . . }Yassah!" While, at a meeting of the Women's Club that same day, Miss Ramona Pfiffner, accompanied by Miss Helga Anderson, presented such a popular musical program that she sang as an encore "Hi, Little Fellow," a "lively negro melody."[25] In October, the Elks Club mounted a fund-raising entertainment, featuring the Elks Tuxedo Minstrels. The club ran a series of advertisements featuring the names of its members and illustrations of very dark, large-lipped strutting caricatures. In one, Joe Pfiffner, a candidate for the job of district attorney, looked remarkably like Ota Binga as he lured patrons with his "Million Dollar Walk."[26]

Newspapers also featured as filler jokes that turned on stereotypical traits of stupidity and laziness and black dialect. There were cartoons like one in a series called "Days You'll Never Forget." The image showed two white boys hiding behind a tree holding a white baby. In the background a fat black woman in apron and full, long skirt, her arms raised in alarm, stood next to a thin black man scratching his head. She exclaimed, "Lawdy! Thar Goes the Chile an' All. Oh!! Save the Chile. That's Wha' Ah Gets for Talking to a Old Fool Lak You Sam Jenkins." The cartoonist's interpretation of the event was expressed by a different caption: "The Day You Frightened 'Aunt Mandy' with the Empty Baby Carriage."[27] In this small city, ethnic difference was a greater cause of strife, but audience response to *The Birth of a Nation,* and the ubiquitous, hateful images of blacks found easily in local media and popular culture, showed one more way Stevens Point fit within the national culture.

The film's review concluded less ambivalently that "in general the pictures are true to history and are a tremendous object lesson in the teaching of American history."[28] Mr. Gregory offered special children's tickets for seats in the balcony, and during the matinee on Tuesday, 28 March, fifty-six chairs had to be brought into the theater to accommodate the crowds. It was estimated that nearly 4,000 people saw *The Birth of a Nation* during Fashion Week.[29] The cartoons, news stories, and fiction to which these overwhelmingly white residents of central Wisconsin had easy access reinforced the film's version of history.

At the end of the week, the *Gazette* crowned the experiment a success and expressed the hope that Fashion Week would become an annual event. Its headline proclaimed, "Hundreds Visit City, Combination of Fashion Week and Birth of a Nation Great Drawing Card."[30] In early April the *Journal* announced, "Fashion Week Grows." A plan was floated to call the event "Stevens Point Week" and to include local manufacturers in addition to the retailers. This would give "both citizens and outsiders a comprehensive idea of the extent and value of industries and various lines of business here. These community shows have been great successes in many places."[31]

Fashion Week gave local businessmen and businesswomen who sold readymade, nationally distributed brands of clothes, hats, and shoes the chance to boost their profits at the same time they "boosted" Stevens Point. *The Birth of a Nation* lent prestige to the occasion—it was famous and spectacular. It demonstrated that Stevens Point could put on a show with the same metropolitan panache as New York or Chicago, and it proved the efficacy of the movies to bring people to town. The road show company mounting the film also saw something of the hospitality of Stevens Point. The Elks, who would stage their own blackface minstrel show later in the fall, invited the orchestra and crew over to their club after the Tuesday night performance. The newspaper reported, "There are thirty-two men connected with the company and some are understood to be Elks. The evening was spent with a smoker, concert, and refreshments."[32] Civic pride would mix with the movies again in the summer, when the opening of a new theater, the Lyric, jibed with the city's Fourth of July festivities.

"One of the Finest, Most Up-to-Date Theatres in the State: The Fire-Proof Idol of Stevens Point"

At its meeting of 6 June, the Stevens Point City Council voted to allot sixty dollars to the Fire Department for its Fourth of July parade decorations.[33] A portion of the money was spent printing a short poem to hand to spectators along the parade route. Opening with the line "Boost your city, boost your friend," this two-stanza verse concluded:

> Boost for every forward movement,
> Boost for every new improvement,
> Boost the man for whom you labor,
> Boost the stranger and the neighbor,
> Cease to be a chronic knocker,
> Cease to be a progress blocker,
> If you'll make your city better,
> Boost it to the final letter.[34]

Boosterism, a heady mix of civic pride, optimism for the benefits of change, and an enthusiastic activism, was the prevailing public sentiment on the city council, in the editorial positions expressed in the city's newspapers, and among the community's businesspeople. "Progress" improved the city's infrastructure, promised to improve its public health, and brought to this "biggest little city" in the state some of the cultural advantages of the big cities.[35] When Stevens Point widened and paved roads, the *Gazette* approved, stating, "Good roads are among the biggest assets any community, any state or any nation can have; where there are good roads it can be taken for granted that there are good homes, good schools, good churches and thrifty, progressive people."[36] An editorial in the *Stevens Point Journal* advocated electric signs on business establishments: "It indicates an increase in pride and interest in improving the appearance of the business houses. It indicates the development of a spirit of progress and regard for the up-to-date."[37] When the Lyric Theatre—sporting an electric sign—opened on July 1, Mayor Walters, who spoke at the inaugural screening, called it a "fine addition to the 'City Beautiful'" scheme." For Stevens Point, the Lyric meant progress.

The new movie theater was first announced in January. Mr. McKinlay, the manager of the Ideal theater, took a lease on land down Main Street next to the post office. The building would be 40 feet by 150 feet in size and one story tall. All the equipment inside would be new, a concrete booth would house the projectors, and there would be a "big-city" front. A newspaper editorial noted, "In fact it will be built for both beauty and safety, meeting all the requirements of the state laws and ordinances."[38] McKinlay went to Milwaukee to talk with architects in February, and ground was broken for the theater in April. Several "landmark" elm trees were cut down when the lot was cleared, but the *Stevens Point Journal* reported they were "sacrificed . . . in the cause of progress."[39]

When it was completed, the auditorium at the Lyric measured 120 feet long by 40 feet wide. Its walls were a light tan, its ceiling was cream, and the seats were "finished in mahogany."[40] The stage was large enough to accommodate vaudeville acts, and there was an orchestra pit with room for twelve to fifteen musicians. The article describing its opening also mentioned the heating and ventilating system, the Danish Diamond Screen, toilet rooms for men and women, and the presence of "eight large exits" should the various fireproofing features fail.[41] It was a building for boosters: with an electric sign, a "tasty and pleasing" interior, "absolutely fireproof," and capable of hosting live shows as well as movies.[42] If that was not enough, on the opening day young ladies of the city served as ushers.

Under Mr. McKinlay's management the Lyric mimicked the shops downtown in other ways. The theater functioned as a civic center. Besides showing movies it also cooperated with local businesses. In October, working with the Moll Glennon clothing and dry goods store and Miss Mayme Ceary's read-to-wear shop, the Lyric hosted a fashion show. The advertising copy favorably compared local merchandise with big-city wares: "Come expecting to see the choicest creations in each line. . . . Come, then, knowing that in Stevens Point you can select garments which for style and quality and moderate prices are not surpassed in the largest fashion centers."[43] The next day, on October 23, the *Stevens Point Journal* reported that the "Style Show Pleases" and described the local young women who modeled suits, coats, dresses, and millinery as participants in a "living moving picture show."[44] In an example of synchronicity, the film showing on October 24 was *The Conflict,* starring Lucille Lee Stewart. Its selling point? "Presented with many beautiful gowns."[45] On October 28, the Lyric advertised *The Scarlet Runner,* which featured, among other enticements, "Big Fashion Shows."[46] In November, the high school music department held a benefit concert at the Lyric. Several days later the embattled Mayor Walters, in conflict with the chief of police as well as the city's newspapers, hinted that he would take his case directly to the people in a public meeting at the Lyric Theatre. This meeting, however, never was held.

Like the retail clothing stores in town, the movie theaters featured brand-name entertainment. Prior to competition from the new Lyric, the two main movie houses were the Gem and the Ideal. The Gem showed Triangle films on Monday, Tuesday, Friday, and Saturday; Fox Equitable on Wednesday and Thursday; and World on Sunday. The Ideal, under Mr. McKinlay's management, provided Paramount, Metro, and VLSE pictures.[47] When he moved from the Ideal to the Lyric, McKinlay took his program with him, and the Ideal entered a period of instability, changing managers three more times before the end of the year. Mr. Rice, McKinlay's immediate successor, instituted a Mutual program.[48] The Della Theater also changed managers twice. P.J. Bresnahan, the theater's owner and manager, leased the building to P. McMann in September, but by November, it was back in the Bresnahan family. Mrs. P.J. Bresnahan took over as manager, offering a program of Universal films.[49]

The entrance onto the exhibition arena of two new venues, the Episcopal parish hall and the Lyric Theatre, also raised the quality of moviegoing at all the theaters in Stevens Point in 1916. After the first screening, *The Last Days of Pompeii,* at the Parish House, the newspaper reported on success of the program. Even though the weather was "unfavorable," the paper noted that the schedule of pictures was "designed to elevate taste and conduce to public improvement" and pointed out that "the machine [projector] is an excellent one."[50] The description of the construction at the Lyric also included mention of two Motiograph projectors using 220 volts of electricity. "The result of this, Mr. McKinlay states, will be to eliminate flickering and reduce the eyestrain of the spectator."[51]

The Ideal, under Mr. Rice, who had been operating the Unique Theater in the nearby city of Marshfield, also installed a new Motiograph projector and brought his former projectionist to run the machine. Rice began his tenure as manager showing serials, *The Girl and the Game* (Mutual, 1915) and *The Iron Claw* (Pathe), two nights a week. This was not an auspicious beginning, and by September he had closed the theater, "the venture not proving a financial success."[52] As the Ideal was changing hands again, the front was painted, the lighting was improved inside and out, and the promise of more remodeling and other improvement was made by the new management team. The year ended much more hopefully. A special road show, managed by the same company that had brought *The Birth of a Nation* to Stevens Point, brought *Ramona,* complete with special operatic score, story based on a very popular novel, and spectacular scenery from the mission country of Southern California to the Ideal.

When the Della shifted from Mr. Bresnahan's control to Mr. McMann's, it also initiated improvements.[53] McMann, too, purchased a Motiograph machine for $285. Although no other major cosmetic, structural, electrical, or lighting changes were reported, the *Stevens Point Journal* did inform its readers that "other minor changes are being made to the theater."[54]

By December 1916, all the theaters showing movies, save the Empire, had purchased new projectors and had accomplished some degree of cosmetic improvements to their buildings. All theaters were still in business at the end of this tumultuous year, and, about 1,400 new seats had been added with the building of the Lyric and the film programming at the Episcopal parish hall. Competition for audience fit into the ideology of "progress"—the theaters vied for viewers by adding a recognized brand of movies, installing new, presumably better, projectors, and sprucing up their interior spaces and their facades. Mayor Walters might well have included them all under the rubric of the "City Beautiful."

*"The Lyric Knows It Can't Show All the Pictures So It Just Shows
the Best . . . Coming . . . Billie Burke"*[55]

*Gem Theatre, "The House That Does Things" . . . Miss Billie Burke
in the $850,000 Photoplay "Gloria's Romance"*[56]

The run of *Gloria's Romance*, a twenty-part serial starring Billie Burke, provides a summary of the themes I have introduced in this chapter. It showed how Stevens Point's two most "wide-awake" theater managers exploited their place in the national and local film distribution scheme. It also demonstrated the competitive spirit that animated movie exhibition in Stevens Point in 1916. Finally, a look at the social context of moviegoing revealed the high degree of referential knowledge an audience member brought with her to the theater. When Russell Gregory, the manager of the Gem, advertised that *Gloria's Romance* was "A Charming Play—Easy to Understand—Worth Understanding," he was right.[57] Residents of Stevens Point knew about fashion trends, Palm Beach, immigrants, wealthy people, and the other elements of a national popular culture that found a place in the plot of this contemporary "romance serial."[58]

Gloria's Romance caused conflict between theater managers in Stevens Point during 1916. Shortly after the Lyric opened on July 1, J. R. McKinlay advertised that Miss Billie Burke's serial would soon be "Shown Only at the Biggest and Best Theatres."[59] This preview of coming attractions ran four more times before Mr. Gregory, manager of the Gem, entered the fray. Taking out a three-column-wide advertisement, he set the record straight:

> **Notice**—The Gem had had contracts signed for the Billie Burke novel for some weeks past. Any advertisement stating that this picture would be run in any other house in this city is incorrect, as the Gem has exclusive first run of "Gloria's Romance" in this city.
>
> The "Billie Burke" novel is run in only the best patronized theaters.[60]

He ran the same ad again the next day. In this battle the "best patronized" theater won. Apparently, distributor George Kleine's exchange agent had made a mistake and booked the serial into both theaters. *Gloria's Romance* premiered at the Gem on Wednesday, September 20, and ran nearly every Wednesday through early December.

This was not the first time these two managers had collided. In February, McKinlay accused Gregory of "knocking" the quality of the films he showed at the Ideal. In an advertisement for Metro's *Song of the Wage Slave* and *The Spell of the Yukon,* he included the following accusation: "I wish at this time to answer a knock recently published by an exhibitor in a vain attempt to 'put something over.' Since I have conducted the Ideal Theater for the past year in such a manner that it is outdistancing all others in patronage, I do not feel at liberty to conduct a correspondence school for the benefit of those who lack both initiative and imitative ability. Nuf sed."[61]

Mr. Gregory won this round, too. He published a rebuttal on the same page, on the same day citing the source of the clever prose about correspondence schools, initiative, and imitative ability. McKinlay had plagiarized from the trade journal *Amusements.* This advertisement concluded, "The Gem knocks no one. . . . We are for truth and HONEST ADVERTISING."[62]

Gloria's Romance was prestigious enough to fight over. Since she arrived from Britain in 1907, Billie Burke had become a well-known and very popular theater actress in America, even in small cities like Stevens Point, where she never appeared onstage. There were articles written about her, interviews with her, and photographs in a variety of women's magazines. These pieces often stressed her beauty, especially her "fluffy" hair, and her stylish clothes, particularly her penchant for pajamas.[63] In February, French, Campbell and Co., the stationery store that carried out-of-town newspapers, alerted customers that the *Chicago Sunday Tribune* would run a series of articles on beauty "based on 'Billy Burke,' the Tribune's $1,000-a-week movie star."[64] In May, the Gem presented Burke's first film, *Peggy,* and introduced her as "The Darling of the American Stage." In a motif that would be repeated in the promotion for *Gloria's Romance,* it was also pointed out that "Billie Burke received a salary of $40,000 for acting this one play and breaking all records as the highest paid actress on earth."[65]

In addition to Burke and her salary, Gregory highlighted the authors of the film, Rupert and Adelaide Hughes. Rupert Hughes was a popular novelist noted for creating characters like Gloria—rich, young, Americans who fell in love and had adventures. *Gloria's Romance* was described as a "film novel," more important than a serial, and it ran in weekly installments in the *Tribune* and other newspapers around the country. The cost of the serial, $850,000, was touted, as was the fact that Burke's leading man was a theater actor, Henry Kolker. Advertisements also noted that "Billie Burke wears $500,000 worth of gowns of the latest models, designed especially for this production." The numbers do not add up, of course. Citing huge production costs and extraordinary salaries for starring actors was a conventional way of boosting the importance of a film.[66] After the serial had been running for a month, the ads would often simply say, "Wednesday Billie Burke."[67] This shorthand saved space in the advertisement, but it also testified to the drawing power of Billie Burke.

Burke made the papers in Stevens Point in other ways during the months the serial ran. In October the *Journal* announced that she had given birth to a daughter, and in November came the news that she was involved in a court case. Interestingly, ads even noted that "Stevens Pointers who find Billie Burke a favorite in the movies will be interested in watching the progress of a $15,000 damage suit against her."[68] Patrons of the public library in Stevens Point had access to *The Delineator, Harper's,* and *Everybody's,* popular magazines that all featured articles about or portraits of "Charming Billie" in the five years before the serial debuted.[69] If they had picked up the Sunday *Tribune* from French, Campbell and Co., citizens could have read the story of the serial, illustrated with both photographs and drawings of scenes featuring young Gloria. And French, Campbell may have also carried copies of sheet music, including incidental music from *Peggy* and the "Gloria's Romance Valse," both featuring portraits of Billie Burke on their covers.[70]

When Billie Burke played Stevens Point, she competed for attention with the war in Europe, a national presidential election, a local antigambling campaign being waged by Mayor Walters against the city's saloon keepers, and an epidemic of scarlet fever and diphtheria that only got worse. Two weeks after the December 6 installment of *Gloria's Romance,* children under fifteen were banned from attending movies, and the schools closed early for Christmas vacation. On December 29 the *Stevens Point Journal* reported, "Movie Crowds Small, Absence of Children under 16 Makes Difference in Attendance."[71] It was a good time for *Gloria* to finish its run.

"Good roads can bring city and country people together . . . it is but a short ride . . . to the city, where they can take in a band concert, a movie or some other attraction . . . "[72]

Stevens Point saw itself as a progressive small city—the "biggest little city in Wisconsin," to borrow Mayor Walters's campaign slogan. Big cities like New York might set fashion, premiere movies, and innovate public health strategies, but Stevens Point residents had access to fashion news, mass-marketed brand-name clothing and other products, and the latest ideas about how best to combat the diseases that preyed on the nation's and the city's children. If a national popular culture can be said to exist, Stevens Point participated in it. Citizens got their information from magazines, newspapers, their own travels, and the travel tales of neighbors that were reported in the *Stevens Point Journal* and in the *Gazette.* Movies also came to the city. Metro, VLSE, Fox,

Triangle, Famous Players-Lasky, Paramount, World, and Universal pictures played the theaters located in and near the city's downtown area. Exchange agents for these distributors vied with each other to get their films into the local theaters. Managers of these houses went to Milwaukee and to Chicago to secure films they felt would appeal to their clientele, or to their own sense of mission in the case of parish hall programming.

Theater managers like Mr. Gregory of the Gem and Mr. McKinlay of the Ideal and the new Lyric saw themselves as boosters and businessmen. In an example of the way that the local movie house tried to fit itself into national as well as local celebrations of commerce and community, Gregory cooperated with local clothing retailers to make Fashion Week a success, and McKinlay timed the opening of the Lyric Theater for the beginning of the week commemorating the Fourth of July.

Fitting itself into a national culture, Stevens Point did not aim to upset any rural-urban balance—although this shift was taking place in America. The quotation from the editorial that opened this section concluded, "Truly good roads pay and they can be depended upon as the surest method to stem the movement from country to city."[73] Still, its citizens wanted to keep up with the trends and the changing times. In fact, Stevens Point's citizens needed to be aware of what was going on in the nation. Some of their sons were already serving in the military in El Paso, and, in 1916, polio began in New York and spread west. Public health administrators, private citizens, and movie theater managers needed to be prepared. The racial issues sparked when folks in the Midwest watched *Birth of a Nation* were part of a much larger problem of race in America. There were race riots in 1919, and the Ku Klux Klan expanded in midwestern states, including Wisconsin, in the 1920s.

The same consolidation of exhibition that occurred on a national level also happened in Stevens Point between 1916 and 1920. In 1916, people could watch movies in four theaters plus the Empire Amusement Hall and the Episcopal parish hall. In the 1917–18 city directory the number of theaters had shrunk to four, and by 1920–21 there were only three movie theaters in Stevens Point.

Taking such a close look at one year in the life of a small city is a very useful exercise for film historians. The quirks and idiosyncrasies of the place, its troubling norms, and the colorful individuals who inhabited its civic spaces stand out in relief against the daily routine. One sees how theater managers tried to fit their work into the leisure-time needs of city residents and how they matched their business strategies to the conventions of the local retailers. Widening the view to accommodate a national perspective is equally important. Movies were made to be seen nationwide and internationally. The business of film distribution also functioned at a national and international level. When the people of this city of 11,000, located in the center of Wisconsin, went to the movies, they were familiar with the genres, the themes, the songs, and the mise-en-scène of the films they watched. The particular history and demography of Stevens Point might cause audiences to respond with nervous applause to the ride of the Klan in *The Birth of a Nation;* their ministers might get more exercised than those in bigger cities about films like *Damaged Goods;* still, Stevens Point was connected to national figures, concerns, celebrations, and trends. The Gem, Ideal, Della, and Lyric, the Empire Amusement Hall, and the Episcopal parish hall were important institutions in the local life of the city, as well as in soldering the connections between Stevens Point and bigger cities of the United States.

Notes

1. Editorial, *Stevens Point Gazette,* 13 December 1916, sec. II, p. 20.

2. A Sanborn Map of Stevens Point published in 1913 stated the population at 10,000. The *Stevens Point Journal,* 29 December 1916, 1, estimated the population at 11,000 based on a count of the houses in town. The *Stevens Point Gazette,* 13 December 1916, sec. II, p. 20, pointed out that the 1910 census pegged the population at 8,692, and "Stevens Pointers have good reason for claiming a population of between 11,000 and 12,000, but they are only estimating it."

3. For references to newspapers for sale, see *Stevens Point Journal* advertisements, 5 February 1916, 6. For a listing of the numbers of books and magazines held at the library, see "More Books Needed," *Stevens Point Journal,* 25 March 1916, 3.

4. "Would Bar Picture," *Stevens Point Gazette,* sec. II, p. 10.

5. Both the *Stevens Point Journal* and the *Gazette* published several columns in each issue detailing the comings and goings of local residents, as well as the visitors coming to the city.

6. "Birth of a Nation," *Stevens Point Journal,* 24 March 1916, 4.

7. "New Theatre Opened," *Gazette,* 5 July 1916, sec. II, p. 7.

8. Advertisement for Fashion Week and the C. G. Macnish Co., *Stevens Point Journal,* 17 March 1916, 3.

9. Advertisement, "Magic Mirror," *Women's Wear,* 3 March 1916, 1.

10. "1916 a Year Full of Events That Will Live in the Nation's History," *Stevens Point Journal,* 26 December 1916, 5.

11. Advertisement, *Stevens Point Journal,* 24 March 1916, 4.

12. "Fashion Week Sure, Thirteen Local Firms Join in Promoting Joint Openings," *Stevens Point Journal,* 14 March 1916, 1.

13. "Parish House Stage Small, Pictures of Birth of a Nation Will Be Shown at Empire," *Stevens Point Journal,* 15 March 1916, 1.

14. "Birth of a Nation Comes," *Stevens Point Journal,* 11 March 1916, 1.

15. "City Briefs," *Stevens Point Journal,* 20 March 1916, 6.

16. Advertisement, *Stevens Point Journal,* 21 March 1916, 6.

17. Ibid.; advertisement, *Stevens Point Journal,* 25 March, 6.

18. "Birth of a Nation," *Stevens Point Journal* 21 March 1916, 3; "Birth of a Nation," *Stevens Point Journal,* 23 March 1916, 4; "Birth of a Nation," *Stevens Point Journal,* 24 March 1916, 4.

19. "Tears Replace Handclaps, 'Birth of a Nation' Is Powerfully Moving Production," *Stevens Point Journal*, 28 March 1916, 1.

20. Ibid.

21. *Fourteenth Census of the United States Taken in the Year 1920*, vol. 1 (Washington, D.C.: Department of Commerce, General Printing Office, 1921).

22. "Patriotism Keynote, Thousands of Flags to Stir Up Glorious Sentiment in Stevens Point July 4th," *Gazette*, 31 May 1916, sec. I, p. 1.

23. "Feature of Fourth, Biggest and Grandest Parade Ever Attempted in This Part of State to Be Held," *Gazette*, 21 June 1916, sec. I, p. 1.

24. Ibid.

25. "Says He Stole Chickens," *Stevens Point Journal*, 27 March 1916, 1; "Club Elects Delegates," *Stevens Point Journal*, 27 March 1916, 1.

26. Advertisement, *Stevens Point Journal*, 26 October 1916, 6.

27. "The Day You'll Never Forget," *Stevens Point Journal*, 12 August 1916, 1.

28. "Tears Replace Handclaps."

29. "Hundreds Visit City," *Gazette*, 29 March 1916, sec. I, p. 5.

30. Ibid.

31. "Fashion Week Grows," *Stevens Point Journal*, 4 April 1916, 3.

32. "One of the Finest" quoted in "Elks Entertain," *Stevens Point Journal* 29 March 1916, 6; Advertisement, *Stevens Point Journal*, 26 June 1916, 3.

33. City Council Minutes, 6 June 1916, University of Wisconsin–Stevens Point Archives, Portage Series 75, vol. 9, p. 567.

34. "Firemen Are Boosters," *Stevens Point Gazette*, 12 July 1916, sec. I, p. 2.

35. Mayor Walters used this phrase when he was headed up the first city council meeting after being elected mayor. "Doctor Still Mayor," *Gazette*, 19 April 1916, sec. I, p. 1.

36. Editorial, *Gazette*, 17 May 1916, sec. I, p. 4.

37. Editorial, *Stevens Point Journal*, 1 May 1916, 1.

38. "New Movie Theatre," *Gazette*, 12 January 1916, sec. II, p. 10.

39. "Elms Are Cut Down," *Stevens Point Journal*, 10 April 1916, 3.

40. "Opening of the Lyric Theater," *Stevens Point Journal*, 1 July 1916, 1.

41. Ibid.

42. "McKinlay Plans to Add Vaudeville," *Stevens Point Journal*, 17 June 1916, 1; "Opening of the Lyric Theater," *Stevens Point Journal*, 1 July 1916, 1.

43. Advertisement, *Stevens Point Journal*, 16 October 1916, 8.

44. "Style Show Pleases," *Stevens Point Journal*, 23 October 1916, 1.

45. Advertisement, *Stevens Point Journal*, 24 October 1916, 3.

46. Advertisement, *Stevens Point Journal*, 28 October 1916, 8.

47. The Della did not advertise regularly in the city's newspapers, and the Empire tended to show specials and road shows. The Episcopal parish hall made its initial deal with George Kleine.

48. "New Theater Owner," *Gazette*, 21 June 1916, sec. II, p. 11.

49. "Takes Della Theater," *Stevens Point Journal*, 2 September 1916, 1; "At the Della Theater," *Stevens Point Journal*, 29 November 1916, 8.

50. "Parish Hall Movie Booms," *Stevens Point Journal*, 31 January 1916, 4.

51. "McKinlay Plans to Add Vaudeville," *Stevens Point Journal*, 17 June 1916, 1; "Opening of the Lyric Theater," *Stevens Point Journal*, 1 July 1916, 1.

52. "Ideal Quits Business," *Gazette,* 13 September 1916, sec. I, p. 1.

53. "Della Gets New Machine," *Stevens Point Journal,* 21 September 1916, 1.

54. Ibid.

55. Advertisement, *Stevens Point Journal,* 26 July 1916, 4.

56. Advertisement, *Stevens Point Journal,* 18 September 1916, 8.

57. Advertisement, *Stevens Point Journal,* 14 November 1916, 2.

58. Advertisement, *Stevens Point Journal,* 7 November 1916, 8.

59. Advertisement, *Stevens Point Journal,* 22 July 1916, 4.

60. Advertisement, *Stevens Point Journal,* 3 August 1916, 4.

61. Advertisement, *Stevens Point Journal,* 11 February, 1916, 6.

62. Ibid.

63. For example, Billie Burke, "My Simple Rules for Beauty," *Delineator* 77 (June 1911): 510; "Alan Dale, "Bonnie Billie Burke," *Cosmopolitan Magazine,* 52 (February 1912): 412–18; Rennold Wolf, "Billie Burke, Married and at Home," *Green Book Magazine,* n.d., c. 1915, Hastings Historical Society, Hastings-on-Hudson, New York; "The First Twinklings of Three Popular Stars," *Woman's Home Companion* 43 (September 1916), 44.

64. "City Briefs," *Stevens Point Journal,* 11 February 1916, 6.

65. Advertisement, *Stevens Point Journal,* 6 May 1916, 3.

66. The various costs do not add up, and even in 1916, creative accounting for publicity purposes was not unusual. In a report about the finances of the serial that he made to stock holders in the film's production company in 1917, George Kleine listed the cost of the negative as $396,222.55. There is no separate line for costume or salary expenses, and the total cost for negative, positive copies, advertising, music and other expenses was given as $1,190,980.46. Letter from George Kleine to John Sidney Burnet, 13 August 1917, George Kleine Collection, Library of Congress, Box 24.

67. Advertisement, *Stevens Point Journal,* 16 September 1916, 6; advertisement, *Stevens Point Journal* 18 September 1916, 8; advertisement, *Stevens Point Journal* 4 October 1916, 8; advertisement, *Stevens Point Journal,* 16 October 1916, 8.

68. "Billie Burke, Well Known Actress in New Role—It's a Girl," *Stevens Point Journal,* 25 October 1916, 7; "Sues Billie Burke," *Stevens Point Journal,* 11 November 1916, 1.

69. For a list of the magazines the library subscribed to in 1916, see "Public Library Notes," *Gazette,* 30 August 1916, sec. II, p. 11.

70. Victor Schertzinger and Thomas Ince, "Peggy" (New York: Jerome H. Remick & Co., 1915); Maud A. Murray, "Gloria's Romance Valse" (New York: Cadillac Moving Picture Music Series, 1916).

71. "Movie Crowds Small," *Stevens Point Journal,* 29 December 1916, 1.

72. "Editorial," *Gazette,* 17 May 1916, sec. I, p. 4.

73. Ibid.

Part IV

MATURITY AND CR

CASE STUDIES

IMAGINING AND PROMOTING
THE SMALL-TOWN THEATER

GREGORY A. WALLER

The key man of the picture business, now and always, is the exhibitor.
"The Road to the Public," *Exhibitors Herald-World* (October 4, 1930)

*We are for the exhibitor, first, last and always, but we would not say that
the exhibitor has not been to blame for many of his own troubles.*
"Skies Look Brighter for the Independent Producer," *Billboard*
(March 8, 1930)

The 200-seat Llamarada Theater in Hilltown, Indiana, unquestionably stands
as one of the most well-documented small-town movie theaters of the early
1930s. Owned and operated by a locally born and raised man who had been
exhibiting films in Hilltown since the nickelodeon era, the state-of-the-art
Llamarada was built in 1930 and managed to remain solvent throughout the
Depression and independent despite the efforts of regional theater chains to
dominate exhibition in the Midwest. From existing records, we know a good
deal about the size and makeup of the Llamarada's staff, the managerial and
programming policies of its owner-operator, and, most important, its audience and its place in Hilltown as "an institution, an important part of the
community."[1]

The problem—or at least the apparent problem—is that the Llamarada
Theater and Hilltown, Indiana, are fictional constructs, created by Margaret
Weymouth Jackson for a series of five stories published in the *Saturday Evening Post* between August and October 1930.[2] That the stories are fiction does
not negate their historical value—or, for that matter, that of the many other
movie-related works of fiction published in the *Post* during this period. In
fact, the Llamarada stories are an important, overlooked resource that, when
read in the context of the motion picture trade press, can help us analyze the
small-town theater as concrete practice, business strategy, and culturally res-
onant myth, particularly during the first years of the Depression. Focusing
on the audiences as well as entertainment providers, this historically specific
analysis will underscore even as it problematizes the role of the local, a topic
of considerable import across twentieth-century media history.

Until recently, film historians have understood the early sound era principally in terms of corporate maneuvering and changes (or continuities) in Hollywood studio practices: the pitching of all-talkies; the westward movement of Broadway personnel; the emergence of new stars, genres, and movie cycles; the refinement of sound recording apparatus; and so on. However, Douglas Gomery's research on the Publix Theaters and Donald Crafton's *The Talkies: American Cinema's Transition to Sound, 1926–1931,* underscore just how sweeping, significant, and even melodramatic the overhaul of the American film exhibition business was during the late 1920s and the first years of the Depression.[3] "The silent exhibitor," in Crafton's words, "was forced to choose between being driven out by competitors, selling the theater to a chain, or converting to sound (probably with borrowed money)." The exhibitor's dilemma hardly ended there: "For all classes and locales of theater owners," Crafton concludes, "the primary issue surrounding the coming of sound was the decreased sovereignty of the local manager."[4] That local "sovereignty" actually mattered is, as might be expected, a governing assumption of the Llamarada stories.

Crafton estimates that by July 1929—several months before the stock market crash—about a quarter of the theaters across the United States were wired for sound. Most of these theaters were in metropolitan areas, but some were in smaller communities.[5] A year later, with life becoming increasingly harder, the *Exhibitors Herald-World* delivered its own (quite optimistic) version of the "true and essential facts of the motion picture market." This trade magazine claimed that as of July 1, 1930, more than 10,000 of the estimated 14,500 "legitimate motion picture houses" (not halls or other venues occasionally used for film screenings) in the United States were equipped for sound. Of the sound-equipped theaters, 6,796 were independently owned; 2,252 were "controlled by producer-owned chains" (Publix, Fox, Warner Brothers, RKO, Loew); and 1,213 were controlled by "independent circuits." The grand transformation, according to *Exhibitors Herald-World,* was virtually complete: the independent owner-operator had survived, the major chains had become stabilized without monopolizing the market, and the remaining 4,500 houses showing silents were sure to be wired by the end of 1930.[6] The story, of course, was neither this tidily nor this equitably resolved, except, perhaps, in the *Saturday Evening Post.*

Tales of the Llamarada

Now, a small-town movie is not like a city movie, and not even sound
pictures and colored pictures can make it so.
Jackson, "Professional," *Saturday Evening Post,* August 30, 1930

In 1930, when the *Saturday Evening Post* maintained its standing as the premier general-interest magazine in the United States, the weekly circulation was purported to be more than 2.75 million. Margaret Weymouth Jackson was among the *Post*'s most frequently published authors. Her first *Post* story appeared in 1927, and she went on to place twenty stories in the magazine between 1929 and 1932, while occasionally publishing in other popular venues as well, including *Women's Home Companion, Good Housekeeping, Ladies' Home Journal,* and, later, the *American Mercury.* In its heyday, the *Post* made much use of series fiction, that is, ongoing stories published across several months (or even years). Each installment offered a largely self-contained narrative that featured recurring characters linked by a consistent locale or environment. In effect, the *Post*'s series fiction collectively mapped a wide-ranging, if still highly selective, vision of America, from New England villages and southern African American communities to Manhattan and Hollywood, from advertising agencies to western ranches, traveling salesmen to Broadway ingenues. In the *Post*'s imaginative cartography, Jackson's turf was the nativist, white, midwestern small town, which she knew and loved and affirmed from the inside. A month before her first Llamarada story was published, Jackson declared in a *Post* self-profile: "I am partial to the Middle West, particularly Indiana . . . the All-American population of the small town where we live—there is only one foreign-born citizen here, an ancient German who came to sweet Owen County [between Terre Haute and Bloomington, Indiana] fifty years ago—makes a fine atmosphere, and I am extremely fond of the friendly, casual, upright manners and methods of my fellow townsmen. In fact, I am Middle Western, middle-class, small-town and Hoosier, and proud of it!"[7] Jackson's fictional Hilltown is not to be confused with the more class-stratified version of Indiana life analyzed by sociologists Robert S. Lynd and Helen Merrell Lynd in their widely publicized study, *Middletown: A Study in Contemporary American Culture.*[8] Hilltown is an "old town nestled between green hills and a shining river, with the limestone mill and quarries lying on the outer edge of it, with the clean, sun-bleached square about its pile of courthouse, with the tidy, well-kept, small stores, the ranging, well-kept, white-painted houses under great trees."[9] It "was a place of its own, a little apart from the world." Yet for all its quaint charm and "old-fashioned" mores,[10] Hilltown was not preserved in amber, aggressively antimodern, or buckling under the weight of the Depression. Hilltown is characterized by its prosperous (when well-run) retail and service businesses, which cater to what in an earlier story are referred to as the community's notoriously "overcareful" consumers: "The town's high and comfortable standard of living on its small incomes bespoke much care in spending."[11]

Jackson introduced Hilltown in a series of stories concerning the publisher and staff of a weekly farm newspaper. In addition to the movie theater series, Jackson wrote stories set in the town's drugstore, its first chain grocery store, a new auto dealership, and a plumbing company (all published in the *Post*). These businesses—not churches or schools, not the bank or the farm—

are where the economic vitality and the durable humanity of this community reside.[12]

Among the biggest commercial success stories in Jackson's modern Midwest is the Llamarada Theater. Significantly, in establishing the ground rules for the Llamarada series, Jackson did not choose to look back nostalgically to the days of the tin-roofed nickelodeon. Instead, she imagined Hilltown's only picture show as a newly constructed venue designed to be highly comfortable, reasonably profitable, and fully equipped with the most up-to-date technology.

In Jackson's Indiana, a brand-new movie theater could be deemed "one of the finest things" in an old-fashioned town.[13] She offers almost no description of the interior decoration, marquee, or foyer, except to note that the compact theater is "beautiful, perfect and finished in every small detail."[14] One story, however, foregrounds the new organist (and his much-appreciated instrument); another is set almost entirely in the projection booth and lays out not only the projectionist's serious work but also the intricacies of the Llamarada's sophisticated sound system.[15] Both the musician and the projectionist-electrician are from Hilltown, as are the two perky usherettes in scarlet satin skirts and gold-brocaded jackets, as well as all the other members of this workplace family, young and old, male and female. No matter what motion pictures fill the Llamarada's screen, this theater is a local enterprise, emblematic of a certain faith in the Depression-proof saving grace of small-town small business, which here requires no urban intervention in the form of technical, aesthetic, or financial expertise.

Presiding over the Llamarada with benign paternalism is the white-haired Mr. McLaughlin, who has built his exhibition business from the ground up, plowing any profits back into the theater. His decency, kindness, and concern for his employees and for the community at large are demonstrated in each story, although we never see him participating in civic activities or opening the Llamarada for charity or public service events. It is enough, Jackson implies, that McLaughlin knows and plays fair with his customers—that earns him and his employees a modest living and makes him ethically unimpeachable. "Know[ing] the town" is McLaughlin's key to success, the result of years spent "studying, wooing and winning Hilltown."[16] He buys the right films and arranges weekly schedules so as to "catch" the many different audiences that constitute the town and its environs.[17] Jackson assumes without question, first, that local prerogative in terms of film booking is possible; and, second, that there is more than enough appropriate Hollywood product from which an exhibitor like McLaughlin can choose. However, Jackson makes only passing reference to what is actually screened at the Llamarada, except for the regular Monday serial, booked especially to draw in "poor farmers" on "dime night."[18]

It is moviegoers rather than movies that fill the establishing shots of the Llamarada stories, perhaps because Jackson seems determined to counter stereotypes about gullible and lowbrow "hicktown" spectators. Hilltown's white, midwestern moviegoers are, these stories insist, neither naive nor homogeneous. The Llamarada's ushers soon recognize familiar faces and seat people according to personal preferences and "all the different little cliques in town," notably by age and gender, for race and class do not register as categories in Jackson's "All-American" stories.[19]

Together, movie-savvy Hilltowners constitute a "discriminating, exacting audience,"[20] whose members are "capricious, discerning, shrewd" about what they expect for their entertainment dollar. Furthermore, they are an active audience, applauding with "good-natured mockery" as local advertisements appear on screen, sometimes singing along with the organist, socializing and joking in those relaxed moments before the show begins.[21] It is a good thing that McLaughlin does his job so responsibly and the audience maintains its high standards because in this small town the movie theater is "an institution, an important part of the community, the light and brightness, the amusement and forgetting, the open door between the hill-and-river-enclosed town and the great world."[22] A reel of film can ignite in the projection booth, but even that potentially life-threatening danger only proves that the Llamarada is in all respects a safe place: the projectionist performs heroically, and the audience files out in an orderly, calm manner. "That's what comes of living in the sticks," an usher effuses, "men and women control themselves. They think as individuals, not as a mob. I tell you, I'm proud of Hilltown!"[23]

Aside from flaming nitrate, the only threats to the Llamarada as independent enterprise and workplace family come from outside Hilltown, either in the form of young men who have left the town and returned or, more seriously, from city men who see Hilltown as merely another market ripe for exploiting. The last story in Jackson's series predictably ups the melodramatic stakes: catastrophe threatens the local picture show, not because of the rising floodwaters that literally isolate Hilltown, but because Michigan Theaters, Inc., decides that it wants to acquire the Llamarada to expand its regional holdings.

In February, 1930, J. C. Penney argued in the *Post* that "the chain store is only one item in the whole great process of nationalizing the business of the United States"—a process that Penney deems inevitable, progressive, and potentially of great benefit to everyone concerned, especially in towns and small cities.[24] But Jackson was having none of it. Michigan Theaters, Inc., stands unambiguously for "the chain movies—the octopus—the great, rich, ruthless company" out to eradicate small business and local capitalism.[25]

Representing Michigan Theaters, Inc., are a Jew and an Irishman, urban interlopers indeed, who are pictured in one gangster movie–styled illustration as racketeers facing off against the defiant, elderly theater owner. As punishment for offering to buy out McLaughlin (who refuses their fair price of $50,000) and then threatening to build a competing theater, the chain-men are stranded for ten days in flooded Hilltown with nothing to eat except pork and no new movies to watch. They flee at the first opportunity, correctly convinced that they could never run the Llamarada at a profit. In the end, market conditions, natural forces, essentialized ethnicity, and a stubborn and decent theater owner keep the Midwest midwestern; the home for nationally distributed entertainment becomes the bastion of regionalism.

It is not as if McLaughlin books movies that are appreciably different or more local than what Michigan Theaters, Inc., would bring to Hilltown. He knows that the chain can buy "better pictures," but in the end the pictures are not the issue for Jackson. On this point, she would likely agree with cultural commentator Gilbert Seldes, who argued in the *Post* in May 1930 that "radio and movie talkies . . . exist for all alike" in the city or the "outlands," and so, we might add, do stories in mass-market magazines like the *Saturday Evening Post*.[26]

Hollywood, of course, is the source of the movies that delight audiences at the Llamarada. Yet Hollywood itself never directly figures in Jackson's stories. Perhaps Jackson and her editors correctly realized that readers could get enough of Hollywood simply by flipping through the pages of the *Post*. In 1930, for instance, the *Post* published a six-part serialized novel *(Happy Landings)*, in which a young stage actress moves to Hollywood, where sound technology holds sway and talkies demand new stars; two stories by George F. Worts, who specialized in fiction about behind-the-scenes studio professionals (in this case, a director of photography and a sound effects man); a story narrated by a female stenographer working at a movie studio; F. Scott Fitzgerald's cynical story "A Millionaire's Girl," about a potential star who leaves Hollywood for an ill-fated marriage.; and J. P. McEvoy's satiric account of a cartoonist who is lured to Hollywood, where his comic strip is set to be directed for the screen by a recently hired Soviet director.

Nonfiction pieces also appeared in the *Post:* a (ghostwritten?) account by Mary Pickford of touring the world with Douglas Fairbanks; feature articles on the color musical revue film and the European market for talkies; and—most interesting—a two-part article by Ben Ames Williams on the "complex and arduous business" of producing a hypothetical movie, a process hemmed in by the competing demands of censorship, the star system, the marketplace, and the author of the original property.[27] Between the stories and the features, the *Post* ran regular weekly ads for Universal under Carl Laemmle's byline and elaborate promotional campaigns for Paramount and Technicolor, as well as a host of ads featuring testimonials by movie celebrities, such as James Cruze on behalf of Mennen shaving cream and John Boles touting Spur bow ties. Jackson's Llamarada stories, then, took their place in the *Post* in a much broader discourse about the movies, a discourse far more likely to spin tales of Hollywood than Hilltown, movie production instead of film exhibition.

Working the Community Angle

*Chain theatre operation can be made dangerous unless, through the
personality, the friendliness, the willingness to work in community
betterment of our representative, our theatre manager is manifest in
that community. . . . Humanize your company, your circuit, through
yourself. Be a pleasant power in your city. Be alive to the opportunity
to serve. Let your neighbors judge the fairness of your company by
your own fairness. Be a well loved and useful citizen—and your
company will gain prestige in that community.*
SIDNEY KENT, general manager, Paramount[28]

For Jackson, imagining the small-town theater was inevitably marking how it
differed from the urban theater, hence her claim that "a small-town movie is
not like a city movie, and not even sound pictures and colored pictures can
make it so."[29] The pictures, which are produced in the metropolis, never
pose any threat to the midwestern and middle-class values that Jackson holds
dear. The important measure of difference between city and small-town theaters is instead to be found in the behavior and makeup of the audience and
in the entertainment experience that McLaughlin provides to his regular patrons. His investment in ensuring that the theater is a first-class, fully modern operation reflects his unshakable faith in his discerning local customers,
in the sound film industry, and in the economic well-being of the nation.
McLaughlin's careful management practices pay off: he weathers the corporate machinations and remains autonomous, able to control his fate as the
Depression looms.

Above all, it is the everyday role of the Llamarada *as* a community and *in*
the community that for Jackson makes this small-town theater worth celebrating, a point driven home in the conclusion of the final Llamarada story.
After rejecting the hostile advances of Michigan Theaters, Inc., McLaughlin
marries the retired schoolteacher who runs his box office. The ceremony is
conducted in the local Presbyterian church, then celebrated with a free show
at the Llamarada for everyone in Hilltown; after all, it is the all-inclusive, non-
denominational movie theater that stands as the true center of Hilltown,
circa 1930.

How does what we could call the myth of the small-town theater in Jackson's
Llamarada stories stack up against the entertainment industry's own rhetoric
concerning such theaters?[30] To chart this particular discursive field, I shall
rely on editorial commentary, news coverage, and letters to the editor from
two different trade magazines: Martin Quigley's *Exhibitors Herald-World,* the
successor to *Moving Picture World,* which subsequently became *Motion Picture
Herald* in 1931 (henceforth referred to in this chapter simply as the *Herald*),
and *Billboard: The Theatrical Digest and Show World Review.* The *Herald* stridently
championed how the motion picture industry was shaping up under the in-

fluence of Will Hays and the Motion Picture Producers and Distributors of America (MPPDA). *Billboard,* as its full title suggests, covered an appreciably wider range of commercial amusements, including stage, radio, and all manner of touring shows. *Billboard* was also much more willing to challenge what it sometimes called the monopolistic "overlords of the cinema," which it saw as engaged in a scorched-earth campaign to destroy vaudeville, theatrical road shows, and other live performance.[31] In fact, *Billboard* dropped its weekly coverage of the motion picture industry in March 1931 (it published only a handful of movie reviews in each issue), when it adopted what it called an "all-flesh" policy.

As the Depression deepened, *Billboard* could run an editorial entitled "Independent Exhibitors Face Results of Their Own Folly" and rejoice over anecdotal evidence that small-town movie theaters equipped for sound had seen the light and were again booking vaudeville acts.[32] The *Herald,* in contrast, reported favorably on any efforts by Publix, for instance, to localize and individualize theater management policies, even as the trade magazine steadfastly insisted that the coming of sound had saved the "small theatre and particularly the small town theatre."[33]

During the early sound era, the trade press discourse made a firm distinction between chain and independent theaters that was not quite the same as the hierarchical divisions enforced by the run-zone-clearance system. (The run-zone-clearance system maximized profits by maintaining the distinction between first-run and subsequent-run theaters, organizing distribution according to geographic locations—or "zones"—and establishing "clearance" times between different runs.) In the trade press, *chain* could refer to theaters owned by national producer-exhibitors such as Fox, Warners, and Publix or to theaters owned by regionally based exhibitors who had no direct link to Hollywood studios. According to trade press accounts, *independent* encompassed a range of theaters found in locations as different as urban neighborhoods, residential areas, small cities, small communities, small towns, and whistlestops "out in the sticks." There is significant slippage—ideological as well as geographic—within and across both categories. (Indeed, the owner of an independent chain of Indiana theaters was one of the most vociferous spokespeople in *Billboard* for "Mr. Small-Town Exhibitor.")[34] No doubt, this slippage is evident through much of the twentieth century's ongoing popular discourse concerning American retail business practices. Yet the relations between "independent" and "chain" (or between independence and corporate affiliation) registered particularly deeply in the Depression with respect to the motion picture industry, which had long promoted itself both as a technologically savvy, forward-thinking big business and as a democratic provider of affordable entertainment for all Americans.

Along with a taxonomy based on size, location, and circuit affiliation, the trade press also resorted to a more figurative vocabulary in which the independent exhibitor—aka the "little fellow"—also became the "safety valve," "shock absorber," or "backbone" of the industry.[35] As such terms suggest, trade discourse never expressed doubt about whether the independent exhibitor should survive; the question was how. What would guarantee his place in the competitive market during the Depression? What could the "little fellow," particularly one operating well outside a metropolitan orbit, teach the corporate bigwigs?

Rule number one, judging from the trade press as much as from the Llamarada stories, is that the manager must accurately gauge the tastes of his audience(s) and, presumably, arrange his programs accordingly. Woe be it to the manager who futilely tried to row against the currents of public opinion. Recall that McLaughlin had no trouble booking movies at the Llamarada that were eminently suitable for Hilltown's different audiences. But listening to regular customers and screening appropriate pictures were not the same thing, as evident in the letters from small-town exhibitors appearing in the *Herald*'s "Voice of the Industry" page. "It is rough how the little fellows out in the sticks are treated," complained G. A. Duncan of Carlisle, Kentucky. "Here is what we pay for: no music, no action in most cases, no picture that the public wants . . . the majority of the people want clean pictures."[36] Other managers drew finer distinctions based on box office receipts and observation of their patrons. A column from December 1930, for instance, included the following assessments: Paramount's *Queen High*, wrote the manager of the Elite Theatre in Greenleaf, Kansas, "gave excellent satisfaction. This is a clever picture and is what the people want to see," whereas *Trailing Trouble* starring Hoot Gibson is so "silly" that "even the 10 year old kids will razz it." Philip Rand from Salmon, Idaho, declared that "the industry has given us two magnificent plays in *Sunny Side Up* and *Rio Rita*. Why can't they give us more like them? We need them. The public wants them! They pay big returns." An exhibitor in Kerens, Texas, lauded *Light of the Western Stars,* which "is great for Saturday," then complained, "Whenever we go highbrow, it gives the small town exhibitor a headache."[37]

The implication of the letters to the *Herald* is that even if the experienced exhibitor knew what his audience wanted, Hollywood rarely provided enough of the right product to suit the tastes of the local market. This problem, according to a *Billboard* article, applied to shorts as well as features, further hampering the small-town exhibitor's programming options.[38]

One could, however, adopt an entirely different booking strategy, based on the movie theater's role as a showcase and conduit for nationally available commercial entertainment. It was entirely possible, as the owner of a theater in Paris, Missouri (population 1,400), put it, that the small-town exhibitor could succeed by offering his patrons "identically the same shows they get in larger towns."[39] From this perspective, there was no rationale for a "localized" show. "Hollywood may be a long way from 'main street' of your town or my town," declared Ken W. Thompson of Adams, Wisconsin, "but talking pictures bridge the gap." In effect, Thompson's logic mirrored the policies announced by Publix chief of "booking and buying," William M. Saal. Saal told his managers and advertising men that while Publix sought to give "the local theatre manager, the district manager, and the division manager a voice in determining the demands of local conditions . . . booking on a national scale, or scope, was advisable in 99 per cent of the cases."[40] Nevertheless, the talismanic word for the trade press was *individuality*—that was what all theater managers most needed to demonstrate.[41]

Both Saal and the small-town exhibitors quoted here made no reference to live performance, the one aspect of the program that could potentially localize (and humanize) the bill at any movie theater. "Locally specialized forms of entertainments, whether stage shows, talent contests, or sing-alongs," disappeared in the early sound era, according to Crafton, who calls this phenomenon the "passing of hometown-generated entertainment."[42] His point is well taken, even though the Llamarada stories more frequently mention organ performances (sometimes with audience sing-a-longs) than on-screen images, and, as I have argued on other occasions, hometown entertainment did not vanish from small-town American theaters after the conversion to sound. It is noteworthy for the purposes of this chapter that the contemporary trade discourse had little to say about the value or liability of live performance and evinced no nostalgia for its supposed heyday during the silent era.

For the *Herald* and *Billboard*, what the exhibitor booked seemed to matter much less than how he dealt with his customers and his community at large. Amusement parks, advised *Billboard*, should "take a tip from the movies": "First of all, gain and HOLD the good will of the people of the community. . . . SERVICE is the keynote."[43] Even the smallest exhibitor presumably had some control over the service he provided, no matter how hamstrung he was when it came to programming. "Chains Have Not Been Able to Meet Small-Town Demands" was the title of a *Billboard* editorial from December 1930, which claimed that "it takes more than business efficiency [always acknowledged to be the undeniable benefit of the chain store] to keep the house out of the red. It takes personality" and the "absolutely essential . . . personal contact" between manager and patron. Also essential was such personal contact between the staff and the public, as in the Llamarada stories, in which ushers direct individual moviegoers to their favorite seats and the projectionist will not rest until he provides Hilltowners with the best possible audiovisual experience.

But even the friendliest welcome and the best service could not necessarily make the movie theater a prominent and valued centerpiece of the local community. In an article reprinted in the *Herald*, University of North Carolina sociology professor Harold D. Meyer—a "playground and recreation

19. "Tears Replace Handclaps, 'Birth of a Nation' Is Powerfully Moving Production," *Stevens Point Journal*, 28 March 1916, 1.

20. Ibid.

21. *Fourteenth Census of the United States Taken in the Year 1920*, vol. 1 (Washington, D.C.: Department of Commerce, General Printing Office, 1921).

22. "Patriotism Keynote, Thousands of Flags to Stir Up Glorious Sentiment in Stevens Point July 4th," *Gazette*, 31 May 1916, sec. I, p. 1.

23. "Feature of Fourth, Biggest and Grandest Parade Ever Attempted in This Part of State to Be Held," *Gazette*, 21 June 1916, sec. I, p. 1.

24. Ibid.

25. "Says He Stole Chickens," *Stevens Point Journal*, 27 March 1916, 1; "Club Elects Delegates," *Stevens Point Journal*, 27 March 1916, 1.

26. Advertisement, *Stevens Point Journal*, 26 October 1916, 6.

27. "The Day You'll Never Forget," *Stevens Point Journal*, 12 August 1916, 1.

28. "Tears Replace Handclaps."

29. "Hundreds Visit City," *Gazette*, 29 March 1916, sec. I, p. 5.

30. Ibid.

31. "Fashion Week Grows," *Stevens Point Journal*, 4 April 1916, 3.

32. "One of the Finest" quoted in "Elks Entertain," *Stevens Point Journal* 29 March 1916, 6; Advertisement, *Stevens Point Journal*, 26 June 1916, 3.

33. City Council Minutes, 6 June 1916, University of Wisconsin–Stevens Point Archives, Portage Series 75, vol. 9, p. 567.

34. "Firemen Are Boosters," *Stevens Point Gazette*, 12 July 1916, sec. I, p. 2.

35. Mayor Walters used this phrase when he was headed up the first city council meeting after being elected mayor. "Doctor Still Mayor," *Gazette*, 19 April 1916, sec. I, p.1.

36. Editorial, *Gazette*, 17 May 1916, sec. I, p. 4.

37. Editorial, *Stevens Point Journal*, 1 May 1916, 1.

38. "New Movie Theatre," *Gazette*, 12 January 1916, sec. II, p. 10.

39. "Elms Are Cut Down," *Stevens Point Journal*, 10 April 1916, 3.

40. "Opening of the Lyric Theater," *Stevens Point Journal*, 1 July 1916, 1.

41. Ibid.

42. "McKinlay Plans to Add Vaudeville," *Stevens Point Journal*, 17 June 1916, 1; "Opening of the Lyric Theater," *Stevens Point Journal*, 1 July 1916, 1.

43. Advertisement, *Stevens Point Journal*, 16 October 1916, 8.

44. "Style Show Pleases," *Stevens Point Journal*, 23 October 1916, 1.

45. Advertisement, *Stevens Point Journal*, 24 October 1916, 3.

46. Advertisement, *Stevens Point Journal*, 28 October 1916, 8.

47. The Della did not advertise regularly in the city's newspapers, and the Empire tended to show specials and road shows. The Episcopal parish hall made its initial deal with George Kleine.

48. "New Theater Owner," *Gazette*, 21 June 1916, sec. II, p. 11.

49. "Takes Della Theater," *Stevens Point Journal*, 2 September 1916, 1; "At the Della Theater," *Stevens Point Journal*, 29 November 1916, 8.

50. "Parish Hall Movie Booms," *Stevens Point Journal*, 31 January 1916, 4.

51. "McKinlay Plans to Add Vaudeville," *Stevens Point Journal*, 17 June 1916, 1; "Opening of the Lyric Theater," *Stevens Point Journal*, 1 July 1916, 1.

52. "Ideal Quits Business," *Gazette,* 13 September 1916, sec. I, p. 1.

53. "Della Gets New Machine," *Stevens Point Journal,* 21 September 1916, 1.

54. Ibid.

55. Advertisement, *Stevens Point Journal,* 26 July 1916, 4.

56. Advertisement, *Stevens Point Journal,* 18 September 1916, 8.

57. Advertisement, *Stevens Point Journal,* 14 November 1916, 2.

58. Advertisement, *Stevens Point Journal,* 7 November 1916, 8.

59. Advertisement, *Stevens Point Journal,* 22 July 1916, 4.

60. Advertisement, *Stevens Point Journal,* 3 August 1916, 4.

61. Advertisement, *Stevens Point Journal,* 11 February, 1916, 6.

62. Ibid.

63. For example, Billie Burke, "My Simple Rules for Beauty," *Delineator* 77 (June 1911): 510; "Alan Dale, "Bonnie Billie Burke," *Cosmopolitan Magazine,* 52 (February 1912): 412–18; Rennold Wolf, "Billie Burke, Married and at Home," *Green Book Magazine,* n.d., c. 1915, Hastings Historical Society, Hastings-on-Hudson, New York; "The First Twinklings of Three Popular Stars," *Woman's Home Companion* 43 (September 1916), 44.

64. "City Briefs," *Stevens Point Journal,* 11 February 1916, 6.

65. Advertisement, *Stevens Point Journal,* 6 May 1916, 3.

66. The various costs do not add up, and even in 1916, creative accounting for publicity purposes was not unusual. In a report about the finances of the serial that he made to stock holders in the film's production company in 1917, George Kleine listed the cost of the negative as $396,222.55. There is no separate line for costume or salary expenses, and the total cost for negative, positive copies, advertising, music and other expenses was given as $1,190,980.46. Letter from George Kleine to John Sidney Burnet, 13 August 1917, George Kleine Collection, Library of Congress, Box 24.

67. Advertisement, *Stevens Point Journal,* 16 September 1916, 6; advertisement, *Stevens Point Journal* 18 September 1916, 8; advertisement, *Stevens Point Journal* 4 October 1916, 8; advertisement, *Stevens Point Journal,* 16 October 1916, 8.

68. "Billie Burke, Well Known Actress in New Role—It's a Girl," *Stevens Point Journal,* 25 October 1916, 7; "Sues Billie Burke," *Stevens Point Journal,* 11 November 1916, 1.

69. For a list of the magazines the library subscribed to in 1916, see "Public Library Notes," *Gazette,* 30 August 1916, sec. II, p. 11.

70. Victor Schertzinger and Thomas Ince, "Peggy" (New York: Jerome H. Remick & Co., 1915); Maud A. Murray, "Gloria's Romance Valse" (New York: Cadillac Moving Picture Music Series, 1916).

71. "Movie Crowds Small," *Stevens Point Journal,* 29 December 1916, 1.

72. "Editorial," *Gazette,* 17 May 1916, sec. I, p. 4.

73. Ibid.

Part IV

MATURITY AND CRISIS IN THE 1930s

CASE STUDIES

10

IMAGINING AND PROMOTING
THE SMALL-TOWN THEATER

GREGORY A. WALLER

The key man of the picture business, now and always, is the exhibitor.
"The Road to the Public," *Exhibitors Herald-World* (October 4, 1930)

*We are for the exhibitor, first, last and always, but we would not say that
the exhibitor has not been to blame for many of his own troubles.*
"Skies Look Brighter for the Independent Producer," *Billboard*
(March 8, 1930)

The 200-seat Llamarada Theater in Hilltown, Indiana, unquestionably stands
as one of the most well-documented small-town movie theaters of the early
1930s. Owned and operated by a locally born and raised man who had been
exhibiting films in Hilltown since the nickelodeon era, the state-of-the-art
Llamarada was built in 1930 and managed to remain solvent throughout the
Depression and independent despite the efforts of regional theater chains to
dominate exhibition in the Midwest. From existing records, we know a good
deal about the size and makeup of the Llamarada's staff, the managerial and
programming policies of its owner-operator, and, most important, its audience and its place in Hilltown as "an institution, an important part of the
community."[1]

The problem—or at least the apparent problem—is that the Llamarada
Theater and Hilltown, Indiana, are fictional constructs, created by Margaret
Weymouth Jackson for a series of five stories published in the *Saturday Evening Post* between August and October 1930.[2] That the stories are fiction does
not negate their historical value—or, for that matter, that of the many other
movie-related works of fiction published in the *Post* during this period. In
fact, the Llamarada stories are an important, overlooked resource that, when
read in the context of the motion picture trade press, can help us analyze the
small-town theater as concrete practice, business strategy, and culturally res-
onant myth, particularly during the first years of the Depression. Focusing
on the audiences as well as entertainment providers, this historically specific
analysis will underscore even as it problematizes the role of the local, a topic
of considerable import across twentieth-century media history.

Until recently, film historians have understood the early sound era principally in terms of corporate maneuvering and changes (or continuities) in Hollywood studio practices: the pitching of all-talkies; the westward movement of Broadway personnel; the emergence of new stars, genres, and movie cycles; the refinement of sound recording apparatus; and so on. However, Douglas Gomery's research on the Publix Theaters and Donald Crafton's *The Talkies: American Cinema's Transition to Sound, 1926–1931,* underscore just how sweeping, significant, and even melodramatic the overhaul of the American film exhibition business was during the late 1920s and the first years of the Depression.[3] "The silent exhibitor," in Crafton's words, "was forced to choose between being driven out by competitors, selling the theater to a chain, or converting to sound (probably with borrowed money)." The exhibitor's dilemma hardly ended there: "For all classes and locales of theater owners," Crafton concludes, "the primary issue surrounding the coming of sound was the decreased sovereignty of the local manager."[4] That local "sovereignty" actually mattered is, as might be expected, a governing assumption of the Llamarada stories.

Crafton estimates that by July 1929—several months before the stock market crash—about a quarter of the theaters across the United States were wired for sound. Most of these theaters were in metropolitan areas, but some were in smaller communities.[5] A year later, with life becoming increasingly harder, the *Exhibitors Herald-World* delivered its own (quite optimistic) version of the "true and essential facts of the motion picture market." This trade magazine claimed that as of July 1, 1930, more than 10,000 of the estimated 14,500 "legitimate motion picture houses" (not halls or other venues occasionally used for film screenings) in the United States were equipped for sound. Of the sound-equipped theaters, 6,796 were independently owned; 2,252 were "controlled by producer-owned chains" (Publix, Fox, Warner Brothers, RKO, Loew); and 1,213 were controlled by "independent circuits." The grand transformation, according to *Exhibitors Herald-World,* was virtually complete: the independent owner-operator had survived, the major chains had become stabilized without monopolizing the market, and the remaining 4,500 houses showing silents were sure to be wired by the end of 1930.[6] The story, of course, was neither this tidily nor this equitably resolved, except, perhaps, in the *Saturday Evening Post.*

Tales of the Llamarada

Now, a small-town movie is not like a city movie, and not even sound pictures and colored pictures can make it so.
JACKSON, "PROFESSIONAL," *Saturday Evening Post,* August 30, 1930

In 1930, when the *Saturday Evening Post* maintained its standing as the premier general-interest magazine in the United States, the weekly circulation

was purported to be more than 2.75 million. Margaret Weymouth Jackson was among the *Post*'s most frequently published authors. Her first *Post* story appeared in 1927, and she went on to place twenty stories in the magazine between 1929 and 1932, while occasionally publishing in other popular venues as well, including *Women's Home Companion, Good Housekeeping, Ladies' Home Journal,* and, later, the *American Mercury.* In its heyday, the *Post* made much use of series fiction, that is, ongoing stories published across several months (or even years). Each installment offered a largely self-contained narrative that featured recurring characters linked by a consistent locale or environment. In effect, the *Post*'s series fiction collectively mapped a wide-ranging, if still highly selective, vision of America, from New England villages and southern African American communities to Manhattan and Hollywood, from advertising agencies to western ranches, traveling salesmen to Broadway ingenues. In the *Post*'s imaginative cartography, Jackson's turf was the nativist, white, midwestern small town, which she knew and loved and affirmed from the inside. A month before her first Llamarada story was published, Jackson declared in a *Post* self-profile: "I am partial to the Middle West, particularly Indiana . . . the All-American population of the small town where we live—there is only one foreign-born citizen here, an ancient German who came to sweet Owen County [between Terre Haute and Bloomington, Indiana] fifty years ago—makes a fine atmosphere, and I am extremely fond of the friendly, casual, upright manners and methods of my fellow townsmen. In fact, I am Middle Western, middle-class, small-town and Hoosier, and proud of it!"[7] Jackson's fictional Hilltown is not to be confused with the more class-stratified version of Indiana life analyzed by sociologists Robert S. Lynd and Helen Merrell Lynd in their widely publicized study, *Middletown: A Study in Contemporary American Culture.*[8] Hilltown is an "old town nestled between green hills and a shining river, with the limestone mill and quarries lying on the outer edge of it, with the clean, sun-bleached square about its pile of courthouse, with the tidy, well-kept, small stores, the ranging, well-kept, white-painted houses under great trees."[9] It "was a place of its own, a little apart from the world." Yet for all its quaint charm and "old-fashioned" mores,[10] Hilltown was not preserved in amber, aggressively antimodern, or buckling under the weight of the Depression. Hilltown is characterized by its prosperous (when well-run) retail and service businesses, which cater to what in an earlier story are referred to as the community's notoriously "overcareful" consumers: "The town's high and comfortable standard of living on its small incomes bespoke much care in spending."[11]

Jackson introduced Hilltown in a series of stories concerning the publisher and staff of a weekly farm newspaper. In addition to the movie theater series, Jackson wrote stories set in the town's drugstore, its first chain grocery store, a new auto dealership, and a plumbing company (all published in the *Post*). These businesses—not churches or schools, not the bank or the farm—

are where the economic vitality and the durable humanity of this community reside.[12]

Among the biggest commercial success stories in Jackson's modern Midwest is the Llamarada Theater. Significantly, in establishing the ground rules for the Llamarada series, Jackson did not choose to look back nostalgically to the days of the tin-roofed nickelodeon. Instead, she imagined Hilltown's only picture show as a newly constructed venue designed to be highly comfortable, reasonably profitable, and fully equipped with the most up-to-date technology.

In Jackson's Indiana, a brand-new movie theater could be deemed "one of the finest things" in an old-fashioned town.[13] She offers almost no description of the interior decoration, marquee, or foyer, except to note that the compact theater is "beautiful, perfect and finished in every small detail."[14] One story, however, foregrounds the new organist (and his much-appreciated instrument); another is set almost entirely in the projection booth and lays out not only the projectionist's serious work but also the intricacies of the Llamarada's sophisticated sound system.[15] Both the musician and the projectionist-electrician are from Hilltown, as are the two perky usherettes in scarlet satin skirts and gold-brocaded jackets, as well as all the other members of this workplace family, young and old, male and female. No matter what motion pictures fill the Llamarada's screen, this theater is a local enterprise, emblematic of a certain faith in the Depression-proof saving grace of small-town small business, which here requires no urban intervention in the form of technical, aesthetic, or financial expertise.

Presiding over the Llamarada with benign paternalism is the white-haired Mr. McLaughlin, who has built his exhibition business from the ground up, plowing any profits back into the theater. His decency, kindness, and concern for his employees and for the community at large are demonstrated in each story, although we never see him participating in civic activities or opening the Llamarada for charity or public service events. It is enough, Jackson implies, that McLaughlin knows and plays fair with his customers—that earns him and his employees a modest living and makes him ethically unimpeachable. "Know[ing] the town" is McLaughlin's key to success, the result of years spent "studying, wooing and winning Hilltown."[16] He buys the right films and arranges weekly schedules so as to "catch" the many different audiences that constitute the town and its environs.[17] Jackson assumes without question, first, that local prerogative in terms of film booking is possible; and, second, that there is more than enough appropriate Hollywood product from which an exhibitor like McLaughlin can choose. However, Jackson makes only passing reference to what is actually screened at the Llamarada, except for the regular Monday serial, booked especially to draw in "poor farmers" on "dime night."[18]

It is moviegoers rather than movies that fill the establishing shots of the Llamarada stories, perhaps because Jackson seems determined to counter

stereotypes about gullible and lowbrow "hicktown" spectators. Hilltown's white, midwestern moviegoers are, these stories insist, neither naive nor homogeneous. The Llamarada's ushers soon recognize familiar faces and seat people according to personal preferences and "all the different little cliques in town," notably by age and gender, for race and class do not register as categories in Jackson's "All-American" stories.[19]

Together, movie-savvy Hilltowners constitute a "discriminating, exacting audience,"[20] whose members are "capricious, discerning, shrewd" about what they expect for their entertainment dollar. Furthermore, they are an active audience, applauding with "good-natured mockery" as local advertisements appear on screen, sometimes singing along with the organist, socializing and joking in those relaxed moments before the show begins.[21] It is a good thing that McLaughlin does his job so responsibly and the audience maintains its high standards because in this small town the movie theater is "an institution, an important part of the community, the light and brightness, the amusement and forgetting, the open door between the hill-and-river-enclosed town and the great world."[22] A reel of film can ignite in the projection booth, but even that potentially life-threatening danger only proves that the Llamarada is in all respects a safe place: the projectionist performs heroically, and the audience files out in an orderly, calm manner. "That's what comes of living in the sticks," an usher effuses, "men and women control themselves. They think as individuals, not as a mob. I tell you, I'm proud of Hilltown!"[23]

Aside from flaming nitrate, the only threats to the Llamarada as independent enterprise and workplace family come from outside Hilltown, either in the form of young men who have left the town and returned or, more seriously, from city men who see Hilltown as merely another market ripe for exploiting. The last story in Jackson's series predictably ups the melodramatic stakes: catastrophe threatens the local picture show, not because of the rising floodwaters that literally isolate Hilltown, but because Michigan Theaters, Inc., decides that it wants to acquire the Llamarada to expand its regional holdings.

In February, 1930, J. C. Penney argued in the *Post* that "the chain store is only one item in the whole great process of nationalizing the business of the United States"—a process that Penney deems inevitable, progressive, and potentially of great benefit to everyone concerned, especially in towns and small cities.[24] But Jackson was having none of it. Michigan Theaters, Inc., stands unambiguously for "the chain movies—the octopus—the great, rich, ruthless company" out to eradicate small business and local capitalism.[25]

Representing Michigan Theaters, Inc., are a Jew and an Irishman, urban interlopers indeed, who are pictured in one gangster movie–styled illustration as racketeers facing off against the defiant, elderly theater owner. As punishment for offering to buy out McLaughlin (who refuses their fair price

of $50,000) and then threatening to build a competing theater, the chain-men are stranded for ten days in flooded Hilltown with nothing to eat except pork and no new movies to watch. They flee at the first opportunity, correctly convinced that they could never run the Llamarada at a profit. In the end, market conditions, natural forces, essentialized ethnicity, and a stubborn and decent theater owner keep the Midwest midwestern; the home for nationally distributed entertainment becomes the bastion of regionalism.

It is not as if McLaughlin books movies that are appreciably different or more local than what Michigan Theaters, Inc., would bring to Hilltown. He knows that the chain can buy "better pictures," but in the end the pictures are not the issue for Jackson. On this point, she would likely agree with cultural commentator Gilbert Seldes, who argued in the *Post* in May 1930 that "radio and movie talkies . . . exist for all alike" in the city or the "outlands," and so, we might add, do stories in mass-market magazines like the *Saturday Evening Post*.[26]

Hollywood, of course, is the source of the movies that delight audiences at the Llamarada. Yet Hollywood itself never directly figures in Jackson's stories. Perhaps Jackson and her editors correctly realized that readers could get enough of Hollywood simply by flipping through the pages of the *Post*. In 1930, for instance, the *Post* published a six-part serialized novel *(Happy Landings)*, in which a young stage actress moves to Hollywood, where sound technology holds sway and talkies demand new stars; two stories by George F. Worts, who specialized in fiction about behind-the-scenes studio professionals (in this case, a director of photography and a sound effects man); a story narrated by a female stenographer working at a movie studio; F. Scott Fitzgerald's cynical story "A Millionaire's Girl," about a potential star who leaves Hollywood for an ill-fated marriage.; and J. P. McEvoy's satiric account of a cartoonist who is lured to Hollywood, where his comic strip is set to be directed for the screen by a recently hired Soviet director.

Nonfiction pieces also appeared in the *Post:* a (ghostwritten?) account by Mary Pickford of touring the world with Douglas Fairbanks; feature articles on the color musical revue film and the European market for talkies; and—most interesting—a two-part article by Ben Ames Williams on the "complex and arduous business" of producing a hypothetical movie, a process hemmed in by the competing demands of censorship, the star system, the marketplace, and the author of the original property.[27] Between the stories and the features, the *Post* ran regular weekly ads for Universal under Carl Laemmle's byline and elaborate promotional campaigns for Paramount and Technicolor, as well as a host of ads featuring testimonials by movie celebrities, such as James Cruze on behalf of Mennen shaving cream and John Boles touting Spur bow ties. Jackson's Llamarada stories, then, took their place in the *Post* in a much broader discourse about the movies, a discourse far more likely to spin tales of Hollywood than Hilltown, movie production instead of film exhibition.

Working the Community Angle

Chain theatre operation can be made dangerous unless, through the personality, the friendliness, the willingness to work in community betterment of our representative, our theatre manager is manifest in that community. . . . Humanize your company, your circuit, through yourself. Be a pleasant power in your city. Be alive to the opportunity to serve. Let your neighbors judge the fairness of your company by your own fairness. Be a well loved and useful citizen—and your company will gain prestige in that community.
SIDNEY KENT, general manager, Paramount[28]

For Jackson, imagining the small-town theater was inevitably marking how it differed from the urban theater, hence her claim that "a small-town movie is not like a city movie, and not even sound pictures and colored pictures can make it so."[29] The pictures, which are produced in the metropolis, never pose any threat to the midwestern and middle-class values that Jackson holds dear. The important measure of difference between city and small-town theaters is instead to be found in the behavior and makeup of the audience and in the entertainment experience that McLaughlin provides to his regular patrons. His investment in ensuring that the theater is a first-class, fully modern operation reflects his unshakable faith in his discerning local customers, in the sound film industry, and in the economic well-being of the nation. McLaughlin's careful management practices pay off: he weathers the corporate machinations and remains autonomous, able to control his fate as the Depression looms.

Above all, it is the everyday role of the Llamarada *as* a community and *in* the community that for Jackson makes this small-town theater worth celebrating, a point driven home in the conclusion of the final Llamarada story. After rejecting the hostile advances of Michigan Theaters, Inc., McLaughlin marries the retired schoolteacher who runs his box office. The ceremony is conducted in the local Presbyterian church, then celebrated with a free show at the Llamarada for everyone in Hilltown; after all, it is the all-inclusive, non-denominational movie theater that stands as the true center of Hilltown, circa 1930.

How does what we could call the myth of the small-town theater in Jackson's Llamarada stories stack up against the entertainment industry's own rhetoric concerning such theaters?[30] To chart this particular discursive field, I shall rely on editorial commentary, news coverage, and letters to the editor from two different trade magazines: Martin Quigley's *Exhibitors Herald-World,* the successor to *Moving Picture World,* which subsequently became *Motion Picture Herald* in 1931 (henceforth referred to in this chapter simply as the *Herald*), and *Billboard: The Theatrical Digest and Show World Review.* The *Herald* stridently championed how the motion picture industry was shaping up under the in-

fluence of Will Hays and the Motion Picture Producers and Distributors of America (MPPDA). *Billboard,* as its full title suggests, covered an appreciably wider range of commercial amusements, including stage, radio, and all manner of touring shows. *Billboard* was also much more willing to challenge what it sometimes called the monopolistic "overlords of the cinema," which it saw as engaged in a scorched-earth campaign to destroy vaudeville, theatrical road shows, and other live performance.[31] In fact, *Billboard* dropped its weekly coverage of the motion picture industry in March 1931 (it published only a handful of movie reviews in each issue), when it adopted what it called an "all-flesh" policy.

As the Depression deepened, *Billboard* could run an editorial entitled "Independent Exhibitors Face Results of Their Own Folly" and rejoice over anecdotal evidence that small-town movie theaters equipped for sound had seen the light and were again booking vaudeville acts.[32] The *Herald,* in contrast, reported favorably on any efforts by Publix, for instance, to localize and individualize theater management policies, even as the trade magazine steadfastly insisted that the coming of sound had saved the "small theatre and particularly the small town theatre."[33]

During the early sound era, the trade press discourse made a firm distinction between chain and independent theaters that was not quite the same as the hierarchical divisions enforced by the run-zone-clearance system. (The run-zone-clearance system maximized profits by maintaining the distinction between first-run and subsequent-run theaters, organizing distribution according to geographic locations—or "zones"—and establishing "clearance" times between different runs.) In the trade press, *chain* could refer to theaters owned by national producer-exhibitors such as Fox, Warners, and Publix or to theaters owned by regionally based exhibitors who had no direct link to Hollywood studios. According to trade press accounts, *independent* encompassed a range of theaters found in locations as different as urban neighborhoods, residential areas, small cities, small communities, small towns, and whistlestops "out in the sticks." There is significant slippage—ideological as well as geographic—within and across both categories. (Indeed, the owner of an independent chain of Indiana theaters was one of the most vociferous spokespeople in *Billboard* for "Mr. Small-Town Exhibitor.")[34] No doubt, this slippage is evident through much of the twentieth century's ongoing popular discourse concerning American retail business practices. Yet the relations between "independent" and "chain" (or between independence and corporate affiliation) registered particularly deeply in the Depression with respect to the motion picture industry, which had long promoted itself both as a technologically savvy, forward-thinking big business and as a democratic provider of affordable entertainment for all Americans.

Along with a taxonomy based on size, location, and circuit affiliation, the trade press also resorted to a more figurative vocabulary in which the

independent exhibitor—aka the "little fellow"—also became the "safety valve," "shock absorber," or "backbone" of the industry.[35] As such terms suggest, trade discourse never expressed doubt about whether the independent exhibitor should survive; the question was how. What would guarantee his place in the competitive market during the Depression? What could the "little fellow," particularly one operating well outside a metropolitan orbit, teach the corporate bigwigs?

Rule number one, judging from the trade press as much as from the Llamarada stories, is that the manager must accurately gauge the tastes of his audience(s) and, presumably, arrange his programs accordingly. Woe be it to the manager who futilely tried to row against the currents of public opinion. Recall that McLaughlin had no trouble booking movies at the Llamarada that were eminently suitable for Hilltown's different audiences. But listening to regular customers and screening appropriate pictures were not the same thing, as evident in the letters from small-town exhibitors appearing in the *Herald*'s "Voice of the Industry" page. "It is rough how the little fellows out in the sticks are treated," complained G. A. Duncan of Carlisle, Kentucky. "Here is what we pay for: no music, no action in most cases, no picture that the public wants . . . the majority of the people want clean pictures."[36] Other managers drew finer distinctions based on box office receipts and observation of their patrons. A column from December 1930, for instance, included the following assessments: Paramount's *Queen High*, wrote the manager of the Elite Theatre in Greenleaf, Kansas, "gave excellent satisfaction. This is a clever picture and is what the people want to see," whereas *Trailing Trouble* starring Hoot Gibson is so "silly" that "even the 10 year old kids will razz it." Philip Rand from Salmon, Idaho, declared that "the industry has given us two magnificent plays in *Sunny Side Up* and *Rio Rita*. Why can't they give us more like them? We need them. The public wants them! They pay big returns." An exhibitor in Kerens, Texas, lauded *Light of the Western Stars,* which "is great for Saturday," then complained, "Whenever we go highbrow, it gives the small town exhibitor a headache."[37]

The implication of the letters to the *Herald* is that even if the experienced exhibitor knew what his audience wanted, Hollywood rarely provided enough of the right product to suit the tastes of the local market. This problem, according to a *Billboard* article, applied to shorts as well as features, further hampering the small-town exhibitor's programming options.[38]

One could, however, adopt an entirely different booking strategy, based on the movie theater's role as a showcase and conduit for nationally available commercial entertainment. It was entirely possible, as the owner of a theater in Paris, Missouri (population 1,400), put it, that the small-town exhibitor could succeed by offering his patrons "identically the same shows they get in larger towns."[39] From this perspective, there was no rationale for a "localized" show. "Hollywood may be a long way from 'main street' of your town or my

town," declared Ken W. Thompson of Adams, Wisconsin, "but talking pictures bridge the gap." In effect, Thompson's logic mirrored the policies announced by Publix chief of "booking and buying," William M. Saal. Saal told his managers and advertising men that while Publix sought to give "the local theatre manager, the district manager, and the division manager a voice in determining the demands of local conditions . . . booking on a national scale, or scope, was advisable in 99 per cent of the cases."[40] Nevertheless, the talismanic word for the trade press was *individuality*—that was what all theater managers most needed to demonstrate.[41]

Both Saal and the small-town exhibitors quoted here made no reference to live performance, the one aspect of the program that could potentially localize (and humanize) the bill at any movie theater. "Locally specialized forms of entertainments, whether stage shows, talent contests, or sing-alongs," disappeared in the early sound era, according to Crafton, who calls this phenomenon the "passing of hometown-generated entertainment."[42] His point is well taken, even though the Llamarada stories more frequently mention organ performances (sometimes with audience sing-a-longs) than on-screen images, and, as I have argued on other occasions, hometown entertainment did not vanish from small-town American theaters after the conversion to sound. It is noteworthy for the purposes of this chapter that the contemporary trade discourse had little to say about the value or liability of live performance and evinced no nostalgia for its supposed heyday during the silent era.

For the *Herald* and *Billboard,* what the exhibitor booked seemed to matter much less than how he dealt with his customers and his community at large. Amusement parks, advised *Billboard,* should "take a tip from the movies": "First of all, gain and HOLD the good will of the people of the community. . . . SERVICE is the keynote."[43] Even the smallest exhibitor presumably had some control over the service he provided, no matter how hamstrung he was when it came to programming. "Chains Have Not Been Able to Meet Small-Town Demands" was the title of a *Billboard* editorial from December 1930, which claimed that "it takes more than business efficiency [always acknowledged to be the undeniable benefit of the chain store] to keep the house out of the red. It takes personality" and the "absolutely essential . . . personal contact" between manager and patron. Also essential was such personal contact between the staff and the public, as in the Llamarada stories, in which ushers direct individual moviegoers to their favorite seats and the projectionist will not rest until he provides Hilltowners with the best possible audiovisual experience.

But even the friendliest welcome and the best service could not necessarily make the movie theater a prominent and valued centerpiece of the local community. In an article reprinted in the *Herald,* University of North Carolina sociology professor Harold D. Meyer—a "playground and recreation

expert"—offered the highest praise for the theater manager in Raleigh, North Carolina, who worked to "fit into the life of the community" by, for instance, arranging special shows for students.[44] Mississippi exhibitor Edward Kuykendahl, newly elected to the board of directors of the Motion Picture Theater Owners of America (MPTOA), advised the small-town manager to engage in even more extensive civic involvement, including consulting with local ministerial organizations, women's clubs, and school officials. "The theatre manager in the small town," Kuykendahl told the 1930 MPTOA convention in a speech quoted extensively in both *Billboard* and the *Herald,* "has a definite and important responsibility in his community, with great opportunity of being of service, since his theatre is essentially a gathering place for local residents." The small-town theater, wrote the operator of the Garrick Theatre in Fond du Lac, Wisconsin, is nothing less than "a necessity in every community. It is the center of social and business life of the community."

For exhibitors like Kuykendahl, the small-town independent theater—not the chain-operated venue—could best provide personalized service, reach out to local audiences, boost Main Street businesses, and assume the mantle of civic responsibility.[45] The lesson was apparently not lost on the major theater chains. Through 1930–31, the *Herald* ran a number of news items, feature stories, and editorials that advised the managers of chain theaters to undertake the kind of civic outreach that had apparently proved so successful for the small, independent owner-operator. "Be a pleasant power in your city," advised Sidney Kent, who also told attendees at the MPTOA convention that "many small houses [in chains] are going back to progressive independents. . . . No business can prosper that prospers at the expense of the small man."[46] In March 1931, Publix provided its managers with an extensive "outline on community analysis," designed to provide full knowledge of the local community's social, economic, religious, ethnic, and racial makeup, as well as its "clubs and societies" and sources of "civic pride." With such information, the manager would better be able to participate in "local activities," thus winning the "respect of his community for his theatre."[47] The same policy was endorsed on the pages of the *Herald* by, among others, the manager of the five Fox theaters in Wichita, Kansas, who explained how he had succeeded by joining the Rotary Club, the Chamber of Commerce, and the Retail Merchants Association.

A *Herald* editorial entitled "The Company—The Manager—The Public" solemnly intoned, "Basic are the advantages of the theatre which is managed by one who is permitted to direct it according to his intimate knowledge of his community."[48] Such knowledge was supposed not only to translate into specific promotional strategies and (occasionally) booking policies, but also, and more significantly, to improve the theater's standing in the community. Proactive civic involvement—including allowing for the localized "individuality" of the chain theater—thus became a cornerstone of public relations for Publix and Fox. Besides encouraging regular patronage and raising the community status of the theater, what the owner of a chain of thirty houses in Tennessee called "a willing spirit of co-operation in all civic movements" would have the important additional benefit of helping to forestall "unfair legislation" and "unreasonable censorship."[49] In effect, theater managers who are "men of local prestige, standing and influence" were the frontline soldiers in the motion picture industry's lobbying efforts at the local and state level.[50]

Speaking of the Small-Town Theater

A host of evidence from the trade press demonstrates that certain qualities associated with the small-town, independent theater—humanization, individuality, personalized service, responsiveness to audience tastes, and civic involvement—were touted in the early 1930s as time-tested business strategies, fully applicable to chain theaters. Whether or not the chains successfully put such strategies into practice remains to be investigated, as does what Richard Maltby calls the "interplay between its [the industry's] typologies of audience groupings, of theatres and of productions."[51] But the trade discourse itself is significant for what it tells us about the symbolic role as well as the day-to-day operation of movie theaters in the early sound era and into the Depression.

Significant as well is another body of information on small-town film exhibition during the Depression that I can only briefly consider here: local discourse, consisting primarily of oral history accounts and advertising, editorials, and reporting in daily or weekly newspapers. In most cases, this material not only provides the best record of programming and promotional practices in small-town theaters but also complements trade press discourse and fictional representations, such as Jackson's stories in the *Post*. For example, an extended series of interviews I conducted with people who worked at or regularly attended the Alhambra Theater in Campbellsville, Kentucky, during the 1930s and 1940s strongly foregrounds the prominent, public role of this theater's owner-operator, who respondents described as a "local man, one of our boys," shrewd but fair in his business dealings, on a first-name basis with his patrons, aware of Baptist sermonizing against the movies, and deeply involved with the everyday commercial life of his town.[52]

If I have focused in this chapter on a discrete historical period, treating only the early sound years, the people I interviewed in Campbellsville were more likely to recollect experiences and describe their hometown theater across the 1930s and 1940s and to remember moviegoing experiences (like the Saturday matinee) or special events (including local amateur shows, beauty contests, and live appearances by touring radio performers). Interviewees also described the many ways the Alhambra figured in the social—

rather than the civic—life of Campbellsville: as a site where folks gathered before the show, where hometown talent sometimes took the stage, where people from the country would be sure to visit on market day, and where the town's codes of racial segregation were made manifest and sometimes stretched (through seating arrangements, special "colored" screenings, and so on). To the idea of the small-town theater as discursive construct, managerial strategy, motion picture industry component, and orphaned "little fellow," oral histories add the notion of the theater as object of recollection and site of social interaction.

The abiding appeal of small-town—as well as ethnic or racially defined neighborhood—America (and Americana) is evident across a range of cultural channels in the 1930s and today. Within this topos, the local picture show exerts its own particular ideological allure, especially when it is depicted as an inviting, accessible, hometown gathering place run by an enterprising, neighborly showman. Thus understood, the movie theater becomes a site in which community was constituted and reaffirmed in the pre–World War II era, a testament to the resilience of the local within a marketplace of commodified mass entertainment, and perhaps even a public sphere that allowed for some measure of transgression, alterity, and novelty in the face of traditional circuits of power—old money, dogmatic religiosity, entrenched hierarchical privilege. Such a vision certainly had and has its allure and a measure of validity.

Much of the trade press material I have surveyed in this chapter echoes with a different sense of the locally situated, independently run movie theater. From this perspective, the picture show—especially the small-town theater—works in concert with schools, seeks out the advice of churches and women's clubs, and vigilantly pays heed to public opinion. This was hardly a novel strategy for realizing legitimation and self-promotion, as Will Hays fully realized in his efforts on behalf of the MPPDA. Thus, to propose that the movie theater had or should have aspired to have not only a prominent position on Main Street but also a civic role as centerpiece of the community provokes a string of questions: What "community"? Who defined the parameters of legitimate "civic" activity? How much of the theater's outreach was a matter of allying itself with the interests of Main Street merchants or with a Chamber of Commerce version of boosterism?

Perhaps a small-town theater's degree of localization could be gauged not by its independence from chains or outside control but by how thoroughly the owner-operator was able to partner with and endorse those empowered individuals and institutions that promoted—and therefore defined—the "good of the community." In light of these questions, Margaret Weymouth Jackson's *Post* stories seem even more utopian, for the Llamarada Theater—independent in all respects—had its home and found its patrons in a world that was unproblematically local.

Notes

This chapter originally appeared as "Imagining and Promoting the Small-Town Theater," by Gregory A. Waller, from *Cinema Journal* 44, no. 3 (2005): 3–19. Copyright © 2005 by the University of Texas Press.

1. Margaret Weymouth Jackson, "The Stars in Their Courses," *Saturday Evening Post,* 25 October 1930, 21.

2. The five Llamarada stories are "Professional," *Saturday Evening Post,* (30 August 1930), 8–9, 44, 46, 48, 52; "'This Way, Please'" *Saturday Evening Post,* 13 September 1930, 26–27, 90, 92, 96; "A Hum in the Llamarada," *Saturday Evening Post,* 27 September 1930, 20–21, 89, 91, 94, 97; "Business Piano," *Saturday Evening Post,* 11 October 1930, 20–21, 90, 92, 95, 99; and "The Stars in Their Courses," *Saturday Evening Post,* 25 October 1930, 20–21, 112, 114, 117.

3. See, for example, Douglas Gomery, "Fashioning an Exhibition Empire: Promotion, Publicity, and the Rise of Publix Theaters," in *Moviegoing in America,* ed. Gregory A. Waller (Malden, Mass.: Blackwell, 2002), 124–37; and Donald Crafton, *The Talkies: American Cinema's Transition to Sound, 1926–1931* (New York: Scribner's, 1997). Scholarly work on film exhibition in the United States has tended to focus on urban areas in the pre-nickelodeon and nickelodeon periods and on the picture palace. For a sense of exhibition in small cities and towns during the silent era, see Gregory A. Waller, *Main Street Amusements: Film and Commercial Entertainment in a Southern City, 1896–1930* (Washington, D.C.: Smithsonian Institution Press, 1995); and Kathryn H. Fuller, *At the Picture Show: Small-Town Audiences and the Creation of Movie Fan Culture* (Washington, D.C.: Smithsonian Institution Press, 1996). See the "Guide to Research and Resources" in *Moviegoing in America* for more information.

4. Crafton, *The Talkies,* 255, 265.

5. Ibid., 253–54.

6. "The Motion Picture Market," *Exhibitors Herald-World,* 26 July 1930, 14–16.

7. "Who's Who—and Why," *Saturday Evening Post,* 19 July 1930, 160, 162.

8. The Lynds discuss film exhibition in the section of *Middletown* titled "Using Leisure," noting that, except for one "college-trained man interested in bringing 'good films' to the city," the nine Middletown (that is, Muncie, Indiana) theaters "are in the hands of a group of men—an ex–peanut stand proprietor, an ex–bicycle racer and race promoter, and so on—whose primary concern is making money"; *Middletown: A Study in Contemporary American Culture* (New York: Harcourt, Brace, 1929), 268. The question of local identity and control recurs throughout *Middletown,* for the Lynds emphasize not only the role of chain stores but also, more generally, the "impossibility of studying Middletown as a self-contained, self-starting community" (271).

9. Jackson, "Stars in Their Courses," 20.

10. Jackson, "'This Way, Please,'" 92.

11. Jackson, "Driveaway," *Saturday Evening Post,* 1 March 1930, 18.

12. Recent commentaries on the *Saturday Evening Post* underscore longtime editor George Horace Lorimer's preference for what Jan Cohn calls "stories of the romance of business," tied to the larger ideological portrait of "a comprehensible society. A society built on fair play and individual initiative and common sense"; *Creating America: George Horace Lorimer and the Saturday Evening Post* (Pittsburgh: University

of Pittsburgh Press, 1989), 6–7. Or, as Tom Pendergast puts it, Lorimer's "goal was no less than to find a place within modern corporate capitalism for the nineteenth-century self-made man of character. What is remarkable is that he clung to that goal for more than thirty years"; *Creating the Modern Man: American Magazines and Consumer Culture, 1900–1950* (Columbia: University of Missouri Press, 2000), 51. See also, for historical information, Frank Luther Mott, *A History of American Magazines, 1885–1905* (Cambridge, Mass.: Harvard University Press, 1957), 671–716; and James Playsted Wood, *Magazines in the United States*, 3rd ed. (New York: Ronald Press, 1971), 155–66. The *Post* also figures significantly in histories of American advertising, such as Roland Marchand, *Advertising the American Dream: Making Way for Modernity, 1920–1940* (Berkeley and Los Angeles: University of California Press, 1985); and Jackson Lears, *Fables of Abundance: A Cultural History of Advertising in America* (New York: Basic Books, 1994).

13. Jackson, "Stars in Their Courses," 20.

14. Jackson, "Professional," 8.

15. For some sense of just how up-to-date the Llamarada is intended to be, see, on the role of the organ and sing-alongs in the early sound era, C. L. Grant, "The Medicine Man for the Blues," *Exhibitors Herald-World*, 8 March 1930, 54; and "The Place of the Organist in the All-Sound Theater," *Billboard*, 12 July 1930, 43; and, on the importance of sophisticated acoustic design, Anna Aiken Patterson, "A Small Town Theatre Built for Sound," *Exhibitors Herald-World*, Better Theatres Section, 15 March 1930, 23–25, 63; and "Small-Town Exhibitors Hurt by Poor Sound," *Billboard*, 23 August 1930, 7.

16. Jackson, "Stars in Their Courses," 112.

17. Jackson, "Professional," 44.

18. Jackson, "Stars in Their Courses," 117.

19. Jackson, " 'This Way, Please,' " 92.

20. Jackson, "Stars in Their Course," 20; Jackson, "Professional," 44.

21. Jackson, " 'This Way, Please,' " 26.

22. Jackson, "Stars in Their Course," 21.

23. Jackson, "A Hum in the Llamarada," 97.

24. J. C. Penney, with Samuel Crowther, "The Community and the Chain Store," *Saturday Evening Post*, 22 February 1930, 10. See also, two weeks earlier in the *Post*, John Winthrop Fleming's commentary, "Cashing In on the Environment," *Saturday Evening Post*, 8 February 1930, 66, which argues that "any business is successful in just the degree to which it adapts itself to its own particular environment."

25. Jackson, "Stars in Their Course," 30.

26. Gilbert Seldes, "The City's Giddy Whirl," *Saturday Evening Post*, 31 May 1930, 43.

27. Ben Ames Williams, "The Arduous Art," *Saturday Evening Post*, May 3, 1930, 6.

28. "Individualism Is Bar to Peril of Chain Arrogance, Says Kent," *Exhibitors Herald-World* 14 June 1930, 102.

29. Jackson, "Professional," 44.

30. In researching the trade press of this period, I have been guided by Richard Maltby's excellent analysis of "the motion picture industry's discursive construction of Classical Hollywood audiences during the 1930s"; "Sticks, Hicks and Flaps: Classical Hollywood's Generic Conception of Its Audiences," in *Identifying Hollywood's Audiences:*

Cultural Identity and the Movies, ed. Melvyn Stokes and Richard Maltby (London: BFI Publishing, 1999), 23–41.

31. "Independent Picture Exhibitors Face Results of Their Own Folly," *Billboard,* 26 September 1931, 28.

32. Ibid.; "Small Exhibitors Find Vaudeville and Circus Acts Business Builder," *Billboard,* 19 December 1931, 28.

33. "Small Theatre and Sound," *Exhibitors Herald-World,* 19 April 1930, 24.

34. See Frank J. Rembusch, "15,000 Exhibitors Can't Be Wrong," *Billboard,* 12 April 1930, 49; and his very long letter to the editor, *Billboard,* 28 June 1930, 13, in which he claims that "the Hays association is the most perfect monopoly ever put together."

35. The expression "little fellow" comes from "The Voice of the Industry," *Exhibitors Herald-World,* 16 August 1930, 52; "safety valve" from "In Which We Say a Few Things Concerning Policies," *Billboard,* 18 January 1930, 48; "shock absorber" from Charles S. Aaronson, "Shock Absorber of Industry—New Name for Small Exhibitor," *Exhibitors Herald-World,* 15 November 1930, 26; and "backbone" from "The 5-5-5 Conference and the Independents," *Billboard,* 5 July 1930, 42.

36. "The Voice of the Industry," *Exhibitors Herald-World,* 16 August 1930, 52.

37. "The Voice of the Industry," *Exhibitors Herald-World,* 20 December 1930, 60–61.

38. "Shorts Fail to Click for Small Exhibitors," *Billboard,* 13 September 1930, 30.

39. "The Voice of the Industry," *Exhibitors Herald-World,* 5 April 1930, 53; Ken. W. Thompson, "Small Town Theatre Needs Consistent Ad Policy, Says Wisconsin Showman," *Exhibitors Herald-World,* 11 October 1930, 50.

40. Jay M. Shreck, "Uniform Operation for Publix Managers Is Outlined by Katz," *Exhibitors Herald-World,* 15 March 1930, 17.

41. See, for example, Joseph Luntz, "Individuality in Theatre Management," *Motion Picture Herald,* 23 May 1931, 69.

42. Crafton, *The Talkies,* 265; Gregory A. Waller, "Hillbilly Music and Will Rogers: Small-Town Picture Shows in the 1930s," in *Moviegoing in America,* 175–88.

43. "The Amusement Parks Should Take a Tip from the Movies," *Billboard,* 15 February 1930, 48; "Chains Have Not Been Able to Meet Small-Town Demands," *Billboard,* 6 December 1930, 60.

44. "The Small Town Grows Up," *Exhibitors Herald-World,* 1 February 1930, 20; Aaronson, "Shock Absorber of Industry," 26; "Small-Town Exhibitor Gives Some Good Advice," *Billboard,* 22 November 1930, 32; W. L. Ainsworth, "The Little Fellow," *Motion Picture Herald,* 18 July 1931, 8.

45. In addition to the material already cited, see two longer pieces in *Billboard:* M. A. Lightman, "The Exhibitor Must Play His Part," *Billboard,* 6 September 1930, 67; Abram F. Myers, "The Independents Are Coming Back!" *Billboard,* 5 September 1931, 43, 46, 76. Much more unusual was the version of localization practiced by the Kemp-Hughes circuit, which opened a new theater in the southern Arkansas pine belt town of Waldron that was designed to offer a "realistic delineation of the pine tree country," including landscape murals and a proscenium designed to resemble a "mountaineer's home"; "A Theatre Designed in Local Motifs," *Exhibitors Herald-World,* 20 December 1930, Better Theatres Section, 58.

46. Jay Shreck, "Chains to Return Many Small Houses to Independents: Kent," *Exhibitors Herald-World,* 15 November 1930, 21.

47. "100% Community Representation Needed for Success of Theatre," *Motion Picture Herald,* 28 March 1931, 19; Nat Holt, "Local Appeal and Civic Contacts!" *Motion Picture Herald,* 23 May 1931, Better Theatres Section, 58; on Fox West Coast theaters, see Leo Meehan, "Theatre Should Be Hub of Community, He Says," *Motion Picture Herald,* 8 August 1931, 143–44.

48. "The Company—The Manager—The Public," *Motion Picture Herald,* 14 March 1931, Better Theatres section, 11.

49. M. A. Lightman, "The Exhibitor Must Play His Part," *Billboard,* 6 September 1930, 67.

50. "Local Influence," *Exhibitors Herald-World,* 23 August 1930, 20.

51. Maltby, "Sticks, Hicks and Flaps," 23. For a preliminary look at Publix activities in Lexington, Kentucky, see Waller, *Main Street Amusements,* 248–55.

52. Parts of these interviews are found in *At the Picture Show* (1993), a documentary film I produced on the Alhambra and the role of the movies in Campbellsville.

11

"WHAT THE PICTURE DID FOR ME"

Small-Town Exhibitors' Strategies
for Surviving the Great Depression

KATHRYN H. FULLER-SEELEY

*Enclosed are a few comments for the "What the Picture Did for Me"
department. I feel somewhat guilty for not submitting write ups
oftener than I do, for I consider these write ups the best guide for a
small theater owner. Situated as we are here in the west so far from
large centers of population, we are almost invariably guided by these
columns in our bookings.*
H. O. EKERN, Rex Theater, Thompson Falls, Montana, *Motion Picture
Herald*, May 11, 1935, 73

For more than twenty-five years, "What the Picture Did for Me" ("WPDFM")
appeared weekly in the *Motion Picture Herald (MPH)*, the largest trade journal for American film exhibitors. But it was not the voice of a random cross
section of the nation's 17,000 movie houses; it was written by a more specialized group—operators of the 10,000 theaters in small towns. The over-
whelming majority of the column's contributors were independent theater
owners who operated 200- to 500-seat houses in towns of 5,000 or fewer
people. Most of these small-town exhibitors were in the Midwest, Plains, and
Mountain states; others were from the Mid-South and northern New England, but very few were from the Mid-Atlantic. In the 1930s, the "WPDFM"
column provided a sounding board for marginalized, nonmetropolitan exhibitors who struggled to survive the Great Depression. It gave these least
powerful—but most numerous—members of the film exhibition industry a
collective voice, a forum in which to air grievances, push for equitable treatment from urban-focused film producers, and lobby for the production of
films that would suit their needs.[1]

"WPDFM" writers focused on challenges that vexed few urban
exhibitors—vagaries of the weather, disingenuous film titles, competition
from tent revivals and baseball games, films too weepy or too swashbuckling,
too "spicy," "high-class," or "urban" to suit their audiences' tastes. Film historians Richard Butsch, Thomas Doherty, Henry Jenkins, and Eric Smoodin,
among others, have made excellent use of these reports as evidence of

nationwide reception of particular films of the late 1920s and 1930s. Focusing instead on a case study of the "WPDFM" columns themselves, this chapter examines concerns stressed by these correspondents, located far from the New York and California centers of the film business, and provides insights into how exhibitors and their patrons in America's smallest communities met the Depression's economic and social challenges.[2]

"WPDFM" began at the suggestion of J. C. Jenkins, self-described "vagabond colymnist" for the *MPH*. In the 1880s, the Michigan-born Jenkins had settled in the northeastern Nebraska town of Neligh (population 1,724), working his way from county clerk and real estate salesman to mayor and state game warden. He built an opera house in Neligh in 1905 and jumped enthusiastically onto the moving picture bandwagon, becoming one of the state's first stationary film exhibitors. Around 1910, Jenkins became a regional correspondent for *Motography* (formerly *Nickelodeon*), a Chicago-based trade journal for movie theater operators. He wrote columns for nearly thirty years, as *Motography* was absorbed first into Martin Quigley's *Exhibitors Herald,* then into Quigley's *MPH*. Adopting the nom de plume "Jaysee," Jenkins provided news, gossip, and folksy stories of fishing, hunting, and dining with some of the thousands of theater owners he claimed as friends "from Pennsylvania to the Pacific" as he passed through innumerable villages. He voiced small-town exhibitors' concerns about a range of issues, including film quality, cranky patrons, hard times, and contentious relations with the film studios.[3]

Jenkins lobbied for the inauguration of a published forum for small-town exhibitors to comment on recent films, and "WPDFM" first appeared in the *Exhibitors Herald* in 1916. It quickly became a staple weekly feature, subtitled "Verdicts on Films in Language of Exhibitor." The column forthrightly identified correspondents by name, theater, town, and state, while a column in the rival *Motion Picture News* attributed comments merely to anonymous exhibitors identified only by region.[4]

Despite the "WPDFM" column's apparent popularity and utility, *Exhibitors Herald* downsized it in 1929, thereafter publishing only a few individual exhibitors' reports in the weekly "Letters to the Editor" column. Although the exact reasons for its diminution remain unknown, it was possibly an indication of the booming film industry's increasingly dismissive attitude toward rural exhibitors. The movie industry was preoccupied with the conversion to sound film and its associated technological upheavals. Henry Jenkins has argued that, at the inception of "talkies," film producers focused on Broadway performers and themes (Eddie Cantor, Al Jolson, and backstage musicals). While these films reaped great profits in northeastern cities, Jenkins notes that a significant "regionalism" in the hinterlands yielded resistance to such films and their urban ethnic performers.[5] Record-breaking attendance at city theaters generated by the "talkies" also might have led *MPH* editors to assume that the industry was riding an endless wave of prosperity, and that small-town exhibition was no longer essential to its profits. (The movie business claimed that film attendance had skyrocketed from 55 million in 1925 to 110 million in 1929.)[6] Walter Odom of the Dixie Theater, Durant, Mississippi, protested the marginalization of small-town exhibitors: "I am through [writing film reports], brother exhibitors, because after all we say and do, and all we have said and all we have done in the past, the big producers still ignore our wants and give us what suits them."[7]

Although the stock market crash in October 1929 did not initially harm the thriving urban exhibitors, nonmetropolitan theaters across the nation were devastated. The expense of wiring for sound was daunting for small independent exhibitors, and the studios had curtailed production of silent features to such an extent that there was not sufficient new product for unwired theaters to remain in business. Then, with the economic downturn, their box office revenues plummeted by more than a third. Widespread unemployment, drought, and falling agricultural prices drained away farmers' and workers' families, and rural middle-class customers were lured to city theaters; the loss of audiences combined with the renovation costs for "talkies" squeezed out many small-town theaters. By 1932, about 8,000 of the nation's 23,000 movie theaters were closed. Densely populated urban areas of the East Coast and West Coast experienced a relatively minor theater closure rate of from 7 percent to 20 percent, but the Midwest, Plains, South, and northern New England lost from 22 percent to 47.7 percent of all their movie houses. The film industry was fearful of making such figures public, but the nonmetropolitan exhibitors were well aware of the damage. "Jaysee" Jenkins published reports in his column estimating that 40 percent of Americans no longer had access to movie entertainment.[8]

In the absence of "WPDFM," nonmetropolitan exhibitors made their plight known in letters to the *MPH, Variety,* and *Billboard,* calling for an end to the Broadway fare and return to westerns, action films, and comic films that children could enjoy. Henry Jenkins argues that "regional" theaters and audiences did not support urban-themed films, even at the dawn of their cycle. In 1931, he writes, Hollywood belatedly began to realize how much it still needed the support of the smaller, noneastern theaters. Studios again began to produce more films geared toward the "sticks."[9]

Chastened from its high state of hubris, the *MPH* also gave more due to its small-town constituents and reinstated "WPDFM" in January 1933 as a three- to four-page weekly feature. While only 10 to 25 exhibitors wrote about 100 total reports for each issue, the reviews expanded from brief sentences to entire paragraphs. Jubilant contributors testified to the column's importance and thanked J. C. Jenkins for championing it. "Bring on those reports!" Joe Hewitt of the Lincoln Theater, Robinson, Illinois, implored his fellow small-town managers. "Give 'em credit{ . . . }or give 'em Hell as the case may justify! Don't think for one minute the producers don't watch these reports! They do! I know from experience, because 'way back, I had letters from directors and stars, which proved that they watch this old column."[10] At this point, the enormous box office tallies and elaborate promotional schemes presented in other *MPH* departments ("At the Box Office," which listed weekly grosses at 100 top theaters, and "Exhibitor's Round Table") must have seemed far-fetched dreams to harried small-town exhibitors. A cartoon of an exhibitor ruefully eyeing a few bills lying on a table accompanied the first revived "WPDFM" column in January 1933. It was captioned, "What the Picture Did for Him—$2.40."[11]

The exhibitors who contributed to "WPDFM" represented the regions where rural exhibitors were the majority. Report writers lived in the states that had the highest percentages of theaters and seats located in small towns of 5,000 or fewer people. A 1938 *MPH* survey of the nation's 17,541 theaters found that in eighteen of the forty-eight states, more than two-thirds of theaters were located in nonmetropolitan areas. These eighteen states had the highest percentages of "WPDFM" correspondents.[12] Conversely, the most urban states had the smallest percentages of small-town theaters; "WPDFM" rarely heard from exhibitors in Connecticut, New Jersey, Massachusetts, New York, or California, unless they operated in distinctly rural upstate areas (see table 2).

States with Highest Percentages of Movie Theaters Located in Small Towns, 1938

State	% Theaters in Towns < 5,000	% Total Theater Seats in the State Found in Small Towns
1. South Dakota	86	71
2. North Dakota	83	65
3. Nevada	83	67
4. Vermont	81	65
5. Utah	80	59
6. Idaho	80	66
7. Wyoming	79	62
8. Nebraska	78	54
9. Maine	76	61
10. Montana	75	49
11. Mississippi	72	58
12. West Virginia	72	51
13. New Mexico	70	55
14. Arizona	69	51
15. Iowa	69	51
16. New Hampshire	69	51
17. Arkansas	68	53
18. Kansas	67	51

Data from "Motion Picture Exhibition Structure of the U.S.; 72% of Theaters in Towns under 50,000 People," *MPH*, May 28, 1938, 62–65.

The middle twenty-five states had significant proportions of small-town theaters within their borders, ranging from Michigan's, Ohio's, and Pennsylvania's 33 percent, to eight states that had more than half (55 to 62 percent) of their theaters located in small towns (South Carolina, Oklahoma, North Carolina, Virginia, Louisiana, Alabama, Delaware, Texas, Kentucky, and Minnesota). Nearly half (48 percent) of the nation's movie theaters in the 1930s were located in towns of 5,000 or fewer people; however, these contained only 27 percent of the nation's 11 million movie theater seats. If seating capacity correlated positively with possible producer/distributor revenue, the small-town exhibitor's suspicions of being ignored by the studios gain additional credence. The urban picture palaces and neighborhood theaters may have represented only half of the nation's film outlets, but they held nearly three-quarters of the seats.

Exhibitors who reported regularly to "WPDFM" throughout the Depression decade felt passionately about their business, and they were not shy about sharing their opinions.[13] Frequent contributors included the following:

L. V. Bergtold, Opera House, Kasson, Minnesota (population 1,150)

Herman J. Brown, Majestic and Adelaide Theaters, Nampa, Idaho (population 7,621)

A. E. Hancock, Columbia Theater, Columbia City, Indiana (population 3,448)

Sammy Jackson, Jackson Theater, Flomaton, Alabama (population 837)

J. P. Johnson and Ingmar Oleson, Sons of Norway Theater, Ambrose, North Dakota (population 389)

Gladys McArdle, Owl Theater, Lebanon, Kansas (population 822)

A. N. Miles, Eminence Theater, Eminence, Kentucky (population 1,317)

Mayme Musselman, Princess Theater, Lincoln, Kansas (population 1,613)

C. L. Niles, Niles Theater, Anamosa, Iowa (population 2,881)

Walter Odom, Dixie Theater, Durant, Mississippi (population 1,870)

A survey of fifty of the most frequent contributors highlights their longevity in the business and their membership in their regions' dominant ethnic and class groups. They were middle- or working-class businesspeople who owned only one or two movie houses. Most had been exhibitors since the nickelodeon days, and many would operate into the 1950s. Many seem to be natives of their region of the country, and those who appeared to be immigrants (like Ingmar Oleson and L. V. Bergtold) shared the ethnicity of their audiences. They noted little racial or ethnic difference in film reception, and only one or two white managers of blacks-only theaters reported with any regularity. Like frequent correspondents Mayme Musselman and Gladys McArdle, perhaps 10 to 15 percent of all correspondents were women, who operated theaters alone, with partner spouses, or as part of a family business. Most of the frequent contributors were personally acquainted with "Jaysee" Jenkins, whose columns mentioned visiting them on his trips. While "WPDFM" correspondents might have operated in locations far outside the metropolitan mainstream, nevertheless, they wrote as knowledgeable critics (and fans), and as seasoned professionals familiar with the tastes and habits of their local customers.[14]

Small-Town Exhibitors' Concerns

When a movie played to a full house, exhibitors reporting to "WPDFM" usually chalked up its success to the quality of the film and its suitability for small-town tastes—usually it included significant elements of action, broad comedy, a fast-paced plot, scenic locations, and an American setting. Correspondents claimed that small-town audiences preferred what exhibitors called "real" characters, not high-society fops, or exotic foreign sirens swathed in elaborate historical costumes. When a film was a box office disappointment, exhibitors sought to identify reasons for its poor performance. Sometimes they blamed the quality of the film production, such as the curt review that Earl McClurg, of the Grand Theater, Preston, Idaho, gave the film *Jealousy* with Nancy Carroll: "Just fair. One of my patrons suggested that the first three letters be stricken from the name. Did poor at BO. Certainly Columbia can do better by us than that."[15] Fault could also be found with the film's national marketing campaign, or local economic and social conditions, or the failure of the film to match audience preferences.

Even the elements could conspire against the unlucky small-town theater owner. Exhibitors in metropolitan areas, whose patrons could easily walk or use trolleys, buses, or subways to reach neighborhood or downtown theaters, did not face the challenges that small-town exhibitors did in just getting customers to their doors. "With roads, streets and sidewalks blocked with snow it's very hard to tell what box office appeal a picture has," lamented G. A. Troyer, of the New Lyric Theater, Rugby, North Dakota. Rudolf Duba, who operated the Royal Theater in Kimball, South Dakota, blamed drought and temperatures of 114 degrees for a poor showing. Heavy rainstorms or bad roads could effectively extinguish even surefire hits. As reported by P. G. Estee of the S.T. Theater in Parker, South Dakota, "15 to 16 below zero weather killed our business [for Will Rogers's *Judge Priest*], but at that, enough came to clear us on expenses." Sammie Jackson noted that a polio epidemic closed his Flomaton, Alabama, theater, ruining showings of a likely success, *The Country Doctor*.[16] The weather affected both Gladys McArdle's box office at the Owl Theater in Lebanon, Kansas, and her audience's reception of *The White Cockatoo,* as she reported: "Ran this while we were having days and days of wind and dust storms, so howling wind and slamming doors [in the film] are no treat to us. Added to this was a lot of French dialect that could not be understood and a crazy cockatoo that solved a murder mystery by flapping his (or her) wings. Pleased about 50 percent." Perhaps the highest praise a film could garner from "WPDFM" correspondents came from J. L. Thayer, of the Raymond Theater, Raymond, New Hampshire, on Wallace Beery's *Man from Dakota:* "They came from the rural district through deep mud to see this one. Everybody seemed to enjoy it."[17]

Small-town theaters were also more vulnerable than their urban counterparts to the impact of other competing local events that might drain viewers away from the theater. Religious tent revivals, high school commencements, county fairs, circuses, itinerant or "jackrabbit" movie shows, and holiday shopping were all identified as threats. Mayme Musselman, owner of the Princess Theater, Lincoln, Kansas, reported: "Have been fighting some stiff competition in night baseball. The town took up collection enough for the lights and the council is donating the field and current. However, with a friendly board of directors, we got the playing time cut to three nights a week, two hours a night. It wouldn't be so bad if the council would allow us to open on Sundays, but they chase all the patrons out of town, nine shows being available within a radius of forty miles. It's tough!"[18]

At the Depression's nadir, weekly movie attendance plummeted to a mere fraction of what it had been. In January 1933, A. E. Hancock, Columbia Theater, Columbia City, Indiana, lamented that even a popular picture "did but average business, which means about forty percent down from the happy days of 1929." Reports dwelling on hard times were liberally sprinkled among other, more matter-of-fact reviews, as exhibitors wished for more hits like *King Kong* or *42nd Street* to fill their theaters for at least a night or two. The nationwide Bank Holiday in March 1933 dragged attendance figures even further below their disastrous 1932 averages. Robert Yancey, who ran the Paradise Theater, Cotter, Arkansas, reported that *"Air Hostess* did well the first night, but the Bank Holiday took 75% off the following night."[19] Some exhibitors accepted bartered goods or IOUs from their cashless customers. Attendance did improve somewhat as New Deal measures put people back to work, but many small-town exhibitors only limped through the decade. As Gladys McArdle noted in her review of *Gentlemen Are Born* with Franchot Tone: "Ran this one on the three coldest nights of the year to below average attendance but it seemed to please nearly everyone who came. Personally I did not like it. We are all fed up with depression, unemployment and hard times without paying to see them." Poor economic conditions lingered throughout the central regions. As late as 1940, Mayme Musselman was still bemoaning the sparse audiences she had for a film that should have been popular, *Farmer's Daughter:* "Poor crops and lack of ready cash keep my farm folks at home or they let the kids come in while they visit."[20]

Unlike the practices of most urban movie houses, small-town theater advertising was not usually done through huge newspaper advertisements or "Exhibitors' Round Table"–like elaborate publicity stunts; it was accomplished directly at the theater, through interest generated by the promise of the film's title as it was displayed on the marquee, the bright images on the posters lining front display cases and lobby walls, and positive word of mouth passed along from patrons to their friends. Details as seemingly minor as the titles of feature films were important to small-town exhibitors. They claimed that customers would stay away if the title seemed to be too dull (if they sought action), or too sophisticated and sexually provocative (if they were morally conservative). Not surprisingly, typical of the kind of titles non-metropolitan exhibitors praised was Janet Gaynor's *Small Town Girl*. Exhibitor P. E. Braun of Cairo, Nebraska, noted: "It seems that when the title contains the words 'small town' or 'farmer' business is good. This drew better than any picture for several weeks." Another example was Paul Muni's *Bordertown*, which Russell Anderson, Casino Theater, Gunnison, Utah, reported as "a splendid picture for rural trade and a western title to get them in from the farm."[21]

Favorable publicity generated by Broadway stage success and the approval of a film by sophisticated urban audiences could be of little help in rural areas for an ambiguously named film like *The Petrified Forest*, as several correspondents groused: "A very fine production with a terrible title. With a title like 'The Arizona Bad Man' the picture would have done 40 percent more business in this town," reported William Powell, Wellington, Ohio. "They came with the expectation to see some actual scenes of the Petrified Forest," wrote J. P. Johnson, Sons of Norway Theater, Ambrose, North Dakota. However, Horn and Morgan of the Star Theater, Hay Spring, Nebraska, did note: "What a swell picture. Held audience almost spellbound throughout the entire length of it."[22]

The visual sales ability of the studio-provided publicity materials was also essential to small-town exhibitors' success. H. M. Johnson of Avon Park, Florida, complimented the Monogram studio, after a fashion, for a poster that made the most of *The House of Mystery:* "A picture crammed with hokum, but it did the business, so I am pleased. The posters all carried pictures of apes and that brought the kids in and they brought the old folks. Business above average on bargain night." Herman Brown of Nampa, Idaho, criticized a studio publicity department for concentrating on urban-focused consumer culture rather than attention-grabbing action in the advertising materials for *Whom the Gods Destroy:* "This picture shows the sinking of a deluxe liner and is a tie-up with the Morro Castle. It does big business. Play it quickly. In the press books no mention is made of the big scenes even if they are gigantic. They confine themselves to the kind of chewing gum chewed by the star and what color the leading lady's shoes are."[23]

Difficulties of Pleasing Small-Town Movie Audiences

"WPDFM" contributors claimed that their audiences reflected the population of their small towns—more native-born whites than immigrants or African Americans, and a fairly equal gender and age balance of men, women, and children—literally, a family trade. Hampered as they were by the strict requirements of the studios' block booking arrangements, theater owners wished to play a steady stream of films that could simultaneously interest all members of this heterogeneous audience. *Meet Nero Wolfe* was a typical feature that seemed to meet those needs, at least in Wellington, Ohio: "Business was good and the picture seemed to have the faculty of pleasing both sexes of all ages."[24]

Having a mixed-gender and mixed-age audience gave exhibitors concerns about how to keep everyone simultaneously engaged with the film program. In his study of 1930s film programming, Thomas Doherty has shown that urban and suburban exhibitors strove to maintain a "balanced program" of feature, cartoon, newsreel, comedy, and short subjects that together constructed a multifaceted program that offered "something for everybody."[25] Nevertheless, the village exhibitors writing to "WPDFM" claimed that they depended heavily on the feature film to carry the entire show. Unlike larger city theaters, which could focus on various segments of the audience at any given show, for rural theaters, the entire potential audience needed to be attracted to each film. Of a film like *Little Shop around the Corner*, J. L. Thayer of Raymond, New Hampshire, warned, "In a situation like ours where children and adults attend the same show, you'll be a nervous wreck keeping the kids quiet because the picture lacks action."[26]

Throughout the decade, nonmetropolitan exhibitors debated whether Hollywood had a lopsided gender balance and was making "too many" films for either only women or men. In 1933, F. M. A. Litchfield of the Morse Theater, Franklin, Massachusetts, worried that frantic film producers, trying to attract attention in hard times, were making too many "horror pictures, weird and gruesome pictures and gangster and underworld sordid pictures" that pulled in males but entirely alienated women. Fearing that women would stay away permanently if the trend were not reversed, Litchfield expressed hope that "when the producers find out that they can't make pictures for men and don't expect every animal picture to be 'Trader Horn' and every gang picture to be 'Little Caesar,'" they would produce more pictures that appealed to women as well; that would create renewed prosperity at the box office.[27]

Other small-town exhibitors, however, charged that it was the men in their audiences who were being neglected. J. A. Milligan, a showman in Schuylerville, New York, pointed to films like *Anna Karenina:* "The women liked Garbo and I still haven't found a man who did. This picture is one of those long drawn out affairs of the heart which men don't care for." He labeled *The Melody Lingers On* "a woman's picture entirely; too draggy to suit the majority." In Dewey, Oklahoma, E. M. Freiburger noted that *Pride and Prejudice* was not a success: "Good picture but poor business. Not a small town picture. The women liked it but the men walked out." In late 1941, an *MPH* editorial writer complained: "One of the fundamental weaknesses that I have been unable to understand is why the producers have overlooked the vast male audiences that we are forgetting want entertainment, too; that want more than just westerns. It seems that the obvious fact that only 51% (recent poll) of our audience is women should imply to Hollywood that they cannot go on making pictures only for the feminine taste."[28]

Swashbuckler films, featuring all the excitement that rural exhibitors seemed to require for male patrons, along with romantic leading men and lovely heroines for the ladies, nevertheless found only tepid small-town business. Of Gary Cooper's *Lives of a Bengal Lancer,* Harry Newman of the Liberty Theater, Lynden, Washington, disappointedly noted: "A wonderful action picture that was a box office flop. The men all came and the women stayed home."[29] Similar complaints were made about *Captain Blood:* "A very fine production with no drawing power. Men and children comprised 90 percent of the audience. Women were afraid it was another 'Mutiny on the Bounty.'" *Mutiny* had been dismissed as a "very good show of the kind, but not a business builder for small towns. Very brutal for ladies to get any entertainment out of it and the big expenses are in vain for the majority of theaters who like to exist yet for some time in the little town. Watch your step, boys."[30]

Some exhibitors chose to categorize their audiences by age rather than by gender. Donald Visger, of Kennewick, Washington, suggested that the "talkie" remake of *M'Liss* was "a good homespun yarn, not too appealing to the younger class of patrons, but liked by the older folks." F. L. Clarke, who operated the Cozy Theater, Hazen, Arkansas, noted of *Freshman Love:* "Fine little picture for your weekend spot, action and comedy aplenty. It will especially please the young folks and that is the biggest part of our customers." Apparently Harry Bubb, of the Sylvanian Theater, New Freedom, Pennsylvania, also felt beholden to his teenage audience. His review of *Mr. Smith Goes to Washington* noted: "One of the best pictures I've played, but no draw. Just one of the mysteries of the game. Ran a matinee for high school and grade school kids. Kids said there must be something wrong with the picture because the school board recommended that they see it."[31]

Other bungled films seemed unappealing to all audience segments. Disgruntled Indiana exhibitor A. E. Hancock roasted *Invitation to Happiness,* with Irene Dunne and Fred MacMurray, as being a "prize fight picture of mediocrity. The ladies don't like the prize fighting and the men evidently didn't like the title. So at the box office you are on a limb and someone had a saw. Second day of run 40 paid admissions and 3 deadheads [free passes].

Bring on the Townsend Plan [a radical plan advocating a redistribution of wealth to elderly Americans to stimulate the economy]." Even westerns, a film genre usually quite successful in small-town theaters, could cause an exhibitor headaches. An Oregon exhibitor complained of *Hells' Highway* with Richard Dix, "The men and children thought it was swell but it didn't get over with the women." While another in Texas remarked of *My Pal the King* with Tom Mix, "My dainty little girl patrons liked it. Thought it was sweet. The boys and the grown ups thought it too juvenile and 'kindergartenish.'"[32]

Nevertheless, some theater owners found ways in their film programming to successfully manipulate the disjunctions between their mixed audiences and the limited choices they had among films they could book for their shows. There were times when appealing to just one segment of the audience, and hinting at the "forbidden," piqued additional community interest in a film. Playing *The Age of Consent,* L. V. Bergtold of the Opera House, Kasson, Minnesota, suggested, "A spicy one like this goes over well once in a while. Recommend [advertising the film as] 'not for kids' and play in the middle of week."[33]

As prominent members of their communities who could not hide when the customers were displeased, and wishing to attract nearly every citizen into their small-town show, these exhibitors worked hard to maintain cordial relationships with their audiences. Gladys McArdle described *Peg of My Heart* as "the kind of a show that makes the proprietor want to stand out in the lobby when the show is over instead of sneaking up to the booth to avoid the patrons." Pleasing audiences impacted the theater owners' bottom line, so theater owners wrote to "WPDFM" in distress when patrons left in the middle of a performance. C. F. Dean, of the Dunbar Theater, Dunbar, West Virginia, vilified *Chatterbox* with Anne Shirley: "Very ungood. They walked out in fours with a $600 Bank Night." Of another poor offering, C. T. Cooney of Waldoboro, Maine, joked, "My head sunk so low in my collar to avoid the scowls of my patrons that I had to cut away my shirt front to find my way home." Half-empty movie houses were not just a sign of poor-quality films, but also, in theater owners' eyes, a poor reflection on themselves.[34]

Contrasting Urban and Small-Town Film Audiences

Against a backdrop of broad social dislocation, urban-rural cultural conflict suffused American culture in the 1930s, as was evident in Robert and Helen Lynd's *Middletown in Transition;* nativist backlash against urban immigrants, blacks, and political radicals; and religious fundamentalists' alarm over the drifting morality of city youth. Concerns about motion pictures as dangerous purveyors of urban attitudes to small-town children became an increasingly prominent part of this cultural anxiety in the late 1920s, just as "talkies" with prominent themes of sex, violence, and urban sophistication swept the nation. In 1933, the Payne Fund studies on movies' putative influence on American youth were published, the Catholic Legion of Decency's disapproval was loud, cries for national film censorship were heard in Washington, and Hollywood studios were frantically formulating a Motion Picture Censorship Code to be overseen by the Hays Office, to calm the public furor over film content.[35]

These concerns about the cultural influence of films were at the boiling point when the "WPDFM" department was revived in 1933. Thomas Doherty has used "WPDFM" reports as evidence of public reaction to the overtly sex- and violence-filled films of "Pre-Code Hollywood," but it is useful to note that these reports represent a particularly rural "hinterlands" point of view. Given the loud censorship struggle occurring at the national level, the number of small-town exhibitors' reviews overtly complaining about film sexuality, immorality, and crime were actually rather small—perhaps only 100 to 200 entries out of several thousand. More often than directly condemning those movies, correspondents simply labeled offending films "urban."[36]

The small-town exhibitors tended to lump together two divergent groups of films into the "urban" category. On the one hand, they argued that "city" films were too sexually provocative and violent and would appeal mostly to the immigrant working class. On the other hand, "urban" films could be wordy drawing room farces featuring indolent aristocrats and operatic warbling; report writers charged that these films would be appreciated only by enervated, upper-class city tastes. "WPDFM" writers represented themselves and their rural audiences as a "wholesome" middle ground that rejected the moral laxity of the city's poorer ethnic thrill seekers and the haughtiness of the city's lascivious rich (who they thought managed to be immoral and boring at the same time). "WPDFM" writers insisted that city movie audiences were the polar opposite of their village clientele in terms of social class, morality, and cultural taste. Yet small-town exhibitors were also frustrated that their audiences complained too quickly about perceived sexual innuendo and that they did not appreciate life's "finer things," and correspondents sometimes displayed superior attitudes toward the "sons of toil" who were their customers.[37]

In "WPDFM" columns of 1934, contributors complained that particular films they had shown were more appropriate for the "classes" than the "masses," and that their small-town audiences would not identify with upper-class film themes. As Harry Musgrave, of Minneapolis, Kansas, reported on *The Stars over Broadway:* "How long can this 'High C' stuff go on? When we were 'sexed' to death, the L. of D. [Legion of Decency] came to the rescue. I for one am ready to start a league of some sort to stop this breed. It's a crying shame to hang this onto Pat O'Brien and Frank McHugh. In the early part of the picture, Pat looks into a traveling bag at a gun lying there. Really, you know I believe he was serious about that." Harold Allison, who operated the Baldwin Theater, Baldwin, Michigan, had trouble with the operetta *The King Steps Out:* "Good singing by good looking Grace Moore. Not a big draw here. When Grace Moore has her mouth open with song, a CCC boy hollers 'toss her a fish.' Ride 'em cowboy suits more people than high C."[38]

Some exhibitors allowed that they had some "urban"-type patrons (upper-middle-class) in their small towns, but hardly enough to pay the bills. Of the film *Barretts of Wimpole Street,* G. A. Van Fradenburg, of Manassa, Colorado, noted, "A wonderful show that will perfectly satisfy adults who have any inclination toward literary and artistic matters, which means about five per cent of our patrons. A fair house the first night and empty seats the second." As A. N. Miles of Eminence, Kentucky, commented on *Barretts,* "I took so many bows for bringing this picture to town that I almost got a 'crick' in my neck. No, we didn't hang out the SRO sign, but we did a nice business. Drew many people who are [not] in the habit of attending pictures, and pleased everybody who saw it very, very much."[39]

Other times the "WPDFM" exhibitors demonstrated their concern for their own cultural status in the film business by denigrating their small-town audiences. "Another rootin, tootin, shootin son of a gun western that the boys with mud on their shoes will get a kick out of. OK for Saturday nights," A. G. Miller, Atkinson, Nebraska, noted of the Ken Maynard film *Smoking Guns.* "We can't remember a more delightful picture," George F. Smith of Lapeer, Michigan, wrote of the film *What Every Woman Knows.* "However it will not please the great unwashed." L. V. Bergtold juggled the difficulties of pleasing not only all gender and age groups, but also all the social class elements of his heterogeneous audience. He reported on *These Three,* "A grand show for the better classes and satisfactory entertainment for the average fan. However, I heard a 'low brow' remark on the way out 'worst show I ever saw.' This was more than offset, however, by the numerous fine comments." Not surprisingly, there were very few instances in the "WPDFM" column of exhibitors feeling less culturally sophisticated than their village audiences.[40]

Several small-town exhibitors described strategies for bridging the social class gaps between their village audiences and Hollywood products. One was to find the perfect film to please all. An example was *Rose Marie.* "This seems to be about half opera and half a Mounted Police story. It appears to be somewhere near to a 'natural' as it will satisfy anyone from a sheepherder to a high-brow professor," reported a pleased G. A. Van Fradenburg, of Manassa, Colorado.[41] Antonio Balducci of Canastota, New York, developed a classification system to deal with class distinctions among his patrons: "This theater enjoys a general patronage, one composed of farmers on farmers' nights, middle class people on middle class nights, and a higher type patronage on their nights. These various nights are designated by the types of picture I run." It is possible these special class-designated nights were only put on for special occasions, but this does suggest that various segments of the audience sorted themselves out by film title, adding weight to the marquee value of a film in nonmetropolitan areas.[42]

"WPDFM" writers sometimes linked both urban working-class sexuality and upper-class sophistication to a debased and diluted urban masculinity, from which they and their audiences distinguished themselves. "There may be a sufficient number of people in the large cities to roll up big B.O. receipts when these ultra-modern, loud sex pictures and plain dirt pictures are shown. But I ask you to turn to the pages of 'WPDFM' dept of the *Herald* and read the fatal verdict in the vast majority of average theaters," scolded B. P. McCormick, Jones Theater, Canon City, Colorado.[43] F. M. A. Litchfield of Franklin, Massachusetts, complained that the inappropriate films favored by city audiences were ruining his solid small-town business:

> The producers find that, in some of the larger cities where their overhead is highest, horror pictures, weird and gruesome pictures and gangster and underworld sordid pictures have taken in fair sized grosses. From this as a beginning they have figured that the whole country wants this type of film fare. In this they are very erroneous—these cities have yielded large numbers of unemployed men who have nothing else to do. They are looking for an extreme that will turn their thoughts from their dire circumstances, hence the popularity of these horrible samples of cinema product.[44]

Small-town exhibitors pointedly stressed the differences between their audiences and city folk. They could target their complaints to put the blame on either high or low class, high in that urban folks must be wealthier and more sophisticated (and immoral when it comes to sex comedies featuring rich folks). On the other hand, in their arguments, the city was also filled with lower-class (immigrant, unemployed, poor), immoral people who liked smut and gangster movies. These class and cultural tensions in the column began to subside by mid-decade; the directives of the Production Code were taking effect to "tame" the more obvious elements of sexual, immoral, and violent displays. Henry Jenkins argues that the Hollywood studios also normalized or "de-Semitized" the more ethnically different performers and film themes to broaden their appeal from the urban, New York show business to a generic kind of Anglo-Americanness more palatable for "regional" or hinterlands tastes (here midwestern cities and rural audiences were melded into one).[45]

As opposed to the urban-themed films that they disparaged, among the highest accolades "WPDFM" contributors could give was to write that a particular film was a "small town natural." Henry Reeve, Menard, Texas, wrote of Janet Gaynor's *Servant's Entrance,* "If ever there was a 100 per cent picture for the small town theater, here it is. Just plain, solid, entertainment, clean as can be." Shirley Temple and Will Rogers were, by exhibitors' accounting, the most popular stars in small-town theaters in the 1930s. Reactions to Temple's early films could be euphoric. Herman Brown, of Nampa, Idaho, noted of one, "The Temple person gets bigger and bigger at the B.O. The starved small town people, sick of the introvert junk based on the decadent novels turned out by a generation of fifth rate writers who have lost the meaning of humanities, turn eagerly to the clever unselfconscious child who says something modern novelists lack genius to say. It's a straight clean mop up." Another reporter from Oklahoma raved, "Swell! Elegant! Supreme. And of course, Colossal. And all other adjectives referring thereto. Packed the house two times in one night, here in a hamlet of 500. They even drove 50 miles to see this one. Actually outgrossed Will Rogers, who has been ace box office here for many moons."[46]

Rogers indeed had a wide following across nonmetropolitan America. "It's just too bad we can't have a Rogers at least once a month. Just let 'em know Will is on the screen and they'll all be there and then we don't see them again until his next picture," reported P.J. Lees, Lake Mills, Wisconsin. Other small-town favorites were the older, nonglamorous comics like W.C. Fields, Marie Dressler, and Wallace Beery, spunky-young-girl figures following Temple such as Sonja Henie, and almost any cowboy film. Of a typical western, *Renegades of the West,* B. McConnell of Hartford, Arkansas, noted, "My audiences like a western once or twice each month, and this one pleased them very much. The real facts are we play westerns because they make us money to pay for the clucks we're forced to run, against our better judgment and the wishes of our audience." Rural exhibitors' enthusiasm for these performers and film genres seemed genuine, although their hyperbole might have been part of their efforts to disparage the sex and crime themes of other then-current films and to lobby for more small-town-friendly fare.[47]

At Decade's End

The final year of the 1930s presented challenges both new and continuing to small-town exhibitors. The studios put increasing pressure on theaters to pay higher percentages of the box office take for films, especially the newest blockbusters. The higher rental fees caused theater owners many problems when the blockbuster films did not perform well locally. Producers demanded 40 percent of the box office for special road show films in 1933 and 1934; in 1935 MGM demanded 50 percent of *Mutiny on the Bo*unty receipts. Rural exhibitors complained with increasing frequency in "WPDFM" that big-picture rental was so expensive that they could not make a profit. On the other hand, some theater owners still prospered with the arrangement on special features. Leslie Smith of the Mayer Theater, Westmoreland, Kansas, showed Disney's *Snow White* earlier than other area theaters and earned twice the returns he normally got. "True, it cost me 50% but 50% on, for example, $200 is better for me than 65% of $100," he reported to a skeptical readership.[48]

Other complaints were long-standing. "People will only come to see pictures that are big, have drama, story and punch and cast," Rudolph Covi of the Covi Theater, Herminie, Pennsylvania, reported in panning the film *I Was an Adventuress,* which apparently shortchanged his audiences on all fronts.[49] If Covi's statement held true for most nonmetropolitan audiences, then small-town theater owners would have been doubly dismayed when the decade's most anticipated film turned out to be a complete disaster for them.

The blockbuster Hollywood picture of the decade, *Gone with the Wind,* still tenaciously holds on to the record (adjusted for inflation) of highest-grossing film in Hollywood history. However, for small-town exhibitors, it was no welcome relief from their Depression woes. "I hope they never make another 'GWTW,'" Robert Wilson of the Palace Theater, Jackson, Missouri, exclaimed. "My theater is located within 10 miles of a 20,000 town where 'GWTW' is being played and has been advertised for months previous. The picture has drained my town of customers and their money. It has taken the spotlight so strongly that the advertising of any other picture is useless." Wilson claimed that he could not afford the high percentage of the box office take that the distributor demanded (MGM took 70 percent of the mandated $1.10 ticket price), so he could not show the film at the usual three weeks after it had been screened in larger towns. Wilson warned that this set a bad precedent: "It impresses the fact upon my customers that my town is too small for big productions."[50]

News of the dreadful results spread in "WPDFM" in the following weeks. "Our town as others were milked by the city run. That we know. Hence we had to go out into the highways and byways for our business. This entailed more money for advertising than it should have done," complained A. E. Hancock, who also lost money on the *Gone with the Wind* engagement. He said he ought to have held off until the following year and played it at popular prices. "The clamor for the picture swayed our judgment. Live and learn." Another Indiana exhibitor wrote, "Beyond a doubt the finest motion picture ever made and with a cast that was perfect in every respect. From a small town box office standpoint, however, a colossal flop. We not only lost money on it but also lost the normal profit that we usually earn on these same days. We are not considering the headaches in preparing for it. These in smaller towns who can afford these prices did not wait for it and the remainder who would liked to have seen it could not afford it."[51]

In mid-December 1941, the week after the Japanese attack on Pearl Harbor finally propelled the United States into World War II, *MPH* published a Christmas film wish list of (small-town) exhibitor "likes" and "don't likes" that highlighted theater owners' fervid desire to have "more Will Rogers and Marie Dresslers." This was certainly a nostalgic look backward, as the two performers had been dead for six and eight years, respectively. Exhibitors longed for the elimination of B pictures, war-themed films, sermon pictures, "highbrow" stories, and drawing room dramas. They favored getting more musicals, action pictures, and two-reel comedies. They asked for less dialogue and more entertainment.[52] At the end of the Depression, small-town theater owners had found ways to survive, but they were being squeezed by higher rental rates, by "bigger" blockbuster films that pointed out how marginalized the rural theaters were, and by "urban" films their audiences did not necessarily like. They continued to make the same requests they had all through the decade, asking for films that would better suit small-town needs—adventure, action, comedy, American characters. But despite the voice they enjoyed through the *MPH*'s exhibitor forums, Hollywood continued to give them only scant attention.

Film historians have utilized the "What the Picture Did for Me" column published in the *Motion Picture Herald* during the 1930s as a representative source of the "vox populi"—a gauge of nationwide exhibitor and audience reception of Hollywood film releases. Closely examining the column delineates more precisely that these were rural and small-town theater owners who used this public space to vent their ongoing frustrations with both the film industry and audiences as they struggled to remain in business in the Dust Bowl. Their reports complain of the difficulties of filling their theaters nightly, of finding films that will be popular with the entire community; of pleasing equal portions of women, men, and children; of mixed social classes and conservative mores. They write of cultural and class friction between local audiences and Hollywood film themes, and even though most of these exhibitors are of northern European heritage, they also comment on their own cultural clashes with their patrons. Reports communicated aggravations about "urban" film themes unsuitable for their audiences, misleading film titles, poor-quality advertising, bad weather, restrictive booking contracts, ruinously high rental fees, and how nonmetropolitan exhibitors (and their audiences) felt overlooked by the studios.

Most of the decade's films considered popular or noteworthy today found little favor in these small-town theaters. Swashbucklers, drawing room comedies, biblical epics, sophisticated dramas, and treacly romances were all given the thumbs-down. Nominated instead as "small-town naturals" were any films in which performers like Will Rogers, Shirley Temple, Janet Gaynor, Marie Dressler, or Wallace Beery appeared, or any low-budget western. In fact, the most disastrous, money-losing film of the decade for these exhibitors was *Gone with the Wind.*

This kind of detailed evidence may guide us in interpreting the varied local and regional reception of films across America's small-town and rural landscapes. It may lead us to more carefully consider in what ways the moviegoing experiences of small-town theater owners and audiences compared with those of their metropolitan picture palace counterparts.

Notes

1. *Motion Picture Herald* trumpeted its prominence in an advertisement, "11,162 Exhibitors Subscribe to Motion Picture Herald," *MPH*, February 11, 1933, 2–3.

2. Richard Butsch, *The Making of American Audiences: From Stage to Television 1750–1990* (London: Cambridge University Press, 2000); Thomas Doherty, *Pre-Code Hollywood: Sex, Immorality and Insurrection in American Cinema 1930–1934* (New York: Columbia University Press, 1999); Henry Jenkins, *What Made Pistachio Nuts? Early Sound Comedy and the Vaudeville Aesthetic* (New York: Columbia University Press, 1992); Eric Smoodin, *Regarding Frank Capra: Audience, Celebrity and American Film Studies, 1930–1960* (Durham, N.C.: Duke University Press, 2004); Eric Smoodin, ed., *Disney Discourse: Producing the Magic Kingdom* (New York: Routledge, 1994).

3. "J. C. Jenkins Dead at 82; Was *Herald* Columnist," *MPH*, March 9, 1940, 60.

4. A typical 1920 "WPDFM" column contained 250 brief reviews submitted by 108 small-town exhibitors in twenty-seven states. Seventy percent of the correspondents lived in the Midwest and Plains; 16 percent represented the South, and 14 percent the West. Few were from the Mid-Atlantic or New England.

5. Jenkins, *What Made Pistachio Nuts?* 162–63; Kathryn H. Fuller, "'You Can Have the Strand in Your Own Town': The Struggle between Urban and Small-Town Exhibition in the Picture Palace Era," in *Moviegoing in America,* ed. Gregory A. Waller (Malden, Mass.: Blackwell, 2002), 88–98.

6. Terry Ramsaye, "A Greater Paper for a Greater Industry," *MPH*, January 3, 1931, 31; "J. C. Jenkins—His Colyum," *MPH*, January 10, 1931, 90; Jenkins, *What Made Pistachio Nuts?* 162–63; "J. C. Jenkins—His Colyum," *MPH*, January 17, 1931, 98; Kathryn H. Fuller-Seeley, "Dish Night at the Movies: Exhibitors and Female Audiences during the Great Depression," in *Looking Past the Screen: Case Studies in American Film History and Method,* ed. Jon Lewis and Eric Smoodin (Durham, N.C.: Duke University Press, 2007).

7. Walter Odom, quoted in "J. C. Jenkins—His Colyum," *MPH*, October 4, 1930, 40.

8. Jenkins, *What Made Pistachio Nuts?* 162; Fuller-Seeley, "Dish Night at the Movies."

9. Gregory A. Waller, in chapter 10 of this volume; Jenkins, *What Made Pistachio Nuts?* Steve Farrar, Orpheum Theater, Harrisburg, Illinois, *MPH*, February 25, 1933, 58.

10. Jenkins, *What Made Pistachio Nuts?* 313–14nn53, 60, 62; "Big Demand for Westerns in All Sections," *Variety*, October 16, 1929, 7; Ernest Rogers, "The Importance of the Sticks," *Variety*, November 6, 1929, 6; Robert H. Brown, "Sticks vs. City on Pix," *Variety*, December 6, 1932, 5; Joe Hewitt, Lincoln Theater, Robinson, Illinois, *MPH*, January 14, 1933, 45. In 1936, *MPH* claimed the "WPDFM" column consisted of "universally read, brief, honest, unedited managers' box office reports in a free weekly forum, voluntarily contributed by thousands of exhibitors." *MPH* advertisement, *International Motion Picture Almanac, 1936–1937* (New York: H. W. Wilson, 1936), 1253. Second-generation film exhibitor Gordon Held testified to the value of "WPDFM," writing, "I have read the exhibitors' reports faithfully every week for as far back as I can remember and place a lot of faith in them." Gordon Held, Strand Theater, Griswold, Iowa, *MPH*, November 11, 1939. 59. A total of 125 different exhibitor-contributors were noted in my survey of twelve issues of *MPH* in 1936. Eighty-nine different exhibitors were noted in twelve issues from 1940.

11. "What the Picture Did for Him—$2.40—Just an Exhibitor in a Small Town," *MPH*, January 7, 1933, 45.

12. "Motion Picture Exhibition Structure of the U.S.; 72% of Theaters in Towns under 50,000 People," *MPH*, May 28, 1938, 62–65.

13. There were also a significant number of onetime contributors in each issue. One "lurker" who had never written in before claimed in defense that he had been forced to run his films too late for his comments to help anyone else; Leslie Smith, Mayer Theater, Westmoreland, Kansas, *MPH*, January 21, 1939, 47. At least half a dozen contributors from 1920 still participated in the late 1930s, and column editors saluted several reporters who reappeared after three-, six-, or even twenty-year absences.

14. A. E. Hancock, Columbia Theater, Columbia City, Indiana, *MPH*, November 24, 1934, 58. Another column reader wrote, "This is my first contribution to your department but it won't be my last. I am like a great many other exhibitors, I guess—let the other fellow do it. But I get so much good out of this department that I have decided to help out my fellow exhibitors as they helped me." L. C. Denton, Rex Theater, Caliente, Nevada, *MPH*, March 14, 1936, 74.

15. Earl J. McClurg, Grand Theater, Preston, Idaho, *MPH*, January 12, 1935, 67.

16. G. A. Troyer, New Lyric Theater, Rugby, North Dakota, *MPH*, March 4, 1933, 59; Rudolf Duba, Royal Theater, Kimball, South Dakota, *MPH*, August 15, 1936, 70; R. W. Hickman, Lyric Theater, Greenville, Illinois, *MPH*, March 18, 1933, 41; W. H. Hardaman, Royal Theater, Frankfort, Kansas, *MPH*, April 8, 1933, 39; P. G. Estee, S. T. Theater, Parker, South Dakota, *MPH*, February 9, 1935, 83; Sammy Jackson, Jackson Theater, Flomaton, Alabama, *MPH*, September 9, 1936, 59.

17. Gladys McArdle, Owl Theater, Lebanon, Kansas, *MPH*, September 19, 1936, 70; J. L. Thayer, Raymond Theater, Raymond, New Hampshire, *MPH*, May 18, 1940, 71.

18. Mayme Musselman, Princess Theater, Lincoln, Kansas, *MPH*, December 2, 1933. Other good films suffered poor box office due to competition. "Business not so hot on it [*Servant's Entrance*] here due to local conditions and an unusually large 'revival' interest, but it is a corker of a picture." Henry Reeve, Mission Theater, Menard, Texas, *MPH*, October 6, 1934, 77; another contributor similarly noted of the film *Carefree*, "Excellent [film], to by far the poorest business we ever had for an Astaire-Rogers feature. Our business has been decidedly off for the past month in spite of the above average showing. Christmas spending and some bad weather are responsible for some of these drops in receipts." C. W. Mills, Arcade Theater, Sodus, New York, *MPH*, January 7, 1939, 45.

19. Hancock, *MPH*, January 14, 1933, 44; Robert K. Yancey, Paradise Theater, Cotter, Arkansas, *MPH*, March 25, 1933, 37.

20. McArdle, *MPH*, January 12, 1935, 67; Musselman, *MPH*, July 20, 1940, 40.

21. P. E. Braun, Cairo Theater, Cairo, Nebraska, *MPH*, November 7, 1936, 75; Russell Anderson, Casino Theater, Gunnison, Utah, *MPH*, April 13, 1935, 42.

22. Hancock, *MPH*, April 13, 1935, 62; William Powell, Lonet Theater, Wellington, Ohio, *MPH*, April 18, 1936, 67; J. P. Johnson, Sons of Norway Theater, Ambrose, North Dakota, *MPH*, September 19, 1936, 60; Horn and Morgan, Star Theater, Hay Spring, Nebraska, *MPH*, April 18, 1936, 71.

23. H. M. Johnson, Avon Theater, Avon Park, Florida, *MPH*, October 27, 1934, 69; Herman J. Brown, Majestic Theater, Nampa, Idaho, *MPH*, October 27, 1934, 69.

24. Powell, *MPH*, September 19, 1936, 57.

25. Thomas Doherty, "This Is Where We Came In: The Audible Screen and the Voluble Audience of Early Sound Cinema," in *American Movie Audiences: From the Turn of the Century to the Early Sound Era*, ed. Melvyn Stokes and Richard Maltby (London: British Film Institute Press, 1999), 143–63.

26. Thayer, *MPH*, May 18, 1940, 71.

27. F. M. A. Litchfield, Morse Theater, Franklin, Massachusetts, *MPH*, April 22, 1933, 50.

28. J. A. Milligan, Broadway Theater, Schuylerville, New York, *MPH*, October 12, 1935, 55; Milligan, *MPH*, December 28, 1935, 88; E. M. Freiburger, Paramount Theater, Dewey, Oklahoma, *MPH*, September 14, 1940, 45; "Exhibitors Continue to Say What They Like and What They Don't," *MPH*, December 6, 1941, 46.

29. Harry A. Newman, Liberty Theater, Lynden, Washington, *MPH*, April 13, 1935, 63.

30. Powell, *MPH*, April 18, 1936, 67; Duba, *MPH*, April 18, 1936, 67.

31. Donald Visger, Liberty Theater, Kennewick, Washington, *MPH*, October 10, 1936, 86; F. L. Clarke, Cozy Theater, Hazen, Arkansas, *MPH*, June 20, 1936, 109; Harry L. Bubb, Sylvanian Theater, New Freedom, Pennsylvania, *MPH*, April 6, 1940, 49.

32. Hancock, *MPH*, August 5, 1939, 91; S. M. Farrar, Orpheum Theater, Harrisburg, Illinois, *MPH*, January 7, 1933, 44; P. J. Eagan, American Theater, Wautoma, Wisconsin, *MPH*, January 14, 1933, 44; M. W. Larmour, National Theater, Graham, Texas, *MPH*, January 7, 1933, 44.

33. L. V. Bergtold, Kasson Opera House, Kasson, Minnesota, *MPH*, January 14, 1933, 44.

34. McArdle, *MPH*, September 30, 1933, 50; C. F. Dean, Dunbar Theater, Dunbar West Virginia, *MPH*, September 19, 1936, 58; C. T. Cooney Jr., Waldo Theater, Waldoboro, Maine, *MPH*, May 13, 1939, 68.

35. Robert S. Lynd and Helen Merrell Lynd, *Middletown in Transition: A Study in Cultural Conflicts* (New York: Harcourt, Brace Jovanovich, 1937); Garth S. Jowett, Ian C. Jarvie, and Kathryn H. Fuller, *Children and the Movies: Media Influence and the Payne Fund Controversy* (London: Cambridge University Press, 1997).

36. Doherty, *Pre-Code Hollywood*.

37. Reporters in the "WPDFM" department also linked lax morality with films that must have been produced for urban markets. Steve Farrar fumed over Wheeler and Woolsey's *So This Is Africa*: "Where are we headed? If pictures like this one and *She Done Him Wrong* are to be what small town exhibitors are to offer their patrons in 1933 and 1934 we might as well close up and quit now, for a few more like this one and we will lose our Sunday shows and have local censorship. These might be hot shows in the big towns but they mean nothing but trouble for us small town theater owners. A few more like this one and we will have Federal censorship and even the mighty Hays Office will not be able to block it. Unless you can get away with murder do not show this on Sunday. It's rotten." Steve Farrar, Orpheum Theater, Harrisburg, Illinois, *MPH*, April 15, 1935, 45.

In 1934 there was a significant amount of urban versus small-town debate in "WPDFM" columns. Yet there is not as much controversy as I had anticipated finding, reading the examples Doherty and Jenkins provide. Although in the earliest years of the "talkies," before 1932, Jenkins notes that many exhibitors complained that films featuring New York vaudeville comedian Eddie Cantor did not play well in Peoria, I located several examples of small-town exhibitors who claimed their audiences loved Cantor (although by 1934 exhibitors were reporting more frequently that Cantor's films were disappointing and he was losing his fan base of support in their towns). Doherty, *Pre-Code Hollywood;* Jenkins, *What Made Pistachio Nuts?;* Henry Jenkins, "Shall We Make It for New York or for Distribution? Eddie Cantor, *Whoopee,* and Regional Resistance to the Talkies," *Cinema Journal* 29, no. 2 (1990): 32–52.

38. Harry Musgrave, Cozy Theater, Minneapolis, Kansas, *MPH,* December 28, 1935, 89; Harold Allison, Baldwin Theater, Baldwin, Michigan, *MPH,* October 10, 1936, 85.

39. G. A. Van Fradenburg, Valley Theater, Manassa, Colorado, *MPH,* February 9, 1935, 84; A. N. Miles, Eminence Theater, Eminence, Kentucky, *MPH,* March 23, 1935, 61. Sometimes exhibitors shared their audience's "High C" opinions. Of *Hound of the Baskervilles,* Bud Davis noted, "To start with, the title was terrible and it is in keeping with the picture because it is the same way." Bud Davis, Ritz Theater, Roanoke, Alabama, *MPH,* August 5, 1939, 92. However, another theater manager noted with surprise, "Didn't know so many people read books 'til we played this." M. L. DuBose, Cotulla, Texas, *MPH,* September 16, 1939, 76.

40. A. G. Miller, Lyric Theater, Atkinson, Nebraska, *MPH,* October 27, 1934, 72; George F. Smith, Lyric Theater, Lapeer, Michigan, *MPH,* December 8, 1934, 73; Bergtold, *MPH,* October 10, 1936, 87.

41. Van Fradenburg, *MPH,* June 20, 1936, 107.

42. Antonio C. Baldacci, Avon Theater, Canastota, New York, *MPH,* February 17, 1934, 68.

43. B. P. McCormick, Jones Theater, Canon City, Colorado, *MPH,* July 15, 1933, 69. Similarly, a review of *Hot Pepper,* with Victor McLaughlin and Edmund Lowe, noted, "Too 'hot' for small town patronage catering to respectable people and family trade. Every town has some who like them 'hot,' but they won't keep you in business." Boom and DuRand, Lyric Theater, Ellendale, North Dakota, *MPH,* April 22, 1933, 53.

44. Litchfield, *MPH,* April 22, 1933, 50.

45. Jenkins, "Shall We Make It for New York or for Distribution?"

46. Henry Reeve, Mission Theater, Menard, Texas, *MPH,* October 6, 1934, 77; Brown, *MPH,* October 6, 1934, 79; Charles Summers and Son, Elite Theater, Seiling, Oklahoma, *MPH,* April 13, 1935, 64. Despite their "cultured" proclivities, some film musicals also succeeded with rural audiences, as B. A. McConnell commented about *Go Into Your Dance:* "Talk about entertainment! Believe me, this musical has everything. Jolson's singing of *A Quarter to Nine* is the hit of the show. We had requests to run reel no. 5 over and did after the last show and did they enjoy it. When you can make a musical to catch the car or sawmill hands and minters, you've got something." B. A. McConnell, Emerson Theater, Hartford, Arkansas, *MPH,* October 12, 1935, 55.

47. P. J. Lees, Majestic Theater, Lake Mills, Wisconsin, *MPH,* December 8, 1934, 73; McConnell, *MPH,* April 13, 1935, 63. A typical rave review for the Marie Dressler and Wallace Beery film *Tugboat Annie* read, "SRO sign hung up for the first time in two years." A. E. Edwards, Orpheum Theater, Orwigsburg, Pennsylvania, *MPH,* September 30, 1933, 52. However, Bert Silver noted of the Richard Dix film *West of the Pecos:* "This is a mighty fine western picture, stars fine and all the case. Very interesting

story. Years ago would have drawn good business as a special, but now it did not do it, though it is extra good entertainment. The highbrows will not go to see a western (not even a *Covered Wagon*)." Bert Silver, Silver Family Theater, Greenville, Michigan, *MPH,* April 13, 1935. 64. Small-town exhibitors even groused about the lauded John Ford film *Stagecoach:* "An excellently made western with good case and story. A little over the head of the average western fan." C. L. Niles, Niles Theater, Anamosa, Iowa, *MPH,* June 7, 1939, 68. The small-town exhibitors and patrons, however, could be just as exacting about the cowboy actors and western films as they were about A-film features, such as this review of *Smoky Trail:* "This is the worst Bob Steele yet played. There are very few good westerns today. Too much singing and comedy. Cowboys have turned 'sissy.'" John Warner, Plaza Theater ("colored patronage"), Greenville, North Carolina, *MPH,* May 4, 1940, 64.

48. Leslie Smith, Mayer Theater, Westmoreland, Kansas, *MPH,* January 21, 1939, 47.

49. Rudolph Covi, Covi Theater, Herminie, Pennsylvania, *MPH,* October 12, 1940, 60.

50. Robert Wilson, Palace Theater, Jackson, Missouri, *MPH,* March 16, 1940, 33.

51. Hancock, *MPH,* May 4, 1940, 64; Ritz Amusements, Incorporated, Park Theater, North Vernon, Indiana, *MPH,* June 1, 1940, 52.

52. "The Exhibitor Has His Say—and Wants to Know What's Next?" *MPH,* December 13, 1940, 42.

12

"SOMETHING FOR NOTHING"

Bank Night and the Refashioning
of the American Dream

PAIGE REYNOLDS

During the 1930s, Americans flocked to the cinema, hoping to escape for a
few hours the devastation and drudgery of the Great Depression by watching gangster films, lavish musicals, and feel-good comedies like *It Happened
One Night* (1934). Even as the economy faltered, 60 to 75 million people attended the movies every week, and Americans spent the majority of their entertainment expenses on filmgoing.[1] Despite the enduring popularity of
film, individual movie theaters and chains were reeling during this tumultuous decade from the increased competition among themselves for the
public's limited entertainment dollars. Consequently, both independent
and studio theaters across the country experimented with a wide variety of
extrafilmic exhibition practices in hopes of luring audiences to their particular venues.

Of these many exhibition practices, perhaps the most famous was Bank
Night, a game of chance first played in 1933 at two independent movie theaters, both located in small, southwestern Colorado towns. A 1936 article on
Bank Night in the *New Republic* described how theater patrons could win cash
through this lottery system:

> The register is set up in the lobby of the theatre and anyone may sign it with-
> out being obliged to buy a ticket. The participants need only sign once to be
> permanently listed for all future drawings (the duplication of signatures has
> been eliminated by an elaborate system of cross-indexes). The number oppo-
> site the signature is dropped into the drum and on the night chosen for the
> drawing someone (preferably a little girl) is selected from the audience to draw
> a number from the drum. The rules require that the holder of this lucky num-
> ber must claim the prize within five, ten or fifteen minutes from the time the
> number is called (the time limit being at the discretion of the theatre man-
> ager).[2]

Though ridiculously simple, this game captured the imagination of the American public and drew crowds, sometimes numbered in the thousands, to movie theaters in towns and cities of all sizes. At their height in 1937, Bank Nights and other "prosperity games" were in place at more than 6,000 of the approximately 15,000 cinemas in the United States.[3] So pervasive was Bank Night that according to one account published in the *Saturday Evening Post*, it "profoundly affected the social life of America, especially in the small town, although movie audiences of the largest cities have gone equally mad over it."[4]

The enormous popularity of Bank Night tells us much about the decade in which it thrived. Dogged by controversy during its tenure in movie theaters, Bank Night's success with film audiences nonetheless demonstrates the resiliency of the American Dream. In the midst of unprecedented economic crisis, this straightforward and almost effortless game cleverly refigured national myths like the Puritan ethos of hard work, the Algerian fantasy of "rags to riches," the wholesome values of the small town, and the parable of the "hometown boy made good" for its legions of audience-players. Some vociferously protested Bank Night and its effect on the civic good, but most raced to their local theater to play the game. Bank Night, I will argue, appealed so poignantly to audiences because it simultaneously tapped into both the lingering fascination and the increasing disenchantment with the American Dream during a historical moment in which the ideal of "something for nothing" held an irresistible allure to filmgoers in cities and small towns across the nation.

The phenomenon of Bank Night can be attributed in part to a convergence of specific social and economic crises and their effects on the film industry. By the late 1920s, most of the film industry was controlled by the "Big Five" studios, vertically integrated monopolies that controlled not only the production of films but also their distribution and, in many cases, exhibition.[5] The "Big Five" owned the majority of first-run theaters in key urban locations, including the elaborate downtown picture palaces. Hence, a studio could exhibit a new film, which it had produced, at one of its first-run theaters and charge the patron a relatively high price to view this newly issued production. Once a certain amount of time had passed, the film would then have a second run at another, less extravagant theater for a lower admission price. This process would continue until the film had completed its run. So while a movie patron who wanted to see a film immediately upon release might pay as much as a dollar, a patron who waited months for the film's fourth or fifth run might pay only a dime. To increase profit, the studios would also sell a full year's worth of films to their exhibitors, a practice known as *block booking* films, which left the independent exhibitor with the remaining, lower-quality films.

As a result of these practices, independents were forced to resort to their own devices to promote and market the film in the most profitable way. The majority of these theaters simply relied on their cheaper ticket prices to attract audiences, an uncomplicated and cost-effective strategy. *Exploitations,* the industry term for film marketing devices, also drew audiences to these independent theaters during the twenties. In their studies of the exhibition practices attending early cinema, film scholars have convincingly argued that these practices allowed for an alternative public sphere in which particular social groups could indulge in filmgoing that nurtured audience participation and expressions of cultural diversity.[6] During the 1920s, however, technological advances, such as sound and standardized film projection speeds, allowed for less diversity in film exhibition practices. These advances also meant that the movie theater experience was increasingly concentrated in the film itself, rather than in the performances and activities surrounding the film. As film production, distribution, and exhibition became more expensive, the industry responded by directing not only filmic content but also film exhibition toward a larger, more homogeneous audience in order to make a greater profit with fewer pictures. Despite these constrictions, exploitations survived and even thrived during this period that saw the genesis of stock exhibition practices such as the double feature and lobby concessions selling popcorn. Games of chance, lotteries and such, were also regularly offered by theaters during the twenties. Yet the majority of independent movie exhibitors continued to rely on lower ticket prices to draw customers.

Until the lowest point of the Great Depression, this system structured by the studios worked well enough for the independent exhibitor. Following the Wall Street crash in October 1929, the domestic box office continued to reap profits, and the Depression had little initial impact on the film industry.[7] The industry credited its immunity to the economic downturn to the novelty of sound film, which debuted in 1929, and the habit of regular moviegoing by its patrons. However, the box office fell sharply in 1932 and suffered its first slump in 1933, four years after the Depression had begun. As hard times hit, the first-run theaters lowered ticket prices to compete with the smaller, independent exhibitors for customers. Since there were now fewer entertainment dollars for which to compete, the smaller chains and independent theaters, which had profited in the recent past from filmgoers eager to pay lower ticket prices, sought new ways to lure customers. In their desperate pursuit of audiences, these theaters offered a hodgepodge of activities, including amateur nights, dish giveaways, organ recitals, community sing-a-longs, double features, midnight previews asking for audience feedback, and beauty contests, among others.

Throughout the 1930s, Bank Night and other games of chance such as Screeno and Prosperity Night, to name a few, were the most successful of the exhibitor's "exploitations." Screeno was a form of bingo in which the theater manager projected a random number on the movie screen, and audience members then punched out corresponding numbers on their Screeno card. As in Bingo, the winner of Screeno was the first player to complete the pattern. Another game, Movie Sweepstakes, asked audience members to bet on a filmed horserace projected onto the screen. Winners usually took home cash in these and other games such as Treasury Night, Cash Award Night, Buck Night, and their hybrids. Initially, exhibitors used these games of chance to draw customers on typically slow nights like Monday or Tuesday. A cash giveaway seemed to solve the problems that exhibitors found accompanied other giveaway schemes: Christmas tree and turkey giveaways worked only during the holidays, and dish giveaways targeted female customers eager to complete a set of china, but when the set was completed, they stayed home.[8] With cash giveaways, exhibitors found a ploy that brought in both women and men, and harnessed an audience that would return weekly in hopes of winning the prize.

Like many exploitations, these games of chance had their start in the independent theaters found in suburban and small towns. According to Tino Balio's history of American cinema during this decade, the domestic exhibition market was composed of 23,000 theaters, of which only 400 were movie palaces located in cities of 50,000 or more. And while 35 percent of the population (43 million people) lived in these cities of 50,000 or more, the remaining 65 percent (80 million people) lived in small towns at the start of decade.[9] Early in the decade, the film industry had recognized the power of small-town audiences to sustain their profits. By 1931, an article in *Variety* entitled "Power of Small Towns" could assert, "Uncle Sam's small town population now dictates the fashion in the entertainment world."[10] According to this report, towns with populations under 50,000 determined which films might generate a profit, and these small-town audiences longing for "clean entertainment" also "represent the greatest bulk of what is known as public sentiment anywhere in the world." By providing films rich with "clean entertainment," small-town theaters hoped to draw customers to a bill that might change as often as three times a week. But as the decade's economic woes persisted, these theaters could no longer rely on the filmic content alone to draw audiences—cash-strapped moviegoers were tempted from their local theater not only by other community activities or by free entertainment like that provided by the radio, but also by theaters in nearby towns promising lower ticket prices, double bills, or other more compelling entertainments to accompany the film.

Charles Urban Yaeger, a manager responsible for a circuit of small-town theaters in Colorado's Rocky Mountain region, responded to these problems by inventing Bank Night. In the winter of 1932–33, Yaeger, an assistant district manager for Fox West Coast Theatre Circuit, developed a cash giveaway to draw and sustain audiences for the company's theaters; he titled the promotion "Bank Night" because the prize money was to be deposited in the bank.[11] The first Bank Nights were staged that winter at the Egyptian Theatre in Delta, Colorado, and the Oriental Theatre in Montrose, Colorado, only twenty minutes apart from each other. The Egyptian had previously reduced its 35-cent admission to 25 cents as a promotional stunt, but Yaeger rescinded the price reduction with the advent of Bank Night. That first evening, the Egyptian's customers were so captivated by Bank Night that, despite complaints about the price hike, hundreds of them waited to play the game outside the lobby, and the theater grossed more in that one night than it had the entire week previous.

Exhilarated by the Egyptian's success, Yaeger instituted Bank Nights at every theater in his district and asked his employer, Frank Henry (Rick) Ricketson, to finance a company providing Bank Night to theaters across the country. Ricketson accepted the offer, and together they formed Affiliated Enterprises, Inc. In December 1933, Yaeger resigned from Fox and turned his full attention to disseminating Bank Night nationally. Affiliated Enterprises began selling the rights for Bank Night to small-town and suburban theaters, and within the first few months more than 1,000 theaters were paying the company anywhere from $5 to $50 a week (depending on the theater's size) for the rights to stage the game. Affiliated Enterprises sold territory franchises to individual promoters; these promoters, in turn, sold the rights to Bank Night to theater owners. Along with the rights to the trademark, theaters received a promotional trailer advertising Bank Night, a register for signatures, record books, and the numbers to be used in the drawing of the numbers.

Because of Bank Night's proven success in drawing audiences, small theaters across the country rapidly purchased the rights to the game. Even in the face of ongoing legal battles to determine if the game violated state lottery laws, local exhibitors in Southern California were "signing bank night contracts at the rate of one a day."[12] By 1935, the game was well established in theaters across the country. A study of movie house exploitations in Dallas, Texas, reveals how Bank Night was typically positioned in cities with suburbs. Of the city's seven downtown theaters, two offered Screeno, one offered Bank Night—while the rest of these studio-owned theaters offered no gifts or giveaway promotions. But virtually all of the smaller "neighborhood" theaters outside of the city center offered regular promotions, of which Bank Night and Screeno were the most pervasive, followed in popularity by dish giveaways and double bills.[13] By 1936, Bank Night was being played in 4,300 theaters, each paying from $15 to $75 a night to Affiliated Enterprises for that privilege.[14]

While Bank Night began as the attempt of small theaters to keep their regular customers and to lure customers from the studio-owned, first-run picture palaces, it was soon adopted by large metropolitan theater chains like

Chicago's Balaban and Katz. Bank Night first arrived in Chicago in March 1935, more than two years after its Colorado debut. By August of that same year, only six months later, 115 Chicago-area theaters were holding Bank Nights once a week. Having acquired the rights to Bank Night, the Balaban and Katz class "A" houses, such as the famous Southtown, Uptown, Marbro, and Tivoli theaters, gave away $150 in their weekly Bank Nights. If the customer was not present to claim the prize, the money was put back in the pot; consequently, individual awards occasionally totaled up to $1,200. The *Motion Picture Herald* described the chaos that ensued when these large cash prizes were available at large picture palaces like the Southtown: "One would think that these huge awards which attract crowds of anywhere from 10,000 to 25,000 persons to the theatre would be fine. They have, however, become a veritable Frankenstein. The theatre has to have from 25 to 150 policemen on duty to handle traffic. Street cars and other traffic must be rerouted and it is rapidly reaching the point where those staging the affairs feel they are getting too big to handle properly."[15] Chicago's Uptown, the sixth-largest theater in the world, could seat only 5,100 people, which gives some indication of the problems that arose when two to five times that number crowded the cinema, lobby, and streets surrounding the building. Bank Nights even spread to venues other than movie theaters. New York's Stork Club offered one each week, and Chicago's Riverview amusement park (owned by two men who also held an interest in Chicago's Essaness theater circuit) famously staged the World's Biggest Bank Night, which offered an award of $2,500 to one of the 260,000 eligible players.[16] Consistently, these games attracted huge crowds, generating enormous publicity for individual movie theaters and the film industry as a whole. Bank Nights were, in fact, so impervious to the economy that they reached the height of their popularity in 1937–38, the second slump of the Depression.

The enormous popularity of Bank Night can be explained at least in part by the particular conjunction of this exhibition practice with classical narrative cinema. The rhetoric surrounding Hollywood films had for years encouraged theater patrons to submit to the narrative at hand, to live vicariously through the movies. In *Middletown*, a sociological analysis of everyday life in the small town of Muncie, Indiana, Robert and Helen Lynd cited a 1929 advertisement reading: "Go to a motion picture . . . and let yourself go. Before you know it, you are living the story—laughing, hating, struggling, winning! All the adventure, all the romance, all the excitement you lack in your daily life are in the Pictures. They take you completely out of yourself into a wonderful new world. . . . Out of the cage of everyday existence! If only for an afternoon or an evening—escape!"[17] As an exhibition practice, Bank Night promoted this same brand of passivity and ease: players simply needed to show up, sign their name to a register, and wait patiently for the winner's name to be called. The game, in tandem with the film, was alluring because it demanded little. Overburdened players could not only watch on-screen characters "winning" but also enjoy an opportunity to see their fellow movie-goers "laughing, hating, struggling, winning"—while gaining access to a chance, however slight, at actually winning themselves.

To American audiences of the 1930s, the imaginative escape offered by films and the surrender to fate offered by games of chance held strong appeal. The American Dream had vowed that with perseverance anyone, regardless of class, could succeed within the capitalist system. Society had promised these individuals a utopia based on the myth of upward mobility, yet this promise had failed the 13 million Americans who found themselves unemployed after the Wall Street crash. While the collapse of the Algerian "rags to riches" fantasy provided a catalyst to awaken revolutionary consciousness in American citizens, many Americans instead sought a new fantasy, one that the film industry was happy to provide. Many of the films Hollywood produced during the Great Depression perpetuated the myth of upward mobility. Rather than replicating the images of idleness, decay, and deprivation that characterized everyday middle-class life of the 1930s, these films insisted that competitive capitalism had not failed. They presented a vision of an American society replete with wealthy characters and opulent goods in order to provide tangible evidence that the social and economic system worked.[18]

Yet most Americans could not afford the affluent lifestyle depicted on-screen, and so audience members were trapped in a futile cycle of desire for the accoutrements of the social and economic privilege placed before them. To stifle the frustration that this futility triggered, the film industry provided a variant of the American Dream that emphasized chance as a crucial element of success. In *42nd Street* (Warner Bros., 1933), for instance, Ruby Keeler plays a chorus girl arbitrarily selected to star in the Broadway opening of *Pretty Lady;* in *My Man Godfrey* (Universal, 1936), Carole Lombard arbitrarily chooses William Powell, an impoverished "forgotten man," to be her butler and the object of her affections; while in *Easy Living* (Paramount, 1937), a fur coat dropping randomly on the head of Jean Arthur could assure that true love and marriage to a wealthy Wall Street magnate lay ahead. According to films like these, hard work and perseverance were no longer critical for success within the economic and social system. Instead, characters gained access to affluence largely through dumb luck.

During the Depression, movies and games worked jointly in further ways to insist that the American Dream continued to serve as a useful road map for individual progress. Both entertainments, for instance, celebrated individual triumph; there can be only one star of *Pretty Lady,* one winner of Bank Night. As a result, they perversely confirmed the ideal of American individuality at a moment when millions of citizens found themselves (or realistically feared becoming) part of a large community of unemployed and impoverished workers. As the films and the games promised individual success, they simultaneously condoned equal opportunity. Each celluloid character and each Bank Night player enjoyed equal access to the luck that brings wealth. Additionally, for vast numbers of destitute Americans, many of whom for the first time were faced with a need for financial assistance, the shared logic of these films and games provided an alternate model of relief that did not wholly refute the ideals of the American Dream. In both entertainments, the passive acceptance of monetary aid was coded as "luck" rather than as desperation or failure. And each insisted that winning was as random as losing—an important message to Depression-era audiences.

The glorification of material success and of the individual that characterizes the American Dream helps to explain the widespread interest in Bank Night's inventor, Charles Urban Yaeger. His "rags to riches" career provided the Depression-weary public a traditional model of entrepreneurial spirit in untraditional circumstances. The *Saturday Evening Post,* a magazine famous for its celebration of American values based on family and small-town life, offered an extensive, albeit incredulous, profile of Yeager and his achievements. The author of this article, Forbes Parkhill, introduced Yaeger by writing, "Few, even in the motion-picture industry itself, are aware that [Bank Night] is the brain child and problem child of a small-towner who made good in the big way."[19] The story of Yaeger's success is portrayed as "a yarn just as cock-eyed as Bank Night itself " in which the readers are asked to be "tickled" by the success of this bumpkin who in spite of "his bland, artless stare" and his eighth-grade education became a millionaire salesman.

This account of Yeager's life further refines the American Dream by insisting that Yeager's success does not stem simply from diligence and thrift. Repeatedly, Parkhill ascribes Yaeger's achievements to ideals associated with small-town Americana. He makes note of Yeager's family values by chronicling his youthful apprenticeship at his father's theater, the Princess in Del Norte, Colorado: "Dad ran the works. Mother sold tickets. I peddled bills and ushered and swept the floors. Sometimes I'd spell dad at the door, and then slide in and double by pumping the automatic piano. When I was old enough, I learned to operate a projection machine" (20). Parkhill does recap Yaeger's history of hard work, describing his pre–Bank Night jobs as a janitor, an usher in Raton, New Mexico, and truck driver for the D & R circuit near Denver, which his eventual partner "Rick" Ricketson then owned. But Parkhill attributes Yaeger's rapid rise from truck driver to checker, booker, and then district manager of the D & R circuit not to his intellect or industry but to Ricketson's recognition that "Yaeger's broad, friend-winning smile was too valuable to be wasted in the cab of a truck" (21). Despite his celebration of Yaeger's work ethic, Parkhill suggests that the greatest commodity Yaeger, or by implication any red-blooded American salesman, might offer is charm. Even as he respectfully describes Yaeger's rustic appeal,

Parkhill notes that he was slow to realize the profit potential of Bank Night and that it was Ricketson who set about copyrighting Bank Night and patenting the game. Affiliated Enterprises is not represented here as a canny business arrangement between peers. Rather, Yaeger is portrayed as a genial, small-towner whose success is to be attributed in part to a man whom he continues to address deferentially as "Mr. Ricketson."

Not surprisingly, the *Saturday Evening Post* article venerates the traditional American values of family, hard work, and a respect for authority. But Parkhill's study of Yaeger reminds readers that the American Dream is not realized through material success alone; it is also defined by a moralistic strain of antimaterialism frequently associated with rural living. In his interviews, Yaeger reflects this belief when he eschews a life in the metropolitan entertainment hubs of Los Angeles and New York and insists, "If we move to New York{ . . . }I'd be too far from the Rose Bowl football games. If we go to Hollywood, I'd be too far from the World Series, and I haven't missed a series in years. Besides, I can't find a city as close to such swell trout fishing as Denver. We're doing okay here" (82). The article's repeated allusions to Yaeger's small-town roots suggest that in contrast to the city, Colorado towns provide safety and order in a chaotic world. Yaeger is cushioned from the madness of sudden wealth and fame not only by his lack of guile but also by his civic, corporate, and family loyalties. His success can be attributed partially to a community so convivial that his employer can become his partner, so cozy that he can leave his tiny Denver office to "drive home to eat luncheon in his four-room apartment with Mrs. Yaeger" (82).

Despite its clever invocation of familiar American ideals, Bank Night was enveloped in a storm of controversy throughout its reign as a successful exploitation, suggesting that some refused to embrace the messages promulgated by its refashioning of the American Dream. Notably, this resistance came from all quarters. Bank Night was condemned by disgruntled players, morally outraged citizens, private businesses, local and state governments, Hollywood studios, and even the independent and studio theater managers who staged the games. Various civic interest groups mobilized to prohibit Bank Night and other cash giveaways, largely because of their associations with gambling and the attendant threat they represented to the moral fabric of local communities. In particular, the women's groups and churches that had organized audience boycotts to control filmic content successfully exerted pressure to encourage municipalities, businesses, and even theaters to ban Bank Nights in their communities. The newspapers in New Orleans responded to this coercion by discontinuing their advertising for theaters offering games of chance. In Pittsfield, Massachusetts—cited by the *Literary Digest* as "the only city to deal effectively with Bank Nite [*sic*]"[20]—the city government doled out Sunday exhibition privileges only to theaters that did not offer Bank Night. Theaters also demonstrated their antipathy for the games by encouraging industry grievance boards and other professional organs to take action against them.[21] Even Quigley Publishing, the producer of *Motion Picture Herald,* which had once provided the industry with legal advice on lotteries, eventually ceased to accept advertising for cash prize games.[22]

While grassroots and industry movements used informal channels to purge their communities of Bank Nights, many of the battles over the game occurred within the confines of the American judicial system. Disgruntled Bank Night players, who felt they had been unfairly cheated of the cash prize, instigated some of the court cases. More frequently, players turned against not the theaters staging the games but the police and vice squads that tried to shut them down.[23] Other legal skirmishes involving Bank Night stemmed from Affiliated Enterprises' aggressive attempts to quell copyright infringements. The company incessantly warned not only theaters but also hairdressers, restaurants, and shops not to stage Bank Night or any of the 1,400 name variations the corporation had copyrighted.[24] Most of the disputes, however, centered on whether or not the game violated state lottery laws. Yaeger and Ricketson deliberately fashioned Bank Night to evade the rulings that outlawed lotteries: patrons did not pay for their Bank Night number, and they could win the game without purchasing a ticket to the movie. In addition, Affiliated Enterprises would not allow Bank Night to be advertised in newspapers.[25] Nonetheless, the game was regularly banned by local and state authorities under state lottery laws, forcing Affiliated Enterprises and hundreds of theaters to spend a great deal of time in litigation.[26]

By early 1936, it seemed that the battle between Bank Nights and the states had been resolved in a landmark case in Augusta, Maine. There, the state supreme court ruled that Bank Night did not violate the state's lottery laws. In late January 1936, the Iowa Supreme Court, located in Des Moines, also ruled that Bank Night was legal. As the presiding judge of this case, Justice Leon Powers justified his ruling with this logic paraphrased in *Time* magazine: "He [Powers] pointed out that a grocer could legally give away candy to children to increase his trade, might determine by child which child to give his candy to, so long as no consideration was required of any of the children for sharing in the chance to get it."[27] The judge's decision likens a Bank Night theater offering cash to adult moviegoers to a salesman giving children free candy, an analogue insinuating both that the game does little harm and that its participants are guileless and immature.

The legal battles over Bank Night were ongoing—as late as January 1937, the supreme court in Topeka, Kansas, ruled Bank Night illegal, just as the court of appeals in Albany, New York, decreed the game legal.[28] Ironically, the litigation surrounding Bank Night was fueled largely by independent theaters, which struggled to ban the game not only from their fellow independents but also from the studio-run theaters.[29] As these battles waged, exhibitors large and small fervently blamed each other for the proliferation of these exploitations. Despite the fact that Bank Night originated and flourished in small-town independent theaters, the independents refused responsibility for its success and instead accused the studio-run theaters of driving them to cash giveaways. In Cleveland, theater owners claimed they had been forced into Bank Night by double-feature competition from the first-run houses.[30] In Kansas City, exhibitors blamed the studios and first-run theaters for both the genesis and persistence of controversial cash giveaways: "The present clearance and restrictions placed upon the exhibitors in playing pictures have forced the lower-admission theatres, which constitute most of the suburban houses, to resort to socalled [*sic*] stimulants such as Bank Night, Jack Pot, premiums, refund checks, two-for-one tickets, gift stamps and other practices which tend to lower the standards of the business. These practices by the suburban theatres have forced the downtown first-runs to adopt similar measures."[31] The studio-run theaters responded in kind. In 1935, for instance, David Loew first threatened to institute giveaways in the Loews circuit in New York unless independents stopped the practice.[32] Loew put the games into his theaters soon afterward, only to drop them three months later from eight New York houses, claiming, "We are going back to the picture business."[33] In truth, he made this decision in light of the threats by New York police against games of chance and rumors in Albany that New York legislators regarded games as violation of lottery law.[34] When yet another ruling affirmed that Bank Night was legal, Loew returned the games to these theaters, only (along with the RKO circuit) to remove them again when another ruling declared them illegal in March 1937.[35]

Underlying all this litigation and controversy were larger concerns about community, morality, and the societal purpose of movie theaters. For many, the destructive effect on local communities was a particularly disturbing aspect of Bank Night's popularity. Even the glowing report on Bank Night in the *Saturday Evening Post* acknowledged that the game disrupted the components of normal small-town sociability. Its popularity was such that, as Parkhill noted, "nobody can schedule a basketball game, a church sociable or a contract party on Tuesday night, because everybody is down at The Gem hoping to cop a cash prize."[36] If the church had once been at the center of the American town, now the motion picture theater sought to provide a similar space for community consolidation. Bank Night and its association with gambling threatened to undermine this status, and as such, many theater owners expressed anxiety about the game's immoral associations.

The discourse surrounding Bank Night revealed concern not only about the destruction of traditional notions of community, but also about the role movies and theaters played in that community. Exhibitors were apprehensive

about how giveaways like Bank Night conflated the space of the movie theater with that of a gambling hall or a store. The Associated Theatre Owners
of Indiana complained about the need for Bank Nights and giveaways, ex-
pressing hope that "someday we shall get back to making good films, exploiting them energetically, and leave the disposal of cheap merchandise to
the 5 and 10 cent stores."[37] Motion picture exhibitors and other commentators
seemed in part to fear that the motion picture could not stand alone, that
films in and of themselves would fail to sustain the movie theater and thus
the entire film industry. The cultural critic Gilbert Seldes related a report
from the *New York Post* that included "the serious suggestion made by the
owner of a Brooklyn movie house, that his colleagues unite with him in elim-
inating feature pictures, movie shorts, and newsreels from their programmes. 'All we need,' he proposed, 'is Bank Nights.' "[38]

Notably, this trepidation regarding the function of the movie theater was
frequently figured in gendered terms, with female moviegoers being portrayed as those guilty of misunderstanding the purpose of the cinema. In its
description of the popularity of giveaways, *Literary Digest* crafted a fictional
account of a woman named "Mrs. Joseph Phau," who attended movie theaters not to see films but to play games. In this account, Mrs. Phau is described as attending the cinema despite the fact that "no portentous film was
to be screened that night. Indeed, the film to be screened that night was of
inferior quality. But Mrs. Phau didn't mind. It is doubtful if she even knew
what the picture was about, or cared."[39] In the end, however, independent
theaters blamed not women but the studios for the problems engendered by
Bank Night. Bad films drove independent exhibitors to employ lotteries and
giveaways, and in turn those games detracted from the positive role the
movie theater might play in the community. A *Motion Picture Herald* editor
lambasted theaters offering Bank Night: "The immediate effect [of lotteries]
is, or is expected to be, big box office business—throngs seeking lucky numbers and coming back to see if they win. It is manifest that there can be few
winners if there is to be a profit. Losers are in the majority and they are disappointed. They buy their disappointment at the box office, where once they
shopped for entertainment. The association of ideas tends toward a community state of mind that will presently be something less than zero as an
asset."[40] Even as it presaged the psychic damage wrought by movie house lotteries, this editorial championed the emergent understanding that the theater had become a space for community consolidation. Like the church or
the school, the movie theater provides the "home town" with wholesome entertainment.

Apprehensive about being identified with vaudeville showmen, exhibitors
of this period were adjusting to their new status as a permanent site for films,
and films alone. This writer suggests that the real danger associated with
games like Bank Night is that "the motion picture with its lottery stays right

in the home town": "The slickers who follow the circus and the carnivals are notoriously and congenitally in bad with the home-town boys. It is healthy for them to move on. But the lottery devices now coursing through the theatres of the land are carnival gambling games, no matter how they may flaunt "copyrights" and garlands of phraseology intended to create an aroma of legality and implied propriety. Hit and run games are played better by those who can run. A theatre is stationary."[41] Here, the movie theater is depicted as a stable local institution at the center of the community, one policed by responsible managers who oppose the itinerant "slickers" associated with the carnival and circus. The subtext of this argument is twofold: one, it associates the theater with the moral, middle-class film audience; two, it reaffirms the distance between the wholesome movie theater of the thirties and the seedy traveling nickelodeon of early cinema. Morality depends here not on filmic content but on the place and context of a film's screening. As the writer continues, "We shall indeed have an anomalous situation if, after all, the Decency comes in the can from Hollywood to contend with home-made sin."[42]

In addition to this apprehension over itinerants and corrupt city dwellers, anxieties about Bank Night also manifested themselves in strange concerns about black audiences and small-town "hucksters." One account of Bank Night's popularity read: "Bank nights broke out in Cleveland last week, when M. B. Horwitz, operating the Haltnorth, playing largely to colored people, instituted the practice."[43] Here, the description of Bank Night as a contagion—something that can "break out" like a disease—merges with the accounts that subtly suggested that this practice was immoral or somehow illicit. Another account of Bank Night in the *Motion Picture Herald* chastised exhibitors who staged these games for manipulating and exploiting their hapless audiences: "The fact, clearly enough, is that depression, unemployment, idleness, relief rolls and the like have conspired to make the dreams of easy money alluring to thousands of persons of low buying power—a situation exemplified continuously in the policy and numbers rackets of New York's dark and hungry Harlem. That there are thousands so afflicted with poverty and bad judgment does not, however, justify their exploitation. There are many ways of getting money that are not worthwhile."[44] The city—or, more specifically, "dark and hungry Harlem"—is a site ripe for moral vices and crimes like racketeering, filled with those who suffer from "poverty" and "bad judgment." The "dreams of easy money" are represented here as the source of urban crime and exploitation, not as the harmless fantasy that made Bank Night so popular with white, middle-class audiences in small towns and suburbs.

Bank Night was steeped in controversy, and the film industry offered a variety of practical solutions that might resolve the ongoing struggle between the studios and the independents, considered the source of many of these legal and rhetorical battles. Issue after issue of the *Motion Picture Herald* and other 1930s periodicals suggested ways to increase movie attendance so that exhibitors would no longer need games of chance. These suggestions included providing better quality films, distributing films more fairly, restricting double features, ending block booking, outlawing giveaways in the major circuits, and simply waiting for the economy to recover so that the first-run houses could restore their pre-Depression ticket prices. William Hatch of the Hayward Theatre in Hayward, California, reasoned, "Like scores of others, I am patiently awaiting the day when the picture product will hold up alone, but until then the best type of showmanship, in my estimation, is displayed by those men who are resourceful and ambitious enough to operate their theatres at a profit."[45] Without quality studio films that audiences want to see, Hatch argued, exhibitors must adhere to a "survival of the fittest" mind-set to make a profit. His celebration of the "resourceful and ambitious" exhibitor also suggested that, even in the midst of the economic crisis, the familiar American ideals of ingenuity and hard work still mattered.

This Darwinian approach to successful film exhibition provides a neat segue into a final examination of Bank Night's controversial standing among Depression-era entertainments. The previously delineated concerns regarding Bank Night and its effects on community—concerns voiced by a diverse group of citizens ranging from morally inclined churchgoers to profit-obsessed theater managers—were refracted in the theoretical work of Depression-era intellectuals on the left. During the late twenties and thirties, many of these intellectuals voiced support for Marxism, agrarianism, and New Deal liberalism as alternatives to faltering industrial capitalism. They imagined that the acquisitiveness and isolation characterizing capitalism's "getting and spending" might be replaced by a new system that valued collectivism and individual freedom equally. A few of these thinkers turned their attention to Bank Night and other games of chance, and argued that these entertainments were pernicious because they jeopardized not public morality or small-town values but rather class consolidation.

Prior to the economic downturn of the American film industry, but in the midst of the worldwide Depression, the German intellectual and film critic Siegfried Kracauer published an essay entitled "Luck and Destiny" that describes the allure a gambling house has for Berliners who, like their American counterparts, have "nothing to lose and everything to gain."[46] In this essay, published in the *Frankfurter Zeitung* in 1931, Kracauer regards the gambling hall as a symptom of the economic and societal changes brought about by the Depression. The dispirited masses are drawn to this site because it offers a flash of hope to all patrons and genuine relief to a lucky few. In dire economic circumstances, the luck promised by the gambling hall replaces the spiritual and material comforts once offered by the nearby Memorial Church and shops. Notably, the Berlin gambling hall stages games and fortune-telling, as well as marionette performances and "men-only" peep shows. According to Kracauer, these diverse activities overtly and mistakenly conflate for players and spectators two different phenomena: luck, a chance happening, and destiny, the preordained or inevitable course of events.

In a similar fashion, the classical Hollywood narrative and Bank Night conflate luck and destiny, as evidenced in one account of games of chance published in the leftist journal *New Theatre and Film*. In this July 1936 essay, Alfred Hayes describes an evening of moviegoing with his mother. They attend the screening of *Magnificent Obsession* (1935), an MGM film about a young woman struck blind in a car accident; years later, the heroine is healed by the doctor she loves, a reformed playboy who was, she discovers, the very man responsible for the accident that blinded her and killed her husband. Though this woman, played by Irene Dunne, falls victim to the bad luck of the accident, an accident caused by reckless drunken driving, she finds her destiny—her true love—as a result of the suffering randomly inflicted upon her.

Hayes is stunned by the audience's sympathetic response to the sentimental film, and by his mother's rabid defense of its escapist fantasy. For him, the images of affluence, compassion, and good fortune jar too radically with Depression-era reality, as does the film's lesson "That What We Do for Others Brings Virtue on Us. Golden Rule by M.G.M. Charity Carries the Day."[47] Following the film, the lights go up and the prosperity game begins. Hayes and his mother attend the Tuesday night screening to participate in a game of Screeno, though Bank Night, he observes, is offered on Thursday nights. The theater is packed with players, each thinking he or she will be the victor. As the winners begin to claim their prizes, Hayes's mother blames the devil, bad luck, and her family for her loss. She laments, "I knew it. The devil watches to see we don't win. You come from a bad luck family, my son" (29).

In the American movie theater, luck and destiny are conflated just as they were in Kracauer's Berlin gambling house. The disappointment of losing a game of chance—that is, the bad luck that your numbers were not called— translates for Hayes's mother into the larger belief that her "bad luck" destiny is inescapable. Upon examination, additional similarities surface between the American movie house game of chance and the Berlin gambling hall. First, Kracauer notes the gambling hall purveyors have discovered a profitable business formula: "To rake some in for themselves they count on the uncontrollable longing for luck by the masses who nowadays have no other chance than luck itself " (53). Likewise, Hayes understands that profit drives Hollywood; he recognizes that the film narrative, the plush surroundings of the picture palace, and the game work in conjunction to lure paying customers to the movies so they might experience the vicarious "winning" that the Lynds noted in *Middletown*. Two, the patrons of Kracauer's gambling hall "who have nothing to lose and everything to gain" participate in games with false hopes of "winning a few pennies" and fortune-telling for assurances of their "own special luck" (54). Similarly, Hayes senses that both the film and the game falsely promise audience members access to prosperity through luck alone. He asks his mother, "Anybody ever give you something for nothing?" and his mother replies, "Nobody gets something for nothing" (13). Infuriated, he watches as she (literally) buys the fantasy, uncritically watching the film, playing the game, and believing she will win this time.

Finally, and perhaps most important, both pieces demonstrate how games of fortune, in the form either of gambling in a vacated Berlin shop or of prosperity games at the theater, undermine collectivity. Kracauer writes: "In addition to the luck in which everyone shares a piece, each person generally seeks his own special luck. And since the possibilities of attaining it in the customary manner by following societal rules are blocked, everyone craves information on the secret powers that he bears in himself and that will indeed ultimately raise him above the rest" (54). The gambler turns his attention not to the practical ways he can access his class power but to how he alone can better succeed within the given system through the use of his "secret powers." As a result, Kracauer asserts, "numerous seekers of luck still want to maintain that they are individuals even though they have for quite some time formed a proletarian mass" (55). In his account of Screeno, Hayes similarly editorializes on the response of audience members to their losses: "Too bad, and there are four hundred other bad luck families here tonight, all convinced that [this] game is just another proof of how they are doomed, and yet still secretly hoping next week maybe my turn will come, we cannot lose forever. Others have money and we have Mickey Mouse and Irene Dunne and the 'Metrotone News,' and the elegant stone ladies in the lobby we pass again on the way out. We have the scarlet ticket taker and the deep rugs and the hushed lights as we turn homewards again" (29). A mass of passive losers, the audience members regard themselves as "bad luck families" rather than illtreated individuals or an entire class abandoned. If fortunes offer the Berlin gamblers respite, then the material comforts of the cinema similarly present American moviegoers evidence that somehow, somewhere there is material relief. Nonetheless, disappointment inevitably inheres in the spectacles and the games of chance offered by the gambling hall and cinema. Yet the audience passively absorbs both distractions, which hold a supplementary relation to each other.

Though writing from different national contexts, Kracauer and Hayes marvel at the same unquestioning acquiescence of the dispossessed to social and economic inequities masked as "destiny" or "bad luck." For both, the coupling of entertainments and games of chance stifles the capacity of individuals to see plainly their pitiable existences. The former critic dispassionately notes the circumstance, the latter reacts in horror to it; both participate in the spectacle at hand. This dynamic of participation, disappointment, and passive acceptance of failure was noted throughout accounts of Bank Night. Oddly, popular discourse surrounding these games focused not on the game's winners or the pleasures derived from playing the game but on the sense of futility players experienced when they lost. Accounts of these prosperity games often include some variant of this satiric tale: A British man becomes fascinated with a very popular American pastime called "Aw Nuts!" After a visit to the States, he returns home to England and describes to his friends this game, which he observed in American movie theaters. The Englishman is amazed by this amusement in which, to quote his own words, "people sat around in a cinema theatre while the management passes out cards. Suddenly one patron would cry 'Bingo!' and the remaining patrons would cry, 'Aw, Nuts!'"[48]

In "King of the Bingo Game" (1944), Ralph Ellison explores these same themes as he describes a bingo game staged at a movie theater following a film that depicts a hero's brave rescue of an abducted young woman. In this short story, luck and destiny are imbued with religious qualities—the black protagonist participates with "faith" in the postscreening bingo game and as "one of the chosen people" wins the right to perform the "ritual" of spinning a wheel onstage for a chance to collect a cash prize.[49] He has, week after week, watched the films and played the game in hopes of winning the jackpot of $36.90 to pay a doctor to care for his dying lover, Laura. When he finally wins the bingo game that gives him the right to spin the wheel for prizes, he "felt a profound sense of promise, as though he were about to be repaid for all the things he'd suffered all his life" (129). Once more in a game of chance, luck masquerades as destiny.

The central character of the story (who, like Ellison's Invisible Man, remains nameless) is consistently represented as alienated from his fellow audience members. In part, his isolation is a function of the game; that is, he wins the bingo game and goes onstage alone "under the spell of some strange, mysterious power" (127) to spin the bingo wheel. He is also disconnected from the audience with whom he shares both a racial and class identity because he hails from "Rocky Mont, North Carolina." The game's white emcee mocks him before the black audience for being from "down South" and choosing "to come down off that mountain to the U.S." (129). This regional difference serves as a false distinction between the bingo winner and the audience members, for as he notes, "All the Negroes down there [in the urban, northern audience] were just ashamed because he was black like them" (132).

The audience's antipathy toward the wheel-spinning protagonist, however, seems to stem primarily not from his regional difference or his special status as the winner of the bingo game but from his refusal to obey the rules of the game. As he presses the button to spin the wheel, the wheel increases speed and "seemed to draw him more and more into its power, as though it held his fate; and with it came a deep need to submit" (129). As he continues to press the button, the audience begins to shout at him, but he realizes: "Those folks did not understand what had happened to him. They had been playing the bingo game day in and night out for years, trying to win rent money or hamburger change. But not one of those wise guys had discovered this wonderful thing. He watched the wheel whirling past the numbers and experienced a burst of exaltation: This is God! He said it aloud, 'This is God!'" (130). The game player enters a hallucinatory state in which he believes himself singled out for recompense. He is "reborn" as "the-man-who-pressed-the-button-who-held-the-prize-who-was-the-King-of-Bingo" and refuses to surrender the button, fervently believing that he will win (133). The audience, which initially "rippled with laughter and applause" at his victory, now shouts for him to come off the stage and encourages the theater management to call the police. His refusal to play by the rules, both literally and figuratively, results both in the forfeiture of the game's prize, even after the spinning wheel miraculously lands on the double zeros, and in his death from a beating given behind the stage's fallen curtain.

In this story, Ellison touches on the allure and danger of these games of chance. The game promises the player individual success, which falsely suggests he is set apart from and above the careworn audience. But the story insists that sense of self is illusory, for immediately after he celebrates his ability to win, the central character forgets his name, even as he realizes that the "name had been given to him by the white man who had owned his grandfather a long lost time ago down South" (132–33). Like the award at the bingo game, his name and consequently his identity are his merely through random chance. His individuality is similarly questioned when he "felt that the whole audience had somehow entered him and was stamping its feet in his stomach and he was unable to throw them out" (133). That consolidation is unpleasant—the audience is his enemy that wants the prize and "the secret for themselves," rather than a community with which he can affiliate, and individual triumph merely singles him out for abuse.

Ellison offers a fictional account of the same dynamic both Kracauer and Hayes observed in games of chance. That is, the player is isolated from members of his class and, as such, falls into a delusive state allowing him to think he is the winner, the one who through luck can escape circumstance. Both the film narrative and the game falsely suggest to Ellison's protagonist that he has a modicum of control over his life, an illusion that literally drives him insane. He earnestly believes that through sheer will he can mimic the film's hero, who miraculously saves the life of a girl in distress, by controlling the outcome of this game of chance. In pursuit of this goal, he weaves together nightmares and reality, violently resists social norms, and indulges in hysterical grandiosity on stage. His mad behavior resists the false promises offered by these games—this is not the murmuring complaint of "Aw Nuts!" famously ascribed to Bank Night players. But ultimately he loses the game, and following a violent blow to the skull, he understands that "his luck had run out on the stage" (136). He is a spectacle, but one that refutes rather than supports this new American Dream of wealth and happiness through good luck. But no one in the audience sees this truth; the police pull the curtain to conceal the fact that the new American Dream results in not prosperity but death.

In spite of the legal and ethical controversies surrounding Bank Night, the *New Republic* would reflect the popular perception of the game when it celebrated Bank Night's role in helping the film industry during the 1930s:

> Bank Night and its imitators have caused more theatres to open during the depression than any other device. There are cases on record showing that circuits operating as many as sixty theatres have been saved from bankruptcy by this system. The fact that it has made converts of a great many former non-moviegoers can be checked by small-town exhibitors, who know the majority of their audience by sight. Box office receipts increase on Bank Night from 100 to 400 percent over normal grosses. In some communities civic and social clubs have changed the dates of their meetings to avoid conflicting with Bank Night.[50]

Bank Night had clearly taken command of the public's enthusiasm and consequently of its pocketbooks. By offering classical narrative films in conjunction with games of chance, independent theaters in smaller markets initiated a practice that provided their Depression-weary audiences across the nation a new American Dream that insisted on chance as the crucial element of success. At first glance, the game seems to affirm the familiar "culture industry" arguments suggesting that mass culture is a totalizing and oppressive force. The game did, in many ways, isolate players and help to subdue any emergent class consciousness by insisting that only one lucky person could enter the affluent culture depicted in many Hollywood films. By providing "a new angle on an old sport called Something for Nothing,"[51] Bank Night might have provided an excessive symptom of capitalism that would expose the irrationality of the system as a whole. But eager Bank Night participants denied the assertion made by Hayes in *New Theatre and Film* that "nobody gets something for nothing."[52] Audiences literally bought the isolation, frustration, and passivity the films and the games engendered, walking away from them only when the economy recovered with the advent of World War II and leaving exhibitors (and critics) still marveling at its hold on the national imagination and its canny restructuring of the American Dream.

Notes

1. Jack Alicoate, ed., *The 1935 Film Daily Year Book of Motion Pictures* (New York: Film Daily, 1935), 301; cited in Andrew Bergman, *We're in the Money: Depression America and Its Films* (Chicago: Ivan R. Dee, 1992), xi.

2. H. O. Kusell, "Bank Night," *New Republic*, 6 May 1936, 363.

3. Ibid., 363–64.

4. Forbes Parkhill, "Bank Night Tonight," *Saturday Evening Post*, 4 December 1937, 20.

5. The "Big Five" were Paramount, Loew's/MGM, Warner Bros., Fox, and RKO, while the "Little Three" of Columbia, Universal, and United Artists produced largely B pictures. Sources for my history of cinema exhibition practices include Douglas Gomery, *Shared Pleasures: A History of Movie Presentation in the United States* (Madison: University of Wisconsin Press, 1992); Philip Davies and Brian Neve, eds., *Cinema, Politics, and Society in America* (New York: St. Martin's Press, 1981); Richard Koszarski, *An Evening's Entertainment: The Age of the Silent Feature Picture, 1915–1928* (Berkeley and Los Angeles: University of California Press, 1994); Robert Sklar, *Movie-Made America: A Cultural History of American Movies* (New York: Random House, 1975); and Barbara Stones, *America Goes to the Movies: 100 Years of Motion Picture Exhibition* (North Hollywood: National Association of Theatre Owners, 1993).

6. Miriam Hansen, *Babel and Babylon: Spectatorship in American Silent Film* (Cambridge, Mass.: Harvard University Press, 1991). Since Hansen's groundbreaking work, a great deal of scholarship has explored audiences and exhibition practices in early film, including articles from the recent collection edited by Richard Maltby and Melvyn Stokes entitled *American Movie Audiences: From the Turn of the Century to the Early Sound Era* (London: British Film Institute, 1999).

7. This brief history is drawn from Andrew J. Neff, "Slump Proof? Not Films: Depression Figures on Profits, Payrolls, Sites," *Variety*, 2 April 1980, 6, 48; and A. D. Murphy, "Trace Recession's Impact on Pix," *Variety*, 6 August 1980: 1, 32. Both articles use film industry grosses and expenditures from the Great Depression to examine the box office during the recession of the early 1980s.

8. Dish Nights were an attempt to lure women to the theater on slow nights, in hopes, too, that they might bring their families to win an inexpensive set of dishware. As with Bank Night, exhibitors feared the film fell second to the giveaway. In a discussion of this topic, *Motion Picture Herald* (13 April 1940, 32) reproduced an advertisement depicting a full set of "Heat Resisting Glassware." In small print at the top of the ad, the reader discovers that the dishes can be found at the Capitol Theatre in Racine, Wisconsin, where "Mickey Rooney in 'Judge Hardy and Son'" is playing. For a critical study of Dish Night, see Kathryn Fuller-Seeley, "Dish Night at the Movies: Exhibitors and Female Audiences during the Great Depression," in *Looking Past the Screen: Case Studies in American Film History and Method,* ed. Jon Lewis and Eric Smoodin (Durham, N.C.: Duke University Press, 2007).

9. Tino Balio, *Grand Design: Hollywood as a Modern Business Enterprise 1930–1939* (New York: Scribner's, 1993), 26–27.

10. "Power of Small Towns," *Variety*, 22 April 1931, 5; cited in Balio, *Grand Design*, 26.

11. Ricketson would eventually write a hugely popular "how-to" guide on motion picture theater management entitled *The Management of Motion Picture Theatres* (New York: McGraw-Hill, 1938). In his discussion of the erratic success of promotional give-aways, he not surprisingly claims, "Ordinary give-aways cannot be considered in the same category with Bank Night as a business stimulator. It was an innovation which helped lift the industry from the depression. Bank Night added literally hundreds of thousands of new theatre patrons, and many showhouses which as a policy did not feature a give-away opened their doors to it" (250).

12. "Two Federal Courts Sustain Bank Night," *Motion Picture Herald,* 18 May 1935, 58.

13. "Subsequent Runs Put Dallas First-Runs on the Sidelines," *Motion Picture Herald,* 10 August 1935, 60.

14. Kusell, "Bank Night," 364.

15. Bill Crouch, "World's Biggest Bank Night," *Motion Picture Herald,* 31 August 1935, 18. Although Bank Night, Screeno, and other games of chance were tremendously successful exploitations for the Balaban and Katz organization, ironically there is no mention of these promotions in Carrie Balaban's history of the chain, *Continuous Performance* (New York: A. J. Balaban Foundation, 1941).

16. Crouch, "World's Biggest Bank Night," 18.

17. Robert S. Lynd and Helen M. Lynd, *Middletown: A Study in Modern American Culture* (New York: Harcourt Brace Jovanovich, 1959), 264.

18. For helpful discussions of the Great Depression and the American Dream, see Lawrence Chenoweth, *The American Dream of Success: The Search for the Self in the Twentieth Century* (North Scituate, Mass.: Duxbury Press, 1974); Charles R. Hearn, *The American Dream in the Great Depression,* Contributions in American Studies No. 28 (Westport, Conn.: Greenwood Press, 1977); Robert McElvaine, *The Great Depression: America, 1929–1941* (New York: New York Times Books, 1984).

19. Parkhill, "Bank Night Tonight," 19.

20. "Bank Night: 'Bingo—Aw Nuts!'" *Literary Digest,* 6 March 1937, 36.

21. In Marshalltown, Iowa, the grievance board ordered Midwest Film Distributors of Kansas City to stop sending films to two Don Thornburg houses offering Bank Night, and grievance boards banned the games in Kenosha and Milwaukee, Wisconsin. See "Two Federal Courts Sustain Bank Night," 18.

22. *Motion Picture Herald,* 10 August 1935, 9. Two weeks later, M. Marvin Berger, a New York lawyer, offered exhibitors a legal account of the legality of prize giveaways: "The popularity of prize nights and similar schemes for attracting customers to the box office has caused many exhibitors to lose sight of the disapproval with which the penal laws of the various States regard such plans." He provides elaborate legal definitions of the terms *price, chance,* and *consideration,* and he encourages exhibitors to seek legal counsel before engaging in lotteries and giveaways. See Berger, "The Law on Prize Contests," *Motion Picture Herald,* 24 August 1935, 33–34.

23. In Los Angeles, a Bank Night winner won his case against the Strand Theatre by claiming that although he failed to claim his prize in the allotted three minutes, he had in fact been in the theater that evening and so deserved the money. In Minneapolis, a Bank Night winner sued the manager of the Fall Theatre for a $2,000 award to compensate for the "humiliation" he suffered when the theater failed to pay him his $150 prize. See "Bank Night," *Time,* 3 February 1936, 58. In Akron, Ohio,

patrons were encouraged to sue theaters to recover their admission price and an additional $50 to $500 damages, if Bank Night were ever ruled a lottery. See "Bank Night Theatres Sued for Damages by Patrons," *Motion Picture Herald,* 17 August 1935, 13.

24. Another prosperity game, Movie Sweepstakes, followed this precedent of copyrighting name variations and aggressively pursuing those who violated their trademark. Movie Sweepstakes, advertisement, *Motion Picture Herald,* 27 July 1935, 72.

25. For other giveaways and games of chance like Movie Sweepstakes, this was not the case.

26. The legal decisions concerning Bank Night amounted to a confusing mess on the federal, state, and district levels. In May 1935, federal courts in Des Moines and San Antonio ruled that Bank Night did not violate state lottery laws, whereas a district court in Brady, Texas, ruled that it did. That same month, Bank Nights were declared legal in Kansas City, Missouri. See "Two Federal Courts Sustain Bank Night," 58. In one week of August 1935, the Milwaukee district court declared Bank Nights illegal as a lottery in a case against Bert Nathan's Hollywood theater; a Dallas theater was fined $100 for employing Bank Night; theaters in Norwalk, Connecticut, ceased staging Bank Nights in the face of court decisions; and the New York Police Department ordered all local theaters to cease Bank Nights. Meanwhile, Bank Nights flourished throughout Ohio, Iowa, and Pennsylvania. See "First High Court Decision Awaited," *Motion Picture Herald,* 10 August 1935, 59.

27. "Bank Night," *Time,* 3 February 1936, 58.

28. "Bank Night Bans," *Time,* 11 January 1937, 56.

29. For instance, the district court ruling in Brady, Texas, was determined in a case brought forward by the independent Ritz Theatre to stop an independent chain, the Brady Amusement Company, from using Bank Night at its Palace Theatre. See "Two Federal Courts Sustain Bank Night," 58. In a similar case, the court of appeals in Cleveland was to decide the legality of Bank Night in a suit between the city's Fountain and Haltnorth theaters. See "First High Court Decision Awaited," *Motion Picture Herald,* 10 August 1935, 59.

30. "Two Federal Courts Sustain Bank Night," 58.

31. "Independents Plead for Cash Night Curb," *Motion Picture Herald,* 17 August 1935, 13.

32. "Two Federal Courts Sustain Bank Night," 58.

33. "Back to Pictures," *Motion Picture Herald,* 17 August 1935, 1.

34. "Bank Night Theatres Sued for Damages by Patrons," 13.

35. "Bank Night: Bingo—Aw Nuts!" 36.

36. Parkhill, "Bank Night Tonight," 20.

37. "Two Federal Courts Sustain Bank Night," 58.

38. Gilbert Seldes, "The Quicksand of the Movies," *Atlantic Monthly,* October 1936, 42.

39. "Bank Night: Bingo—Aw Nuts!" 36.

40. "On Lotteries," *Motion Picture Herald,* 10 August 1935, 1.

41. Ibid.

42. Ibid.

43. "Two Federal Courts Sustain Bank Night," 58.

44. "Back to Pictures," *Motion Picture Herald,* 17 August 1935, 1

45. Ibid.

46. Siegfried Kracauer, "Luck and Destiny," trans. Courtney Federle, *Qui Parle* 5:2 (1992): 53.

47. Alfred Hayes, "A Night at the Movies," *New Theatre and Film,* July 1936, 13.

48. *Literary Digest,* 36. Also described in Kusell, "Bank Night," 364.

49. Ralph Ellison, "King of the Bingo Game," in *Flying Home and Other Stories* (New York: Random House, 1996), 128.

50. Kusell, "Bank Night," 364.

51. Parkhill, "Bank Night Tonight," 20.

52. Hayes, "A Night at the Movies," 29.

Part V

LOOKING BACKWARD, LOOKING FORWARD

BAD SOUND AND STICKY FLOORS

An Ethnographic Look at the Symbolic Value
of Historic Small-Town Movie Theaters

KEVIN CORBETT

Most film studies research focuses on film-as-text. Of the relatively little film theater research there is available, much of that tends to focus on architecture and/or economics. These approaches gloss over or all but ignore the audiences who go to see films and value the experience on a symbolic and cultural level. If the analysis of film audiences represents just a fraction of the film studies canon, then the *ethnographic* analysis of film audiences represents just a fraction of that fraction. This is unfortunate because certain issues can be explored effectively only by engaging real moviegoers in conversations about their moviegoing, as opposed to relying on secondary sources. One of those issues is the symbolic value the very act of going to movies has had and continues to have for people, an issue that much of the literature on film audiences has overlooked. The reasons for this oversight are many and complex, and they have as much to do with the "turf wars" that go on among some film historians, cultural studies scholars, and other media studies practitioners as with the difficulty of simply "doing" ethnography.

For many people, the act of going out to see a movie can be at least as important as the movie itself. This is especially true in social contexts where the act of movie watching holds symbolic value.[1] But another—often overlooked—aspect of the movie-watching process is the movie theater itself, and important symbolic meanings may be tied to these theaters. Furthermore, the symbolic meanings that surround historic movie theaters in small towns where, for many decades, the theater was the primary (if not the only) venue for entertainment and socializing, may differ from those associated with their big-city counterparts.

This chapter explores the role of the historic small-town theater in towns where such theaters still stand and attempts to describe that role from the perspective of the townspeople in those locations. These descriptions are derived from the initial stages of a long-term large-scale documentary project.

Historic Movie Theaters: Threats and Resurgence

Despite significant fluctuations in theater attendance in recent decades—caused perhaps by the spread of the VCR, cable TV, and now satellite and DVDs—people still go out to the movies. The film distribution and exhibition industries, obviously, have a vested interest in making sure people go out to theaters, wherever else they might also watch movies, and, historically, they have made a variety of efforts to ensure that the practice continues. These efforts range from technical "gimmicks" like 3-D and Cinerama in the 1950s to changes in architectural design like the twenty- to thirty-screen "megaplex" theaters that sprung up across the United States in the 1990s. But the continued practice of theatrical moviegoing also has to do with audience motivation, and while some people are motivated by things like stadium-style seating, it is just as likely that there is a symbolic dimension to these motivations. Furthermore, that symbolism is closely tied to the histories of both individual moviegoers and the movie theaters they have gone to.

At the same time the "megaplexes" were appearing, historic theaters across the country—and in small towns especially—were being saved and restored. In some cases private entrepreneurs took it upon themselves to save their old small-town theater. In other cases local governments purchased and revitalized these old theaters as a way of revitalizing the local economy. In still other cases volunteer groups have formed to save their local old theater out of appreciation for its architectural and/or historic value. These efforts, which suggest that there is a certain symbolic value attached to old movie theaters, have been reasonably well documented as "human interest" pieces in local newspapers. But little systematic research has been done to fully understand this phenomenon. One way to understand the symbolic role of the historic small-town movie theater, then, is to explore that process ethnographically.

The Interviews

Interviewees who participated in this new project included former and current theater owners, longtime and recent theater patrons, and former and current theater employees—including volunteers at nonprofit theaters. These interviews were conducted at more than forty theaters in small towns in Michigan, New York, Pennsylvania, Connecticut, Maine, Virginia, North Carolina, and Tennessee. The interviewees ranged in age from nine to ninety-six years, but most of them were between forty and sixty-five years old. All interviews were conducted on camera, with lengths ranging from thirty to ninety minutes. All interviewees were asked a basic list of questions,[2] but in most cases additional lines of questioning emerged based on the interviewees' responses and situational factors: their age, the range of their experience with the theater, and so on. Furthermore, additional questions emerged based on the current status of the theater.[3] In places where the theater was thriving, the interviews tended to focus on the history and current value of the theater. In towns where the theater had recently been (or was currently being) renovated, the interviews tended to focus on the renovation process. In still other towns where the theater was struggling (or had been closed), the interviews tended to focus on the fight to save the building.

The Themes

Over the course of the interviews, several interrelated themes began to emerge, revealing the complex and symbolic role of historic small-town movie theaters. Many of these themes are typically not addressed by the bulk of film studies research. The following is a presentation of some of these themes, along with supporting excerpts from the interviews.

"Something Different with People You Know"

Throughout the interviews, theater owners and patrons described what made their local old movie house special or unique, especially when compared with the multiplex theaters that some saw as leading to the disappearance of the historic single-screen theater. One theater owner-manager seemed to see maintaining his theater as part of a public responsibility:

> It's a question of providing for the public an alternative. . . . I say that because the large multiplexes, with their sixteen and eighteen screens, offer a lot for the public, but of course I also see that there's some way I can offer a lot in reverse to the public, whether it be lower prices, whether it be a feel of the quaint theater from yesteryear, something that maybe some parents will say this is how theaters used to be, and this is what I grew up with this is what the theater used to be. . . . we do offer a lot of services the big theaters don't, whether it's the friendliness, whether it's knowing our patrons by name, I really feel that there is a niche in the market in America for this kind of theater. . . . to be honest with you, you can never compete with a multi-million-dollar multiplex theater, but you can also offer them something that they can't get someplace else. And that's what I do.

Another theater owner had a similar feeling:

> I run it because I think the community needs a theater like this. I think they have to have a place where the kids—and the adults that still enjoy movies I think it's—I owe, I owe 'em that much, because they've been good to me over the years. . . . I made a good living and I feel I really owe that to the community.

A regular patron at another theater extends the idea of the historical and nostalgic significance of old movie theaters, something that differentiates them from multiplexes:

> It's a, an amazing piece of architecture that has survived the ravages of economic hard times, when movie theaters of course went by the way of the current videos. But if you want to see a movie on a large screen you gotta come here. You can go up to the eight-screen complex over here in the plaza, or you can go to the five down here. But if you want to see it in the splendor of the 1930s, you gotta come here.

Aside from an "alternative" and/or historical experience, some theater owner-managers provide other services that make their theaters unique:

> It is so special because [the manager] will give you a cup of coffee for free. . . . He [her husband] was late for the movie but he wanted a cup of coffee. [The manager] said, "How do you take it? Go sit down, I'll bring it to you." That is not going to happen at Showcase. . . . That's what makes it special.

The same manager would often provide another service for late arrivals:

> [The manager] would be in the lobby, and whenever anybody is a little bit late, he would, you know, while you're buying your popcorn and getting your ticket, he would give them a little synopsis on what they've missed.

The same manager, who emerged as a sort of local hero in the fight to save his theater from being sold and subsequently destroyed by an "evil" landlord, often went to extraordinary lengths to accommodate his customers:

> Yeah, we walk in, and he says it's only half the price today, which is already nominal. . . . I said "why," and he said, "Oh, because I'm late in turning the air conditioning on, so it's going to take you about thirty minutes for it to cool—so you'll be uncomfortable, so I don't think it's proper." I mean, where else can you have that kind of integrity?

When asked what made the theater she ran different—in terms of service—from the multiplexes, the co-owner–manager at another old movie house replied:

> My name is Louise—I'll go up and introduce myself to people. We have someone that stands out—as people enter into the auditorium to let them know who works here and who's here and that we really care if they're comfortable, what their needs are. When somebody walks through our door—we are so happy to have them here. It's like, you know, somebody, you know, an invited guest coming to you home.

The superlative customer service that so frequently characterizes the operation of historic small-town movie theaters means that customers are frequently willing to forgive—sometimes even enjoy—the quirky shortcomings (the bad sound and sticky floors) that go along with attending such theaters. In the following comment, one patron summarizes what makes attending many of these theaters going "someplace different with people you know":

> The film would usually break down in the middle of the movie. . . . But you know it was like—it wouldn't be right if it didn't. It was just kind of a whole, fun thing and everybody would clap and you know this kind of thing, it was just fun it's just something you don't get in the big theaters. . . . Just the warmth and the friendliness, also just knowing that the kids were right nearby. So I didn't worry about them. I knew I could get at them quickly and that they were with people we knew.

Because, for so many people, going to an old small-town movie theater is simultaneously a special event and a familiar one, a volunteer at one nonprofit theater offered the following analogy in comparing a visit to the historic theater she helped reopen to the larger multiplexes:

> It's kind of like eating Thanksgiving dinner with your family, or going to a restaurant where everyone's a stranger.

"All in the Family"

The idea that going to a historic small-town theater is like visiting with family is reflected in the fact that many of these old theaters are family-run businesses. One seventy-year-old former theater owner described how his eight children had all worked at the theater over the forty years he ran the place.

> I had the kids all working in the . . . I finally learned an old trick. I'd take maybe eight or ten quarters, you know, and I'd place 'em here and I'd place 'em there, you know, and every once in a while they'd find a quarter and that would (laughs) well that would, they'd be real happy. And I never did tell 'em about hiding a few things for 'em, you know. And I said of course you can keep any candy bars as long as they're wrapped up, but, but if there's any open you don't dare keep it, so I, once in a while I'd plant a few Life Savers here and there and that always kept 'em interested you know.

The following quotation from another theater owner echoes this family-run idea and reemphasizes the role of the old theater for the small town:

> I've been in the business all my life, but my family too. My wife, my two sons, like I said, they work here, they do everything for the theater, whether it be the fixing or the painting or so forth, they do a lot of physical work as well as the operation itself, so it's definitely a family affair. And the customers expect that . . . and I think they appreciate that. There's something about, especially in a small town, a resident, when they see the owner of the establishment work there, I think they appreciate it more.

"For the Kids"

Perhaps because of this family-run approach, many owners and managers of historic small-town theaters take great pride in the traditions associated with their old movie houses. Among those traditions is a history of taking care of the young ones in the community. The following response is from an interview with an owner and his wife. The man's grandmother had gotten into the movie business in 1911, and at one point there were five theaters in different towns in southwest Michigan owned by members of his family. This family emphasized discipline and decorum in their theaters, and the man's wife notes that this was later appreciated by some of the young ones they had to discipline:

> *Man:* We were always very strict on discipline in any of the theaters owned and operated by any members of our family.
>
> *Woman:* Some of those kids, after they grew up, thanked us, for making them behave.
>
> *Man:* That's true (laughs).
>
> *Woman:* They said, "We were brats, and we know we were bad. You did what you had to do, and we're glad (laughs).
>
> *Man:* We had one lady we were talking with here in town, she said to the effect, she says, "I don't know how you put up with me in that theater all those years when I was a teenager" (both laugh).

This selection is from the owner of the only theater in not just the town, but the county, which was located just down the block from the town's—and the county's—only stoplight:

> For years and years, this is where kids came and spent their evening. Safely, without any problems at all. Parents dropped their kids off knowing that we would take care of them, and we still do, we still, if a parent doesn't show up, we make sure to get the call out. You know sometimes a parent goes home and falls asleep on the couch, and they're supposed to come back and pick up their kid at 10:00, and it's quarter after 10:00 and there's a twelve-year-old sitting around there, you better find out what's happened.

This passage comes from a longtime patron who is now also a volunteer at the nonprofit theater in his town:

> And the parents feel secure about sending the kids, that's another big thing. They'll let the young people come down here of an evening, and, uh, be together and whatever and know there's nothing going to happen that shouldn't be happening. And we watch, we don't lock up the theater until all the kids are out and have been picked up, or arrangements made for them to get home. I know a couple of times I've had to take a couple home because the parents didn't show up, car broke down or something (laughs).

"Labor of Love"

While the people who run historic small-town movie theaters seem to genuinely enjoy their work, they also recognize the difficulties and challenges of maintaining their old picture parlors. One former theater owner described this as a "labor of love," and many of the owner-managers interviewed echoed this sentiment:

> I mean, you can talk, but it takes physical help to get down here every day . . .
> I mean it's go go go go go.

Another theater owner described the way he approached his "labor of love":

> It's like this problem we want to solve: how to keep a small-town theater going?

Running an old small-town theater becomes a particular challenge when it involves renovating it. Here a theater patron recognizes this:

> There are only certain people that seem to care enough to step up and take risks and spend the time, this is a huge task to save a building like this. . . . this has been an incredible, incredible job, if you saw the way it used to be.

In this selection another patron expresses his appreciation of the local theater manager's apparent dedication to the old movie house, as well as a possible explanation for that dedication and the dedication of other old theater owners and managers. In doing so he invokes some interesting imagery, including the notion of such managers as being on "missions" not unlike that of Don Quixote:

> We love the cinema mainly because of these human touches. Because first of all the guy—I don't know where he makes money, because we pay nothing, we eat all the popcorn for which again we pay nothing, we get refunded every time something goes wrong. And I've gone to these megaplexes where they don't have a conscience . . . but it must be true by and large that these proprietors must be of this type, because why are they fighting the impossible if they're like Don Quixote against the windmill, why do they take on the challenge? I think by and large they love movies more than they love money. If you find this trait among more than the average number of such people I would not be surprised, because that's their mission.

"David versus Goliath"

Related to the idea that running a historic small-town movie theater is a labor of love is the idea that the owner-managers who endure this labor are sometimes seen as local heroes of sorts. In describing these local heroes, some interviewees used language and imagery that, for scholars who eschew ethnographic accounts and other primary sources (if not audience analysis altogether) in favor of textual sources, might appear to be quite eloquent and surprisingly analytical. Specifically, these descriptions not only reemphasize the value of these old theaters but reveal a recognition and critique of the political and economic forces that otherwise dominate the American entertainment industries, capitalism more generally, and, perhaps, American culture as a whole. Especially prevalent in these descriptions was the notion of one "little guy" against many "big guys":

> But there are people out there that are independents . . . that like the business and they want to make it thrive and they'll do everything they can to do that, and if it weren't for guys like [the local owner-manager] the little theater just wouldn't survive because the big chains are interested in numbers of screens, how many screens can I get in and how many people can I pack in every night, it's a corporate level of thinking rather than—than somebody that really cares about, really cares about it.

In Cheshire, Connecticut, a somewhat serious battle was waged in the press and on picket lines to save the local cinema, a simple brick structure with no ornamentation or other architectural significance, built in 1939. One of the interviewees, asked why he got involved with trying to save the cinema and what the fight meant to him and to the town as a whole, responded passionately:

> *Interviewee:* It's just a beautiful old thing, and big business and big corporations are coming in, with the help of town councils and the help of the court system to just sweep it away, we're being inundated by corporate America, and I hate it. And to me it's important to save something like that.
>
> *Interviewer:* So is it about the underdog?
>
> *Interviewee:* Oh, yeah, oh absolutely the underdog and fighting city hall, fighting town hall, and you know the big corporate megaliths trying to come in and take over our lives, and if we can win it'll feel good for a little while. I'm kind of a cynic. I don't have too much hope, in the long run, but this might—this'll make us feel good for a while.

A relatively recent arrival in Cheshire, a native of India, offered an interesting comment that revealed how the fight to save the Cheshire Cinema was actually a fight to preserve American democratic ideals:

> We want it [the cinema] back. And I will be very surprised if we don't get it back because this is a society run by the people, for the people, this is what the people want, and if it doesn't work I will be very cynical about the whole process.

He went on to further describe his motivations, as well as the larger implications of saving not just the theater itself but also the job of the seemingly heroic manager:

I really believe if an individual of such character is allowed to go down, the system has failed. And we cannot take any pride in the system if a person like this cannot stand up to these big institutions. That is the only reason a person like me who is typically apolitical got involved, it's not a political issue at all, the issue was a sense of values: can an honest businessman make it in this world? We like to believe so, believe the answer is yes. So we are involved, we are doing what we can. . . . And we hope that . . . the rest of the world will know that they are not alone, they too can launch a massive fight, and fight these big guys, it's okay to have the big guys, but why destroy the small ones? . . . We have very few models of character, and we can go to Washington and come back empty. Here you find in a small town, some person, who's not a religious leader or anything, showing character in what he does. Are we going to support that, and are we going to perpetuate that or are we going to destroy that, that's the question. I think it's very clear what the people want to do. In a democracy what the people want should happen. Let us see if it's true or not.

"Revitalization"

Many of the efforts to save historic small-town movie theaters have been marked by this symbolic battle between the "little guys/Davids" and the "big guys/Goliaths." But even in these cases, there are often more pragmatic motivations behind attempts to save old small-town movie theaters. One reason many people fight to save their local old theater is that they see the potential economic benefits in doing so. In many towns such renovation represents hopes for the revitalization of the downtown area. The $2 million renovation of the Smith Opera House in Geneva, New York, is one example of this characterization, as described by one of the people heavily involved in the project:

> We think that the Smith Opera House is central to the revitalization of downtown Geneva. I believe that personally, and I think that the people in the city administration believe that, and they are working hard and in conjunction with us to make sure that this remains a viable part of downtown Geneva.

In another interview, a Geneva historian described the role of the Smith in the town's "upswing":

> Really the Smith has led the upswing of downtown because this happened first and everyone else figured, you know, we need the rest to go along with it. And I think you see a lot of—a lot of progress in the downtown, and the city has really embraced the Smith Opera House as a focal point of, sort of a symbol of the reemergence of Geneva.

Just up the road from Geneva, in Auburn, New York, a local group is trying to save and eventually renovate the Schine's Auburn Theater, a unique outer-space-themed art deco design by renowned theater architect John Eberson. The leader of that group described the potential impact of that renovation in the following terms:

> Downtown has been a graveyard, and over the past couple of years some of the historic buildings have been bought and renovated, and it's bringing more business back. Once this theater is opened again, it's phenomenal what it can do for a city. . . . Just everything will turn around, it will bring the focus back to downtown and bring life back to downtown again. It could very easily do this. It did it during the 1930s, it was the hub of downtown, and it could very easily do it again.

Another volunteer working on the project to save the Auburn Theater described how the project had already helped increase town morale:

> If you look at the attitudes just since we've taken over and started working on this theater . . . attitudes in the past have been "Oh, they ought to just tear the place down, it's just an old relic, it's falling apart and who needs it, who needs the past?" And now that they see that we're working on it, people are clamoring to get in. . . . Nobody is anymore saying that they ought to tear it down, that there's nothing good, there's a lot more positive attitude in the air. And I think that's, it's a wonderful thing. If just what we've done so far has had a great impact on Auburn's self-esteem, people are feeling better about Auburn, with what's going on so far, and we've not done that much yet.

A volunteer at another theater noted the positive impact the reopening of the theater had on other local businesses: "Even the ice cream stand, down by the river, sold less ice cream." Describing a proposal to demolish the theater for another purpose she added, "And it really wouldn't make that many parking spaces" (laughs).

"A Community Place"

Even local residents who see the economic benefit of the revitalization of their old theater also recognize the theater as a unifying social force. Historically, these theaters often served this function simply because small towns frequently offer few entertainment options. Here, an eighty-six-year-old woman describes the importance of going to her local theater for her group of childhood friends:

> When I was a child, we got two dimes—allowance. And the—matinee Saturday afternoon was ten cents. And next door was a confectionary, ice cream and confectionary. . . . And we had ten cents for the matinee and ten cents for a sundae or soda, and that was our big do for the weekend. . . . We'd get a gang together and walk down to the theater and do our thing Saturday afternoon. Then, uh, after we were in high school, and we were dating, why the theater was the place for the date, the date for the movie theater and the soda."

In this quotation a longtime patron from a small town in an extremely rural area describes the role of the theater as an entertainment option: "Well,

I mean, in a small town, what else do you do? In the big city you have lots of choices, but you don't have a lot of choices here."

Here a local historian discusses the role his local theater (and others) played in maintaining the community prior to the advent of television:

> At the time there was no television, there was no really entertainment . . . like there is today. They had to come to a community place, and this was the place that they would see and be seen, this is where you would see who was out with whom this weekend, and it was a very community-oriented experience. . . . there was the ability to come together and share news, especially during wartime. . . . People who would come three or four times a week, just to catch up on what was happening.

In this quotation, an elderly patron of another theater comments on the seemingly timeless appeal of, and need for, the local movie house:

> The teenagers I still noticed would come—reminded me of my own teenage years—they didn't seem to have changed much, it was a place to go out to. . . . they'd get one car, and they could pick up a crowd or a lot of times bunches of teenagers would walk to a movie. And it was nice because it would give them a Saturday night out, locally. . . . And I don't think teenagers, despite of all the stories we hear about all the wild stuff—a lot of teenagers haven't changed that much. They still like to go out in a crowd, they like to go to the movies. . . . So in my older years I began to notice how wonderful it was for the old and the young to have this facility.

A patron of the same theater describes her experiences there during her preteen years of the late 1950s and early 1960s—experiences that likely resonate with preteens of today:

> I remember going there probably on Friday night, and a lot of other girls who were maybe eleven or twelve or thirteen were there. And of course we'd watch the movie, but also we'd go in the ladies room and have social meetings.

Another patron recalls how her local theater served not only as a meeting place for friends but as a dating arena, adding that these functions served to unify the town:

> Everybody went to the movies. Either Friday night, or Sunday afternoon. And if you had a date, you went on Saturday night. And it was great. It's something that held the town together, once it came.

Contrary to the implication inherent in much film reception research, which seems to suggest that "everyday" movie patrons are not equipped to analyze the underlying cultural aspects of their moviegoing, many of the interviewees readily identified the symbolic role played by their local old movie house:

> It's part of the fabric of life. . . . it's as much a part of the community as the church. It's up there with the post office, with the grocery store—the ice cream

place, the place where you bring your laundry, it's part of what makes a town a town. Without a theater in the town . . . there's something missing. . . . It's what makes home home. It's just that simple, it's what makes home home.

Another patron discussed the importance of these theaters on both a personal and a national scale:

It's a little bit of America that's disappearing, and there's no reason for it to disappear. Let's keep it . . . it's something that I have a memory of from my childhood, it was a really nice thing. And it's nice to preserve something of old American culture, and it's a dying thing.

Even when patrons did not address symbolic value directly, they frequently emphasized the value of the theater to the community as a unifying force. An elderly patron—who was also an employee at the theater in the 1940s—nearly broke into tears as he made the following statement about his former place of employment:

It's a family theater. If you go there, you become knit, you know each other. You know he sits there, oh, he's missing, is he sick today, I better call him on up, see if he's all right. You get to know people, by a theater like this.

"It's Our Cinema/Our Town"

Underlying all the symbolic, economic, and even political issues that surround the historic small-town movie theater is the fact that, for many towns where these theaters have managed to survive, the theaters are central to the identity of the town. Theater owners and patrons trying to hold on to these old movie houses, then, are trying to hold on to the quality of life that characterizes many small towns and to the towns themselves. In this quotation, the city manager of one small town describes the importance of saving the local theater as part of a larger project of preserving the history of towns like his:

Historic preservation is important to small towns basically per se. Without historic preservation we'd become just another four-lane highway with strip malls on either side.

Saving small towns, therefore, is about saving the quality of life they represent, as this quotation from a theater owner-manager illustrates:

If you take away a theater such as this in a small town, then the quality of life loses quite a bit. First of all the downtown retail section, which is comprised of a few blocks, would probably be, I would say, 60 percent less active. And from that everything kind of snowballs. For instance, if the theater's not here and doesn't draw people, for instance, on weekends and evenings there's nobody downtown. . . . It would probably be, and I hate to use the word ghost town, but it would be close to it. . . . I think that the people want a small town and live in a small town because of the services they provide because of the atmosphere, and the residential life in a small town. And with a theater it adds a lot to it.

Here the Indian American man who spoke so eloquently on democratic ideals states that he and his family (and, by extension, his adopted hometown) love the theater simply because "it's our cinema," and despite some otherwise bothersome technical problems:

> So we like the fact that it's a smaller cinema. It doesn't have the greatest sound in the world, and we weren't paying the greatest bucks in the world to see it. The fact is that it's our cinema, we love it with all its plusses and minuses.

Here a mother and daughter, interviewed together, further illustrate this theme:

> *Mother:* It's just kind of a part of the life of a small town, and I think we need small towns.
>
> *Daughter:* I understand that change happens, and you know change is for the better. I don't think all change is good, I don't think everything needs to be built up, and you know bigger and better and more money. I think that a lot of people, maybe even a lot of my generation, are realizing that things are too rush-rush. You know the pace is too fast, and you know, just kind of want to go back to a simpler, you know, lifestyle, and in some small way, you know, that represents that—the simpler lifestyle.
>
> *Mother:* But I think we need a theater, I think we need these theaters in these small towns, I do. I think that it makes a community.

The mother later explains why she got involved in the fight to save her local theater and therefore the town in which it stands, as well as the extent to which she will continue that fight. She starts by mentioning the town's recent population growth, which she suggests might actually have negative consequences for the community and its inhabitants:

> So it is getting bigger, and I'm not crazy about that, because I'd like my children and her children to—grow up in a small-town atmosphere. I think it's healthier, I think it's better, I think you live longer. They want to put this mammoth Stop&Shop in here . . . and I guess I'm going to fight it to the last breath.

One of the most interesting commentaries on the role of an old movie theater in a town's identity came from a young man who was just twenty-two when he bought a theater that had been closed for a decade. After working for more than a year to restore and reopen the theater, he bought another old theater in another small town nearby. An economics major in college, this young man was able to speak quite intelligently about how old theaters like his represent the center of small-town life and, therefore, the center of American culture:

There aren't many theaters like this left in the country, they are, you know, but they're not theaters anymore, they're, they're empty buildings or they've been converted to something else. People don't build theaters in cities this size, so a lot of times, when a smaller city loses its theater, nothing will go there to replace it. . . . Expansion can only happen so much, and it is, you know, good, you know, obviously if we don't expand and grow, you know as a country and a community we're not going to get anywhere. But, at the same time, we have to look at what got us there. You know, when this city was built or most cities, you know, they'd always start out small and grow and grow. Well, the negative effect is that, the inner city, you know, dies, and it keeps growing out this way (gestures with hands: an expanding circle). I think a lot of people stopped and said, you know, well we wouldn't be here, you know, if it wasn't for small businesses in America, and small-town businesses, you know, we couldn't have got started. . . . There's already hundreds of empty places in this country that do nothing and that may never be used for anything. I think it's, you know a lot of people are seeing that, you know, we need, we need to protect this [old theaters and other small businesses] 'cause it's essentially, it's the core of, you know, the country, it's how everything became, you know, it just branched out. And, you know, if you forget the center part of it then, you know, your outer ring isn't going to be any stronger if your center part's dead.

Discussion: Doing Ethnography and Its Rewards

The excerpts from the interviews reveal the deep-rooted symbolic value of historic small-town movie theaters. The people who took part in this exploratory study continue to support their local old cinema not because it offers the latest releases presented via the most up-to-date sound and screen enhancements. Instead, they go to these old theaters knowing that they may encounter things like bad sound and sticky floors, even breaks in the film. They go because they appreciate the historical significance of the buildings themselves and/or because they enjoy the social and cultural benefits of going to theaters like these. This suggests that something other than technological capability or even media content underlies audience motivation for choosing one medium or distribution channel over another. That "other" often has to do with the symbolic value a medium or technology can hold for its users.

The symbolic value and cultural implications of movie theaters are not especially new topics in the film studies arena. Lary May explores the topic is some detail.[4] Kathryn Fuller, meanwhile, has discussed the symbolic implications of the naming of small-town movie theaters in the early twentieth century,[5] and Gregory Waller has discussed the social and cultural role movie theaters played in small towns during the same period.[6] But these cultural and symbolic issues have not been explored from an ethnographic perspective in any systematic way. One reason for this apparent gap in the literature is that, even in the field where it has been practiced the most—cultural studies (especially in the British tradition)—ethnography as a research tool has been debated more than it has been employed.

Ethnography has been practiced by cultural studies scholars for more than two decades, resulting in a compelling body of research.[7] This research, however, is marked by two traits: a focus on the political dimensions (e.g., gender, race, class, and other identity issues) related to "everyday" media use, and a focus on the television medium. It is not surprising that cultural studies scholars would choose to focus on the political dimensions of media use. Explaining the relative shortage of cultural studies research projects focusing on film audiences, however, is another issue. One reason for this shortage may be that, for many cultural studies scholars, ethnography as a research tool is as problematic as it is promising. If cultural studies scholars have embraced ethnography, Patrick Murphy categorizes that embrace as an "uncomfortable" one, noting that "critical culturalists . . . have produced a substantial pool of scholarship that calls for the ethnographic study of media audiences while questioning the mission of such studies."[8] The result has been that many of the publications regarding ethnographies of media audiences are debates on the tool's problems and promises as opposed to actual examples of ethnographic studies. These debates focus on issues such as the duration and depth of involvement with the individuals or groups under study, and the degree to which that involvement encroaches upon and impacts the power relationships among those individuals and groups. Since a concern for political relationships underlies much of the cultural studies tradition, it is no surprise some cultural studies scholars would hesitate before undertaking an ethnographic study. It should also be no surprise, then, that the variety of media studied by cultural studies ethnographers is somewhat limited.

The problem of talking about doing ethnography instead of actually doing ethnography may, however, be changing. One recent book, rooted in the identity politics heritage of the popular culture and cultural studies tradition, presents an ethnographic analysis of the role of filmgoing in the identity of Indian males.[9] Meanwhile, in another recent book, a traditional film historian almost inadvertently employs ethnography. Tom Stempel used written responses to a questionnaire in compiling his deliberately "freewheeling" look at moviegoers' responses to specific films and moviegoing more generally.[10] Hopefully, these efforts and this chapter will inspire other scholars, from a variety of disciplines, to explore film audiences from an ethnographic perspective. In fact, an interdisciplinary approach to the study of film audiences—an idea often championed but seldom exemplified—might be the best way to explore the rich and complex issues that weave through past and present film audience experiences, and that might weave through such experiences in the future. Because historians, cultural studies scholars, and other media scholars spend a lot of time debating the primacy of the text versus the potential of the audience and, therefore, the political and practical problems of doing ethnography, it is easy to forget how valuable simply talking with people about their experiences can be. Even in a worst-case scenario—where ethnographies of movie audiences provide merely a brief glimpse of what some folks were saying about some aspect of their film experiences at some point in time—these studies can provide valuable insight and, at least, leave a record for future scholars to interpret. Culture, like history, is an ongoing process. Therefore, even brief snapshots of that process in action can help current and future scholars study that process.

Conclusion

The turn of the twenty-first century brought with it an onslaught of new communications technologies, many of which have promised to impact the production, distribution, consumption, and reception of motion pictures. A similar, though less radical, transformation faced motion pictures at the turn of the twentieth century, as movies were transformed from "peep shows" to projections on a screen. We have little record of how real movie watchers reacted to this transformation, how they experienced and valued movies themselves, much less the act of watching them within social contexts. Then, film scholarship began in earnest in the 1920s with the Payne Fund studies, the purpose of which was to explore and ultimately denounce the power and negative effects of films and other media on their audiences. Since then, the majority of film research has taken films themselves—including film stars, directors, and production processes—as the object of study. This emphasis on film-as-text (however rigorously critical and insightful) has left a gap in film studies research. We have little systematic and reliable evidence on how and why "everyday" moviegoers (people who are not film critics or university professors) experience film, and how they use and value the act in their social lives. Similarly, into this gap has fallen the movie theater—as both a site for social interaction and a film distribution technology. As the curtain opens on another century of film, it is important that we explore these issues. This study at least hints at the value of making that exploration via ethnographies of movie audiences.

Notes

1. See Kevin Corbett, "Empty Seats: The Missing History of Movie-watching," *Journal of Film and Video* 50, no. 4 (1998–99): 34–48.

2. The basic list of questions asked of each interviewee included the following:

"What can you tell me about the history of the theater?"

"How long have you been coming to this theater?"

"How often did/do you come to this theater?"

"What do you like or dislike about the theater?"

"Are there other theaters you go to in addition to this one? If so, which do you prefer and why?"

"Is this theater an important part of this town? If so, why?"

"How would you feel if you found out this theater was going to be converted for another use? What if it was just going to be closed? What about if it was going to be torn down?"

"Do you have a particular memory about going to the theater you'd like to share? An experience at the theater you'd like to tell me about?"

3. Interviews were conducted at the following theaters: the Palace (Lockport, New York); the Strand (Brockport, New York): the Smith Opera House (formerly Schine's Geneva Theater—Geneva, New York); Schine's Auburn Theater (Auburn, New York); the Cheshire Cinema (Cheshire, Connecticut); the Alamo (Bucksport, Maine); the Roxy (Northampton, Pennsylvania); the Franklin (Franklin, Tennessee); the Lincoln (Marion, Virginia); the Parkway (West Jefferson, North Carolina); the Strand–Capitol Center for the Arts (York, Pennsylvania); in Michigan: the Broadway Theatre (Mt. Pleasant); the Pines (Houghton Lake); the Rogers (Rogers City); the Calumet (Calumet); the Star (Brooklyn); the Park (Augusta); the Regent (Allegan); the Alco (Harrisville);

4. Lary May, *Screening Out the Past: The Birth of Mass Culture and the Motion Picture Industry* (New York: Macmillan, 1980), 147–66.

5. Kathryn H. Fuller, *At the Picture Show: Small-Town Audiences and the Creation of Movie Fan Culture* (Washington, D.C.: Smithsonian Institution Press, 1996), 49–56.

6. Gregory Waller, *Main Street Amusements: Movies and Commercial Entertainment in a Southern City, 1896–1930* (Washington, D.C.: Smithsonian Institution Press, 1995), 164–77.

7. The oft-cited landmarks include Ien Ang, *Watching Dallas* (London: Metheun, 1985); Tamar Liebes and Elihu Katz, *The Export of Meaning: Cross Cultural Readings of Dallas* (New York: Oxford University Press, 1990); James Lull, *Inside Family Viewing: Ethnographic Research on Television's Audience* (New York: Routledge, 1990); David Morley, *The Nationwide Audience* (London: British Film Institute, 1980); Morley, *Family Television* (London: Routledge, 1986); Janice Radway, *Reading the* Romance (Chapel Hill: University of North Carolina Press, 1984).

8. Patrick Murphy, "Media Cultural Studies' Uncomfortable Embrace of Ethnography," *Journal of Communication Inquiry* 23 (1999): 205–21.

9. Steve Derne, *Movies, Masculinity, and Modernity: An Ethnography of Men's Filmgoing in India* (Westport, Conn.: Greenwood, 2000).

10. Tom Stempel, *American Audiences on Movies and Moviegoing* (Lexington: University Press of Kentucky, 2001).

14

CONCLUSION

When Theory Hits the Road

RONALD G. WALTERS

Let us imagine a theory about popular culture as a fancy new car, perhaps a European import—sleek, appealing, complex, its inner workings unfathomable to the layperson. In its natural habitat, the dealer's showroom, it is perfect and self-contained, a universe of imagination and desire. We buy it. Then we take it on the road. Imperfections appear: dings, rattles, and the inevitable breakdown. It depreciates. New models arrive, promising more. The cycle begins again.

In making this analogy, I am not declaring myself against theory, as Walter Benn Michaels and Steven Knapp urged colleagues in literary studies to do in the mid-1980s, or looking "post-theory," to borrow from the title of a recent collection of essays on film studies, or even to join Sonia Livingstone in bemoaning a loss of theoretical diversity in audience studies.[1] Good theory helps us to see what we might have missed, to understand connections that might have remained invisible, and to believe that we have a clearer comprehension of how things work. When theories fail to do that, it is time either to schedule a major overhaul or to trade in for a new model.

I want to suggest how recent theoretical and empirical work on popular culture generates, but does not resolve, problems that become all the more apparent when we look at a wide variety of audiences, especially less familiar ones like those represented in this collection. In the end, I will focus on one very important theory that is both powerful and problematic for understanding rural and small-town moviegoers. It is the so-called modernity thesis that posits crucial links between the movies and modernity—I will leave open the question of whether this really is a full-blown theory or merely, as a proponent claimed, one of the "Big Ideas."[2] Be that as it may, the modernity thesis frames much excellent work on early film and other forms of popular culture. The difficulty is that the "modernity" in it usually serves as a starting point for the rest of the analysis—one that is assumed more than examined critically. In this chapter, I want to suggest places where such an examination might be in order and to see what issues arise when we take the modernity thesis out on the road, to early moviegoing in rural areas and small towns. My goal is not to call into question scholarship that I very much admire, as I do books and articles I cite and criticize in this chapter. For the most part, they work very well within the terms their authors set for them. I want to suggest where those terms might prove restrictive or in need of some preventative maintenance.

Historians naturally want to believe that history matters. That said, I nonetheless find it striking that several trends in scholarship seem to point ever more insistently to the need to understand popular cultural in general, and film in particular, in terms of *historicity*. By that I mean the degree to which performances and audiences—in this case movies and moviegoing—are embedded in particular times and flows of time. The choice of plural words, *times* and *flows,* is not accidental. When we look broadly at contemporary work on popular culture, the message clearly is that multiple histories converge or diverge at whatever particular moment and place we choose to look, whether the subject is the silent film era in small-town America or 1980s heavy metal music and its fans.[3] I will give only a few instances to make the point.

Let us again enter an imaginary space, not a car dealership, but a movie theater of any vintage, from nickelodeon to cineplex (although quite obviously *where* we see a movie is itself a function of history). The film on the screen reflects the stage of the industry—how its economic organization and system of distribution have developed. What we see likewise represents a moment in the evolution of cinema and in its relationship to other forms of popular culture such as vaudeville or video games (which also have histories). We, moreover, very likely are viewing the state of the art in moviemaking technology, as it has developed, and perhaps are watching a film commenting on, and drawing from, earlier films. Our imaginary movie may have a future, as well as a past and a present. It, too, will pass into memory, available to be appropriated and reappropriated over time.

The audience around us also contains many histories, beginning with the individual ones of its members, with their assumptions, prejudices, and preferences. These are also, in part, a product of the histories of the groups with whom audience members identify and of the positions of those groups within the larger society. In addition, our fellow viewers approached the film with prior knowledge about it and about movies and moviegoing—a personal and collective history of viewing. Quite probably they will talk about it later and use it as a point of comparison with other bits and pieces of popular culture. It may influence how they represent themselves and what they buy.

All these histories, and others, converge at the point of movie spectatorship. Among the strengths of the case-study method taken by many of the chapters in this collection is that it enables us to see several such histories operating simultaneously in real lives, in specific settings, and in relation to individual films or genres. But fitting these complicated particulars into any larger understanding of cinema and its history is an extraordinarily difficult challenge for theory and for interpretation and one that I think has yet to be met fully.

The task is made all the harder by several decades of very creative scholarship, coming from different disciplines and theoretical perspectives, dedicated to showing that texts do not have single, transparent meanings, but rather are open to multiple, even contradictory interpretations. Audiences may be physically passive and yet culturally active in making meaning out of what they view. If audience members are interpreters of movies, and if the multiple histories we already discussed shape their interpretations, it then becomes difficult to talk about *an* audience. At best, we are left with audiences that we can define roughly by some primary social or cultural category, such as age, gender, race, ethnicity, religion, class, or type of community.

Here enters the "modernity thesis," which locates cinema within a specific historical moment, the birth of the "modern" world, in contrast to my suggestion that it is best understood as the convergence of multiple histories. "Cinema is the quintessential product of fin de siècle society," Ben Singer declares. "It stands out as an emblem of modernity."[4] Indeed, the words *modern* and *modernity* abound in the titles and subtitles of important recent works on film.[5] Nor are film scholars alone in their quest for links to modernity: colleagues working on other areas of turn-of-the-century popular culture have recently found it in such places as the Wild West Show, Tarzan, and Harry Houdini's magic.[6] The modernity thesis in American cinema studies appears to be part of a much larger intellectual project of identifying the components of modernity now that we believe we are safely into postmodernity, or beyond.

In a thoughtful and nicely shaded defense of the thesis, Singer traces its origins to the late 1980s, when "a number of film scholars began drawing upon [Siegfried] Kracauer's and [Walter] Benjamin's suggestive remarks on modernity and cinema, and upon seminal figures, especially [Charles] Baudelaire and [Georg] Simmel." Such views "coalesced" into "something akin to a school of thought" in the 1990s.[7]

According to Singer, the "modernity thesis" has three major components. The first is that "in certain salient respects cinema is *like* modernity."[8] The two resemble one another, for example, in reordering time and space and in presenting men and women with abrupt discontinuities. The view leads naturally to an analogical interpretation of films, as when Tom Gunning, in his masterful book on Fritz Lang, writes of a murder in *While the City Sleeps* that "the violence of modernity's modes of representation and information matches the aggression of the crime itself."[9] In such instances the claim is that there is a similarity or resemblance, rather than a tight set of causal connections between modernity, cinema in general, and the elements of a particular movie.

A second assumption underlying the modernity thesis is that film is a part of modernity and, according to Singer, "in dynamic interaction with a range of adjacent similar phenomena."[10] Leo Charney and Vanessa R. Schwartz agree, insisting that "cinema must be reunderstood as a vital component of a broader culture of modern life which encompassed political, social, economic, and cultural transformations."[11] From my social and cultural historian's perspective, one of the virtues of the modernity thesis is that it provides a framework for locating early cinema in relation to other contemporary phenomena, such as department stores, world's fairs, imperialism, and amusement parks.

The third, most controversial and difficult of Singer's components of the modernity thesis is a causal proposition: that cinema "was a *consequence* of modernity." In one of its most radical (and intriguing) formulations, this assertion amounts to a claim not only that there is a causal connection between modernity and the birth of cinema, but also that movies mark a new stage in human perception—what David Bordwell (who is unsympathetic to it) calls "the history-of-vision thesis."[12] Framed that way, the history of film, and of modernity, is one of rupture and discontinuity. The assertion is that there is both a very different world after the movies, and very different ways of seeing that world. This is a bold proposition and one that arouses skepticism in historians trained to look for continuities and to regard assertions of radical change as a sign that an author may not know much about the earlier period.

Helpful as Singer's list is, I think a fourth item needs to be added to it. In some versions of the modernity thesis there is an assumption that cinema serves simultaneously as both a reflection and a critique of modernity. Such a view pervades Gunning's perceptive reading of Fritz Lang's films. Gunning claims, for example, that Lang, more fully than any other director, understood "that cinema would provide the image by which the twentieth century, the era of late modernity, would grasp itself." He "likewise understood that the cinema would have to provide the twentieth century with visions of both its future . . . and its past."[13] Thus modernity does not confine film in the prison of its own logic, but rather sometimes frees it—even in its most popular and commercial forms—to dissect the larger process of which it is a part.

Attempts to root the emergence of cinema in "modernity" have a great deal to recommend them, but they also have begun to draw criticism and are open to some obvious questions and objections. What are the opposites of *modern* and *modernity*? Although most modernity thesis scholars seem to dodge that question, the obvious answer is *traditional* and *tradition*. That dichotomy, however, is an old one that proved enormously troubling when applied elsewhere, notably in modernization theory.[14] It also seems problematic when applied to rural and small-town America, much of which was undergoing great demographic change in the nineteenth century and had long been involved in regional, national, and even international markets, hardly the stuff of a traditional way of life. With that in mind, I will use *traditional* in this chapter as the presumed opposite of "modern," but with considerable skepticism about its implications and utility for describing the United States when the movies were born.

There are other obvious questions about the modernity thesis more specific to film studies. How well can it explain the persistence and incorporation of earlier performance practices, such as those coming from vaudeville, burlesque, and even the minstrel show? If the modernity thesis is most powerful in explaining early film—which presumably emerged simultaneously with modernity itself—can it tell us anything significant about later cinema? Gunning believes that it can, but there is a suggestive shift from the application of the concept of "modernity" to early film and his application of it to Fritz Lang's movies.[15] In the former case, it is supposed to help us understand cinema in general; in the latter case it serves much more narrowly to inform a reading of a particular director's work. But even if we grant the utility of "modernity" in both of those projects, how well can it explain elements in cinema that appear, at least on the surface, to be antimodern, or at least unmodern, such as the enormous popularity of westerns or what Lary May calls "the radicalism of tradition" in Will Rogers in the 1930s?[16] Finally—in a question to which I will eventually return—where do rural and small-town viewers fit into any narrative of discontinuity and the sudden emergence of modernity?

Before going back on the road and into the hinterland, however, I want to look at some key—and debatable—assumptions embedded in the modernity thesis. One of the most basic is that there is a clear, agreed-upon definition of *modernity*. The title of Matei Calinescu's book *Faces of Modernity* (1977) should have been an early warning signal against that notion.[17] Some of the most influential thinkers of the past few decades—Jacques Derrida and Jürgen Habermas, for example—disagree over *modernity* and its discontents.[18]

Even scholars in other fields whose work might appear congenial to the modernity thesis have rather different perspectives on modernity from that of its proponents in film studies. Literary scholar Simon During, for example, places magic, not movies, at the heart of modernity, writing of cinema that "it embalmed the older genres it drew upon."[19] Perhaps more challenging for the modernity thesis are two important books by Ann Douglas and Christine Stansell, both dealing with cultural life and modernity in New York in the early twentieth century, *Terrible Honesty: Mongrel Manhattan in the 1920s* and *American Moderns: Bohemian New York and the Creation of a New Century*.[20]

Each associates the rise of the "modern" with a different social groups from the ones central to the modernity thesis—intellectuals and artists, not moviegoers—and pays scant attention to cinema. Of her New York bohemian modernists (not filmmakers), Stansell writes that they "made modernity local and concrete, tangible to a popular American audience," later characterizing the period as "an age when the movies had yet to take hold."[21] At minimum, we have a disagreement over who and what spread modernity outward from New York City, as well as perhaps a sign that it is a good idea to read across disciplinary lines.

The "modernity" envisioned by modernity thesis proponents is one of sensory overload—the assumption is that fragmentation, discontinuity, spectacles, and sudden juxtapositions are at the heart of the modern experience. Here are some propositions about modernity, taken and presented more or less randomly from the authors I have been using as exemplary of the thesis, mostly because their works *are* important and challenging: "Urban spectacle has been understood as a defining quality of 'modernity' generally construed"; "construction and deconstruction of identity within modern systems"; "general anonymity of modern existence"; "abstraction and fragmentation, the master tools of modern process"; "a fundamental desire to dominate the world, the ambition for systematic mastery which lies behind the project of modernity"; "a project of abstraction and dehumanization"; "modern society's extraordinary discontinuity"; "the crowd, in the form of the masses, became a central player in modernity"; "modernity, or the development of 'modern consumer society'"; "post-1870 transformations of modernity generated a perceptual climate of overstimulations, distraction, and sensation"; and "Modernity . . . was conceived of as a barrage of stimuli."[22] Whatever place such language describes, it sure isn't *Main Street*.

Although a bit overwrought, as these examples indicate, the view of modernity embedded in the modernity thesis is consistent with how many observers themselves saw turn-of-the-century life. But even that rationale is a thin one: other contemporaries saw modernity quite differently. For some it was a story of progress and order, not one of fragmentation, spectacles, unstable identities, and discontinuity. For others it was an object of disgust. "My dear fellow," complains a character in a 1901 English novel, "modernity simply means democracy. And once democracy has been forced upon us there's no good protesting any longer."[23] The fundamental fact is that there were—and are—various conceptions of what it meant to be modern, and the modernity thesis privileges one of them at the expense of others.

If I were acting as an academic attorney in defense of the thesis, I would advise my client that there are several ways of responding to the problem of multiple definitions of modernity, short of junking the concept altogether. One is simply to regard the matter as undisturbing to anyone truly knowledgeable, as Jonathan Crary appears to do in writing, "It may be unnecessary to emphasize that when I use the word 'modernity' I mean a process completely detached from any notions of progress or development."[24] That dismisses as unworthy of consideration one of the major ways in which early twentieth-century Americans regarded modernity.

Perhaps more persuasive is the approach taken by Ben Singer and Vanessa R. Schwartz, although each goes about it in a somewhat different manner. It is to cite diverse aspects of modernity, roughly corresponding to different views of it, and then to present them as complementary or as components of a larger definition.[25] The danger of that strategy is that it will obscure disagreements and differences. Singer's six "conceptions of modernity," for example, include *modernization* in a way that glosses controversies over the term. His list also includes *rationality*, which he regards as encompassing both the rise of bureaucracies and "individualism," concepts some of us have problems including in the same sentence.

A third approach to the issue of multiple modernities would be to acknowledge more clearly and critically that there are, and were, competing concepts of modernity, but to assert that film connects most directly to one of them. That scales the thesis back a bit but preserves its core. A fourth approach, however, might be more interesting. It would involve conceiving of modernity as multiple, uneven, and contradictory, with cinema participating in more than one of its varieties. Consider, for example, a notion of modernity very different from the one on which the modernity thesis rests—that it is defined by processes of consolidation, bureaucratization, professionalization, specialization, and globalization. That view may have little to offer in helping us understand the visual effects of early cinema, but it is not a bad description of the development of the film industry.

If, however, we take *modernity* solely in the sense in which it appears in the modernity thesis, the timing of its emergence is crucial for establishing the nature of the relationship between it and early cinema. If the two coincide, there might well be a case for film helping *constitute*, or *create*, modernity. The evidence, however, suggests a different chronology and a looser connection, with cinema following modernity (as understood within the modernity thesis) and being one of its many manifestations. The oft-cited witness of modernity Charles Baudelaire died in 1867, well before the advent of motion pictures. Recent works by Jonathan Crary and Vanessa Schwartz, as well as essays in a collection edited by Schwartz and Leo Charney, suggest important changes in spectatorship and visual stimulation prior to the birth of film.[26] There is also fragmentary and tantalizing evidence from the United States and Europe that new modes of visual representation were emerging before cinema and even before impressionism and other forms of modernism appeared in the arts. In France, for example, Charles Joseph Minard produced in 1861 a famous and remarkable chart of the Russian campaign of Napoleon's army, capturing six different variables on one page. Edward R. Tufte declares, "It may well be the best statistical graphic ever drawn."[27] Even earlier, in Prussia and the United States, Alexander von Humbolt and Matthew Fontaine Maury did innovative and remarkable work in devising visual representations of land and sea.[28] From these scattered but intriguing examples it appears as if there may well have been a "modern" visual revolution already under way prior to the invention of cinema, perhaps driven as much by trade, imperialism, and capitalism as by the experiences of modern life.

The question of *where* modernity emerged is as important as the one of *when* it emerged. The "modernity" of the modernity thesis is explicitly urban, in other words, not in places treated in these chapters. "Modernity," Charney and Schwartz declare, "cannot be conceived outside the context of the city."[29] The jostle and bustle of late nineteenth-century metropolises, with their variety and wonders, were its manifestations and perhaps its creator. "The basic hypothesis," as Ben Singer puts it, "involves the notion of a general reconditioning or re-calibration of the individual's perceptual capacities and proclivities to correspond to the greater intensity and rapidity of stimuli" in urban life.[30] The chief sites of this modernity were Paris and New York, no matter how atypical they may be of the nations whose cultural capitals they are.

It would be silly to argue that this notion is entirely wrong. Late nineteenth-century New York and Paris were modern by any reasonable definition of the word. But let us return to how the modernity thesis imagines the urban experience to have been there, and in other major cities—one of spectacle, extreme visual stimulation, discontinuity, disorientation, and unstable identities. That surely does not describe life in the countryside, but does it truly describe the lives of the majority of urban moviegoers? For three decades or more, historians writing about early twentieth-century working-class and immigrant men and women, an important part of the audience for early film in major cities, have told a different story. The world they portray is not that of the flaneur, taking in the spectacle of urban fragmentation, but rather one of community, ethnic allegiances and institutions, religious life, family bonds, and selective use of commercial popular culture for personal and group ends.[31] The modernity thesis posits a "shock of the modern" that a sizable portion of the audience for early film—urban as well as nonurban—may not have experienced.

Even if we put that possibility aside for a moment, there is a further difficulty in locating the modernity of the modernity thesis spatially. To make the point I will shift terms from *modernity* to *modernism*, recognizing that the two are not synonymous, but also that the latter shares much visually with cinema and was likewise a part of modernity, however the term might be understood. Can we make the case that modernism is a product of urban modernity? If so, how can we explain the nonurban origins of, and antiurban currents among, artists whom we regard as modernists, or their flights from New York and Paris to places like Provincetown, Taos, or the south of France? For that matter, how well can the modernity thesis explain the remarkable flowering of visual modernism, including in cinema, in Russia, among the least modern of European nations? Were such artists in the cultural outlands simply marching to orders from Paris, or were they participants in a variety of transnational experiences and experiments, not necessarily confined to the most "modern" of cities? "Every center of European culture," Peter Jelavich wrote, "left its particular local imprint on modernism."[32] If nothing else, observations such as this raise questions about whether it makes most sense to conceive of modernity as having special sites, each with its own inflection, or, alternatively, to posit an abstract fin de siècle urban experience that fits a few cities better than others. In other words, are we really talking about New York and Paris or about a general urban model best approximated in those places? If the answer is the latter, are we then to imagine gradations of modernity—Chicago, pretty modern; San Francisco, less modern; small-town America, traditional and watching modernity from afar? At minimum, arguments that connect the birth of cinema to urban modernity must eventually explain the relationship of film to both creators and audiences who lived outside the presumed capitals of modernty.

And that brings me back to this collection of chapters and to the question of where placing early film within the context of "urban modernity" leaves rural and small-town audiences. One possibility would be simply to dismiss small-town audiences and assert that the real action was in the sites of urban modernity, with the rest of the country following, some places rapidly, others slowly. Even people within the industry saw it that way at times. As late as 1946 a *Variety* headline asked, "Hick's Buck as Good as the City Slicker's, So Why Doesn't Hollywood Angle More Pix for Fans in Stix?"[33] To dismiss audiences outside of the great metropolises as insignificant, however, would, as Robert C. Allen reminds us at the beginning of this collection, write off as peripheral the majority of the potential audience for film in its first two or three decades. Noteworthy in this respect is the case of early cinema in France, America's great competitor at the time, as described by Vanessa R. Schwartz, a supporter of the modernity thesis. "Although it emerged and eventually returned to the urban context," she wrote, "between the years 1896 and 1901 cinema probably witnessed its greatest popularity as an attraction at itinerant fairgrounds."[34] Even without cautionary notes such as that, or the scholarship that is now emerging on diverse audiences in the United States, any general argument about cinema that simply ignores nonurban audiences sounds intellectually suspect. Three decades of postcolonial and subaltern studies provide a reminder that the world imagined from an imperial metropolitan center is quite different from the world lived in the great lands beyond.[35] The same may well be true of cultural metropolises and their peripheries.

Another conceivable relationship between modernity, films, and nonurban audiences also follows something of an imperial model. It would be to argue that cinema was a missionary of modernity, bringing it to the boon-docks. That is an attractive thought, including to those of us raised in the boondocks for whom movies opened up new worlds of glamour, sophistica-tion, and sophomoric humor. Books, however, did the same thing. A more fundamental problem with the missionary view of rural and small-town moviegoing is that it requires either a good deal of shading or taking a step backward from what scholars have been saying for some time about audi-ences for popular culture: that they are active interpreters of it, not passive recipients. The natives made up their own minds and arrived at their own conclusions, whether the subject was religion or westerns. At minimum, we need to know about the moviegoing practices of nonurban audiences before consigning them to an analytical, as well as geographic, periphery.

That leads to a third way of conceiving of the relationship between cine-matic modernity and hinterland audiences: to regard the latter as active but selective, filtering out what they liked and did not like. That approach fits with what some observers thought, and it can be tested empirically by look-ing at what played well outside of New York. Much harder to judge is how clearly urban/rural differences in taste divided along modern/traditional lines—or even if such a dichotomy really makes sense.

However that may be, any approach that denies cultural creativity to moviegoers, or severely limits it in the case of some audiences and not oth-ers, forecloses at least two potentially fruitful approaches. The first would ex-plore how multiple histories operated simultaneously in movie spectator-ship, the path I suggested at the beginning of the chapter. Once we assume any audience to be passive or irrelevant, the conception of converging multiple histories I suggested earlier either vanishes or is relegated to formal analysis of the film itself, not to an examination of its viewers. A second per-spective that would similarly be lost is one of understanding cinema as en-gaged in a dialectical (or dialogic) relationship with multiple audiences. To accept for the moment the traditional/modern distinction that I dislike, might there not be instances when traditional trumps modernity—when the values of small-town audiences prevail, as well as instances when they are challenged, or instances when the differences are compromised, perhaps even creatively? The modernity thesis may be better at explaining the visual qualities of early film than, for example, the rise of movie censorship.

When there are problems with a car, trading in for a new model is an option, although not always the best one. A great deal of significant work on film and other varieties of popular culture rests upon the modernity thesis, so perhaps an overhaul will do, at least until a newer, better model comes along. We have to take seriously the notion that connections existed between something called modernity and early cinema, if only because men and women at the time believed that to be the case. What we do need, however, is a clearer sense of what *modernity* means in any given context. It is likewise important for any theory to be able to encompass the multiple histories that converge in film and film spectatorship, rather than to focus on a historical moment, the birth of modernity. Also in order are theories that better comprehend the diversity of movie audiences, the variety of interpretive skills they bring to moviegoing, and the unevenness of culture—the ability of *modern* and *traditional* to coexist and transform each other. In other words, we need a theory to take out on the road.

Notes

1. W. J. T. Mitchell, ed., *Against Theory: Literary Studies and the New Pragmatism* (Chicago: University of Chicago Press); David Bordwell and Noël Carroll, eds., *Post-theory: Reconstructing Film Studies* (Madison: University of Wisconsin Press, 1996); Sonia Livingstone, "Audience Research at the Crossroads: The 'Implied Audience' in Media and Cultural Theory," *European Journal of Cultural Studies* 1 (1998): 194.

2. Ben Singer, *Melodrama and Modernity: Early Sensational Cinema and Its Contexts* (New York: Columbia University Press, 2001), 127.

3. An especially good example of what I have in mind, dealing with a different realm of popular culture, is Robert Walser, *Running with the Devil: Power, Gender, and Madness in Heavy Metal Music* (Hanover, N.H.: Wesleyan University Press, 1993).

4. Singer, *Melodrama and Modernity*, 102.

5. For example, ibid.; Tom Gunning, *The Films of Fritz Lang: Allegories of Vision and Modernity* (London: British Film Institute, 2000); Leo Charney and Vanessa R. Schwartz, eds., *Cinema and the Invention of Modern Life* (Berkeley and Los Angeles: University of California Press, 1995).

6. Joy S. Kasson, *Buffalo Bill's Wild West: Celebrity, Memory, and Popular History* (New York: Hill and Wang, 2000); John F. Kasson, *Houdini, Tarzan, and the Perfect Man: The White Male Body and the Challenge of Modernity in America* (New York: Hill and Wang, 2001); Simon During, *Modern Enchantments: The Cultural Power of Secular Magic* (Cambridge, Mass.: Harvard University Press, 2002).

7. Singer, *Melodrama and Modernity*, 101.

8. Ibid., 103.

9. Gunning, *Films of Fritz Lang*, 439.

10. Singer, *Melodrama and Modernity*, 103–4.

11. Charney and Schwartz, *Cinema and the Invention of Modern Life*, 10.

12. Singer, *Melodrama and Modernity*, 103–4; David Bordwell, *On the History of Film Style* (Cambridge, Mass.: Harvard University Press, 1997), 142ff.

13. Gunning, *Films of Fritz Lang*, 476.

14. On the political implications of modernization theory, see Nils Gilman, *Mandarins of the Future: Modernization Theory in Cold War America* (Baltimore: Johns Hopkins University Press, 2003).

15. Gunning, *Films of Fritz Lang*, x–xi.

16. Lary May, *The Big Tomorrow: Hollywood and the Politics of the American Way* (Chicago: University of Chicago Press, 2000), 14.

17. Matei Calinescu, *Faces of Modernity: Avant-Garde, Decadence, Kitsch* (Bloomington: Indiana University Press, 1977).

18. See, for example, Maurizio Passerin d'Entreves and Seyla Benhabib, eds., *Habermas and the Unfinished Project of Modernity: Critical Essays on The Philosophical Discourse of Modernity* (Cambridge: Polity Press, 1996).

19. During, *Modern Enchantments*, 173.

20. Ann Douglas, *Terrible Honesty: Mongrel Manhattan in the 1920s* (New York: Farrar, Straus and Giroux, 1995); Christine Stansell, *American Moderns: Bohemian New York and the Creation of a New Century* (New York: Metropolitan Books, 2000).

21. Stansell, *American Moderns*, 3, 121. The index has no entries for cinema, film, or movies, although she mentions them in the passages cited.

22. Vanessa R. Schwartz, *Spectacular Realities: Early Mass Culture in Fin-de-Siècle Paris* (Berkeley and Los Angeles: University of California Press, 1998), 3; Charney and Schwartz, *Cinema and the Invention of Modern Life*, 4, 73, 183, 279; Gunning, *Films of Fritz Lang*, 113, 236, 245, 446, 448; Singer, *Melodrama and Modernity*, 19.

23. This quotation may be found under *modernity* in the online version of *The Oxford English Dictionary*. It comes from May Sinclair's *Divine Fire*. Also note the two strands of modernity suggested in Louis Menand, "Diversity," in *Critical Terms for Literary Study*, ed. Frank Lentricchia and Thomas McLaughlin, 2nd ed. (Chicago: University of Chicago Press, 1995), 337.

24. Jonathan Crary, "Unbinding Vision: Manet and the Attentive Observer in the Late Nineteenth Century," in *Cinema and the Invention of Modern Life*, ed. Leo Charney and Vanessa R. Schwartz (Berkeley and Los Angeles: University of California Press, 1995), 47.

25. Singer, *Melodrama and Modernity*, 20ff.; Schwartz, *Spectacular Realities*, 4.

26. Charney and Schwartz, *Cinema and the Invention of Modern Life*; Schwartz, *Spectacular Realities*. The most recent book-length statement of Crary's position is Jonathan Crary, *Suspensions of Perception: Attention, Spectacle, and Modern Culture* (Cambridge, Mass.: MIT Press, 1999).

27. Edward R. Tufte, *The Visual Display of Quantitative Information* (Cheshire, Conn.: Graphics Press, 1983).

28. On Humbolt and Maury, see William H. Goetzmann, *New Lands, New Men: America and the Second Great Age of Discovery* (New York: Viking Penguin, 1986). Other examples of changes in cognitive styles—including in visual thinking—before the invention of cinema can be found in Daniel Calhoun, *The Intelligence of a People* (Princeton, N.J.: Princeton University Press, 1973); Anthony F.C. Wallace, *Rockdale: The Growth of an American Village in the Early Industrial Revolution* (New York: Knopf, 1978), 237–39.

29. Charney and Schwartz, *Cinema and the Invention of Modern Life*, 3.

30. Singer, *Melodrama and Modernity*, 119. For a work not centrally concerned with film that also makes a case for Paris as the birthplace of modernity, see David Harvey, *Paris, the Capital of Modernity* (London: Routledge, 2003). Harvey's notions of what comprises "modernity," and how and when it emerged, however, are far more complex than those found in the "modernity thesis."

31. See, for example, Lizabeth Cohen, *Making a New Deal: Industrial Workers in Chicago, 1919–1939* (Cambridge: Cambridge University Press, 1990); John E. Bodnar, *The Transplanted: A History of Immigration in Urban America* (Bloomington: Indiana

University Press, 1985); Susan A. Glenn, *Daughters of the Shtetl: Life and Labor in the Immigrant Generation* (Ithaca, N.Y.: Cornell University Press, 1990); Kathy Lee Peiss, *Cheap Amusements: Working Women and Leisure in Turn-of-the Century New York* (Philadelphia: Temple University Press, 1986).

32. Peter Jelavich, *Munich and Theatrical Modernism* (Cambridge, Mass.: Harvard University Press, 1985), 5.

33. Hayden Talbot, "Hick's Buck as Good as the City Slicker's, So Why Doesn't Hollywood Angle More Pix for Fans in Stix?" *Variety*, October 2, 1946; May, *Big Tomorrow*, 122–24, appears to consider such audiences as peripheral until the 1930s.

34. Schwartz, *Spectacular Realities*, 189.

35. For an example, note the perspective in Dipesh Chakrabarty, "Postcoloniality and the Artifice of History," in *The Post-colonial Studies Reader*, ed. Bill Ashcroft, Gareth Griffiths, and Helen Tiffin (London: Routledge, 1995), 382–88. A classic that should be a cautionary tale for any of us who use the word *tradition* loosely is Eric Hobsbawm and Terence Ranger, *The Invention of Tradition* (Cambridge: Cambridge University Press, 1992).

CONTRIBUTORS

RICHARD ABEL is the Robert Altman Collegiate Professor of Film Studies at the University of Michigan. He is the editor of *Encyclopedia of Early Cinema* (2005) and *Silent Film* (1996) and the author of *The Cine Comes to Town: French Cinema 1896–1914* (1994), *The Red Rooster Scare: Making Cinema American, 1900–1910* (1999), *Americanizing the Movies and "Movie-Mad" Audiences 1910–1914* (2006), and other works in French and American film history.

ROBERT C. ALLEN is the James Logan Godfrey Professor of American Studies, History, and Communication Studies at the University of North Carolina, Chapel Hill. His research focuses on the history of American popular entertainment and popular culture. He has written on film history and historiography: *Vaudeville and Film, 1895–1915: A Study in Media Interaction* (1980); *Film History: Theory and Practice*, coauthored with Douglas Gomery (1985); popular theater: *Horrible Prettiness: Burlesque and American Culture* (1992); and television: *Speaking of Soap Operas* (1985), *Channels of Discourse: Television and Contemporary Criticism* (1987, 1992), and *The Television Studies Reader*, coedited with Annette Hill (2003); and other works in media criticism and history.

KEVIN CORBETT is Associate Professor in the School of Broadcast and Cinematic Arts at Central Michigan University. He specializes in the social history of film, including the cultural history of small-town movie theaters. He also has expertise in television and video production. He has published widely in cinema and media journals and has created numerous documentaries, including *Little Palaces: Michigan's Historic Small Town Movie Theaters* (2000) and *Crazy or What?* (2007).

LESLIE MIDKIFF DEBAUCHE is Associate Professor in the communication department at the University of Wisconsin–Stevens Point. She is the author of *Reel Patriotism: The Movies and World War I* (1997). Her areas of research interest include silent film history, haute couture, mise-en-scène, Billie Burke, and film actresses in the second decade of the twentieth century.

KATHRYN FULLER-SEELEY is Associate Professor and Associate Chair of the Department of Communication at Georgia State University. Her research interests include moviegoing and film exhibition history, radio history, and media reception studies. She is the author of *At the Picture Show: Small Town Audiences and the Creation of Movie Fan Culture* (1996), *Children and the Movies: Media Influence and the Payne Fund Controversy* (1996), coauthored with Garth Jowett and Ian Jarvie, and *Celebrate Richmond Theater* (2001). Her current projects are studies of early moviegoing in Cooperstown, New York, and the Jack Benny radio program.

TERRY LINDVALL is the C. S. Lewis Chair of Communication and Christian Thought at Virginia Wesleyan College in Norfolk, Virginia. He has taught at Regent University and Duke University's Divinity School and was the Walter Mason Fellow of Religious Studies at the College of William and Mary. He is the author of *Surprised by Laughter: The Comic World of C. S. Lewis* (1996), *The Silents of God: Selected Issues and Documents in Silent American Film and Religion, 1908–1926* (2001), and *Sanctuary Cinema: Origins of the Christian Film Industry* (2007), among other works.

ANNE MOREY is Associate Professor in the Department of English at Texas A&M University. Her research interest is American silent and early sound film. She has published on aspects of British film history, American women screenwriters and commentators on film during the silent period, children's film, and genre film. She is the author of *Hollywood Outsiders: The Adaptation of the Film Industry, 1913–1934* (2003).

GEORGE POTAMIANOS is Associate Professor of history in the Department of Humanities and Communications at College of the Redwoods. His research interests are in film history and television studies. His book in progress is *Hollywood and the Hinterlands: Mass Culture in Two California Communities, 1896–1938.*

CALVIN PRYLUCK (1924–96) taught film production and media theory at the University of North Carolina, Chapel Hill, and later at Temple University. His articles "Toward a Psycholinguistics of Cinema," coauthored with Richard Snow (1967), and "Structure and Function in Educational Cinema" (1969) were among the first to translate semiology to film studies. His essay "Ultimately, We Are All Outsiders: The Ethics of Documentary Filming" (1975) remains a classic, and his early adoption of new computer and Internet technology greatly encouraged others to follow his lead.

PAIGE REYNOLDS is Associate Professor in the English department at the College of the Holy Cross. Her research areas include modern and contemporary Irish literature; Irish studies; twentieth-century British and American literature and culture; modern drama and performance, as well as a long-standing interest in film history. Her book in progress is *The Audiences for Irish Modernism: Drama and Irish Spectacle, 1890–1925.*

CHARLES TEPPERMAN is Assistant Professor in the Faculty of Communication and Culture at the University of Calgary. Tepperman has published articles on early cinema in Canada and nontheatrical film technology; he is currently working on a book about the Amateur Cinema League and midcentury amateur film culture in North America.

GREGORY A. WALLER is Professor and Chair of the Department of Communication and Culture at Indiana University. His work covers a range of topics in film studies, including the history of exhibition and distribution, American popular movie genres, and New Zealand cinema. He is currently working on "Movies on the Road," a study of traveling film exhibitions in the 1930s and 1940s, and on "Japan-in-America," a comprehensive look at the representation of Japan in the United States from 1890 to 1915. He is the author of *Main Street Amusements: Movies and Commercial Entertainment in a Southern City, 1896–1930* (1995), and editor of *Moviegoing in America: A Sourcebook in the History of Film Exhibition* (2002).

RONALD G. WALTERS is Professor of history at Johns Hopkins University. He is the author of *The Antislavery Appeal: American Abolitionism after 1830* (1976, 1984) and *American Reformers: 1815–1860* (1978, 1997) and editor of *The Authority of Science and Twentieth-Century America* (1997). His research interests range widely in American cultural and social history, and his works in progress include essays on radical and reform movements and on twentieth-century popular culture, and an interpretive history of twentieth-century American commercial popular entertainment.

SELECTED BIBLIOGRAPHY

Articles

Allen, Robert C. "Motion Picture Exhibition in Manhattan: Beyond the Nick-elodeon." *Cinema Journal* 18, no. 2 (1979): 2–15.

———. "From Film Exhibition to the History of Film Reception." *Screen* 31, no. 4 (1990): 347–56.

———. "Manhattan Myopia, or Oh! Iowa." *Cinema Journal* 35, no. 3 (1996): 75–103.

———. "Relocating American Film History: The 'Problem' of the Empirical." *Cultural Studies* 20, no. 1 (2006): 48–88.

Aronson, Michael. "The Wrong Kind of Nickel Madness." *Cinema Journal* 42, no. 1 (2002): 71–76.

Bernstein, Matthew. "Selznick's March: The Atlanta Premiere of *Gone with the Wind*." *Atlanta History* 63, no. 2 (1999): 7–33.

Carbine, Mary. "Best Show outside the Loop: Black Audiences in Chicago." In *Silent Film,* ed. Richard Abel, 243–62. New Brunswick, N.J.: Rutgers University Press, 1996.

Cohen, Lizabeth. "Encountering Mass Culture at the Grass Roots: The Experience of Chicago's Workers in the 1920s." *American Quarterly* 41, no. 1 (1989): 6–33.

Fuller-Seeley, Kathryn. "Viewing the Viewers: Representations of the Audience in Early Cinema Advertising." In *American Movie Audiences: From the Turn of the Century to the Early Sound Era,* ed. Melvyn Stokes and Richard Maltby, 112–28. London: British Film Institute, 1999.

———. "Dish Night at the Movies: Exhibitors and Female Audiences during the Great Depression." In *Looking Past the Screen: Case Studies in American Film History and Method,* ed. Jon Lewis and Eric Smoodin. Durham, N.C.: Duke University Press, 2007.

Gomery, Douglas. "The Growth of Movie Monopolies: The Case of Balaban & Katz." *Wide Angle* 3, no. 1 (1979): 54–63.

———. "Movie Audiences, Urban Geography and the History of the American Film." *Velvet Light Trap* 19 (Spring 1982): 23–29.

———. "Thinking about Motion Picture Exhibition." *Velvet Light Trap* 25 (Spring 1990): 3–11.

Gunning, Tom, "The Cinema of Attractions: Early Film, Its Spectator and the Avant-Garde." In *Early Cinema: Space, Frame, Narrative,* ed. Thomas Elsaesser, 56–62. London: British Film Institute, 1990.

Haralovich, Mary Beth. "Film Advertising, the Film Industry, and the Pin-Up: The Industry's Accommodations to Social Forces in the 1940s." In *Current Research in Film: Audiences, Economics, and Law,* ed. Bruce A. Austin, vol. 1, 127–64. Norwood, N.J.: Ablex, 1985.

Singer, Ben. "Manhattan Nickelodeons: New Data on Audiences and Exhibitors." *Cinema Journal* 34, no. 3 (1995): 5–35.

Streible, Dan. "The Literature of Film Exhibition: A Bibliography on Motion Picture Exhibition and Related Topics." *Velvet Light Trap* 25 (Spring 1990): 80–119.

Waller, Gregory. "Introducing the 'Marvelous Invention' to the Provinces: Film Exhibition in Lexington Kentucky, 1896–1897." *Film History* 3 (1989): 223–34.

———. "Situating Motion Pictures in the Pre-nickelodeon Period: Lexington Kentucky 1897–1906." *Velvet Light Trap* 25 (Spring 1990): 12–28.

———. "Robert Southard and the History of Traveling Film Exhibition." *Film Quarterly* 57, no. 2 (2003–4): 2–14.

Books

Abel, Richard. *The Red Rooster Scare: Making Cinema American, 1900–1910.* Berkeley and Los Angeles: University of California Press, 1999.

———. *Americanizing the Movies and "Movie Mad" Audiences, 1910–1914.* Berkeley and Los Angeles: University of California Press, 2006.

Allen, Robert C. *Vaudeville and Film 1895–1915: A Study in Media Interaction.* New York: Arno Press, 1980.

Allen, Robert C., and Douglas Gomery. *Film History: Theory and Practice.* New York: Macmillan, 1985.

Altman, Rick. *Silent Film Sound.* New York: Columbia University Press, 2005.

Austin, Bruce. *Immediate Seating: A Look at Movie Audiences.* Belmont, Calif.: Wadsworth, 1989.

Butsch, Richard, ed. *For Fun and Profit: The Transformation of Leisure into Consumption.* Philadelphia: Temple University Press, 1990.

———. *The Making of American Audiences: From Stage to Television, 1750–1990.* New York: Cambridge University Press, 1998.

Couvares, Francis. *The Remaking of Pittsburgh: Class and Culture in an Industrializing City 1877–1919.* Albany: State University of New York Press, 1984.

Fuller, Kathryn H. *At the Picture Show: Small-Town Audiences and the Creation of Movie Fan Culture.* Washington, D.C.: Smithsonian Institution Press, 1996.

Fuller-Seeley, Kathryn. *Celebrate Richmond Theater.* Richmond, Va.: Dietz, 2001.

Gomery, Douglas. *Shared Pleasures: A History of Movie Presentation in the United States.* Madison: University of Wisconsin Press, 1992.

Hanson, Miriam. *Babel and Babylon.* Cambridge, Mass.: Harvard University Press, 1991.

Hark, Ina Rae, ed. *Exhibition: The Film Reader*. London: Routledge, 2002.

Headley, Robert J. *Motion Picture Exhibition in Washington DC*. Jefferson, N.C.: McFarland, 2000.

———. *Motion Picture Exhibition in Baltimore*. Jefferson, N.C.: McFarland, 2006.

Levine, Lawrence. *High Brow Low Brow: The Emergence of Cultural Hierarchy in America*. Cambridge, Mass.: Harvard University Press, 1988.

Musser, Charles, with Carol Nelson. *High-Class Moving Pictures: Lyman H. Howe and the Forgotten Era of Traveling Exhibition, 1880–1920*. Princeton, N.J.: Princeton University Press, 1991.

Peiss, Kathy. *Cheap Amusements: Working Women and Leisure in Turn-of-the-Century New York*. Philadelphia: Temple University Press 1985.

Rabinowitz. Lauren. *For the Love of Pleasure: Women, Movies and Culture in Turn-of-the-Century Chicago*. New Brunswick, N.J.: Rutgers University Press, 1998.

Rosenzweig, Roy. *Eight Hours for What We Will: Workers and Leisure in an Industrial City, 1870–1920*. Cambridge: Cambridge University Press, 1983.

Staiger, Janet. *Interpreting Films: Studies in the Historical Reception of American Cinema*. Princeton, N.J.: Princeton University Press, 1992.

———. *Media Reception Studies*. New York: NYU Press, 2005.

Stewart, Jackie. *Migrating to the Movies: Cinema and Black Urban Modernity*. Berkeley and Los Angeles: University of California Press, 2005.

Stokes, Melvyn, and Maltby, Richard, eds. *American Movie Audiences: From the Turn of the Century to the Early Sound Era*. London: British Film Institute, 1999.

Waller, Gregory. *Main Street Amusements: Movies and Commercial Entertainment in a Southern City 1896–1930*. Washington, D.C.: Smithsonian Institution Press, 1995.

———, ed. *Moviegoing in America: A Sourcebook in the History of Film Exhibition*. Malden, Mass.: Blackwell, 2002.

INDEX

Abel, Richard, 4, 14
African-Americans (in the movie audience), 4, 12–13, 23, 27–30, 41, 46, 53, 59–60, 62–63, 69, 72n31, 91–101, 121n9, 154–156, 171, 181, 190, 193, 206–207n47, 220, 224
Airdome, 59, 64, 66, 69
Alabama, 12, 195; Flomaton, 190, 191; Roanoke, 206n39
Alaska, 43
Allen, Robert C., 4, 6, 8, 10, 12, 16, 103n71, 121n10, 258
Altman, Rick, 4
Amusement parks, 5, 29, 122n18, 178, 258
Arizona, 45, 56, 189
Arkansas, 189; Cotter, 192; Hartford, 200, 206n46; Hazen, 195
Automobiles, 6, 7, 10, 12, 45, 94, 137, 150, 171, 259

Balaban and Katz (theater chain), 14, 213, 228n15
Barron, Hal S., 7, 11
Baseball, 8, 76, 154, 192
Baudelaire, Charles, 252, 256
Benjamin, Walter, 24, 225
Bernstein, Matthew, 4
Billboard, 41, 46, 61, 169, 175–181, 188
Birth of a Nation (1915), 14, 150, 151, 153–157, 159, 163, 164
Black Diamond Express (1896), 6, 41

Block booking, 14, 194, 209
Blockbuster films, 200–202
Boosterism, 110, 156, 157, 179
Bordwell, David, 253
Bowles, Kate, 16
Bowser, Eileen, 61n80, 80, 121n6, 123n37
Butsch, Richard, 4, 186

California, 116, 150, 187, 189, 212; Hayward, 221; Los Angeles, 228n23; Placerville, 5, 13, 75–87; Sacramento, 75–76, 81, 86; San Francisco, 76–77, 80, 86, 258
Canada, 13, 23, 39; Ontario, 13, 14, 44, 130–145
Carbine, Mary, 27–28
Censorship (film), 8, 13, 14, 26, 27, 93, 132, 174, 196–197, 205n37
Chain stores, 67, 171, 173, 178, 183n24
Chain theaters, 67, 173–175, 176–181, 215, 240
Charney, Leo, 253, 256, 257
Chaser theory, 4, 39, 43–44
Chautauqua, 77, 150
Children (in the movie audience), 60, 66, 67–68, 82, 85, 93, 133–134, 156, 162, 192–196, 205, 235, 237–238
Church as site of film exhibition, 7, 10, 56, 77, 99–100, 150, 153, 163
Church events held in theaters, 95–96, 98–100
Churches, 8, 77, 81, 85, 92, 149, 150, 153, 192, 221

Circuses, 8, 39, 40, 42, 44, 46, 47, 48, 55, 59, 60, 192, 220
Cities (urban areas), 3–15, 20–22, 37–38, 186, 193, 197–201, 202, 209. *See also* New York City
Cohen, Lizabeth, 4
Colorado, 13, 45, 208, 215–216; Canon City, 199; Del Norte, 215; Delta, 212; Denver, 126n66; Manassa, 198; Montrose, 212
Connecticut, 189; Cheshire, 240, 249n3; Middletown, 71n17; Norwalk, 229n26
Corbett, Kevin, 15, 16, 248n1
Couvares, Frank, 4
Crafton, Donald, 170, 178
Cripps, Thomas, 20
Curtin, Michael, 8–9

DeBauche, Leslie Midkiff, 14
Delaware, 190
Depression (Great), 11, 14, 27, 48, 89n37, 169–181, 186–202, 208–226
Derrida, Jacques, 254
Disease (closing movie theaters), 83, 162, 163, 191, 220
Dish Night, 210, 211, 212
Doherty, Thomas, 186, 194, 197, 205n37
Double features, 210, 212

Edison Manufacturing Company, 38, 43, 46, 59, 77, 99, 141, 159, 163
Education (films used in), 95, 130–145
Eisenstein, Sergei, 136
Electric lights, 5, 9, 45, 158
Electricity, 7, 39, 56, 137, 144
Ellison, Ralph, 224–225
Ethnography, 8, 15, 223–248
Ewen, Elizabeth, 68
Exhibitor's Herald–World, 169, 175–181, 187
Exhibitors, 3, 9–14, 37–48, 51–53, 70, 186–204, 236, 239. *See also* itinerant exhibitors
Exhibitor cooperation with local business and community, 14–15, 75–87, 110, 149–165, 169–181, 233–246

Famous Players (film company), 107, 113, 117, 163
Fan culture, 8, 101n1, 117–120
Farmers (in the movie audience), 5–12, 15, 24–25, 30, 75, 130–145, 149, 172, 188, 192–193, 198

Feature films, 84, 85, 112–114, 120, 193
Film Index, 64
Fisher, Claude, 7
Florida: Avon Park, 193; Palm Beach, 160
Fuller-Seeley, Kathryn, 4, 14, 69, 128n91, 182n3, 203n5, 203n6, 227n8, 246

Gaines, Jane, 4
General Film Company, 84, 110, 111, 112, 113, 120
Georgia, 155; Atlanta, 66, 94
Giveaways at theaters, 67, 227n8m 210, 211, 212, 228n11
Gomery, Douglas, 4, 18n16, 67, 121n6, 170, 182n3, 227n5
Gone with the Wind (1939), 201–203
Government, regional (impact on movie-going), 14, 130–145, 216
Government, local (impact on moviegoing), 8, 89n40, 216–217
Grieveson, Lee, 146n6
Gunning, Tom, 4, 5, 142, 147n34, 252, 253, 254

Habermas, Jurgen, 254
Hansen, Miriam, 4, 69, 71n5, 147n33, 227n6
Haralovich, Mary Beth, 4
Hays Office, 176, 181, 197, 205n37. *See also* Production Code
Herzog, Charlotte, 60–61
Higashi, Sumiko, 69
Historiography, 3–17, 20–31, 37–38, 43, 108, 250–260
Howe, Lyman H., 38, 56, 57, 150
Huettig, Mae, 37, 38

Idaho, 177, 189; Nampa, 190, 193, 199–200; Preston, 191; Salmon, 177
Illinois, 46; Chicago, 4, 9, 14, 22, 24, 27–28, 44, 63, 67, 92, 113, 115, 149, 150, 161, 163, 187, 213; Harrisburg, 205n37; Robinson, 188–189
Illustrated songs, 39, 45, 57, 62, 63, 79, 83, 84, 93, 107
Immigrants (in the movie audience), 4, 6, 10, 11, 13, 23, 27–28, 31, 43, 44, 50n26, 62, 63, 109–110, 121n7, 122n37, 149, 155, 179, 190, 193, 196, 197, 199, 257; German, 46, 110, 149; Italian, 27–28, 109; Jewish, 10, 21, 27–28, 46, 54, 55, 68, 109, 123n26, 155, 173, 199

Independent theaters, 14, 180, 186–201,
217–218, 233–248
Indiana: Columbia City, 190, 192, 195, 201;
Hilltown (fictional town), 13, 169–181;
North Vernon, 207n51
Iowa, 189, 206–207n47; Anamosa, 10, 13, 31,
190; Des Moines, 4, 5, 13, 14, 107–120,
229n26; Griswold, 203n10; Marshalltown,
228n21
Itinerant exhibitors, 7, 8, 10, 13, 14, 19, 29,
37–49, 51–52, 55–58, 69, 75–79, 192, 220

Jackson, Margaret Weymouth, 169–181
Jenkins, Henry, 186, 187, 188, 199, 205n37
Jim Crow (laws and practices), 28–30, 60, 63,
69, 71n20, 72n40

Kansas, 4, 177, 179, 189; Greenleaf, 177;
Lebanon, 5, 13, 15, 190, 191–192, 196;
Lincoln, 190, 192; Minneapolis, 197;
Topeka, 217; Westmoreland, 200;
Wichita, 179
Kentucky, 13, 27, 177, 180–181, 190; Camp-
bellsville, 180–181; Carlisle, 177;
Eminence, 190, 198; Lexington, 4, 27, 53,
54, 58, 65–66; Owensboro, 27
Kleine, George (film company), 80, 88n24,
107, 113, 150, 161, 166n66
Koster and Bial's Music Hall, 38, 39, 43,
47, 48
Kracauer, Siegfried, 24, 221–223, 225,
250
Ku Klux Klan, 154–157, 163, 164, 196

Laemmle, Carl, 37, 44, 47, 48, 73n55, 111,
174
Lang, Fritz, 252, 253, 254
Legion of Decency, 197
Levine, Lawrence, 4
Lindvall, Terry, 8, 13, 26
Locally made films, 48, 68, 85, 87
Louisiana, 190; New Orleans, 23, 94, 116
Lynd, Robert and Helen, 171m, 182n8, 196,
213, 222

Magazines, 5, 10, 14, 107, 150, 161, 162,
169–181, 208–209
Maine, 16, 189; Augusta, 217; Bucksport, 16,
249n3; Portland, 45; Waldoboro, 196
Maltby, Richard, 4, 18n16, 20, 146n15, 180,
183n30, 227n6

Marchand, Roland, 183n12
Marvin, Carolyn, 7
Maryland: Baltimore, 23
Massachusetts, 23, 189; Boston, 92; Franklin,
194, 198, 199; Pittsfield, 216–217;
Somerville, 16; Worcester, 4
McArdle, Gladys, 15, 190, 191, 192, 196
McKenna, Chris, 30
Medicine shows, 8, 39, 40, 47, 48
Men (in the movie audience), 68–69,
194–196
Michigan, 15, 39, 43, 87n1, 190; Allegan,
249n3; Augusta, 249n3; Baldwin, 197,
198; Brooklyn, 249n3; Calumet, 249n3;
Detroit, 116; Greenville, 207n47;
Harrisville, 249n3; Houghton Lake,
249n3; Kalamazoo, 43; Lapeer, 198; Mt.
Pleasant, 249n3; Rogers City, 249n3
Mid-Atlantic (region), 11, 22–23, 28, 45, 186,
203n4. See also individual states
Middle class movie audience (white) 13, 55,
64, 68, 92–101, 114, 171–181, 196–199,
220
Midwest (region), 11, 12, 13, 14, 22, 28,
45, 47, 48, 50n28, 59, 61, 155, 169–181,
186, 188, 199, 203n4. See also individual
states
Minnesota, 58, 83, 190; Kasson, 190, 196,
198; Redwood Falls, 83; St. Paul, 116;
Winona, 47, 48
Minstrel shows, 31, 48, 55
Mississippi (state) 12, 179, 189; Durant, 189,
190; Vicksburg, 72n31
Missouri, 177; Columbia, 72n31; Jackson,
201; Kansas City, 218, 229n26; Paris, 177;
St. Louis, 58, 59, 154
Modernity, 5–8, 10–15, 21–26, 137, 143–145,
250–260
Montana, 189; Thompson Falls, 186
Morey, Anne, 13
Motion Picture Herald, 14, 169, 175–181,
186–202, 213, 216, 219, 220
Motion Picture News, 187
Motion Picture Patents Company (MPPC),
80, 81, 84, 87, 110, 117
Motion Picture Story Magazine, 117
Motography, 187
Moving Picture World, 59, 61, 62, 65, 67, 107
Munsterberg, Hugo, 130, 133–134, 140–141,
145, 146n15, 148n39
Musser, Charles, 4, 56, 57, 65, 92, 97

Mutual (film company), 107, 111, 112, 120, 159

Muybridge, Eadward, 115

Nebraska, 12, 20, 189, 198; Atkinson, 198; Cairo, 193; Hay Spring, 193; Neligh, 187

Nevada, 189; Caliente, 204n14

New England, 11, 16, 23, 28, 51n28, 171, 186, 188. *See also individual states*

New Hampshire, 189; Raymond, 192, 194

New Jersey, 189

New Mexico, 189; Raton, 215

New Republic, 208–209, 226

New Theatre and Film, 222, 226

New York (state), 11, 23, 189, 218; Albany, 217; Auburn, 241, 249n3; Brockport, 249n3; Brooklyn, 11, 219; Canastota, 198; Cooperstown, 11; Geneva, 241, 249n3; Lockport, 249n3; Poughkeepsie, 11; Schuylerville, 194; Sodus, 204n18. *See also* New York City

New York City, 4–10, 20–24, 38, 53–55, 63, 70, 86, 93, 108, 113, 150, 162, 187, 199, 213,

New York Dramatic Mirror, 55, 112

New York Clipper, 38, 39, 40, 41, 46

Newspapers, 14, 16, 29, 81, 92, 108–120, 149–164, 193, 216

Nickelodeons, 4, 7, 13, 21–28, 31, 41–48, 57–65, 75, 86, 94, 107–120, 131, 169, 172, 182n3, 190, 220

Non-theatrical exhibition, 130–145, 146n8, 146n9

North Carolina, 4, 17, 20–27, 29–31, 179, 190; Asheville, 54, 58; Charlotte, 22, 51; Concord, 51, 57; Durham, 73n36; Gastonia, 13, 26; Goldsboro, 54, 57; Greensboro, 54, 56, 57; Greenville, 206–207n47; Raleigh, 179; Rocky Mount, 224; West Jefferson, 249n3; Wilmington, 5, 13, 53–74; Wilson, 57; Winston–Salem, 54, 57; Wrightsville Beach, 56

North Dakota, 12, 189; Ambrose, 190, 193; Ellendale, 206n43; Rugby, 191

Northeast Historic Film, 16

Nye, David, 7

Ohio, 46, 118, 122n17, 124n39, 190; Akron, 228, 229n23; Cleveland, 4, 46, 116, 117, 118, 210, 218; Toledo, 116, 118; Port Washington, 43; Wellington, 193, 194; Youngstown, 128n95

Oklahoma, 154, 190, 199, 200; Dewey, 195; Idabell, 154; Seiling, 206n46

Opera house, 7, 10, 29, 55, 58, 75–83, 150, 187, 241

Oregon, 46, 196; Portland, 45

Organ, 65, 84, 172, 173, 178, 210

Ownby, Ted, 18n7

Paramount (film company), 10, 65, 66, 110, 145, 159, 174, 175, 177

Pathe (film company), 59, 112, 113, 114, 116, 118, 146n7, 159

Payne Fund Studies, 197, 248

Pearson, Roberta, 108, 146n15

Peiss, Kathy, 4, 129n108

Pennsylvania, 11, 23, 187, 190; Herminie, 201; New Freedom, 195; Northampton, 249n3; Orwigsburg, 206n47; Philadelphia, 9, 22; Pittsburgh, 4, 23; Wilkes-Barre, 38; York, 249n3

People not in the movie audience, 7, 8, 12, 26, 28–29, 60, 198

Phonograph, 5, 39, 42, 78

Picture palaces, 4, 10, 14, 20, 26, 58, 84, 107, 190, 202, 209, 211, 241–242

Potamianos, George, 13

Price, Gertrude, 115–120

Prizefight films, 40, 55, 56, 77, 79

Production Code, 14, 199. *See also* Hays Office

Progressive Era reformers, 21, 26, 108, 131

Projectionists, 40, 47, 61, 172

Projectors, 7, 10, 38–48, 59, 64, 77, 108, 130, 159, 172, 178, 196, 215

Promotions and giveaways in movie theaters, 67, 81, 83, 85, 89n37

Pryluck, Cal, 13

Publix theaters, 110, 170, 176, 178, 179, 180

Queen Elizabeth (1912), 113, 116, 124n50

Quigley, Martin, 175, 187

Rabinovich, Lauren, 4, 129n108

Racial attitudes toward movies and moviegoing, 6, 13, 27–30, 59–60, 181

Racial conflict, 12, 27, 28–30, 54, 59–60, 62, 113, 154–156, 163, 181

Radio, 5, 7, 10, 174

Railroads, 53–54, 108, 130–137

Ramsey, Terry, 49n5, 92
Religious attitudes toward movies
    and moviegoing, 13, 26, 31, 56,
    91–101
Religious conflict, 11, 18n7, 26–27, 96–98,
    193, 196–197, 216, 218
Religious groups, 8, 13, 26, 81, 92–101,
    179
Reynolds, Paige, 14
Riefenstahl, Leni, 136
Rogers, Will, 191, 199, 200, 201, 202, 254
Rosenzweig, Roy, 4
Run-zone clearance system, 176, 209
Rural areas, 3–15, 22–29, 37–48, 130–145,
    188, 197, 199

Saloons, 8, 61, 68, 91–92, 162
Saturday Evening Post, 14, 169–181, 209,
    215–216
Schwartz, Vanessa, 253, 256, 257, 258
Scott, James C., 143–144
Sears, Roebuck catalog, 38, 40–42,
    50n13
Seldes, Gilbert, 174, 219
Serials, 60, 86, 114, 125n64, 151, 159,
    160–164, 172
Sheldon, Karan, 16
Simmel, Georg, 24, 252
Singer, Ben, 10, 21, 24, 121n10, 125n64, 225,
    252, 253
Sklar, Robert, 32n6, 227n5
Small cities, 4–15, 53–50, 91–101, 107–120,
    149–164, 208–229
Small towns, 3–15, 22–29, 37–48, 75–87,
    169–181, 186–202, 208–229, 233–248
South (region), 12, 13, 18n7, 20–31, 22, 23,
    27–28, 53–74, 91–101, 203n4. *See also
    individual states*
South Carolina, 54, 190
South Dakota, 12, 189; Kimball, 191;
    Parker, 191
Spanish American War, 43, 56
Stacey, Jackie, 4
Staiger, Janet, 4, 69
Stamp, Shelley, 125n64
Stereopticon, 39, 40, 41, 42, 55, 77–78
Studlar, Gaylyn, 69
Suburban (context of moviegoing), 15, 194,
    218
Sundays (movie theater closings), 57, 74n58,
    82, 96–98, 192, 216

Talkies, 39, 57, 75, 170, 174, 176, 178, 187,
    188, 191, 210
Telephone, 5, 7, 9, 10, 45
Television, 8–9, 15, 46, 234
Temple, Shirley, 199, 200, 202
Tennessee, 180; Franklin, 249n3
Tents (outdoor movie shows), 29, 42, 48, 59,
    60, 61, 63, 64
Tepperman, Charles, 14
Texas, 46, 177, 190, 196; Brady, 229n29;
    Cotulla, 206n39; Dallas, 212; Kerens,
    177; Menard, 199, 204n18; San Antonio,
    229n26
Thissen, Judith, 21
Time (magazine), 217

Uncle Josh at the Moving Picture Show (1902),
    141, 147n33
Universal (film company), 37, 67–68,
    107, 111, 112, 113, 120, 159, 163,
    174
Upper–class (audiences and film themes),
    197–198, 206–207n47, 214
Urricchio, William, 108, 146n15
Ushers, 172, 173, 178, 215
Utah, 189; Gunnison, 193

Variety, 20, 22, 188, 211
Vaudeville, 4, 8, 10, 39–45, 48, 53, 65–66, 69,
    73n46, 77, 84, 92–94, 97, 109, 122n18,
    150, 158, 176, 205n37, 219
Vermont, 189
Virginia, 29, 54, 67, 190; Marion, 249n3;
    Norfolk, 13, 26, 91–101; Portsmouth, 95;
    Shenandoah Valley, 13, 46–47; Williams-
    burg, 17
Vitagraph (film company), 118, 151,
    159

Waller, Gregory, 4, 14, 16, 27, 53, 54,
    63, 64, 65, 69, 121n6, 182n3, 184n42,
    246
Walters, Ronald G., 5, 12, 15
Washington (state): Kennewick, 195;
    Lyndon, 195
Washington, D.C., 46–47, 150
Washington, Booker T., 95
Weather (affecting movie shows), 191–192,
    159, 202, 204n18
Wells, Jake and Otto, 92–101
West Virginia, 189; Dunbar, 196

Western (region), 11, 12, 13, 43, 45, 75–87,
186, 203n4. *See also individual states*
Westerns (films), 46, 60, 118, 193, 195, 196,
198, 200, 206–207n47
Wisconsin, 178, 179; Adams, 178; Black River
Falls, 48; Fond du Lac, 179; Grand
Rapids, 153; Kenosha, 228n21; Lake
Mills, 200; Milwaukee, 158, 163, 229n26;
Oshkosh, 37, 47; Racine, 223n8; Stevens
Point, 13, 14, 149–164
Women (as exhibitors), 48, 122n21, 190–191,
192, 196

Women (in movie audience), 4, 56, 60,
67–68, 71n5, 82, 83, 118–120, 160–164,
194–196, 202, 219, 227n8
Women's Christian Temperance Union, 56,
92, 155
Working class (in movie audience), 4, 25, 26,
57, 109, 197
World War I, 48, 64, 67, 151, 162,
World War II, 15, 201, 226
Wyoming, 189

Yaeger, Charles, 211–212, 215

Text: 10/12 Baskerville
Display: Syntax
Compositor: BVC
Printer and Binder: Maple-Vail